THE ROAD BEFORE ME WEEPS

THE ROAD

On the refugee route

BEFORE ME

through Europe

WEEPS

NICK THORPE

YALE UNIVERSITY PRESS
NEW HAVEN AND LONDON

For information about this and other Yale University Press publications, please contact:
U.S. Office: sales.press@yale.edu   yalebooks.com
Europe Office: sales@yaleup.co.uk   yalebooks.co.uk

Set in Minion Pro by IDSUK (DataConnection) Ltd
Printed in Great Britain by Gomer Press Ltd, Llandysul, Ceredigion, Wales

Library of Congress Control Number: 2018962173

ISBN 978-0-300-24122-8

A catalogue record for this book is available from the British Library.

10 9 8 7 6 5 4 3 2 1

This book is for M'baye

CONTENTS

ACKNOWLEDGEMENTS

I would like to thank the hundreds of men, women and children who shared their stories with me during some of the most difficult moments of their lives. Many of their names appear in the text, others preferred to remain anonymous. The courage of those who set out into the unknown is matched only by the courage of those who stay at home, come what may. This book is dedicated to M'baye, wherever he may be, who rescued my sister and I when we were lost and afraid, long ago, on our first night in Dakar.

I want also to thank the many volunteers, aid workers, translators, government officials, police and border guards who gave information, permissions, tea or advice in many countries. In particular, staff of the United Nations refugee agency, the International Organisation for Migration, Médecins Sans Frontières, the Hungarian and Bulgarian Helsinki Committees, Frontex and numerous volunteer groups and activists were generous with their time and help.

My work for the BBC gave me the opportunity to spend many months along the borders of the Balkans. My thanks to commissioning editors and colleagues too numerous to mention for their interest in the story and their companionship.

In Budapest Bálint Ablonczy, Suzanna Zsohár and Michael Ignatieff, and in London Xandra Bingley and the anonymous readers at Yale, read early drafts of the book and offered valuable suggestions. Gerald Knaus magnanimously shared with me his recollections of the gestation and birth of the EU–Turkey deal.

ACKNOWLEDGEMENTS

Huge thanks are due to my Hungarian publishers, Scolar Kiadó, and in particular Nándor Érsek and Andrea Illés for encouraging me to write the book in the first place. At Yale University Press, Robert Baldock, Rachael Lonsdale, Julian Loose, Marika Lysandrou, Clarissa Sutherland and many others worked assiduously to produce this beautiful edition. Finally, I would like to thank my wife Andrea and my sons Jack, Caspar, Daniel, Matthew and Sam, my mother Janet, my sister Mish and my brother Dom, for tolerating my long absences, and for all their love and support.

ILLUSTRATIONS

All photos taken by the author.

1 Afghan boys by the roadside near Ásotthalom, Hungary, June 2015.
2 Eric Özeme, from the Democratic Republic of the Congo, near Ásotthalom, Hungary, June 2015.
3 Refugees queue for the buses at the Röszke cornfield that will take them to a registration centre, Hungary, September 2015.
4 A field of tents at Röszke, Hungary, September 2015.
5 A Syrian boy holds up his new design for the flag of his country, East Station, Budapest, September 2015.
6 Hungarian police, East Station, Budapest, September 2015.
7 Yazidi refugees, Dimitrovgrad, Serbia, November 2015.
8 A volunteer serves food to Afghan refugees beside the police registration point at Dimitrovgrad, Serbia, November 2015.
9 A sister and brother at the One Stop Centre refugee camp, Subotica, Serbia, September 2016.
10 Refugee women cooking supper on the Serbian side of the Hungarian border at Kelebia, September 2016.
11 Women at the water tap, Horgoš illegal encampment, Serbia, September 2016.
12 Lunchtime at the Horgoš illegal encampment, Serbia, September 2016.
13 A young Somali at Adaševci, with the lists of those queuing to get into the Hungarian Transit Zones, September 2016.

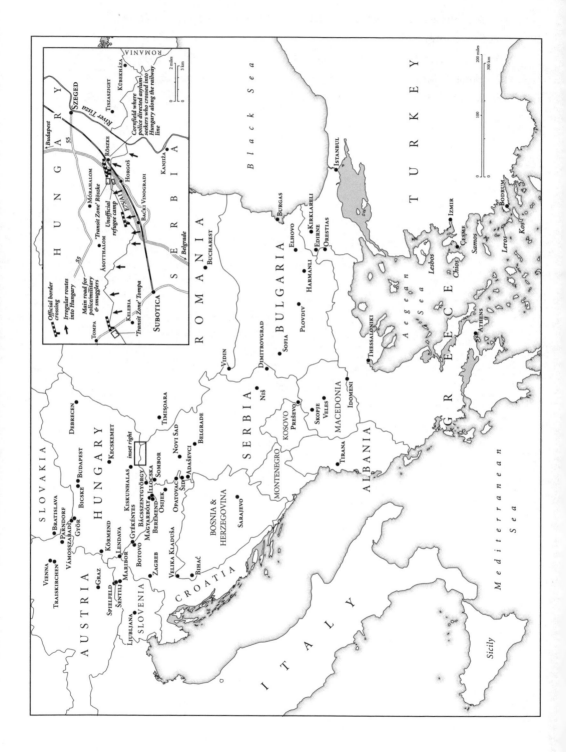

THE FACES AT THE FENCE

Imagine that you see the wretched strangers,
Their babies at their backs and their poor luggage,
Plodding to the ports and coasts for transportation . . .
              William Shakespeare, *The Book of Sir Thomas More*[1]

On a world scale emigration has become the principal means of survival.
              John Berger[2]

This is a book about refugees and migrants along what became known as the western Balkan route, from Turkey to Western Europe, from 2014 to 2018. This is just one of the five main routes into Europe, but in 2015 and the start of 2016, it was the most trodden.

'Migration is like a balloon,' an official of Frontex, the European border control agency told me, 'you squeeze it in one place, it grows bigger somewhere else.' The deals done in distant capitals, the walls and fences built, and the detection equipment installed have had a certain deterrent and delaying effect. But those who are determined enough will always find a way through. All the means taken to stop them simply increase their suffering, the cost of the journey and their dependence on the criminal underworld which facilitates their movement.

Much changed in the world while I was writing this book. What began as a chronicle of a mass influx turned gradually into detective work, tracing individuals from the mid-point to the end-point of their journeys. Such is the fragility of their status, some of the characters may be in other countries by the time you read these words. Some may have struggled gladly or reluctantly home.

It is my hope that this book, as a chronicle of an age-old phenomenon during a certain short period in modern European history, will remain a useful reference for readers many years from now. The book raises questions of human freedom and hospitality, of rights and obligations which are of crucial importance in any age.

From my home in Budapest, I returned over a four-year period to the same tracks across fields and forests, and to the same villages and towns where people rested on their journeys or were temporarily incarcerated. When the fence on the Hungarian-Serbian border was completed in September 2015, I traced the flow of people through Croatia and Slovenia. When the trickle of people over and through the Hungarian fence fell almost to zero, in the autumn of 2017, I traced people across Romania into Hungary, through Slovakia and the Czech Republic into Germany. Others took the route through Albania or Bosnia, into Croatia, Slovenia and Italy. Since their arrival in Western Europe, I have continued to follow the fate of several dozen people. Some of their stories conclude this book.

This is also the story of the help and hostility they met on their way, and when they arrived. My adopted homeland of Hungary produced the fiercest political opposition, in the form of Viktor Orbán's Fidesz government, to both refugees and migrants. My familiarity with the Hungarian prime minister – I have known him since 1988 – gave me a useful perspective from which to follow the refugee phenomenon across Europe and the world. Though I write in the shadow of his fence, my privileged status as a BBC correspondent gave me the opportunity to zig-zag through it at will, and to speak to whomsoever I wished.

I place the experiences of those along the route in the wider context of European and global migration, and the growing fear of terrorism. And in conversations at the end of the book, with some of those who are now accepted in Germany, France and Switzerland, I explore the successes and setbacks of integration.

The title, *The Road Before Me Weeps*, was first suggested to me by my friend Balázs 'Dongó' Szokolay, a brilliant Hungarian musician and master of all manner of flutes, saxophones, bagpipes and other wind instruments. It is taken from a folk song of the Szekler people, first recorded by the collector and composer László Lajtha in the village of Bözöd in Transylvania in what is now Romania, on the eve of the First World War.[3] There are several versions of the text. In the best-known, a man walks down the village street, so sad that even the road weeps before him, to visit the girl he loves, who has forsaken him for another man. No door opens to him.

In 1987, the Hungarian film-maker Sándor Sára gave the same title to a series of four films about the plight of the Szeklers of Bukovina, forced from their villages as refugees during the Second World War, never to return.[4] In yet another version, sung by the Vízöntö (Aquarius) rock band in the 1990s, a Hungarian is far away across the seas, an emigrant, and his family don't even know if he is dead or alive.[5]

While I was writing, the people of Britain voted to leave the European Union (EU) and Donald Trump was elected forty-fifth president of the United States. Both outcomes were strongly influenced by the desire of the electorate to 'regain control' of their countries from those portrayed as political and business elites who favour globalisation. Both the champions of Brexit and Donald Trump's campaign leaned heavily on public concern about immigration. It is ironic that while East European governments opposed 'migrants' from outside Europe, many people in Britain were swayed to leave the EU because they resented the influx of East Europeans to their own countries. New business elites came to power in many countries, and stayed in power in others, because they were better able to speak 'the language of the people'.

'Real greatness is able to give and accept, to be national and international at the same time,' László Lajtha, the musician to whom I owe the title of this book, once commented in a radio interview. 'It widens the boundaries of national culture, accepts every trend of the universal human coming his way and does not know the narrow, secluded animosity mocked as national.'[6]

That 'narrow, secluded animosity' however, rarely runs very deep. People everywhere prefer what is 'local' – including local Gypsies, local Syrians, Latinos or Kurds, once they get to know them. It is easy, on the other hand, to demonise newcomers and strangers, especially those who arrive overnight. Another of the ironies of the influx is that many of the newcomers were from the educated middle classes. They could otherwise never have scraped together the funds for the journey. The poorest and most vulnerable had few ways out. The final irony is that relatively few came to Europe, despite all the fuss – 1 million Syrians, for example, compared to 5 million who stayed in neighbouring countries.

The education and skills of the new arrivals will work to the advantage of the economies of the countries which welcomed them. But it will be a disaster for Syria and Iraq if their teachers, doctors, engineers and construction workers never go home. This can also be used as an argument against integration – 'Please don't settle down here, you will soon be sorely needed at home.'

The arrival of so many asylum seekers provoked a political backlash in many countries. Nationalist governments were elected in Austria (2017) and Italy (2018), and reelected in Hungary (2018). In Germany, Angela Merkel hung on to power, but with a reduced majority as the rise of the Alternative für Deutschland (AfD) with its fierce anti-immigrant rhetoric, robbed her Christian Democrats of votes (2017). Elsewhere in Europe, centrist parties grew tougher on immigration, in an attempt to reduce the growth of far-right parties.

In the summer of 2015, I watched Hungarian police gaze in bewilderment at petrol stations beside the motorway from Serbia, unable to distinguish between 1 million Turks returning legally from their holidays to their jobs and homes in Germany, and the hundreds of thousands of people who traipsed, irregularly, across the same border in the same direction. Similarly, a million Moroccans and other North Africans travel legally to and from France each year through Spain.

In an age of migration and climate change, of changing work patterns, demographic decline and population explosions, and of falling travel costs to Europe, it is impossible to draw a sharp line between migrants, refugees and the temporarily displaced. The word 'refugee' was originally applied to the French Protestants, known as Huguenots, who fled to Britain, the Netherlands and other countries after the Revocation of the Edict of Nantes in 1685. The 'wretched strangers' referred to by William Shakespeare at the beginning of this chapter, refers to earlier arrivals – 'wealthy Lombard bankers and Flemish labourers' – attacked by a mob in London on May Day 1517. Thomas More was deputy sheriff of the city and attempted to calm the crowd.

Immediately after the First World War, what is regarded as the first 'refugee crisis' of modern times took place, as up to 2 million Russians fled the Bolshevik Revolution, and hundreds of thousands of Armenians, Greeks and Balkan peoples were forced from their homes. The Norwegian Arctic explorer and diplomat Fridtjof Nansen, as the first High Commissioner for Refugees of the League of Nations, worked tirelessly to enable their freedom of movement. The idea of redistributing asylum seekers from the country of first arrival, Greece or Italy, to other countries in Europe, can be traced back to the 'Nansen passports' issued under his authority in the 1920s. These were subsequently adapted to give the bearer more rights – including that of being allowed to travel on to another European country, in search of shelter and work. To that extent, the Nansen passport was more advanced than current European legislation, which requires that those granted protection stay where they are.[7]

During the Second World War, an estimated 60 million people fled their homes. Today over 68.5 million are displaced, of whom some 23 million are regarded as refugees.[8] When the United Nations Refugee Convention was agreed in 1951 there were still a million refugees in Europe. Refugee camps, and international law, evolved to address refugee crises during the Cold War. The United Nations refugee agency (UNHCR), alongside national governments, is now struggling to adapt its practices to a world in which refugees remain refugees much longer, and where civil wars, rather than wars between separate countries, often force them out. Climate change, and the refugee waves it is expected to produce, is another challenge. Drought in north-eastern Syria, and the subsequent influx from affected rural districts to the cities, is regarded as one of the contributing factors to the civil war.[9]

'For the first time, the rights of individuals have been recognised by the international state system,' writes Michael Ignatieff. 'No other language of the human good has proved so influential, in large part because the language used addresses every single human being alive as a sovereign individual.'[10] As I stood on the railway track from Serbia into Hungary early one morning in September 2015, I asked a Syrian man with a broken leg, in a suit and tie, supported on both sides by his nephews, who he was.

'I am, Sir, a sovereign man,' was his reply. In an age when national sovereignty is once again being trumpeted from the rooftops, it is well to remember the value of individual sovereignty.

As the average length of 'refugee-hood' is now over ten years, refugee camps hardly offer a sustainable solution. The alternative, a precarious, semi-legal or illegal existence in a nearby city is what most choose in preference to the enforced idleness of a camp, deprived of meaningful economic activity, dependent on handouts.

In their book *Refuge: Transforming a Broken Refugee System*, Alexander Betts and Paul Collier explain the need to turn refugee flows from a humanitarian issue into a development one.[11] Only if those who flee are given the opportunity to find work, education for their children, and proper health care, will they stay in the countries where they first arrive, like Turkey, Lebanon and Jordan, which would be their first choice. But they will stay there only if the international community helps those countries enough to restore their autonomy and dignity.

There are far more 'displaced' people in the world than refugees. The displaced are motivated by the simple human desire to stay as close to home as possible, in the hope that they can soon go back. If this is a 'crisis' at all, it is a 'crisis of the displaced' rather than a refugee or migrant crisis. A displaced person becomes a refugee at the point where they flee their country. In Syria by the end of 2017, of a pre-war population of 23 million, 6 million were displaced within the country's borders, 5 million were refugees in neighbouring countries, 1 million had come to Europe and approximately half a million had been killed. The Syrian refugee crisis began with the crushing of the peaceful protests against President Bashar Assad's rule, in 2011.

More often than not the words used for those 'on the move' are political definitions. A government, political party or media organisation which dislikes 'aliens', sees them wherever it looks. The humanity of those fleeing the horrors of war in Aleppo, Mosul or Sinjar is devalued with the disdainful epithet of 'economic migrant'. The failure of the international community to do enough to help the refugees, and the host countries, where they first arrived, created the problem of secondary 'migration' as asylum seekers hurried from countries neighbouring Syria, towards Western Europe. They were compelled first and foremost by the information that it was about to get harder – Viktor Orbán's fence initially acted as a magnet, rather than a barrier. By the time that Chancellor Angela Merkel said that Germany had suspended deportations of Syrians to the first country of entry, many were already on the move.[12]

The statistics and costs are hard to tie down but offer a certain insight into the processes at work. Around 3.7 million people claimed asylum in Europe during the four-year period addressed in this book.[13] EU governments spent €2 billion either to keep them out or reduce the flow – €1,000 for each person on the move.[14] While most East European countries excelled in the rhetoric of anti-migrant xenophobia, many West European countries quietly built their own walls. New fences went up, or older fences were reinforced, on sections of the Greece–Turkey, Bulgaria–Turkey, Greece–Macedonia, Hungary–Serbia, Hungary–Croatia, Slovenia–Croatia, Austria–Slovenia, Austria–Italy, Latvia–Russia and Russia–Estonia borders, and along the entrances to the ferry and Channel Tunnel on the France–UK border. By 2018, the 828-kilometre wall built by Turkey on its border with Syria was the most effective of all.[15]

The old Iron Curtain was built by Communist regimes to stop their own populations fleeing to the West. The new Iron Curtains are designed to stop the influx into Europe (that northerly continent) of the poor and the oppressed of the global South, and of refugees from the war-ravaged East.

Confusion over who is coming to Europe and why has added to the confusion over who to let in and who to keep out. The Common European Asylum System (CEAS) in 2005 was an attempt to make sure that all EU member states protected the rights of asylum seekers and refugees, with a set of minimum procedural standards. A cornerstone of the CEAS was the so-called Dublin procedures, revised in 2013, under which a person must seek asylum in the first EU country in which they arrive. This worked relatively well when the numbers were comparatively small, as transit countries turned a blind eye to those traipsing through their fields in the hope that they would soon leave, and target countries either absorbed the new arrivals – or sent them back under the Dublin procedures.

From 2014 the system became unworkable – hundreds of thousands of people did not want to stay in Greece or Italy, nor be deported there if they reached their goal. Instead, the system fell apart, and each country came up with its own, more closed or open solutions, often improvised from one day to the next, with little or no consultation with neighbouring countries. What has emerged since is the beginnings of an agreement, to redistribute those recognised as genuine refugees more fairly, and absorb only as many 'economic migrants' as a country needs. During this same period, from 2014 to 2018, EU countries also spent around €20 billion rescuing refugees from the sea, feeding and housing them in transit on land, sheltering them, and beginning the integration process.[16]

Parallel to, and often in contrast to the approach of state institutions, tens of thousands of volunteers devoted months of their lives to help the new arrivals. Aid agencies led by the UNHCR, the International Organization for Migration, the Red Cross, Save the Children, Médecins Sans Frontières, Médicins du Monde, the Norwegian Refugee Council, Oxfam, and numerous church-related and secular groups mobilised their resources to soften the pain and suffering of the journeys. And, hidden from view, thousands of smugglers made billions of euros – an estimated €6 billion in 2015 alone – guiding the refugees across one border after another, despite the ever-increasing security.[17] Without them, there could have been no journey, no influx. Over four years, 2 million people paid smugglers €8–10 billion – four to five times as much as was spent on all the walls, fences, surveillance equipment erected in their path. By any calculation, that was a huge waste of precious resources. If the new arrivals could have reached Europe with even part of that money in their pockets – as the Russians fleeing Bolshevism did – their integration could have got off to a better start.

In response to the influx, the EU has also spent around €16 billion on funds for Turkey, Syria and African countries, to keep potential refugees from setting out from their shores. EU countries have spent close to €30 billion processing and integrating the new arrivals. Whatever one calls it, this is a complex and contradictory process.

The way Europeans reacted to the new arrivals was strongly influenced by their experience of the wider issue of migration, and immigration. This helps explain the hostility to refugees in Eastern Europe, where few people have experience of meeting, let alone living with strangers from other cultures. Only 1.6 per cent of Hungarians were born outside their own country, compared to an EU average of over 8 per cent. It was easy for politicians to turn that genuine concern into fear.

According to the German immigration authority, in 2014 there were 16.3 million people with an immigration background living in Germany, one in five of a population of 80 million.[18] More than 8 million did not have German citizenship. Most were of Turkish, East European or Southern European background. Yet Germany continued to allow people in, both to fill vacancies in the labour market and for humanitarian reasons. In 2016, there were 20.7 million people with non-EU citizenship living across the EU, in a continent of over 500 million – 4 per cent of the population. A further 16 million EU citizens lived in another member state.[19]

In Eastern Europe one frequently comes across the argument that migrants represent some kind of a threat to 'Christian Europe'. This ignores the universal nature of Christianity, preaching not to one tribe or nation, but to all humanity. In the parable of the Good Samaritan, the Samaritan, who is not just a stranger but also an enemy of the Jew who lies wounded in the ditch, is the only one who comes to his aid. The point here is not that we *have* to help the stranger, but that we have the *freedom* to help him or her. And when we walk by, on the other side of the road, we are impoverished as human beings as a result. In Eastern Europe, where the churches played a central role in the creation of nation-states in the nineteenth century, and their survival through the vicissitudes of the twentieth century, that universalist tradition was diluted or lost.

'What it comes down to is this,' Michael Ignatieff told an audience at the University of Toronto in October 2016, 'Come in. I, the citizen, give you this gift of hospitality.'[20] In return, the citizen expects the newcomer to acknowledge that gift and be grateful for it. The Canadian refugee experience has been so successful because it is framed in these terms, of local hospitality, rather than the language of universal human rights. My own conclusions are much the same as those of William Shakespeare, 500 years ago:

Why, you must needs be strangers: would you be pleas'd
To find a nation of such barbarous temper,
That, breaking out in hideous violence,
Would not afford you an abode on earth,
Whet their detested knives against your throats.
Spurn you like dogs, and like as if that God
Owed not nor made not you, nor that the elements
Were not all appropriate to your comforts,
But chartered unto them? What would you think
To be thus us'd? This is the strangers' case;
And this your mountainish inhumanity.

CHAPTER ONE

NEW YEAR 2015

To live and die amongst foreigners may seem less absurd than to live persecuted and tortured by one's fellow countrymen. But to emigrate is always to dismantle the centre of the world, and so to move into a lost, disoriented one of fragments.

John Berger[1]

'Today many people are once again coming onto the streets on Mondays, and shouting: "*Wir sind das Volk*" – "*We are the people*," ' German chancellor Angela Merkel said in her 2015 New Year address. '*But what they really mean is: you are not one of us, because of your skin colour or your religion.*'[2]

The new round of Monday evening demonstrations was organised by the Pegida movement, founded in the East German city of Dresden in October 2014.[3] Pegida stands for 'Patriotic Europeans Against the Islamisation of the West'. Patriotic Europeans, not patriotic Germans. The founders wanted to underline their idea of their *European* identity. Of the continent, not of the Fatherland. For many Germans since the Second World War, Germany was a difficult concept to belong to. Europe had become a substitute for their allegiance, and since German reunification that Europe was modelled and centred on Germany.

A week before Christmas, 20,000 Pegida supporters marched through Dresden demanding a stop to immigration. Twenty-six years earlier, in the autumn of 1989, opponents of the Communist Party marched through the streets of East German cities each Monday, chanting 'We are the People'.

Pegida picked the same day of the week and the same chant. As an East German herself, and the daughter of a Lutheran pastor, Angela Merkel understood this very well, and was deeply affronted.

East European societies under Communism were largely homogeneous. Socialist man and woman lived in regimented societies where they earned the same money, wore the same clothes, ate the same food and learnt the same version of history at school. There were few people from other cultures apart from the North African and Middle Eastern students at the medical or engineering faculties of the universities. That was a big contrast to Western Europe where hundreds of thousands of immigrants arrived from former colonies in the wake of the Second World War, as in Britain or France. Or where large numbers of Turkish or Yugoslav *Gastarbeiter* arrived from 1961 onwards, as in West Germany. Those influxes had considerably changed the complexion of those societies by the end of the twentieth century. When Germany was reunified in October 1990, many East Germans were shocked to find so many people from other cultures and faiths in their country. That made them natural allies of nationalists in West Germany or France or Belgium, who resented their continent's physical openness to the rest of the globe. The fact that the newcomers or their children were doing menial jobs which other Germans no longer wanted to do, cleaning the streets, driving the buses, or wheeling the elderly through the corridors of their hospitals, was little consolation.

By 2014, there were 4.8 million Muslims in Germany, 5.8 per cent of the population. Interestingly, more Turks were returning home by then, than arriving – so-called 'circular migration' is often forgotten in the heated debates.[4] But there were new waves of immigration, mostly from the wars in the Middle East – in 2014, nearly 300,000 refugees applied for asylum in Germany. Also that year 199 hostels where asylum seekers were living were attacked. German society was ill-prepared for the arrival of more than a million more asylum seekers in 2015. Those who didn't want them there were prepared, however. In 2015, the number of attacks on hostels increased fivefold, to 1,005. In 2016, it showed a slight decline, but the number of physical attacks on migrants soared to over ten a day.

As well as the almost uniformly pale skin reflected in the East European early morning mirror, there was another factor which made Eastern Europe different and which would also influence the approach to the new influx of

11

refugees and migrants. National feeling was a central element in all the East European revolutions of 1989. This was ignored or underestimated by those commentators who identified only the 'embrace of capitalism' and the 'Western victory in the Cold War' in the events which unfolded. But without the outburst of patriotic fervour, long suppressed but never eradicated by four decades of 'socialist internationalism', the fall of Communism was unimaginable. The refugee crisis was now to reignite German as well as East European nationalism.

Like Angela Merkel, French president François Hollande also used his 2015 New Year address to emphasise an inclusive message, aimed at all the different communities of France. 'When France forgets her principles, she loses herself,' he said. 'I am making the fight against racism and anti-Semitism a national priority.'

The Muslim population of France is 4.7 million, or 7.5 per cent of the population, mostly of North African origin, from the former French colonies in Algeria and Tunisia or from Morocco.[5] France also has the largest Jewish population in Europe at around 600,000, or 1 per cent of the population, mostly of Sephardi and Mizrahi origin. Like French Muslims many French Jews came from North Africa when their countries gained independence. In 2014 French police registered 851 incidents of 'an anti-Semitic nature', 810 attacks on Christian places of worship or cemeteries, and 199 attacks on Muslims. French Muslims were responsible for many of the anti-Semitic incidents.[6]

On 7 January 2015, exactly a week after President Hollande's appeal, two men born in France of Algerian parentage, the brothers Chérif and Saïd Kouachi stormed the Paris offices of the satirical weekly *Charlie Hebdo*, asked for individual journalists by name, and shot them dead in cold blood. Eleven people died in or just outside the newspaper offices in the Rue Nicolas-Appert, including a receptionist, a bodyguard and nine journalists.

The perpetrators got back into their black Citroën and drove off. A policeman on foot patrol on the Boulevard Richard Lenoir, forty-two-year-old Ahmed Merabet, pulled out his service pistol and tried to confront them. They stopped their car, shot him once in the groin, then walked up to him as he lay helpless on the pavement and shot him again at point blank range in the head. Like them he was a Muslim, born in France to parents of Algerian origin.

As the Twitter hashtag 'Je suis Charlie' went viral, in solidarity with the newspaper journalists killed for posting cartoons mocking the Prophet Muhammad, others tweeted a 'Je suis Ahmed' hashtag, in solidarity with the policeman. 'I am not Charlie, I am Ahmed the dead cop. Charlie ridiculed my faith and culture and I died defending his right to do so,' @Aboujahjah, posted.

On the Saturday after the attacks Ahmed's brother Malek gave a press conference. 'I address all the racists, Islamophobes and anti-Semites. Do not mix the extremists with Muslims. Stop confusing them, stop unleashing wars, stop burning mosques and synagogues, stop attacking people. That will not give us back our dead, and will not comfort our families.'[7]

The following day 2 million people gathered for a peace march through the streets of Paris. Forty heads of state and prime ministers from around the world attended. Among them was Viktor Orbán, the Hungarian prime minister. After the march he gave an interview to Hungarian state television, MTV.

> We must make very clear that we will never allow Hungary to become a target country for immigrants, at least as long as I am prime minister and as long as this government is in place. We do not want to see significantly sized minorities with different cultural characteristics and backgrounds among us. We want to keep Hungary as Hungary.[8]

Mr Orbán had mentioned his aversion to immigration in previous speeches. The previous August, at the annual gathering of Hungarian ambassadors in the Foreign Ministry building at Bem Square, Péter Szabadhegy, the Hungarian ambassador to London, asked him whether he saw immigration as one of the solutions to falling population.

Hungary's attitude to immigration should be 'as hard as stone', the prime minister told his diplomats, 'because it sees no value in breaking up a homogenous society'. The immigration policy of the EU, Orbán continued, was 'hypocritical, lacking moral foundations, and purposeless'.

During the hour he spoke, 1,800 people were forced from their homes around the world – 42,500 a day, according to the UNHCR. During the whole of 2014, 43,000 people were detected crossing the Hungarian-Serbian border, according to Frontex, making it the third most popular route into the EU after the central Mediterranean (170,000) and the eastern Mediterranean (51,000).

'We are witnessing a paradigm change, an unchecked slide into an era in which the scale of global forced displacement as well as the response required is now clearly dwarfing anything seen before,' the UN High Commissioner for Refugees António Guterres wrote. 'It is terrifying that on the one hand there is more and more impunity for those starting conflicts, and on the other there is a seeming utter inability of the international community to work together to stop wars and build and preserve peace.'[9]

After the *Charlie Hebdo* attack, Orbán and his advisers discovered the political value of migrants, or rather the fear of them. Elected in 2010 with a landslide victory, his party Fidesz, won a second two-thirds majority in May 2014. Since then Fidesz had lost a million voters, and several by-elections. Although it was still the largest party in parliament by far, it no longer had a two-thirds majority. Many centre-right voters had lost their faith in Fidesz, gravitating to Hungary's weak and disintegrated liberal or centrist parties, or towards the radically nationalist Jobbik. Now Orbán had found what would prove to be the magic weapon to get them back on board his ship.

His ploy was all the more remarkable as next to none of the migrants beginning to embark in Europe wanted to stay in Hungary anyway. Orbán's speechwriters solved that problem by saying that the prime minister wanted to defend Europe. Another peculiarity was that the Hungarians themselves, at their particular crossroads of Europe, were a mixed bunch themselves. One of the most common surnames is Németh, meaning German, another is Tóth meaning Slovak, and Horváth – Croat. At times over the years to come, as Orbán whipped up then played on the public fear of refugees and migrants, he came close to portraying his people as ethnically pure. At other times, he was the first to admit that to be Hungarian was a matter of language and commitment, rather than race.

The new government message was underlined the day after Orbán returned to Budapest from Paris by Antal Rogán, leader of the Fidesz parliamentary faction. Muslim communities, he said, were already demolishing the internal order of Christian countries in Western Europe. 'It is not in Hungary's interest to accept "economic migrants" with traditions completely different from Hungarian ones.'

14

On 30 January the Hungarian prime minister was in the parliament building, handing out prizes to deserving students. The speeches dragged on. Orbán was wearing a bright silk tie, of a colour somewhere between the bright yellow of a lemon and freshly squeezed gold. The ceremony took place beneath the central dome of the building, next to the Crown of St Stephen, Hungary's most precious heirloom, thin hammered gold, encrusted with jewels and pictures of the saints, preserved in a glass case. I photographed Orbán through the case from several angles – the King of Hungary. The lights from the dome overhead reflected on the glass, like frogspawn. Before the ceremony was over, the prime minister's press chief and constant companion, Bertalan Havasi, noticed me lurking with a BBC colleague near the braided rope which separated the crowd from the dignitaries. We had positioned ourselves there on the assumption that he would walk past us at the end, and we might be able to get a quick question to him.

'Don't you dare even try!' Havasi growled at me. A few minutes later our guess proved accurate. 'Prime minister, would you please answer a question on the Merkel visit?' I asked.

'Maybe next time,' said Havasi, trying to move Orbán away from us. But the prime minister would not be moved. We asked about Merkel's visit the following week and that of Vladimir Putin on 17 February. 'Plus the prime minister of Turkey, plus the prime minister of Georgia ...' he added, in conversational mood, 'the diplomatic life is going on.'

'How difficult for Hungary is the balance between East and West now?' my colleague Hugh Sykes asked. 'That's part of the life if you are born here,' he replied, before his minders swept him on his way. A video of our encounter, filmed by the commercial channel ATV gathered 200,000 views on YouTube. It was very unusual for a reporter to successfully doorstep the Hungarian leader.[10]

On 4 February I visited Ásotthalom for the first time, a sprawling village of 4,000 people down on the Hungarian-Serbian border. Articles had begun to appear in the Hungarian media about a big influx of migrants. 'What Lampedusa is to the Mediterranean, Ásotthalom is to the Balkan route,' wrote the conservative weekly *Heti Válasz*.[11] Hungarian police sources suggested more than a thousand people, mostly Albanians from Kosovo, were crossing into Hungary each day.

It was a damp, cold, grey February morning, the temperature 4 degrees Celsius. In front of the covered market in Mórahalom I saw a group of thirty or forty migrants waiting patiently beside two police minibuses, their blue lights flashing. Several smaller groups of six to twelve people straggled along the road towards Mórahalom from Ásotthalom. A slight majority were men but there were also many families, pale, thin and determined. They reminded me of the Kosovars who fled Slobodan Milošević's police and army in 1998 and 1999, through the snows of the Pashtrik mountains into Albania. These Kosovars were fleeing the country whose independence their compatriots died for.

On the roads of southern Hungary the Kosovars wore anoraks or denim jackets, woolly hats and scarves. Some rolled babies along the tarmac in pushchairs, others carried children on their shoulders. They didn't run away when the police stopped them. Some even waited for the police to come, to hand themselves in. Hungary was just a transit country, and they knew they would not be turned back. The rain got heavier, and I turned on my wind-screen wipers. The Kosovars kept coming, smudges of pink and blue and black in the flat green Hungarian countryside.

My name is Drita. I'm twenty-three, from Mitrovica in Kosovo. I left because the mafia is in charge in Mitrovica. They run everything, hand in glove with the politicians. I can't get a proper job there. I finished two years at college, then quit to make this journey.

Drita set out with his brother and a group of friends. First by bus to Merdare, on the Serbian border. Ever since Kosovo declared independence from Serbia in February 2008, the Serbian authorities had refused to recognise the dark blue Kosovo passports, and considered the fist-shaped map of Kosovo imprinted on the front an insult to the memory of the province as the cradle of Serbian culture. But in 2014 the Serbs began to implement an agreement with the Kosovar authorities, brokered by the EU, to allow freedom of movement across their territory. At the border crossing point at Merdare they were issued with a laissez-passer, a single sheet of paper with their name and date of birth and a round purple Serbian stamp. There wasn't even a photograph.

From Merdare they took another bus to Belgrade. From Belgrade Drita took a taxi to the Hungarian border, though it would have been cheaper to take the bus to Subotica and walk. He and his friends had been walking all morning. They were on their way to Germany, they said, to find properly paid work.

Arafat, from Vushtrri in Kosovo, was in his late forties, travelling with his wife and five children. We spoke as he walked down the road, trying to balance his two-year-old son on his shoulders. The boy was fast asleep and much heavier as a result. He had left Kosovo, Arafat said, because his salary was pitifully low. Somewhat better off than most of his compatriots, his plan was to find a small hotel for the family for the night. I left him and his family, walking towards Mórahalom, burdened down with their luggage.

László Toroczkai sat in a bright red chair in the conference room of the village council in Ásotthalom, beneath a painting of the royal crown of Hungary, two hands, and the Virgin Mary. He was a controversial figure in his country, radical instigator of an impromptu roadblock on the Elizabeth Bridge across the Danube in Budapest in 2006, as part of a protest against the then Socialist government. In 2013 he was elected mayor of Ásotthalom in the colours of the radical nationalist party, Jobbik.

'The migrants were not a problem here until 2012 but their numbers have been growing ever since,' he said. Now they were causing untold suffering for his community. About half the population of the village lived in outlying farms, dotted through the woods which covered most of the municipality. Waiting outside his office I had studied a detailed map of the area and noticed one part of the woods close to the border called 'the home of the curse'. Cursed, the mayor explained, because there was no water in the wells, no matter how deep they drilled into the sandy soil.

The migrants crossed into Hungary at night under cover of darkness. They set the dogs barking, knocked on the doors of the inhabited houses asking for food or water, and broke into the unoccupied houses to shelter for the night. They made fires in the woods to keep warm. He was afraid of a major forest fire breaking out when the drier weather came.

Did he not feel any sympathy for them? I asked.

I feel responsibility first and foremost for the 4,000 Hungarians who live here, my constituents. Of course I believe we should help those who are genuine political refugees. But most of these are from Kosovo, a safe country. I cannot understand why they set out in freezing temperatures in mid-winter with babies just a few months old. Every week we have to call ambulances to save them. There is poverty here too. I understand people who fear poverty. But some of these Kosovars are better off than we are!

Toroczkai reorganised the civil defence of his village. He appointed three field rangers, with four-wheel drive Lada Nivas, to patrol the rough tracks along his 30-kilometre stretch of border with Serbia. And eighteen volunteer civil guards, to keep order on the streets. He spoke disparagingly of the police.

'They simply act like taxis for the migrants. What we really need here is a fence, like on the Bulgarian-Turkish or US-Mexican border, and the reestablishment of the Border Guard.' The Hungarian Border Guard, as a separate body within the armed forces, was disbanded in 2008, and its duties given to the police. The only help he had received from the state to cope with the ongoing migrant influx, Toroczkai told me, was a grant of 6 million forints (€20,000) from the Interior Ministry the previous autumn to be spent on seven or eight night-vision cameras. Two dozen police reinforcements had also been stationed temporarily in the Pinetree bed and breakfast for the past weeks, which had also helped 'a bit' he concluded, grudgingly.

I went on patrol with one of the rangers, Barnabás Heredi. As we bumped over the rough ground towards the border, he told me his typical day. Up at 4.25. Check the bus shelters in the village for sleeping migrants. The cleaning woman was usually already there, swabbing down the huts with disinfectant. Then out on the sandy tracks all day, occasionally returning to the asphalt roads. Local people rang him when they spotted migrants. In camouflage uniform, in a jeep with official markings, Barnabás was assumed by the newcomers to be police, although he carried no gun or handcuffs. His job was to ring the police and stay with the group until they arrived. Depending on the numbers that day, it could take anything from two to eight hours for the police to get there.

As we drove through the wet grass a startled deer jumped out and fled our approach. After we parked and went ahead on foot four men suddenly appeared out of the trees. We communicated in my poor Serbian. They were Kosovars from Vushtrri. They wanted to know if they were on Hungarian soil yet and were delighted to find out that they were. Could we please tell them the way to the nearest railway station? We pointed in the rough direction of Szeged, 35 kilometres to the east. They thanked us and set out stoically. No point in calling the police for such a small group, Barnabás told me. They would round them up on the main road anyway and take them to Szeged themselves.

Then we came to the border, a shallow drainage ditch or canal, known as the Körös-éri channel. Much of it was overgrown with reeds. In one place a small bridge crossed to Serbia on the far side. The bridge was strewn with a tangle of thick rusting steel cables to prevent an earlier generation of smugglers from bringing stolen cars across here. The actual border was marked with white-painted concrete waymarks every few hundred metres, with the letter M for Magyarország on one side and RS for the Republic of Serbia on the other. A few disused control towers still rose above the fields on the far side, from the era of tension between Socialist Yugoslavia and Socialist Hungary during the Cold War. We could see the roofs of outlying farmsteads in Serbia, many of them abandoned and useful resting places for migrants.

Footpaths were clearly visible in the reeds which crossed the canal, worn down by the constant tread of feet during the night. The paths into Hungary were lined with litter. Discarded bottles, biscuit wrappers, a packet of Lucky Strikes with a health warning in Albanian, socks discarded after getting soaked crossing the canal. And documents, dumped in the long grass, often torn to shreds, but still legible. I stooped to study some of the crumpled pages, issued to the Kosovars to cross Serbia.

Basrije Havolli. Born 8 June 1979. Identity card number 1015386092. Crossed at Merdare, 1 February 2015. Only the February rains, the marshy land, and the mole hills dotted through the dead yellow grass slowed the new arrivals. Above the birdsong the traffic on the motorway from Belgrade to Budapest hummed through the morning. Ásotthalom had become the main bottleneck for migrants entering Hungary from the Balkans, and the reason was abundantly clear. At one point the motorway ran only 500 metres from the Hungarian border.

When I returned to the village a few days later, the rain had turned to snow. This time there were Afghans, Africans and Syrians beside the Kosovars, huddled round small fires beside the main road, watched over by nervous policemen. The Kosovars were treading the grass flat on the Balkan route, for all the other nationalities to follow.

'Where the fuck are the Maltese?' one of the police shouted into his walkie-talkie, referring to the Hungarian Charity Service of the Order of Malta. A grey-bearded Afghan man approached us in tears carrying a child in his arms. The three-year-old boy had not been able to sleep or keep food or water down for several days. He vomited everything back immediately and had a high fever. We laid the child on the back seat of my car and explained the situation to the police. A coach was supposed to arrive soon to take all the refugees to the police registration centre in Szeged where the child would get medical care. Around the embers of a fire, the man's three other children crouched with their mother, eating apples given them by locals.

Also huddled in the wet grass were several men from Mali in West Africa, and two Syrians from Homs. The Afghans seemed the hardiest, the Malians the most despondent, incongruous in the Hungarian winter. The Syrians stood a little to the side, better dressed, better organised for their journey than the others. Eventually the coach arrived and took them all away. I found the Afghan child's blue woolly hat on the floor in my car.

I met László Toroczkai again in the mayor's office. He was preparing for a debate on the migration issue in parliament a few days later, to which he had been invited as mayor of the most affected community. László was indignant about the ease with which potential terrorists or weapons' smugglers could cross the border here, so soon after the *Charlie Hebdo* attacks: 'They could just walk in with rocket-propelled grenade launchers. They could even drive in a tank, and nobody would notice!' His men had noted cars with Lithuanian and Portuguese licence plates recently, he said, as well as the usual German and Austrian ones. The nearest official crossing at Királyhalom closed at seven each evening. Like the migrants, local people simply walked over the green border when they felt like it. The beer was cheaper in Serbia.

On this visit to Ásotthalom I went out with Vince Szalma, another of the rangers. His record 'catch' in one day, as he put it, was 1,140 migrants. That was down now to 80–100 whom he personally encountered each day. He put the improvement down to police reinforcements, brought in from Vas county and elsewhere in the country.

I watched a group of Kosovar Albanian men being rounded up. It was a humiliating affair, for both sides. The officer put on blue rubber gloves and made them stand against the side of the police minibus, to search them before they were allowed aboard. They had crossed the border illegally, therefore they had to be treated as criminals, the police explained.

I crossed into Serbia at Királyhalom. At the bus station in Subotica, a handsome, former Hungarian city, I noted the arrival times of ten buses a day from Belgrade. Poorer, or better organised migrants, able to dodge the shark-like taxi drivers who haunted the streets around the bus and railway stations in Belgrade, paid a small sum for the two-hour journey up the motorway here. But not all were as successful in crossing the border as those I had met at Ásotthalom, or on the approach roads to Mórahalom. Among a cluster of Kosovars in the waiting room, I found one man who spoke a little English. He had taken a taxi from Subotica to the border with his young son but was turned back by a Serbian police patrol. 'Go back to Kosovo,' they told him. Discouraged, he had returned to the bus station in Subotica, where he met up with some more Albanians who had just arrived from Belgrade. They were planning to try to cross the border again that night, this time in a larger group of ten to fifteen people.

Back in Hungary I took pity on a group of men, women and children sheltering from the snow in a bus shelter, waiting for one of the infrequent buses to Szeged from Ásotthalom. Twelve people squeezed enthusiastically into my seven-seater Volkswagen.

'We are heading to Germany because the economic situation in Kosovo is catastrophic. That's why we have to leave our country. All our politicians are corrupt, from top to bottom.'

'I'm travelling with my wife,' explained another. 'We are leaving because we lack even basic living conditions.'

'Everyone there is trying to make ends meet but it's just not possible,' said a third. 'It's not easy to leave your country, but we have no choice.' I dropped them at the railway station in Szeged.

Back in Kosovo, alarmed by the exodus, the president and prime minister launched a publicity campaign and even toured bus stations, trying to persuade their citizens to stay.[12] I calculated that at the current rate of 1,000 a day, it would only take six years to empty Kosovo completely of its 2 million inhabitants. In Pristina, some commentators even alleged that the Serbs were letting them go on purpose, to make the new state unviable. The police in Belgrade said they had already issued 60,000 laissez-passer papers.

21

In Szeged, József Seress, the head of the regional inspectorate of the Office for Immigration and Nationality (OIN), placed the increase in numbers crossing Hungary in a longer perspective: 'In 2013 we processed more than 17,000 asylum claims here in the southern Alföld region. In 2014 more than 37,000.' In the first six weeks of 2015, his office registered 18,000 claims, more than the total for the whole of 2013.

Of these claims, 80 per cent were from Kosovars, and 40 per cent were children. The exodus from Kosovo began in September 2014 when Serbia, which had previously refused to recognise Kosovan passports and therefore would not let them cross their territory, relaxed the rules under pressure from the EU. From now on, they were just asked to stamp a single, photo-copied paper, saying they had passed into Serbia.

Once in Hungary, they could be held under EU regulations for no more than twenty-four hours before they were put in an open camp. 'What happens to them then?' I asked, feigning innocence, fully aware that Hungary had no more than 2,000 places in its three refugee camps at Bicske, Debrecen and the new one at Vámosszabadi, opened in 2013. 'It can happen that they set out for the camps, but never arrive,' Seress said cautiously. It was the understatement of the year. Only the most vulnerable, or those in need of rest, actually reached the camps. For several years the Hungarian authorities, like the Serbian author-ities to the south, had been simply turning a blind eye to the tens of thousands of migrants crossing their territory. That was all now about to change.

The police chiefs of Hungary and Serbia held a crisis meeting at the motorway border crossing point at Röszke. Károly Papp spoke first, for the Hungarian side. The two counties on the Serbian border had over 1,000 officers at their disposal and had already received 136 reinforcements. His officers were coping with the situation, he said, by renting new premises, notably a hangar at Röszke and coaches with which to transport the migrants from the roadside to the registration centres at Röszke and Nagyfa. He used none of the alarmist language used by Hungarian politicians but spoke of the situation simply as a professional challenge. Twelve police officers had arrived from Austria and Germany to monitor the situation, with fifteen more due soon, under the auspices of the European border control authority, Frontex. The numbers of migrants arriving had already fallen to around 600 a day, from a peak of 1,200, thanks to joint patrols organised with the Serbian colleagues, he said.

'We see the Kosovo Albanians as our own citizens,' explained the Serbian police chief, Milorad Vejović, 'we have to give them travel documents if they ask for them, according to the Brussels agreement with the EU.' Nevertheless, the Serbian authorities were looking into ways to stem what he called 'an explosion' in the numbers of those coming. Four gangs of traffickers in the border area were broken up in 2014, thanks to cooperation with the Hungarian police. One particularly notorious hub for the smugglers, the Hotel Lira in Palić on the main road into Subotica, had been bought by an Albanian the previous summer. It had recently been raided by police and closed down.

I spent a day at the east railway station in Budapest to find out how the migrants were travelling on to Western Europe. Chaos reigned in the waiting room beside platform 9. Some Albanian families had been living there for ten days. The Hungarian police were preventing them from boarding trains to Vienna, they complained. They had no money left, not even to pay the toilet attendants to use the bathrooms. One woman told me she would go back to Kosovo immediately if she just knew how. '*Bitte zurück Kosovo oder bitte raus Germania!*' she shouted into my camera.

'All of us here are from Kosovo,' another man told me, in a quieter, cleaner waiting room further up the platform, where they had been grouped by Hungarian police. 'All we want is a better life, to go forward, to work and make something with our lives. We have no work, no money, no prospects in Kosovo. And we've been here for four days and four nights without sleeping even a minute.'

Would he consider going home to Kosovo? I asked.

'Maybe we can't go home. The Serbians wouldn't let us. That is their policy,' he said. 'Anyway, I have family members in Germany, and Austria . . . everywhere. They will help me.'

A white Hungarian prison bus pulled up outside. Names were read out. The men filed obediently along the platform, beneath loudspeakers announcing the next train to all the places they were being denied – Vienna, Linz, Munich. A dark red Siemens intercity train slid elegantly into the platform beside them. They kept their eyes lowered, to avoid seeing it. They were led in silence out onto the station forecourt and into the waiting buses. They would be taken to the OIN to be registered, and to launch their asylum claims, if they had not done so already. Then they would be

23

put in open camps, I knew, and would be free to continue their westward journeys.

On 22 February, an eighteen-month-old Kosovar baby with Down syndrome died of pneumonia at the refugee reception centre at Vámosszabadi, probably contracted in the damp woods at Ásotthalom. She was the youngest of a family of six who arrived in Hungary on 9 February.[13] By then, there were 160 asylum seekers at the open reception centre. According to a statement from the UNHCR, by mid-February 22,394 Kosovars had applied for international protection in Hungary, 85 per cent of applicants.

'It is also important to remember that 72 per cent of the asylum seekers in Hungary who are not Kosovars come from Syria and Afghanistan, two countries plagued by war, insecurity and instability,' said Montserrat Feixas Vihé, regional representative of the UNHCR in Budapest.[14]

'This is a kind of invasion of refugees or rather economic refugees, coming mostly from Kosovo, but also from Afghanistan and Syria and other parts of world, so it is increasingly difficult to cope,' Zoltán Kovács, the government spokesman told me.

I wouldn't say we are overwhelmed, but we are facing new challenges, such as finding new shelters. We also have to rethink the legal framework, which is becoming insufficient. We are keeping our obligations under the Schengen treaty, the Geneva Convention and other European rules. What is missing is an overall European strategy for handling this issue.

The interview took place in the wind and rain in Kossuth Square, in front of the Hungarian parliament. As we spoke, an uncharacteristic tear ran down the government spokesman's face. We repeated his answer to that question, to avoid the false impression that he was crying. What did he think of László Toroczkai's idea of building a fence? I asked.

'We would most definitely like to avoid as much as possible the introduction of any kind of fence or wall. We have bad memories of that from the Cold War, and most definitely we don't think this is going to be the solution,' Zoltán Kovács explained.

CHAPTER TWO

A TIME OF FEAR

The world is a bridge, across which the way of the king and the poor man passes.

> Inscription on the bridge over the River Harmanli, Bulgaria

The most frustrating thing about life there was the waiting. After all, in spite of the 'advantages' you have there, you are a prisoner. You just sit and wait, and your whole life is waiting.

> Former inmate, Busmantsi detention centre, Bulgaria[1]

The old red locomotive had round windows along the side, like portholes on a ship. I laughed when I saw the number on the front: 007. James Bond. It was March 2015, and I was waiting on the platform at Belgrade railway station for the night-train to Sofia, to investigate reports of Europeans going to fight for Islamic State (IS). One route led across Bulgaria, so they could keep below the radar of Western intelligence on their way to and from Syria. In the wake of the *Charlie Hebdo* attacks, the Hungarian government was determined to paint the migrants and the terrorists with the same brush. I wanted to find out if there was any basis for that claim.

Though the engine looked powerful, the carriages were falling apart. Painted dark blue long ago, they seemed held together now by layers of swirling graffiti. *Thins1* was painted just beneath my window, in yellow, red and green curls, in contrast to the block capitals of *LIEGEWAGEN*, which suggested German second-class comfort, designed for students with Inter-rail tickets in the 1970s.

I paced the platform like a trainspotter, taking photographs of the scene. From the compartment next to mine, a young man leant out, watching me suspiciously. In the photographs he has a square, Slavic jaw. In the early spring night the station looked like a film set. Puddles of orange light spilling from the windows, drowning in the gloom of tracks and platforms, the facade of the station, crowned with Cyrillic letters, lit up in Habsburg yellow.

I had a six-person sleeping compartment all to myself. This delighted me until I realised that the lights didn't work. Maybe they would come on when the train started? They didn't. A quick inspection of the other empty compartments proved that mine was the rule, not the exception. After a while a grumpy attendant passed through with a pile of starched white sheets, ironed thin as paper.

I made my bed with the rough, musty-smelling blankets I found on the bunk above me and was finally glad I couldn't see into the filthy corners of the compartment. What was I doing, dragging myself across the Balkans in late winter, on a wild goose chase? I cursed myself for not paying extra for a comfortable Austrian Airways flight from Budapest to Sofia via Vienna.

When I awoke it was still dark, but the train was motionless. I heard knocking on the compartments, one after another, doors sliding open, and gruff male voices. We had reached the Bulgarian border at Dragoman. I unlocked the door, pulled my ragged bedclothes around me to present a modicum of dignity, took my passport out from under the pillow, and waited.

The voices reached the next compartment to mine where my square-faced fellow traveller was sleeping. The door slid open. Barked instructions. A silence. Then a single sentence. 'So, you've been in Syria?' The question was in English. I sat up sharply. Strained to hear the reply but couldn't decipher it. Soon the border guards were in my compartment. They studied my own passport, stamped it, then were gone. I mulled over what to do about my widely travelled companion. My search for people of his ilk was, after all, the reason I had chosen this route. It was three o'clock in the morning. Light snowflakes had just started drifting past the windows as the train moved sluggishly off again. He could have been a construction worker there. An engineer. A security guard. A soldier even, in Bulgaria's NATO contingent in Iraq. The train was due into Sofia station at 07.30. I resolved to strike up a conversation with him as we got off the train together.

Standing behind him in the corridor in the slowly dissipating gloom of the Sofia morning, I noticed he had no luggage. He wore a grey hoodie with the name of some non-existent university or sports team. Once we were down on the platform, I thought, I would make some passing comment about the discomfort of the journey. But the moment his foot touched the ground, he started running. He jumped down onto the tracks and sprinted across the wooden sleepers towards the exit. It all happened so fast, I hardly had time to consider, and reject, the idea of running after him.

Later that morning I sat down with Nikolai. An agent of DANS, the Bulgarian counter-intelligence service, until a few months earlier, he had agreed to our meeting surprisingly easily. After a coffee in my hotel we went for a walk, Cold War-style, in a nearby park. He promised to make enquiries about my fellow traveller, and in the meantime told me stories from his own time in the service.

'There was a foreigner in Bulgaria whom we suspected. As a West European citizen, he could travel freely. We placed him under surveillance. But it took a whole month to get the information we needed from the secret services in his home country. Can you imagine? Not hours, but weeks!' By that time the bird, like my flighty fellow at the railway station, had flown.

Nikolai compared tracking down potential terrorists to making a cake. You assemble all the ingredients in your kitchen, then discover that one is missing. Vanilla, for example. But you planned a vanilla cake! So you go to the shop. But it's closed. It's Sunday night. If Bulgarian intelligence asks its partners for a specific piece of information, it is given, in due course, he explained. But only that. Not all the other background, connected to that person, that might provide the missing clue, the missing ingredient. His or her friends, relations, network. There's a sort of patriotism within secret services, he suggested, about sharing sensitive information about their own citizens. It is as though they don't want their own people to carry the can, or at least, no more of the can than they actually deserve. The services are also jealous of one another and reluctant to share information which has often been gathered in illegal or semi-legal ways.

A French citizen of Haitian origin, Fritz-Joly Joachin was arrested at the Kapitan Andreevo border crossing from Bulgaria to Turkey on 1 January 2015, six days before the *Charlie Hebdo* attack. He was on a bus bound for Istanbul with his three-year-old son. The initial European Arrest Warrant was filed in Paris by police acting on information provided by his wife, who thought he might take the boy to Syria. Fritz-Joly was already sitting in a Bulgarian police cell when the *Charlie Hebdo* attacks happened. Another warrant was issued after the French police discovered that he was in regular contact with Chérif Kouachi, one of the men who attacked the *Charlie Hebdo* journalists. After three weeks in detention in Bulgaria he was extradited to France.[2]

One of Nikolai's jobs in counter-intelligence was to interview asylum seekers at the Elhovo and Harmanli refugee camps close to the Turkish border. 'I can say with full confidence that 99 per cent of all those I spoke to were genuine refugees, tortured people fleeing to safety, often with their families,' he said. The problem might lie with the remaining 1 per cent, usually from the Maghreb countries of Algeria, Tunisia and Morocco. Each case was handled in a room with three or four officials present: himself, another officer, and an interpreter. Questions were based on knowledge about the place the person claimed to come from, the different dialects spoken there, even the layout of that particular town. Interviewees might even be asked the names of teachers who taught at the school where they said they had studied.

The interview lasted fifteen minutes. When a person was judged suspicious, he or she – there were some women among the refugees – was sent to the asylum detention camp at Busmantsi, near Sofia. There they could be held for up to twelve months legally, up to eighteen months in practice, while more information was gathered about them. If no link to a terrorist organisation could be proved, as happened in about 90 per cent of cases, they were then set free to continue their journey, Nikolai explained. Those judged to be a serious security threat, a mere handful, were extradited to their countries of origin, provided the country accepted them.

The refugee influx into Europe was being carefully monitored, and in some cases assisted, for political reasons, by the Turkish intelligence service MIT, Nikolai told me. He gave as an example the sudden influx of about 10,000 migrants over a 50-kilometre stretch of the mutual border in November and December 2013. At that time Turkey and the EU were locked in talks about eventual Turkish membership, and the Turkish government clearly wanted to increase the pressure. The border police managed to stop one group of 150 migrants from entering the country at their first attempt. Several hours later, the same group reappeared inside Bulgarian territory. Someone had reorganised, and transported them to another place, very efficiently.

'The MIT has been able to establish relations with many other intelligence organizations in accordance with the interests of Turkey,' reads the entry on international cooperation in the 'Frequently Asked Questions' section of the organisation's website.[3]

I made contact with a Syrian who had recently been released from the high-security detention facility at Busmantsi, where Nikolai's dodgy characters, who failed the questions at the interview, were sent. 'The guards tried to impose discipline, as it was a prison-like institution, but they treated us with respect and care. It was like a prison, but without the abuse. If it was in our country, it would have been really different in a bad way,' he told me, in written answers to my questions.

What kind of people did he meet there? I asked.

'Mostly refugees, trying to escape to Western Europe via Bulgaria, but unfortunately caught at the border.' He had not heard of anyone who was a real security threat. Some of the inmates had been there as long as eighteen months. Some didn't even want to leave, because at least they had food and shelter, and were safe from the dangers of the outside world.

Most of the conversations between the inmates were just small talk, he said, about their families, or about their relatives, waiting for them in other European countries. They often watched television, played cards, smoked or drank coffee together, 'but that switch for concealing the truth is on all the time'.

The most frustrating thing about life there was the waiting. After all, in spite of the 'advantages' you have there, you are a prisoner. You just sit and wait, and your whole life is waiting. You know there will be an end to all this and one day you will be out, but at this moment you have nothing to do but wait. While waiting, some of the inmates became angry because of the slow procedures, because of the suspense and the uncertainty and the vague future out there. Most of the people there just want a better life for themselves and their families.

Back in the park, Nikolai reverted from the image of the chef in his kitchen, to the older one of finding a needle in a haystack. 'Finding the needle is only the first step, though it's hard enough. Most important is what you do after that. How to react, because of the lack of time, the lack of information.'

I interviewed Philip Gunev, deputy interior minister of Bulgaria, in Sofia. He stressed that Bulgaria was doing all it could, and that whenever a tip-off arrived the Bulgarian services acted swiftly and effectively. Three Moroccan and Brazilian citizens, allegedly planning a bomb attack in Barcelona, were arrested in Bulgaria the previous December and extradited to Spain. Imran Khawajah, a British man convicted of terrorist offences, passed through Bulgaria on his way home in summer 2014, after faking his own death in Syria.[4] 'If a future terrorist attack takes place somewhere in Europe,' Philip Gunev told me, 'and the perpetrator passed through Bulgaria, then that would be a failure of security services across Europe to identify such an individual and to notify us, rather than our failure for not stopping him.'

*

In May 2015, the Hungarian government launched its National Consultation on Immigration and Terrorism.[5] This was a follow-up to Viktor Orbán's interview on state television in Paris, after the *Charlie Hebdo* attack – an attempt by the government to consolidate the link in voters' minds between migration and terrorism. A single A4 page with twelve questions was sent to all 8 million Hungarian voters. The questions prompted the desired answers. Each was followed by a choice of three boxes to tick. An envelope was provided for the completed form, with pre-paid postage. The questions included:

Do you agree that mistaken immigration policies contribute to the spread of terrorism?

Do you agree with the opinion that economic immigrants endanger the jobs and livelihoods of the Hungarian people?

In your opinion have Brussels' policies on immigration and terrorism failed?

Would you support the government in its efforts to introduce stricter immigration regulations in opposition to Brussels?

Would you support a new regulation that would allow the government to place immigrants who illegally entered the country into internment camps?

Do you agree with the government that instead of allocating funds to immigration we should support Hungarian families and those children not yet born?

It was not a questionnaire in the classic sense of trying to find out what the population thinks, the government spokesman, Zoltán Kovács, cheerfully admitted. It was a 'political' questionnaire, he explained, intended to seek support for the government's own stance, that immigration and terrorism were tightly interwoven. And it was a classic example of the Fidesz government's governing methods and style, which a small group of communications experts were perfecting. You tell people who to fear one day, and you ask them the next day who they are afraid of. And you store their data carefully, so that at the next election, you know who to address, and who to encourage to vote – nationwide. This was the third such campaign, all with an anti-migrant theme, organised by the government between the elections in 2010 and 2018.

The regional representative of the UN Refugee Agency, Montserrat Feixas Vihé was not impressed: 'We are deeply concerned by the way the government increasingly vilifies people who have fled from war zones like Syria, Afghanistan and Iraq and who desperately need safety and protection in Hungary,' she said. 'The UNHCR believes the questions intentionally attempt to confuse refugees and asylum seekers with so-called 'economic migrants' and wrongly blame refugees for a number of purported threats to Hungary and Europe.' And she concluded: 'We need to remember that around the world the primary threat is not from refugees, but to them.'[6]

The justice and interior ministers of the rest of Europe had not been idle since the Paris atrocities in January. At a meeting in Latvia on 29 January they issued the Riga Statement. Counter-terrorism efforts were now a priority at national and international level.[7]

'The carefully planned attacks demonstrated the elevated threat to the EU from a fanatic minority, operationally based in the Middle East, combined with a network of people born and raised in the EU, often radicalised within a short space of time, who have proven to be willing and able to act as facilitators and active accomplices in terrorism,' Rob Wainwright, director of Europol, the European police agency, wrote a year later, looking back at 2015.

31

The difference in the Hungarian government's approach was that instead of a fanatic minority, they saw a fanatic majority. And where EUROPOL identified a network of people born and raised inside the EU, radicalised inside or outside prison, Viktor Orbán's government saw immigrants. In the sixty-page EUROPOL report on the terror threat to Europe during 2015, published in 2016, migrants are only mentioned five times.[8]

> Due to the continuous rise in the number of irregular migrants entering the EU, including asylum seekers, and the increasing difficulties in accommodating them, the migration issue may remain the focus of social discourse and media coverage for a non-foreseeable period of time. In addition, *it is likely that right-wing extremists and groups will reinforce their efforts to portray the asylum policy in a polarising manner and exploit the debate for its own purposes* [italics added].

It could have been a description of the position of the Hungarian government. The 'war on migrants' was about to restore the sliding popularity of Fidesz.

On 22 February 2015, the party lost the safe seat of Veszprém in western Hungary to an independent candidate backed by the (unusually united) opposition. On 12 April, Fidesz lost the Tapolca by-election to the far-right Jobbik. Immigration was not an issue in the election, which focused mostly on the threatened closure of the town hospital, and the low pay of medical staff, which forced many to leave the country.

The numbers of asylum seekers were falling on the southern border. While in January nearly 15,000 and in February 17,000 were registered, only 6,000 arrived in March. This was a result of heavy intervention from the Kosovar authorities and warnings from Germany to the people of Kosovo that new arrivals would simply be sent home. Under heavy pressure from Germany, the Hungarian and Serbian authorities agreed to expedite that process, and busloads of reluctant Kosovars began to take the long, lonesome road back down the Balkan route in a southerly direction. But as their numbers fell, the numbers of other peoples, especially those fleeing the wars in the Middle East and Afghanistan, began to rise, along the tracks through the fields which the Kosovars had created.

In April, 8,224 migrants entered Hungary. Entering the country without the proper documents – a passport, stamped with a visa for the Schengen group of countries to which Hungary belonged, was defined under Hungarian law as a misdemeanour. The Justice Ministry were working on new regulations to turn it into a criminal offence.[9]

In May 11,606 arrived, an average of 374 a day. The police had few buses of their own. Through the spring of 2015, most of their requests to the government for funds to hire buses from private companies were turned down.

The police had developed a system to deal with the Kosovars at the start of the year. They collected all migrants at one place beside the road, then took them by bus to a blue hangar at Röszke for registration. The hangar, rented since January, had a capacity of 500. As it overflowed, rows and rows of green army tents were set up in the field next to it.

'We were under enormous pressure from the Austrians and Germans at that time,' recalled Gizella Vas, then head of the border police for the southern counties of Hungary, bordering Serbia and Croatia. 'The Austrian attaché came to see me one day, very aggressively. "Where are all the finger-prints?" he demanded. In fact, we did a good job, registering everybody and taking their fingerprints, until early September [2015].'

The police were also under huge psychological pressure, many of them drafted in from other parts of the country, with few language skills and little or no experience of handling foreigners, let alone refugees. In the circum-stances, they did their best.

In early June 2015, giant government-sponsored roadside posters went up all over the country, to complement the 'National Consultation', which had received a disappointing response from the public. Ostensibly aimed at the migrants, the messages were in Hungarian, targeting Hungarian voters: 'If you come to Hungary, don't take our jobs', or 'If you come to Hungary, you must respect our culture!'

A wave of disdain for the crude style of the posters ran through Fidesz, but there were no resignations or serious protests within the party. It was a similar story in the Catholic and Protestant churches. Some bishops even took up the government's crusading tone, echoing the prime minister's call to 'defend Christian Europe from the Muslim invasion'. The Catholic archbishop of Veszprém, Gyula Márfi, was particularly extreme.[10] This flew in the face of the pro-refugee approach taken by Pope Francis. Relations between the Catholic bishops in Hungary and the Vatican deteriorated, as the refugee crisis continued. The Pope made clear his own sympathy, his own desire to help refugees at every opportunity. His first visit outside the Vatican after taking office was to African refugees on the Italian Mediterranean island of Lampedusa in 2013. Asked about relations between the Hungarian Catholic Church and the Pope, one dissident priest told me that 'Most of my church is praying for the Pope to die.'

The churches, especially the Calvinists (Orbán is a Calvinist), have a long tradition in Hungary as defenders of the nation at times of foreign occupation. By describing the influx of asylum seekers as exactly that, Orbán tapped a rich vein of patriotic feeling which the churches were unwilling, or unable to resist. At the same time, his government spent lavishly on the churches, and their schools. 'They have bought the churches' loyalty,' one Greek Catholic priest lamented.

Rival, humorous posters began popping up across the country in strategic locations. Funded by the scurrilous Twin-Tailed Dog Party, the messages, usually in English, included: 'We are sorry about our prime minister' and 'Come to Hungary! We've got jobs in London!' When police were deployed to protect the official posters from attempts by activists to deface them, the party produced a new one. 'Dear police, there is no need to guard this poster. Please keep the public order somewhere else!'

In preparation for 20 June, International Day of the Refugee, the Central European branch of the UNHCR in Budapest put up its own posters on the walls of the metro.[11] Four successful immigrants to Hungary were identified: Begum Ali, a Bangladeshi woman who owned a restaurant in the eighth district, Dariush, a young Afghan man who worked as a tourist guide, Sophie, thirty-one, from Togo, now working as a nanny in a kindergarten, and Zeeshan, nineteen, from Pakistan, a prominent figure in Hungary's little-known national cricket team. I went to the open day at Begum Ali's restaurant.

Begum and Moshaid Ali fled their home in Bangladesh in 2000, when their shop was burnt down during political violence. Begum was eight months pregnant with their first son, Ferdoz, at the time. He was born in Pakistan, where they first found refuge. Their daughter Lutfa, now seventeen and their second son, Kalam, fifteen, were also born there. Violence in Pakistan forced them to flee again, first to Iran, then Turkey and Greece, where they spent nine years in a refugee camp, but failed to get refugee status. Of the three children, Kalam, the youngest, spoke most easily of his childhood as a refugee. 'The worst experience was on the Greek-Macedonian border, when a fight broke out between Afghan and African refugees in early 2013, when we were trying to cross,' he told me. 'Hungary was the first country to make us welcome, and we are very grateful for that.'

They spent their first six months in a refugee camp in Debrecen in the east of the country. When they were granted refugee status, they borrowed money from a family friend to open a small restaurant, the Al Modina. As we spoke, Kalam's mother rushed around the kitchen putting the finishing touches to various curries, including one made from Danube carp. Samosas sizzled in a vast pot. There were only six tables but it seemed a popular and cheap spot to eat in a neighbourhood where almost every second building boasts a restaurant. According to Kalam, the family had only been the target of racist insults once in their three years in Hungary, when a man shouted at them, 'but he was drunk,' explained Kalam. 'We came to Hungary to try to find a better life, and we found it here.'

*

The Bulgarian land border with Turkey stretches along the rough granite rocks of the southern Rhodope mountains. In early June, giant purple this-tles, their heads like the busbies worn by the ceremonial guards outside Buckingham Place, grew everywhere. Towering above them, glinting threat-eningly in the morning sunlight, a tall fence topped with razor wire was also growing. The Bulgarian fence grew out of the same seed as the short, stubby Greek one nearby.

This is the ancient province of Thrace, the gateway to Europe from Asia.[12] Bordered by the Danube to the north, the Black Sea to the east and the Aegean to the south, the first farmers brought their livestock to the narrow strip of land between the Marmara Sea and the Black Sea in the sixth millennium before Christ. They also brought grain, and the art of winning copper from rock and fashioning elegant tools, weapons and jewellery from it.

West of Istanbul, the granite Yildiz or Star mountains climb gently for 300 kilometres to their highest ridge, 1,031 metres near the Turkish town of Kirklareli. The forests on their slopes are mostly of beech and pine. Beyond Kirklareli is Edirne, once famous for the manufacture of drums, used on the

Ottoman military campaigns up through the Balkans. I bought one for my sons here, long ago.

Bulgarian museums are rich in stone images of the lone figure of 'the Thracian horseman', his spear held at the ready. This was probably the archetype of later images of the Christian figure of St George. The Christians simply added a dragon.

The flow of migrants has never stopped through Thrace, in the footsteps of those first farmers. The Evros River is 480 kilometres long; it rises in the Rhodope mountains in southern Bulgaria, where it is known as the Maritsa. The last 205 kilometres of its course forms the border between Turkey and Greece, before it flows into the Aegean near the port of Alexandropoulis. Throughout history, its valley has guided invading armies, traders and adventurers up into the Balkans and beyond. In the new migrant crisis, it was to play a similar role.

Between 2006 and 2008 most refugees crossed the narrow stretch of water from the Turkish coast to the Greek islands nearby. By the summer of 2009, that number reached more than sixty a day. The conditions in which they were detained on the islands were often atrocious. The removal of land mines left over from the 1948 Greek Civil War beside the Evros River in 2009 opened a new route for refugees coming from Turkey who were disillusioned with the sea route. But crossing the Evros River was already hard, and about to get harder.

In the winter of 2010, Italian photographer Giovanni Cocco captured the determination and despair of migrants trying to cross the marshy reaches of the Evros River on their way to Western Europe.[13] His photographs include many of the river itself in the early morning, of migrants from Africa and the Middle East drying their clothes after swimming over, or crossing the river in inflatable boats. There are pictures of men huddled around fires trying to warm themselves in the frosty Balkan winter. One of the most poignant is of the little mounds of earth, mostly unnamed, at the 'illegal migrants cemetery' at Sidiro, on the Greek side.

Foreign photographers and reporters were not the only ones to notice the migrant influx. In 2011, 55,000 people were intercepted by police trying to enter Greece along the Evros border. In January 2012, the Greek authorities began to build a 4-metre high razor-wire fence along the drier 12-kilometre bottleneck through which most migrants crossed, between the villages of Kastanies and Nea Vyssa.[14] This was the Greek equivalent of the woods at Ásotthalom. Mórahalom in Hungary was similar to the Greek town of Orestiades nearby. Twenty-three night-vision cameras were installed along the Greek fence, partially financed by the EU, and Greek patrols were backed up by Frontex, the European border guard service.[15]

In response, the smugglers simply rerouted their clients back to the Aegean coast. They established a flotilla of rubber dinghies to take them across to the nearer islands, risking the lives of those in their care by over-packing the boats. In 2014, 43,500 migrants and refugees arrived in Greece by sea alone, triple the number for the previous year. By far the largest number were from Syria, followed by Afghanistan, Somalia and Eritrea. The Greek reception centres barely improved. In its December 2014 report the UN Refugee Agency recommended that other European countries not return asylum seekers to Greece. The French medical charity Médicins Sans Frontières noted 1,000 attempts to reach the Greek islands in the last week of September 2012. By the end of the year, attempted crossings of the Evros River border near Orestiades were down 95 per cent.[16]

In Bulgaria, construction of the fence on the Turkish border began in January 2014. There was no plan initially to build a fence along the whole 288 kilometres of the border, just along what was regarded as the most vulnerable stretch, the 30 kilometres between the Kapitan Andreevo check-point and the checkpoint at Elhovo to the east. That took seven months to complete at a cost of €5 million. EU funds were provided for a large number of night-vision cameras along the whole border. Most were small and fixed, but there were also one or two super-powerful cameras, with a range of 18 kilometres, deep into Turkey. By the summer of 2015, a new 100-kilometre section of fence was under construction. The British government presented Bulgaria with fifty ex-army land rovers. Cameras were mounted on many of the new vehicles.

Kapitan Andreevo is a big modern checkpoint, renovated by the EU, with five lanes in each direction. Approached from the Bulgarian side, giant posters advertise the ancient Via Diagonalis, which once ran from this point diagonally north-west across Bulgaria to Serbia just below the city of Vidin on the Danube. If any of the migrants glanced at it, they might have noticed that it runs more or less exactly along the route they hoped to take.

During 2014, 11,000 people applied for asylum in Bulgaria; 5,000 applications were granted, almost all from Syria, 3,000 more were given 'protected status' and 3,000 people simply disappeared – through Serbia or Romania, towards the West. In the first three months of 2015, 4,700 people crossed the land border and applied for asylum in Bulgaria.[17]

Captain Aleksandar Andreevo, nicknamed Chapata, was a guerrilla fighter against the Ottoman empire in the early twentieth century. In Bulgarian eyes then, a revolutionary, while for the Turks, a terrorist.

For the Communists too, the border had a great symbolic value. In the corridor of the border police control centre at Elhovo, there is a large oil painting. It shows a determined soldier with a red star on his cap, his arm locked across the neck of a desperate young man in everyday clothes clutching a machine-gun, while a dog sinks its teeth into his arm – a border guard seizing a guerrilla fighter opposing the Communist takeover of Bulgaria in 1948. In the background, the rocky terrain with snatches of forest had changed little, but the trees gave precious cover now to thousands of desperate people fleeing war and poverty. Or so they thought.

The bank of screens in the control centre each portrayed the view from eighteen cameras, six across, three down. Black and white images, of the fence, the road running beside it, or of craggy outcrops of rock, flickered on each. The perspective from the larger cameras was amazing – the rolling hills with darker patches of trees and woodland, stretching into the far distance. The camera was powerful enough, I was told, to zoom in and read a car number plate at a distance of more than 10 kilometres. Beneath it, on a pop-up menu, the corresponding map could be brought up. Men and women in camouflage uniforms craned over the screens, scanning them for intruders. If any were spotted, two calls were made. One to the Turkish army on the far side, and the other to their own border police. I was shown a short video of a recent, night-time interception. Four small white figures could be seen, white because captured on night-vision cameras. The two in the middle were taller, the one ahead slightly smaller, possibly a woman. The figure at the back held the hand of a child. Each carried a small rucksack, which showed up black on the screen. They turned a corner, where the track got wider. At that point it turned out that there were six people in the group. Another white light appeared on the horizon. The figures scattered across the screen. One man seemed to kneel down, perhaps to protect a child. An army jeep raced down the track towards them. Then they all scattered, back into Turkey.

Harmanli, in Bulgaria, is a town set back 45 kilometres from the Kapitan Andreevo border crossing. It's a sleepy place with a fine Ottoman bridge, built in 1585, over the dried-up River Harmanli. 'The world is a bridge, across which the way of the king and the poor man passes,' reads the plaque on the middle.

The town museum was firmly shut, but in its courtyard a bust of Lenin, chiselled from grey granite lay on its side. Someone had thoughtfully placed a flowerpot with a tall thin plant growing out of it, by his head. The plant was clearly watered regularly, as it would hardly survive otherwise in the June heat. An act of consolation for the fallen giant of Marxism-Leninism, or gentle mockery.

A large tourist map on a stand in the main square promoted the glories of the Haskovo region. There were Thracian tombs and monuments, including one called the Deaf Stones, and Roman roads and Orthodox churches dedicated to the Virgin Mary, St Constantine and St Helena.

The Harmanli refugee camp is a former army camp, opened in 2013 when the first large waves of migrants caught the Bulgarian authorities unprepared. The atrocious conditions drew the ire of human rights groups, and a big effort was made to improve the place. The pink-painted barracks are still crumbling, but the rooms and corridors have been renovated. Cabins and tents were added to absorb up to 3,000 people at a time.

In a classroom I met an English teaching volunteer, Sadie Clesby and her mother.[18] They came for a month, and stayed. The classroom was brightly painted, with stacks of games, and the Arabic and Latin alphabets on the wall. Girls kneaded multi-coloured play dough into funny shapes, a boy challenged his sister to yet another game of table football, the sun shone in the window and grateful mothers pottered by to check their children were alright. Two boys climbed in and out of the ground floor window. Most of the inmates were Syrian Kurds, but there were also Iraqis and Afghans. Refugee girls, teenagers who had learnt some English at school, helped Sadie and her mother talk to the children.

'They learn so fast, communication is not a problem,' she explained.

When the children first arrive, it is as though they are shell-shocked. Some cling to the walls of the classroom. They need their parents to be there at first, which would be normal behaviour, until you see the worry lines on their faces. They often have the worried, facial expressions of adults. When some of the older refugees set off fireworks in the court-yard to celebrate Nowruz, the Kurdish New Year, the children went completely silent – not like normal children when they see fireworks. They clung to us. They were terrified.

Before we came here there was no school, no play area. We just set up something to keep them busy and let them have fun.

Most of the children in the classroom were from Al-Hasaka. As we spoke, a major drama was unfolding in their home town. IS had launched an offensive to capture the city, which had 190,000 inhabitants before the war. On 5 June, the Kurdish YPG militia (Syrian Kurdish People's Protection Units) joined government troops to fight IS forces which were taking the city district by district. By the time IS forces were finally driven back, after two months of fighting, large parts of the city, and the homes of the children I met at Harmanli, lay in ruins.[19]

In a room off a corridor near the schoolroom, I met some of the adults. Idris, from Afren, near Aleppo, said he had been in the camp for seven months. He knew people here who had been waiting for five years, he said. His own story was typical. It took him fifteen days on foot to reach Turkey from Syria in September 2014. In May 2015, he joined migrants attempting the land route through the Balkans to Germany. From Istanbul he took a bus to Edirne, where he stayed five days. A smuggler told him where to cross the border into Bulgaria. New smugglers got him and his travelling companions as far as the Bulgarian-Romanian border, but there they were caught and sent first to the asylum detention camp at Elhovo, and from there to the open refugee camp at Harmanli.

Days earlier, a baby died from a snake bite in the camp, the men told me. Since then, another larger snake had been caught and killed. They took me to see it. A man held up a harmless grass snake, minus its head, as the children gathered round to laugh nervously. A police minibus arrived, and disgorged more refugees, mostly women and children. One woman wore the full black chador, while other women, probably Kurds, were dressed in

Western style with their hair flowing down their shoulders. The adults seemed exhausted, the children full of energy and excitement at arriving in a new place. The same journey which almost turned their parents' hair white with anxiety and fear often seemed nothing more than a great adventure for the children.

I asked the men milling around outside, gazing at the snake, if any had direct experience of the IS group. One said his friends had told him that many Europeans come to fight for them. He didn't understand why. Another man butted in. 'Everyone is fighting just for the money, not for freedom, not for their fellow man. The fighters say they are fighting for Islam, but deep in their hearts, they just need money.'

Were there people in this camp who lived in areas under IS control?

'Yes, but they won't speak to the media because they are afraid for their families, who stayed behind. One man here told me how they killed his brother. First they took him to prison for a long time. There was no information about him. Then he found out they had killed him.'

He too, he said, had met Da'esh (a pejorative name for IS) fighters as he was fleeing from Aleppo. You cannot trust them at all, he said. 'Maybe this man today is very handsome, very kind, a very good man. But from one hour to the next, he turns into a killer, a murderer, who might kill you. No one knows why they change so fast.'

The refugees at Harmanli were nervous about the Dublin procedures, a cornerstone of European asylum law. They were afraid that by giving their fingerprints they might be returned to Bulgaria even if they did make it to Germany. The Dublin III procedures entered into force in 2013, an addition to the European asylum rules agreed in 2005. The country in which a refugee was first registered assumed a legal responsibility to care for that person. If the person travelled on to another country they could be returned to the first. Also implicit in the Dublin procedures was the principle that asylum seekers should be distributed fairly among EU member states. It was this principle which would later be opposed so bitterly by East European governments.

By 2015 the Dublin procedures were breaking down, both under the weight of numbers and because of reservations in Western Europe about how asylum seekers would be treated if they were returned to the East. In the whole of 2014, only eighty migrants were sent back to Bulgaria from Western Europe.[20]

The asylum seekers at Harmanli asked me for advice. What could I say? They could hardly expect Bulgaria or any other country to let them in, or let them through without registering them and recording their identity. Most had been persuaded by the smugglers to hand over their passports or other identity documents as they crossed Turkey. Others had torn them up or abandoned them at the roadside. Many later came to regret this, as in order to pick up money from a Western Union or MoneyGram office, you have to prove who you are.

In a plain whitewashed room on the first floor of the main building I was allowed to attend a security screening. There were three officials, from the secret services, the State Agency for Refugees (SAR) and an interpreter. The session lasted about fifteen minutes. The man was young, perhaps in his mid-twenties with a small, pointed face and chin, wearing a red T-shirt. He seemed earnest and confident in his innocence. The officials had notepads open. The man from the secret services asked most of the questions. I thought of Nikolai and his needle in a haystack.

Back in Sofia I met Nikola Kazakov, head of SAR. Bulgaria has the longest land border of the EU directly affected by the current refugee crisis he explained, almost proudly:

All are escaping wars in their countries, from Syria, Iraq or Afghanistan. They are afraid of executions, afraid for their lives.

For most of these people Bulgaria is a transit country to their final destinations. But we would like them to regard Bulgaria as their country. We want whoever wants to stay here, to integrate here, to be part of the society. And that is why the Bulgarian government just started to implement a national strategy for immigration and integration.

Our position is that we want all the countries in the EU to share responsibility towards refugees, and to distribute them fairly between them.

Under the quota scheme under consideration by the EU, Bulgaria had been asked to take 788 refugees and had agreed to the request. In return, as the poorest country in the EU, Bulgaria was asking for three kinds of assistance. Financial help, expert advice, and for an EU-level assessment of the refugee situation in each country, to decide what resources were needed.

If Bulgaria is so welcoming, why build a fence? I asked.

'The aim of fence is not only to stop people but also to redirect them to the checkpoints, so they can cross legally. The second purpose of the fence is to fight the human smugglers.' By the end of April, 50 per cent of new arrivals came through the official border crossings. They hid in the back of trucks, and freight cars on trains.

As we finished the interview, sirens wailed across Bulgaria. It was noon on 2 June, the day Bulgarians celebrate their nineteenth-century poet and revolutionary fighter against the Ottomans, Hristo Botev. Botev was shot dead aged only twenty-eight. Traffic stopped. People stood to attention beside their cars or on the pavements where they were walking. The siren parted the red sea of the city. Then the sound wound down, and the waters came cascading back in.

Krassimir Kanev, head of the Bulgarian Helsinki Committee, began by praising the Immigration Directorate, when we met for coffee in a quiet street near my hotel: 'We have one of the highest rates of asylum granted in Europe.'[21] Almost all Syrians were granted asylum. Hidden behind the numbers however, was the Bulgarian government's desire not to integrate the new arrivals, but to get rid of them as quickly as possible, Krassimir claimed. Knowing that they regarded Bulgaria first and foremost as a transit country, the sooner they got their documents, the sooner they would leave, he argued. In the light of the experience of other countries, I wasn't sure. The Serbian authorities gave them twenty-four hours to leave the country, while the Hungarians gave them seventy-two hours.

The Bulgarian fence was also the butt of much criticism by human rights groups. 'The government is trying to stop the influx by all means possible, without regard to who is coming. There are many reports of physical ill-treatment, including deaths in suspicious circumstances,' Kanev said. He also suggested that the efforts at integration of those who wanted to stay were half-hearted at best. Bulgaria might pay lip service to the idea of a fair distribution of refugees based on a quota system, but its Members of the European Parliament (MEPs) voted against the concept in the European Parliament.

In defence of the fence, I suggested, surely it was only fair that a country knows who is crossing its borders? What about the threat of terrorism?

'They want to end one illegal situation by creating another, with more risks. The government says they should go to the official checkpoints. But as

they have no Schengen visas, they will be turned back. So the fence is actually pushing them into the hands of the smugglers, not saving them from
them.' This also meant that only the better-off refugees, who had the money
to pay, stood a chance of getting through. The poorest, and most in need of
international protection, could not even set foot on Bulgarian soil. The
answer would be the creation of a sensible policy at European level, and the
fair distribution of refugees through a quota system. On this at least, he
agreed with the government.

CHAPTER THREE

VIKTOR ORBÁN'S JIHAD

The Arabic word 'jihad' is often translated as 'holy war', but in a purely linguistic sense, the word 'jihad' means struggling or striving. The Arabic word for war is: 'al-harb.'

Islamic Supreme Council of America[1]

With huge shortages of funding and wide gaps in the global regime for protecting victims of war, people in need of compassion, aid and refuge are being abandoned. For an age of unprecedented mass displacement, we need an unprecedented humanitarian response and a renewed global commitment to tolerance and protection for people fleeing conflict and persecution.

António Guterres, UN High Commissioner for Refugees[2]

In his regular, bi-weekly interview on public service radio on 12 June 2015, Viktor Orbán said that 'every possibility [to block the migrants] will be analysed, including the possibility of full, physical border closure'. A decision, based on the options drawn up by the Interior Ministry would be announced the following Wednesday.[3]

On 17 June in parliament, during a break in the cabinet meeting, Foreign Minister Péter Szijjártó announced that Hungary was going to build a fence along the whole 175-kilometre length of the border with Serbia. It would be 3 metres high, with 70-centimetre coils of razor wire along the top. The poles would be buried 1.7 metres into the ground. The components would be manufactured by the inmates of Hungarian prisons and erected by them, with the help of soldiers and those on government work schemes, to reduce the burden on the Hungarian tax payer. Initially, the foreign minister said it would be finished 'by the end of November'. That message was quickly altered to 'the end of August'.

'Iron Curtain!' proclaimed the banner headline the following morning in the *Blikk* tabloid. The fence could cost 30 billion forints – €100 million – the paper's readers were told. 'And might keep out 125,000 migrants a year.' Beneath the article was an advertisement for holidays in Tunisia. Non-Europeans should stay out of Europe, apparently, but Europeans wanted to keep enjoying the sun and sand in North Africa.

In fact, the fence was not a new idea. The first secret studies on the viability of a border barrier were commissioned by Interior Minister Sándor Pintér in 2013. Police officers were despatched to study existing fences, and Hungarian embassies in countries with border fences were required to submit information about their efficacy. But Viktor Orbán's government initially showed no interest in the information submitted. It was only after the loss of two 'safe' Fidesz seats in by-elections that the government's communications gurus dusted off the reports. Orbán now produced them unexpectedly from his top hat like a magician: 'This is not a *wave* of migration,' he said, 'but a *process* of mass migration which we can expect to last a long time.'

Central to the government's argument was the valid point that before reaching Hungary, unless they arrived by air, the newcomers must have passed through at least one EU member country – Greece or Bulgaria. Under EU law, they should have sought safety there. Hungary now began changing its own laws, to criminalise the migrants in accordance with its own ideology.

On 1 August 2015, a new law came into force, declaring all countries south of Hungary 'safe' for refugees. This was a logical extension of the fence idea. If anyone got through it, they would henceforth be pushed back into Serbia. This broke international refugee law, which explicitly ruled out such push-backs, which are usually referred to by the French word *refoulements*.[4]

How safe were Greece and Bulgaria for refugees? In December 2014 the UNHCR declared Greece unsafe, because of poor facilities and ill-treatment of refugees.[5] The UNHCR and human rights groups also judged the Bulgarian response to the needs of refugees seriously lacking.[6] The

Hungarian government was either unaware of such reports or chose to ignore them.

Serbia was also regarded internationally as unsafe for refugees, despite the relatively friendly official attitude to migrants. 'Reception conditions were inadequate for the numbers arriving, and insufficient care was provided to vulnerable individuals . . . Police continued to ill-treat and financially exploit refugees and migrants,' wrote Amnesty International.[7]

Turkey was a special case. The country's leaders had signed the 1951 Refugee Convention in 1962 but imposed a geographical limitation on the 1967 protocol to it, under which it could only be applied to European citizens. In practice this meant that not a single refugee or migrant from the ongoing wave could legally be returned there.

On 18 June in Geneva, the day after the new Hungarian fence was announced, the UNHCR released its annual Global Trends report.[8] A record 60 million people around the world were displaced in 2014, up from 51 million in 2013, and 37.5 million in 2003. Of these, 13.9 million were newly displaced. The report listed the outbreak of fifteen new conflicts in the past five years. Eight in Africa (Côte d'Ivoire, Central African Republic, Libya, Mali, north-eastern Nigeria, Democratic Republic of the Congo, South Sudan and Burundi); three in the Middle East (Syria, Iraq and Yemen); one in Europe (Ukraine) and three in Asia (Kyrgyzstan, and in several areas of Myanmar and Pakistan).

'Worldwide, one in every 122 humans is now either a refugee, internally displaced, or seeking asylum. Were this the population of a country, it would be the world's 24th biggest.' It would fall between Italy and South Africa on the list. A refugee nation.

Before the Hungarian fence was announced, 400 migrants a day were crossing through the narrow bottleneck between Ásotthalom and Tiszasziget. That number doubled by the end of the month to over 1,000 a day. Why did you come and why now? I asked those I met at the border. 'We set out because we heard it would be much harder in the future,' they told me in the second half of June and July. The sparkling new razor-wire fence acted as a magnet for the tens of thousands of people it was supposed to keep out. For those agonising over whether to brave the dangerous journey to Europe, and the uncertainties and indignities of life as a refugee, news of Viktor Orbán's fence tipped the balance.

47

The response of other European countries to Hungary's fence and the new rules was swift. Serbian Foreign Minister Ivica Dačić warned the Hungarian government that it risked creating a 'human tragedy' at the border, as migrants piled up in makeshift camps, unable to cross. Much was still unknown about how the push-backs would happen in practice. Once construction began, fence-watchers noticed that small gates were being left in the fence, every 500 metres, presumably to enable people to be deported without the trouble of reaching prior agreement with the Serbian authorities on the other side.

The Serbian government largely turned a blind eye to the migrants travelling across their country. The Serbian police had almost given up patrolling the border with Hungary. If they came across a large group of migrants they would simply check if they had enough water and point them towards Hungary. The parks around the train and bus stations, starting from Belgrade and finishing in Subotica, the town furthest to the north, were full of resting people. International organisations, led by the French medical charity Médecins Sans Frontières, mobilised to help.

A photographer from *Dél Magyarország*, a regional daily newspaper based in Szeged, filmed Serbian police alighting from a coach on the motorway which runs just a few hundred metres from the Hungarian border, to be followed down by a large contingent of migrants. They immediately set out across the fields, across the drainage canal into Hungary.[9]

There were three main crossing points from Serbia into Hungary: beside the River Tisza and its oxbows, up a largely disused railway line which stretched through the cornfields between Horgoš and Röszke, and through the scrubby woodland near Ásotthalom. Many migrants gathered to rest at a disused brick factory known as 'Ciglana' on the outskirts of Subotica. A crumbling red brick chimney, long low buildings roofed with tiles, and the surrounding fields of wheat and weeds, became home to a transient population of thousands over the next two years.

On an early June evening the sandy tracks around Ásotthalom were full of migrants once again. Where I had seen mostly Kosovar Albanians in February, now the largest number were from Syria and Iraq, closely followed by Afghanistan. The Syrians had the best mobile phones and were the best organised. In the village of Horgoš on the Serbian side I sat with a group of them. They didn't want their faces to be filmed, but we could record their voices, and the backs of their heads, as they set out up the railway track to cover the last 3 kilometres to the Hungarian border.

On the Hungarian side, a wide road of mud and sand had been cleared of trees and undergrowth as far as the eye could see. The fence began as an experiment, supported by concrete posts in some places, timber ones in others, with one coil of razor wire along the bottom, and another along the top. At regular intervals there were white signs with the words, 'state border' in three languages. And the Hungarian flag.

In a quiet moment, the cameraman I was working with, Mark Hewitt, who had served in the army, struck up a conversation with the soldiers building the fence. What did we think of it? they asked, clearly rather proud of their handiwork. 'In the British army, they taught us to cross these things in about three seconds,' Mark told them. They were crestfallen.

A glass bottle of perfume with a silver screw top lay in grass flattened by human bodies. A colourful striped shawl in pastel reds, browns, purples and yellow lay nearby, either lost in the hurry to leave or placed carefully for others to find, to mark the easiest place to cross the narrow Körös-éri canal which marks this section of the Hungarian-Serbian border. I picked it up, as a souvenir, then thought better of it, and put it carefully back in its place in the morning dew. The grass beside it, leading to a parting in the reeds on the overgrown canal, had been trodden flat. And the water shone clear in the daylight, marking the path. *Patrin* is the Gypsy word for signs left behind as waymarks for those who follow. It means leaf. But there were no Gypsies here. Through the trees on the far side were the occasional red tiled roofs of Serbian farmsteads. As there was no one about, I took off my shoes and socks, rolled up my trouser legs and waded through the water, into Serbia. The soil seemed better there, richer and browner, in contrast to the sand on the Hungarian side. A field of sunflowers grew in orderly rows. I crossed back, illegally, fearing detection, but there was nothing to fear, only the flies which buzzed around my mouth and eyes. A warm breeze brushed the hair of the long grass.

Biscuit wrappers and other litter, discarded after a hurried snack before dawn, were strewn across the track which led inland, towards the main road. Lost things from a long journey. The canal bristled with sword-shaped leaves, and willows leant over it protectively, as though to hide what was going on here from prying eyes. At one point, the canal was crossed by a

49

small bridge, just big enough for a car to cross. But it was decorated, long ago, with thick steel cables, to prevent car smugglers using it to take their stolen vehicles in one direction or the other. Now the cables had rusted, they looked like loops of spaghetti left on a child's plate. Beyond the canal, white-painted concrete border stones stood out in the grass, with metal plates with the letter M for Magyarország on one side, RS for Serbia on the other. There was another plaque on the side with the number 432 – 432 kilometres from somewhere. There were no border guards, no police, just the din of birds and frogs, and the traces left by refugees. On the far side, in the distance, maize plants, already knee high, added another shade of green to this mostly green world. In the Hungarian language, corn is known as *tengeri*, meaning sea, because it came from beyond the sea, from the Americas. Other fields were already dotted with the cylindrical shapes of hay bales, winter fodder for the animals. In the middle of a field of sunflowers, already as tall as a man but with their flowers still tightly shut, a lookout tower rose like the turret of a Gothic castle. Halfway up the tower had a sort of belt made up of concrete flames. Above that what looked like a house, with windows and sloping grey roof, but no doors, was suspended, and rising from that, instead of a chimney, another square tower bristling with aerials. The whole peculiar structure appeared to be abandoned.

A maze of sandy tracks riddled the woods on the Hungarian side of the border. Close to the village of Ásotthalom, there were storks' nests atop telegraph poles, and stately black and white birds minding their chicks while their mates cruised gracefully among the open fields between the woods for food. Wild daisies grew everywhere, and crude purple flowers with leathery leaves I did not recognise. The woods were mostly spindly poplar, freckled with shrub acacia. No tall or stout trees graced these woodlands – the result of Communist-era forestry practices which favoured mass planting, and mass cutting. Thirty years later the same approach was the norm. Near the main tracks, fir trees thrived in the sandy soil.

'Don't bother to go down there and get eaten by mosquitoes! Just wait on the main road, the migrants will come to you!' advised a friendly local man. He was staying with his wife and daughters in an outlying farm. There was a swing in the yard, a blue plastic slide, and behind the house on the edge of an open field, three wooden lookout towers for hunters, side by side, each with eight wooden steps. People here must be selling them, I thought.

What did he think of all the people, from far flung corners of the world, traipsing down the path beside his house? I asked. His face darkened. 'I'm a hunter – and they disturb the wild animals,' he grumbled. If I give him my phone number, would he text me if he saw another group of migrants coming?

'No mobile phone coverage!' he complained. On the map in the village hall in Ásotthalom, this area is called 'the accursed forest' – a reference to the lack of water, or perhaps now to the lack of mobile coverage. Driving back to the main road, two deer crossed my path, almost lazily, then watched me from a clump of acacias, oblivious to the danger of men with guns. I passed a signboard advertising the presence of other mammals. There are three kinds ground-dog (*Spalax leucodon*), the Transylvanian, the Hungarian, and the Southern Great Plain variety. All three can be found in this region, but the latter is the most endangered, with only 300 individuals left. In the picture below, it looked like a small otter, 15 to 25 centimetres long, brownish-grey, with a flat head. Completely blind, without earlobes or tail, it lives its whole life underground. Forestation, deep ploughing, and the destruction of the grasslands beneath which it builds its shallow burrows, are wiping the animal off the face of the earth. There was also an appeal to save the poor animal from extinction. Anyone who sees one should ring the nearest branch of the national park.

Just off another sandy track, watching suspiciously from her front porch, a middle-aged woman replied in short sentences to my questions. She had lived in this neighbourhood all her life, and had a son aged twenty-six and a daughter of sixteen.

The situation is bad. They knock on my door at night. I don't dare let my daughter out in the evenings. Sometimes they call out to her. Once they threw gravel. I'm more afraid for her than she is for herself. And this has been going on for almost a year already.

Mostly we see them at dawn. Some ask for water. Others just walk past our gate. I never let them in, And I don't give them anything either.

There was a time when the police patrolled here, in March and April, then the migrants kept their distance. But now the police had disappeared, and more and more migrants were coming. Mostly in groups of five or six young people, around five in the morning. She'd seen three groups already today. They shook her garden gate but she hid inside. They called out for water or shouted 'police' in English. And her dog, and all the dogs on nearby farmsteads, barked from evening till morn. Would a fence help?

'That's what we need,' she said. 'It would protect us . . . but what we really need is for the Border Guard to be reestablished.' Ordinary police took over the Hungarian Border Guard's duties in border areas. There was no solution in sight. She just wanted the migrants to stop coming.

I needn't have worried about finding refugees. They were already resting at the roadside when I reached it. Almost all those in this first group were from Africa. The Hungarian police in their smart blue uniforms and red caps stood guard over them, like peacocks guarding wild, migrating birds. But there was no desire to escape. They had reached what they hope would be the promised land. Hungary. And they were very, very tired.

Eric was twenty-one, from a village near Kinshasa in the Democratic Republic of the Congo. He had been walking for four months, across Turkey, Greece, Macedonia and Serbia. He was wearing a red and white baseball cap, denim shorts, and a grey hoodie jacket. He had a short beard, which helped him look older than his real age. In Istanbul he teamed up with the fifty or so people he was with now. 'We are all together.'

They crossed from Turkey to the Greek island of Kos on a small rubber dinghy – he gesticulated just how small it was between his two hands. The boat journey was too hard. 'Like death itself' his travelling companion interjected. The French word for death, *la mort* rebounded between them like a ball on a table tennis table.

From the island of Kos, they took a ship to the Greek mainland at the port of Athens, Piraeus, then continued northwards, on foot. Eric had a Refugee Certificate from the UNHCR in Turkey.

To whom it may concern. This is to certify that the above named person has been recognised as a refugee by the United Nations High Commissioner for Refugees, pursuant to its mandate. As a refugee, he is a person of concern to the Office of the UNHCR, and should, in particular, be protected from return to a country where he would face threats to his life or freedom. Any assistance afforded to the above named individual would be most appreciated.

The document was dated Ankara, 1 November 2011, when Eric first arrived alone in Turkey, a few days after his sixteenth birthday. The last sentence reminded me of the beginning of 'Paddington' by the British children's author, Michael Bond. A bear arrives at Paddington station in London from 'darkest Peru', with a small suitcase containing marmalade sandwiches, and a sign around his neck: 'Please look after this bear.'

What did you know about Hungary before you came? What kind of welcome do you expect? 'C'est la paix, quoi' – it's a country at peace! – he replied, and that was quite enough.

He fled war and mistreatment by the authorities in Congo, he explained. As we spoke, the radios of the policemen guarding them crackled into life. The southern Hungarian dusk was deepening. The headlights on the police van were turned on and the Africans exposed, as though on stage. On his radio, one officer related how many were in this group, while another reported how many had been caught somewhere else. The tone in which they spoke about the migrants was not racist, rather pragmatic. Twenty here, ten there, a straggling group of six or seven somewhere else. All spotted at the roadside and told firmly to sit down and wait. They could easily have run away – the police were at full stretch, with just two or three guarding thirty of forty migrants, but they had no reason to run. They felt they had arrived somewhere and were actually keen to be registered. The first question many asked was, 'Where can I find the police?' The influx already represented a logistical problem for the authorities, who didn't have enough buses.

Life has always been difficult in Africa, I suggested to Eric. What was the final straw, what propelled him to leave? 'So many of my friends were killed in the street.' He said so quietly, gazing at me, his eyes gleaming white in the peaceful European roadside dusk. I was ashamed of my question. A horse and cart passed, the old Hungarian peasant looked down from his seat, uncomprehending – an emotion shared by the asylum seekers as they watched him slowly go by. Had they really fled to a country where people travel by horse and cart? A police helicopter hovered overhead like an angry dragonfly, then flitted away over the tree tops. The Africans were silent. The only chatter was from the birds, settling down for the night, and the police, who wished they could too.

Another man from Congo, called Israel, said he left his country because he wanted to live in peace. 'In Congo there are so many political problems, so much manipulation. Corruption and theft are huge problems.'

'The police surrounded the area and accused me and my friends of being bandits, delinquents, but that was not true. We were just petty traders.' He described his terror when he saw his friends killed by the police. 'That's why we came here, to look for a life free of fear.' What would have happened to you and your friends if you had stayed in Congo?

'I would have died. You cannot live all your life in terror. When they follow you, and accuse you of something you didn't do, that is very hard to take. And when they come for you, and take you away, very few survive to tell the tale.' He left his brother and sister behind in Greece, where he met Eric and the others. They crossed the country, sleeping rough as they went. They were registered by the police, but never 'admitted'. There were no humanitarian centres where they could find shelter, or food. Without money, they collected scraps of food from dustbins.

'Sometimes we give fingerprints, sometimes we don't.' They would prefer not to, because the big fear of most is that they will one day be deported back to one of the poor countries on their route, like Greece, or Hungary.

Most of the people from Congo spoke French but another man in the group, Omar from Mauritania, spoke English too. He had left his country five years earlier by plane to Turkey and had travelled on foot ever since. He spent more than four years in a refugee camp in Greece but left when his request for asylum was rejected.

'This is my family now!' he laughed, putting his arms round Issa and his wife, Fatouma, from Congo. 'We came together from Thessaloniki!' He was a Peulh, also known as Fulani. 'In my country the white Moors are in power, and the black, like me, are shut out of everything.' He would be twenty-five in February.

Did he have a profession? I felt like a job interviewer.

'I have three professions!' He grinned. Information technology, plumbing and electricity. When did he last drink water? 'The police gave me some, when they caught me. I felt so happy in my heart!'

Later I looked up his country on the internet. The fresh water beneath the capital, Nouakchott, is expected to run out in around 2054, and is already expensive.[10] The Fulani number 40 million, spread across West and Central Africa; 13 million are nomadic, the largest pastoral nomadic people in the world.

The first European to 'discover' Congo, or the source of the River Congo at least, was the Hungarian László Magyar, an adventurer from the western Hungarian town of Szombathely.[11] He died in Ponte de Cuio, Angola in 1864. A prolific linguist who spoke five European and five African languages, his writings are most valued for his descriptions of the people whom he travelled among, and their customs. He was known as 'Mister What-is-this?', on account of his insatiable curiosity.

Our roadside conversations were cut short by the arrival of a white police bus. The Congolese picked themselves up wearily from the side of the road, and dragged themselves towards it, Issa supporting his pregnant wife on his arm. On the steps, a policeman with a torch noted gender and nationality. Forty-eight people in all. As they waited, I talked to Sefala Han, twenty-six, from Jalalabad in Afghanistan. He fled first to Pakistan, where he stayed two or three years. There were big problems there. Then he travelled for four or five months through Iran, Turkey, Bulgaria and Serbia. At home he worked as a sales assistant in a sweet shop.

'If your country will give me refuge,' he said, assuming I was Hungarian, 'I will stay here.' He had lost track of the rest of his family, who fled in another direction. 'I am very happy to reach Hungary, insh'allah, with God's help.' Among this mostly African gathering, there were just four Afghans, including two children standing slightly apart, looking too young to be here, a brother and sister. Salman was twelve and Zahra fifteen, from Afghanistan. Their mother was very ill, in Athens. They teamed up with the Africans somewhere in the Balkans. I wanted to ask more, but the police were impatient to leave. A policeman called Norbi called the countries on his list, like football scores. Pakistan 2, Afghanistan 4, Cameroon 1, Congo, 48. Fifty-five people in all. The Mauretanian had clearly gone unnoticed among the Congolese. Thirty-six men, eighteen women and one child. Zahra was counted among the women. Only her brother was a child now. The bars on the inside of the bus clanged shut. Through the small windows, the refugees made little V for victory signs to me, as they were driven away to the blue hangar and white tents of the camp at Röszke.

It was almost dark by now. I took a room in the Pinetree Guesthouse on the corner where the road from Ásotthalom reaches the main road. The boarding house, true to its name, was overhung with pines. This was where the extra police, brought in to catch the Kosovars in February, were quartered. I was the only guest.

The next morning I was up at five. I wanted to witness people at the very moment they entered Hungary. I drove back down the sandy tracks to the same places I found the day before, to the cable strewn bridge and the overgrown canal. Cobwebs glittered gold in the early sunlight. Layers of mist lay on the fields along the border, like fine pastry. The din of the birds and frogs was deafening, but there were no migrants. I was too late – they came at first light. By the time the sun was up, they had reached the road. The first group I met, as yet undiscovered by the police, were eight young Afghan men, hardly more than boys, walking slowly along the road between Ásotthalom and Királyhalom. They hadn't eaten for four days, they said. I had six melons in the back of the car, three watermelons, three honeydew. The eyes of the Afghans lit up as I unpacked the big fruit. Do you have a knife? One of the boys asked. No? He shrugged, lifted the fat green cylindrical melon into the air, and let it crash onto the tarmac at his feet. It split into five pieces. Soon we were all perched at the roadside, our faces buried in the red, sugar-sweet, black-seeded flesh.

CHAPTER FOUR

THE DOG'S BREAKFAST

> The sharing of migrants across member states, the processing of asylum
> claims, the creation of legal routes into Europe – there should be pan-
> European coordination of this. Instead, there is a dog's breakfast of
> national policies, some more enlightened than others.
>
> *Financial Times* leader column, 31 December 2015[1]

On 31 July 2015, British prime minister David Cameron announced that he
was sending sniffer-dog teams and extra security fencing to France to help
reduce the growing chaos in Calais.[2] For the past year, informal tent camps
of migrants dubbed 'the Jungle', close to the motorway which leads to the
port area, had grown from 800 to around 5,000 people. Each night they
tried to clamber on to the back of, underneath, or into the containers carried
on trucks bound for the UK. Most of the migrants were young and desperate
enough to risk their lives. Eurotunnel, the company which manages the rail-
link under the English Channel which the trucks were queuing to get onto,
said they had prevented 37,000 people from entering Britain so far that year.
A security fence costing £7 million was already in place. The new fencing
was sent to reinforce it.

There was no figure available for the number who had got across, but
media reports in Kent, the first county on the far side, suggested over 600
unaccompanied children succeeded in just three months. The numbers were
small compared to those funnelling up through the Balkans, but psychologically important. Britain was just a year ahead of a crucial referendum on EU

57

membership. Most people thought of 'immigrants' not as Syrians or Iraqis fleeing war, but as East Europeans flooding the country in search of work. The double impact of Poles, Hungarians, Lithuanians and Romanians already legally present in the country, and the nightly images of kids from the rest of the world trying to storm lorries at Calais was already fuelling the argument for Britain to leave the EU.

The British prime minister's choice of the word 'swarm' to refer to migrants, was fiercely criticised in Britain:

> David Cameron crudely described this flow of migrants as a 'swarm' this week, but worse was the Prime Minister's subsequent decision to send British sniffer dogs to fortify the channel crossing. This is the shallowest gesture politics, a ploy to keep the press sated for a few days. If Mr Cameron lacks vision, so too does the European Union itself.

The solution, the *Financial Times* leader writers argued, was complex but not impossible for a club with the wealth and diplomatic and military resources of the EU. A quota system for the relocation of asylum seekers from pressure points like Greece and Turkey should be one of the elements – exactly the quota system so fiercely opposed by the East European states. Longer-term measures should include Europe welcoming and streamlining applications from those who had already reached Turkey, Lebanon and Jordan. British and French military forces should help impose some order on the North African ports, especially in Libya, from which many African migrants were setting out to cross the Mediterranean. And much more should be done to improve the economic prospects of North and sub-Saharan Africa, to reduce the exodus. And the *Financial Times* concluded:

> Governments invest too much hope in technical fixes: a security measure here, a raid on people-traffickers there. The real problem is structural. As long as chaos reigns close to Europe, people will risk their lives to come here. The solution to the migrant problem lies at the source.

*

A new Hungarian law came into force on 1 August 2015, turning illegal entry into Hungary from a misdemeanour into a criminal offence.[3] It also created a unilateral legal provision for Hungary to send migrants back to any country its parliament declared safe. Until that point, Serbia and Hungary had a bilateral agreement allowing for the deportation of up to sixty people a day in either direction. That agreement had been successfully implemented with hundreds of Kosovars in the spring. Upset by the fence, and deeply alarmed at the prospect of tens of thousands of people getting stuck in Serbia when the fence was completed, Serbia announced that it was suspending the deportation agreement. Hungary's fast-track courts might be able to sentence dozens of people a day to expulsion, Serbia made clear that it would not accept them.

On 4 August reporters were allowed into the old Dunaferr iron works in Dunaújváros, on the River Danube, south of Budapest. We were shown into the vast assembly hall where inmates from four Hungarian prisons were preparing steel rods as stanchions for the new border fence. They wore yellow high-visibility jackets over their grey prison uniforms, blue or orange helmets, and heavy-duty gloves. Many were of Roma origin. Hungarian prison governors privately admit that more than half of all inmates are of Roma ethnic background. Dark-skinned Hungarians were being conscripted into Viktor Orbán's war against dark-skinned refugees.

The men stacked the steel rods under the watchful, but not unsympathetic, gaze of prison warders in dark trousers and pale blue shirts. Handcuffs glimmered on the back of their belts like Christmas decorations. Other stanchions hung at an angle from the high ceiling on wires, like solar panels. The wires looked from a distance like steel rain, falling in shafts of sunlight across a futuristic industrial landscape.

The men were manufacturing the basic components of the fence itself, not the razor wire which was made at another factory. In the next-door workshop, more inmates, meticulously kitted out in safety gear, used welding torches to cut the steel rods to the right length. In yet another workshop, the steel was galvanised with zinc to increase its resistance to corrosion, and thus lengthen the life of the fence. János Lázár, the head of the prime minister's office, had commented a few days earlier that the fence was only a temporary, not a permanent measure. The work we observed in Dunaújváros suggested it would be around longer than we would.

The inmates tolerated our intrusive lenses pretty well. The border fence, everyone knew, was a kind of political circus, and we reporters no less than the men building sections of it, or the soldiers unrolling it, fixing it into place and guarding it, were all performing animals. Outside, great rusting drums lay like discarded toilet rolls. Dunaferr is just a shadow of its former self. Dunaújváros was built on the fields around the village of Dunapentele in the mass industrialisation period following the Communist takeover after the Second World War. From 1951 to 1961 it was called Sztálinváros, Stalin-town. The ore melted into steel in the furnaces here was brought across the Black Sea from Ukraine and Russia, then up the Danube in long, flat-bottomed barges.

On 12 August, twenty-year-old Marah El Saeed left the Syrian city of Aleppo with her mother, her sister and two younger brothers, after four years of war.

> We always hoped that it will end soon. We told ourselves we had to be more patient, although the lack of the water and electricity and every-thing we needed made life so difficult. The part of the city we were living in was bombed daily for three years. Despite the bombing and the short-ages, we tried to lead a normal life. My sister and I were going to univer-sity and my brothers to school. But in the final year IS and the other Islamic groups were so close to where we live. They threatened people that they will come in and kill us horribly. They are monsters, and they were our biggest fear and our biggest reason to leave.
>
> From Aleppo we travelled to the Lebanese border. From Beirut we flew to Turkey – this part of the journey we did legally. Then on 20 August, just before sunrise, we boarded a rubber dinghy on the west coast of Turkey. The journey took exactly one hour, across the sea to Mytilene on the Greek island of Lesbos.
>
> We took the big ship to Athens, then a bus to the Greek-Macedonian border. We walked through the borders at night in a big group and the police were all around us, as though they were guiding us. We crossed Macedonia by train to the Serbian border. The Serbian police tried to stop us from getting in, but there were not so many of them, so we ran past them, into Serbia.
>
> Then we travelled by bus to a region whose name I have forgotten. We paid the smugglers to make us fake papers there, which meant we could reach Belgrade without having to stay in a camp first. From

Belgrade we tried to go to Hungary by train, but the Serbian police in the train near the Hungarian border caught us, and we just got off the train.

At night a man persuaded us to let him accompany us, as he was also going to Germany. So we started walking with him. Then we discovered that he had lied. He didn't have internet or GPS on his phone. I told my mum I thought we should go back. We found a nightclub and they ordered a taxi for us and we went back to Belgrade.

In the morning we took a bus to the Hungarian border. Then we walked across the border. The police in Hungary caught us and told us to sit at the roadside. We waited in the hot sun without any water for more than seven hours. Finally they took us by bus to the camps but in fact they were like prisons. We were treated so badly for two days.

As the numbers of those crossing into EU countries increased, so did the tensions between Hungary and its Balkan and EU neighbours. On 20 July EU leaders accepted a plan to redistribute 32,000 asylum seekers from Greece and Italy across the block – less than the 40,000 proposed by Jean-Claude Juncker in June, but respectfully close to that number. Most were Syrians and Eritreans. 'We are almost there,' Dimitris Avramopoulos, EU home affairs commissioner, said confidently. 'The remaining 8,000 will be allocated by the end of this year.'

While most other European countries grappled with the question of how many asylum seekers to accept, the Hungarian government stuck to its policy of not accepting a single one. In speech after speech, Orbán insisted that these were not genuine refugees at all, but economic migrants. The government also announced plans to close the two long-established refugee camps at Debrecen and Bicske, and move asylum seekers to tent camps instead.

The Hungarian police, and László Toroczkai's field rangers, were struggling to cope with the influx at Röszke and Ásotthalom. The blue hangar at Röszke had long since overflowed, with an average of 1,500 people crossing a day, mostly up the railway track from Horgoš to Röszke. Those rounded up by the police were taken there first, for preliminary registration. The field next to the hangar filled with green and white tents. The Hungarian Red Cross put up a white tent at the entrance. It was a closed camp, patrolled by the police, but relatively easy to get into or break out of. On the far side of the road the authorities were building a larger, more secure camp with taller fences.

The people-smugglers were having a field day. The Serbian, Albanian and Romanian traffickers who had been plying their trade from the OMV petrol station beside the motorway at Röszke had begun to be edged out by more home-grown 'taxi drivers' – mostly people of Roma origin from Baranya and Borsod counties. Word spread fast that Syrian migrants would pay €200 per person for a ninety-minute ride to Budapest. The stupidity of the situation was that they could have got a bus ticket into Szeged for a couple of euros, then an intercity train ticket for €20.

Non-governmental organisations (NGOs) and volunteer groups struggled to step into the huge vacuum the state refused to fill. In Szeged, a Migration Solidarity group set up by local teachers Balázs Szalai and Mark Kékesi had around 200 volunteers. With the permission of the Socialist mayor of Szeged, László Botka, they set up semi-permanent wooden booths in front of the railway station, and distributed leaflets, tea, food, clothes and information about the onward journey. Everywhere the refugees went they left a trail of litter which did little to endear them to the local population. But here in Szeged, a city of 160,000, the volunteers made sure that all litter in the area around the station was cleared almost before it hit the ground. The volunteers even cleaned the station toilets, to the astonishment of the local toilet attendant, who wept with emotion as she told me she had never seen them so clean. Those registered and fingerprinted at one of the Röszke camps, or at the OIN office on the main boulevard in Szeged, or at the new camp at Nagyfa, just to the north of the city, were brought to the railway station by bus, in several convoys a day. Each was issued with a single A4 page, telling them to report to one of the camps at Debrecen, Bicske or Vámosszabadi within seventy-two hours. But little information was provided about how to get there. The volunteers took them over, arranged translators, and gave them the information they actually needed. The volunteers drew maps with instructions in Arabic, Farsi and English, on how to get to the designated camps. They also clashed with some Szeged taxi drivers, who resented the fact that, armed with the information that one could travel so cheaply to Budapest on public transport, many began to shun their expensive offers.

Within the police, there was also a degree of corruption. One local person described how the migrants were taken in groups of three cars, which the police were paid to ignore. I had no way of checking the information, but it tied in with the procedures used by smugglers in Bulgaria. By prior arrangement, the first car would be stopped by police. While they were occupied checking the bona fide identity of the passengers, the second car would sail through, unscathed by the law. A third vehicle would drive along behind, guarding the smugglers' rear from over-inquisitive police who were not party to the plot. In April, May and June 2015, 3,000 suspected smugglers were arrested across the EU, according to Frontex.

On 22 August I moved down to Szeged, and hardly got home for the next three months. Each morning I drove down to the cornfield at Röszke to do my early reports for the BBC beside the railway track as the sun came up, and long lines of asylum seekers appeared from the fields of maize and sunflowers.

These are the flattest and lowest-lying lands in the whole of Hungary. Not far from the border at Gyálarét near Tiszasziget is the lowest point in the country, just 75 metres above sea-level.[4] In the marshland nearby, the *Lúdvári Venus* was found by archaeologists in the 1960s. A clay figure resembling a woman, estimated at 7,800 years old, she was the product of one of the civilisations which grew up in the lower Danube basin in the late Neolithic and Copper Ages.

The numbers of migrants grew through August, passing 2,000 a day on the 16th and topping 3,000 for the first time on the 25th.[5]

*

In Germany on Friday, 21 August 2015, a private memo signed by Angela Wenzel, a senior official at the Federal Office for Migration and Refugees (BAMF), fell into the hands of a pro-asylum NGO, the European Council on Refugees and Exiles (ECRE) who immediately published it on their website.[6] The memo made it clear that Germany had suspended the hitherto obligatory tests for Syrian asylum seekers, which all asylum seekers had to undergo, to establish which country they first entered the EU. That test was the necessary prerequisite to fulfil the Dublin III Regulation. In practice this meant that Syrian refugees need no longer fear deportation to the first country where they were registered after they entered the EU.

Hungary had already announced on 23 June that it was suspending implementation of the Dublin III regulation, but this was much bigger news. Germany, as the main target country, had made clear that it would not send any Syrians back to the fringes of the EU. The message to Syrians was clear: from now on, you are welcome here.

The Dublin system appeared to work as long as manageable numbers of migrants arrived in Europe. But large numbers rendered it unworkable, as it put an unfair burden on EU countries with borders along the southern and eastern edges of the EU. The German action, even though it was declared as a 'suspension' of the Dublin procedures that would be applied only to Syrian refugees, looked very much like the final nail in the Dublin coffin.[7]

The EU refugee system had long been withering on the vine. In 2014 Germany asked Italy and Greece to take back 35,100 asylum seekers under the Dublin procedures. In practice, only 4,800 of those were actually deported.[8] At the same time, German and French leaders called on Greece and Italy to do more to register all migrants in the first place. Greece protested that it did not have enough fingerprinting machines. Frontex complained that member states were not fulfilling their promises to provide more personnel and equipment. The argument went round and round in circles, and illustrated how hard it was for a club of twenty-eight states to coordinate unpopular policies. Meanwhile the UNHCR pointed out that countries neighbouring Syria – Turkey, Lebanon and Jordan – continued to bear the brunt of the refugee crisis, and only a fraction of the funds pledged to make their lives more bearable there had actually arrived. Thus it was little wonder that they continued their journeys to Europe, in search of a less precarious life.

The Pro-Asyl NGO in Germany welcomed the news from BAMF, but called for it to be extended to others. 'Unfortunately the fiction persists that this only works for Syrians, not other nationalities,' said the group's leader, Günther Burkhardt: 'Now the German Federal government must face up to reality and suspend the system for other refugees too.' 'The values of European civilisation are at stake,' he added. 'A Europe surrounded by fences will not work.'

Close to midnight on Tuesday 11 August, two Kurdish cousins watched the headlamps of their bus pull into the station at Dohuk in northern Iraq. It was more than three hours late, and they were irritated and nervous. The delay had given their relatives more time to try to persuade them not to leave. But now nothing could stop them.[9]

Semian Nasser Mohammed, twenty-five, and Nashwan Mustafa Rasoul, twenty-five, boarded the bus from Dohuk to Istanbul. Both had fought in the Kurdish Peshmerga army against IS, especially in Tel Asqof, a Christian village north of Mosul. Both were disillusioned and frustrated by conditions in Iraq, according to Rasoul's older brother, Sarbast. They had not been paid for three months and wanted to get to Europe to start a proper life. Mustafa sold his car for €14,000 to finance their trip.

In Istanbul they met a man called Sediq Sevo, an Iraqi Kurd from Zakho, to whom they had each already paid €6,600 for the through-trip to Munich, before setting out. 'I have been working for more than seven years in the smuggling sector,' Sediq Sevo told reporters from the Reuters news agency. 'I used to take people from Kurdistan to Turkey and from Turkey to Greece all on foot and by car.' This time he arranged transport for his clients to the Turkish-Bulgarian border. The cousins walked for at least seven hours across the mountains, then were met by Bulgarian smugglers on the far side who took them to Sofia.

After several days hidden in a Sofia apartment they were driven to the Serbian border, trekked through more mountains and were registered by the Serbian police at Dimitrovgrad. From there, a bus took them to Belgrade. After several days in an apartment they were driven by car to Horgoš on the Hungarian border. On the night of 24 August they followed the railway track into Hungary, accompanied by an Iraqi Kurdish smuggler called Bewar.

Two brothers, also Kurds from Iraq, thirty-four-year-old Hussein and twenty-one-year-old Raman Khalil, left their hometown of Qamishli in 2013, also fleeing IS. After two years in Turkey they continued their journey to Europe through the Balkans. They met Semian and Rashwan either on the railway track near Horgoš, or at the rendezvous point just inside Hungary. Just before dawn, the four of them and fifty-five other men, eight women and four children squeezed into the back of a small refrigerated meat lorry with the word HYZA on the side. It was to be standing room only, all the way to Munich.

The Volvo meat truck was driven by Bulgarians of Roma ethnic background from the Humata district of Lom in north-west Bulgaria. The usual driver was sick that day, so another man drove the truck, who did not understand how to keep the doors only partially shut, in a way that air could still come in. He inadvertently sealed the migrants into the airtight container. Half an hour after leaving the border area, the two men in the cab heard muffled banging from inside. They rang their Afghan boss. 'Ignore it, and just keep driving,' he told them.

One of the Bulgarians, Mitko, aged twenty-nine, had started in the used-car business, first repairing then driving minibuses full of Bulgarian migrants to workplaces in Western Europe. He was always in a rush, according to people who knew him in Lom, to make money and get home to Bulgaria. He ran up speeding fines in Austria and Germany and never paid them. When he was finally caught, he lost his driving licence. He robbed a filling station, was caught, and spent time in prison. There was always easy money to be made smuggling cigarettes across the Serbian border into Bulgaria. When the influx of refugees and migrants gained momentum in 2014, Mitko's band and others like it shifted their business to human trafficking.

'Arabs in Turkey organise everything,' a Bulgarian smuggler from a rival gang told me. 'They have their own people everywhere. Mitko was very close to one of them.'

The truck headed up the M5 motorway towards Budapest, round the M0 ringroad, then out on the M1 towards Vienna. By now the banging in the back had stopped. The pictures of cheerful hens and Slovak writing advertising fresh meat on the side, and the 'Z' registration plate showing that it had recently been imported into Hungary, lifted the truck above the suspicion of Hungarian police trying to intercept minibuses and taxis full of migrants. The temperature that day rose to 35 degrees Celsius.

Each day the Hungarian police intercepted Lithuanians, Romanians and Serbs with vehicles packed with asylum seekers. Some had been picked up directly at the border, like those in the Hyza, without being registered and fingerprinted first, but most had already been through at least a preliminary identification process.

The Hyza lorry was found abandoned beside the motorway near Parndorf, 30 kilometres inside Austria, on the morning of 27 August. Motorway maintenance workers who first noticed it thought it had broken down. Then they noticed fluid leaking from the back and a terrible stench, and called the police. The truck was driven to the border crossing point with Hungary at Nickelsdorf, where the gruesome task of disentangling and identifying the bodies began. The work was done so meticulously, that only one of the victims could not be identified. €2,000 in notes soaked in body fluids, extracted from the pocket of one of the victims were returned to one family. Some Syrian and Iraqi families paid €6,000 for the return of the bodies to be buried in their home soil – a similar sum to that paid by smugglers to get them to Austria alive. Twenty-nine were from Iraq, twenty-one from Afghanistan and fifteen from Syria. The last fifteen victims, mostly of Afghans whose families could not afford to pay for the return of the bodies, were finally buried in October, in a Muslim cemetery in Vienna.[10]

On the day of the discovery of the truck, European leaders including the German chancellor Angela Merkel were meeting in Vienna for a routine gathering to discuss the enlargement of the EU, which turned into an emergency summit on the refugee crisis. Commenting on the discovery of the lorry at Parndorf, Angela Merkel said the leaders were 'all shaken by this terrible news'. She called on Europe to act together to solve the migrant crisis.[11]

The Austrian interior minister Johanna Mikl-Leitner called it 'a dark day'. Europe needed to work together to fight people smuggling, she said. 'The solution is not to make more border checks. We need a solution to protect the refugees and I think the best way is to build legal ways through Europe. With legal ways we can protect the refugees and the criminals have no chance for the business.'

Austrian and Hungarian police moved swiftly to catch those responsible. Acting on Austrian police information and their own intelligence on the traffickers plying the Hungarian-Serbian border, four men were arrested within twenty-four hours. Three Bulgarians aged twenty-eight, twenty-nine (Mitko) and fifty, and one Afghan, aged twenty-eight. On Sunday 30 August they appeared in court in Kecskemét in central Hungary, the town where the lorry was registered.[12] The men arrived in the courthouse in a convoy of black police cars on another hot August morning. They looked bewildered as they were led down a corridor packed with photographers and cameramen. They were charged with aggravated human smuggling. All pleaded not guilty.

Later, Police Colonel Zoltán Boross of the Hungarian National Investigative Agency (NNI) told me some more of the background of the case. 'That vehicle required a very serious logistical background, with very serious money and a very serious circle of people able to carry out their tasks. We know this was not the first trip they organised, and not the last either.' Even after the Parndorf tragedy, other members of the network kept working. The money was too good to give up.

Throughout August the numbers of those reaching Greece by boat from Turkey, and from there pressing on through the Balkans towards Hungary, continued to grow: 50,000 migrants arrived on the five Greek islands by boat in July alone – the same number as for the whole of 2014. Nine out of ten were Syrians. Many were fleeing directly from Syria, but some had grown weary of an uncertain future in Turkey or one of the other refugee-hosting countries and decided the time had come to try to build a new life in Western Europe.

Operation Poseidon was organised by the European Border and Coast Guard Agency Frontex in the Aegean to help the Greek authorities police 15,000 kilometres of borders, including all 200 islands. Frontex had eleven coastal patrol boats, one larger offshore patrol boat, two helicopters and two planes – all the property of national services, temporarily donated to the organisation. Just what they were authorised to do during their daily interceptions of overcrowded dinghies full of migrants on the choppy waters between Turkey and the Greek islands was a moot point. International law is laid down in three main documents: the United Nations Convention on the Law of the Sea (UNCLOS), the International Convention on Maritime Search and Rescue (SAR Convention), and the International Convention for the Safety of Life at Sea (SOLAS Convention).[13] The obligations on all states were pretty clear: to rescue all those in trouble at sea. This fact was played on by the smugglers – ironically, the less safe the boats on which they sent people across, the more chance the boat had of reaching its final destination. They were simply asking to be rescued. The UN Convention also made clear that it referred to 'any person' in distress. So no difference could be made between a supposed 'economic migrant' and a refugee. Any ship's master finding people in distress at sea has a legal obligation to take them to what is called 'a place of safety'. Unlike on Europe's land borders, the law meant that migrants picked up at sea stood a good chance of being taken exactly where they wanted to go – hence the temptation to risk their lives in wretched overcrowded boats on both the Aegean, and the much longer route to the Italian island of Lampedusa in the central Mediterranean.

From mid-August onwards the Hungarian authorities, presumably under Austrian and German pressure, made it harder for refugees to travel on from Hungary by train. They were either prevented from boarding trains in Budapest or taken off them at later stations. The police also tried to prevent them boarding the train at Györ, halfway to Vienna, even if they had bought tickets. According to the single-page document issued to all migrants when they were first registered at Röszke or Szeged, they should report to a refugee camp within seventy-two hours. For years, however, most had simply used that time, and often that piece of paper, as a ticket out of the country towards Austria. There was a sort of unspoken agreement with the Hungarian authorities, that this was how the game worked. Hungary, after all, only had 2,000 places in its refugee camps, and few migrants wanted to stay in Hungary anyway. Ending that game meant that Hungary risked becoming a holding pen for refugees – as other countries further down the route would, later in 2015.

In stark contrast to the state's mobilisation of its resources to stop migrants, thousands of Hungarian volunteers began tending to their needs. The Hungarian Helsinki Committee, active since the 1980s, had a long tradition of offering legal advice to asylum seekers, as well as to the Hungarian poor.[14] Menedék, meaning 'Shelter' was established in 2010 and offered practical help including food and clothing.[15] Kalunba is a group of Christian aid volunteers, established in the spring of 2015 when the Reformed Church organisation they worked for decided it no longer wanted to work with refugees at all.[16] In June, Migration Aid was set up by a small group of volunteers, initially as a Facebook page.[17] Within days, several thousand people joined it. In mid-July, the Budapest police chief rang Zsuzsanna Zsohár, one of the Migration Aid founders to ask for advice and offer cooperation. He was soon followed by representatives of the city council. New groups sprang up near existing camps in Debrecen, Bicske, Fót and Cegléd. Official state or church-backed groups, Caritas and the Maltese charity, were slower to react to the crisis, and worked mainly in the official camps, alongside the Hungarian Red Cross. The voluntary groups provided food and cold drinks in the hot summer, hygiene packs for women and babies, and above all information – where to seek help, and advice on how to travel on. They worked in tandem, sometimes hand-in-hand, but often in a state of tension with the 'official' charities. The volunteers often accused the charities of working only eight-hour days, and of wearing the same latex gloves and face masks as the police, which suggested fear or disrespect, and hindered empathy. The volunteers worked overnight, welcoming the refugees with sympathy and affection.

Only a tiny fraction of the migrants saw Hungary as their final destination, and they could not understand why the Hungarian state was putting obstacles in their way. 'They marched across our country like soldiers of a foreign army,' the Hungarian government spokesman Zoltán Kovács told me, and a similar sentiment was reflected daily in the coverage of the crisis in pro-government media.

While the NGOs criticised government inaction, Jim Knies, a Baptist preacher who had lived in Hungary for twenty-two years, was more appreciative: 'The volunteer effort is pretty much unorganised, everyone just stepped in,' he told me in an underpass of the Budapest east station, where more than a thousand refugees were camped out, prevented by police from travelling on.

The needs are incredibly overwhelming, it would be impossible to meet them all. The Hungarian government I believe has done a good job. It has been criticised in the media but it is doing an excellent job in controlling a very bad situation.

They're setting up transit zones. New ones at the railway station and in the park near here. There's no danger here, just people trying to find a better life, and Hungarians have been very welcoming.

If you strip aside politics and people's opinions, everyone believes they're right. All people want is a better life for their families, just as you or I do, that's the bottom line.

By government help, he was referring to the actions of the Budapest city council, rather than central government. In coordination with NGOs like Migration Aid, taps were set up in the underpasses at the east station and in the new zone beside the west station, with drinking water and a place to wash, even to shower. Mobile toilets were laid on, but never enough. Volunteers organised clown shows, drawing, bubble-blowing and ball games with the children. The newly renovated underpass at the east station had an air of carnival by day, and a refugee camp by night. It was very colourful, but often tense and certainly unsustainable over a longer period. The city council began to prepare a strip of waste ground not far from the station as a future, more permanent site. Then the rains came.

'The situation is escalating because this week there was heavy rain in Budapest so everything overflowed. I think the system of the Hungarian Migration Office collapsed,' Zsuzsanna Zsohár told me. 'So we have many, many people here without papers, who had to be registered again. The Migration Office computer system collapsed. We had 200 people more than usual on Monday evening, and we had to find them places to sleep, to give them lunch and breakfast and then help them back to the stations.'

She estimated about 100 volunteers worked with Migration Aid alone, plus others who just showed up, or worked with other NGOs. We spoke next to a giant pile of donated clothes. 'It's incredible, its chaotic. Everybody wanted new clothes because they couldn't wash. There are no washing machines in the camps. They are washing here by hand . . .'

Thanks to the cooperation between the NGOs and the city council, hygiene was improving. She estimated a thousand people each night, sleeping at the east station, and hundreds more at the Pope John Paul Park nearby, and at the west station. The 'transit zones' established by the city council were very different from those with the same name established later at Horgoš and Kelebia on the Serbian border, built into the fence. Those in Budapest were simply more organised points designed to offer basic services and information to those travelling through, not to police them or restrict their movement. Even simple things like drinking clean water or access to public toilets were difficult for people with no common language or Hungarian currency. The transit zones in Budapest were a temporary, but relatively effective solution.

'Our message to the government is that you can build a wall, but you should put a roof on it, so there will be some shelter,' said Zsuzsanna. 'I think when someone flees from a war, when someone is a refugee, they shouldn't be handled like animals. It is our goal to help them.'

As the Hungarian authorities stepped up their efforts to stop the migrants, or slow down their migration, the numbers went up and up, as word of the fence-construction spread down the Balkan route. The fence, just as much as news of a possible welcome in Germany, was fuelling the momentum. Many refugees felt it was now, or never – the chance of a life-time to reach Europe before it became impossible.

I met Omar, aged twenty-eight, from Mosul in Iraq at 8.30 one morning on the Serbian side of the railway track. We stood beside the white stones which marked the Hungarian border. Triple coils of razor wire, stacked on top of each other, reached both sides of the track, but the Hungarian railway authority insisted that the fence not cover the track. In normal times, one cargo train a day came through this way. For now at least, the Hungarian authorities agreed to keep it open, and this passing quarrel between two separate Hungarian state authorities, the railways and the police, transformed a single railway line into the main entry point into Hungary.

Omar wore a thin brown pullover over a T-shirt, sunglasses, jeans, and a camouflage pouch round his waist. He was dejected. He and his friend had just been robbed of €1,500 each by a smuggler who promised to take them to Austria. The previous night the smuggler walked with them in the dark along the railway track, then suddenly disappeared and didn't come back. They slept the night by the track.

Omar was an English teacher in Mosul when IS troops took over the city, almost without a fight, in the summer of 2014. 'Come home quickly, there is a problem,' his father told him on the phone. He picked up a few belongings then fled the city with his university friend Ahmed, crossing Turkey, Greece and Macedonia to get to Hungary.

After our meeting, he and Ahmed hid in the forest near Röszke for two days, with other refugees. They were determined to avoid registration and giving their fingerprints to the police, out of fear of extradition to Hungary later on. Children were crying from hunger and thirst. On the second night Ahmed negotiated with the owner of a petrol station nearby, to drive them to Budapest for €250 each. 'We knew it was a lot, but we had no choice.'

In Budapest they found a hotel and each paid €50 a night for a room. The hotel manager warned them not to go outside, because they might get caught by the police.

Once, when we went out, the police started chasing us, but we were faster, and we got away. Then we found a WiFi signal in the street, I guess it belonged to a restaurant. Anyhow we had a Hungarian phone number for a smuggler, which someone in Turkey had given us. He was Lebanese and had been living in Hungary long enough to know the language. We called him and sent him our location. Half an hour later he found us and took us to a flat. There were nearly twenty persons there, and all of them had been fingerprinted except me and Ahmed.

The smuggler drove them as far as the Austrian border in an Audi saloon, for €400 each. Three of them in the car plus the driver. They just drove on the main motorway to Hegyeshalom in the late afternoon, and saw no police on the way. 'The police were all in the railway stations and bus stations. We crossed the border by car. He stopped at a big supermarket inside Austria. We picked up other refugees there, then he took us to Vienna.' They stayed three nights in a hotel, then got as far as Munich before police took them off a train and sent them to a camp.

Back at the railway track at Röszke, I interpreted one morning for a Syrian man and the Hungarian police. He only spoke Greek and explained to me that his wife and young daughter were hiding in the maize field nearby. At that moment, a Hungarian police Skoda was parked across the track, manned by two young policemen, and he was afraid to cross. I explained his predicament to the policemen.

'If he's worried about our presence here, we'll just drive off and get out of his way,' the policeman told me kindly, and he did just that. While the Hungarian police often got a bad press, many I met were polite, friendly, and thoughtful.

There were also tragedies. One Syrian woman I met, distraught, had just heard that her friend's baby died in childbirth in the camp at Kiskunhalas, because, she said, officials did not take her desperate requests for help seriously. 'The police just laughed at her, like she was a dog. The water we were given there stank. We only got food once every twenty-four hours. It was a terrible place.'

Most of the refugees carried a single rucksack with as many things as they could squeeze into it, but some carried two or three tied together, helping weaker members of their group. There were still just two or three mobile toilets in the police collecting point in the cornfield at Röszke.

I met two Syrian girls, Haneen and Rama early another morning in the cornfield. Both were seventeen, from Aleppo, and were travelling with Haneen's father and uncle. I let Haneen use my laptop to Skype with her aunt in Aleppo, to tell her they were safe.

A few days later I bumped into them again at the east station in Budapest. They had been through the registration process and were looking for ways to get to Germany now the station was closed to refugees. The same day an old friend, Viktor Bori, a jazz musician who had a flat near the station told me he would like to offer it to refugees, as his contribution to their journey. That evening, Viktor and I let Haneen and her extended family into the small flat in Marek József Street. They were delighted to have a little privacy, to have warm running water, a shower, and real beds for the first time in weeks. Later, Viktor took them shopping for basic provisions. They stayed there for nearly a week. The streets around the station were full of refugees, smugglers and police on the prowl. I was worried for the girls in particular, and we devised roundabout routes, to get them to the flat. I could hardly believe I was doing this in twenty-first-century Hungary – helping refugees down a tightrope between those trying to lock them up, and others trying to rob them.

Refugees like Haneen and Rama had spent two days at Kiskunhalas, before being put on a train to Budapest. From there, they were supposed to go on to a more permanent camp at Debrecen or Bicske. Each morning trains from Kiskunhalas, packed with several hundred refugees, arrived at the Köbánya-Kispest suburban station in Budapest. They were supposed to change for the Debrecen train. Instead, they changed to a different platform, and travelled the short distance into the west station instead, swelling the numbers already there, trying to move on westwards. Volunteers from Migration Aid were waiting for the trains, and distributed aid packages from the stocks pouring in each day from Hungarian well-wishers. One man I spoke to, Zaid Majid from Baghdad, said he had climbed over the fence with his friends. It was only half a metre high he said. But some were not so lucky, suffering bad cuts as they clambered over the razor wire.

Each of the passageways beneath the east station was overcrowded with people resting and sleeping. Some put up tents, others just slept on mattresses or cardboard, like the homeless who lived there in less troubled times.

'Every day in Syria, we died several times,' a young woman, Zana, twenty-one, told me. 'How come the world sees this, and does nothing? Look at the babies, the children!'

Meeran, also twenty-one, from Afghanistan, said he had seen so much death in his home country. The killing of his friends and his brothers. He wanted to reach the UK or Ireland, he said, anywhere where he could live in peace, in freedom, with human rights. He, like the others, was overwhelmed by the kindness of the volunteers.

The Hungarian government's decision to build the fence, block the refugees and criminalise the migrants earned it the approbation of governments across Europe. Hungary's young foreign minister Péter Szijjártó, thirty-six, appeared at times both abrasive and undiplomatic. In quick succession in late August his government's policies were attacked by the French foreign minister Laurent Fabius and the Austrian chancellor Werner Faymann, as going 'against European values'. In an interview in *Le Monde*, also carried by French public service radio and the rolling TV news channel I-Télé on 30 August, Fabius described the conduct of East European countries towards the refugees as 'scandalous'.[18] He condemned 'in the strongest possible way' Hungary in particular, for building a fence 'which would not be put up for animals, let alone for the protection of values'. The new fence should be taken down, and the EU should lead serious and tough talks with the Hungarian leadership.

Szijjártó summoned the French ambassador and told the press he was 'shocked' by Fabius's words.[19] 'Some people in Europe still don't understand how big and how dramatic the pressure is in Hungary because of the arrival of so many illegal migrants across its borders. A good Europe is one which keeps its own rules,' he said, referring to the Schengen agreement, rather than the Dublin one which Hungary had suspended the previous month. 'Instead of attacking one another, we should seek a common solution – how to stop the migrant pressure.' Hungary was just defending its own, and the EU's outer boundaries, he said. And if their countries, starting with Greece, were to do the same, at least part of the problem would be solved.

Jean-Claude Juncker, the president of the European Commission, whose election Hungary had, with Britain, bitterly opposed, also took the side of the asylum seekers. 'The EU will never turn away those people who need our help.' The real Europe is personified, he said, by 'those Hungarian volunteers who give food and toys to hungry, exhausted refugee children'. Europe is 'those students in [the German town of] Siegen who opened their dormitory to refugees . . . the baker on the island of Kos who distributes bread to hungry and weary people. This is the Europe I want to live in.' 'By hiding behind fences we can't barricade ourselves from all fears and sufferings,' he added, to rub salt into the wounds. The article was published in the opposition daily, *Népszabadság*.[20]

The biggest problem Szijjártó faced was not the migrants themselves – they were suffering a sort of malign neglect from his government – but rather the gulf opening rapidly between his policies and those of Western Europe. The Fidesz government's vision of a 'Fortress Europe', barring those it regarded as 'illegal migrants', was on a collision course with the policies of other countries – Austria, Germany, Sweden, the Netherlands, the

Scandinavian countries and to some extent France, that Europe should be a 'safe haven' for 'genuine refugees'. This was also an argument about time, and legislation. Critics of the Hungarian government, at home and abroad, argued that the new fence, the transit zones which would be built into it, and the fast-track legal procedures, including putting those caught crossing the fence on trial in Szeged, broke Hungary's humanitarian obligations under the 1951 UN Convention on Refugees. Hungarian officials argued that the convention was out of date, and that this was not a humanitarian crisis, but a security one.

On 28 August, I interviewed Babar Baloch, the regional spokesman for the UNHCR, in the cornfield at Röszke. By now the encampment had spread to the other side of the road as well. As we spoke, police tried to keep the road open for traffic. Every new hour a cream and orange coloured bus or coach, hired by the police, pulled up to take the refugees in the field to the registration centre near the motorway crossing, just 3 kilometres away. The migrants would happily have walked the distance if it had been explained to them. But as usual, there was no communication. The police had not been provided with interpreters, and as a result, no one understood what was going on, and why the people in the field had to spend twenty-four, thirty-six or even forty-eight hours waiting in the hot sun, with too little food, water and toilet facilities.

'When desperate people like refugees have no legal avenues to cross over into Europe and continue the journeys where they're seeking safety, they fall into the hands of ruthless smugglers – and this is what happens,' Babar, himself from the troubled Baluchistan region of Pakistan, explained. I put it to him that the authorities were at last, though painfully slowly, getting organised to cope with the influx.

It is encouraging to see that people who need access to help in Hungary are being allowed in. But the worry is also the fence. People crawling under the barbed wire fence or trying to come over it. That shouldn't be there for refugees and asylum seekers.

We are asking, not only from the Hungarians but from the Europeans also, for a robust system which works in helping these people. So far this system is dysfunctional here.

CHAPTER FIVE

A REFUGEE VICTORY

This is a good country, in a good condition ... And it makes me proud to see so many people from civil society selflessly helping refugees ... The number of helpers is many times higher than the number of rabble-rousers and xenophobes.

Angela Merkel[1]

The new Iron Curtain is for us, not against us.

Viktor Orbán[2]

On Monday 31 August, German chancellor Angela Merkel spoke at the traditional summer federal press conference in Berlin.[3] It should have been held on 17 July but was delayed because of talks in Greece on the financial crisis. Dressed in a bright pink trouser suit and looking surprisingly relaxed after a summer with little time for a vacation of her own, the German chancellor took the lead that no other statesman in Europe dared to – one which surprised friends and foes alike. Rewatching her speech on YouTube, news from the front lines of the crisis flashes along the bottom of the screen: 'Bavaria and Austria sharpen their border controls in the struggle against smugglers', 'Hungary allows refugees in trains to leave for Germany.' And a strange one from the Pro-Asyl group: 'Number of Balkan refugees falls sharply.' Ever a cautious leader in her ten years in the job, she now made clear that Germany was prepared to help. In August alone 104,460 asylum seekers had entered her country and many more were on their way.

'What is happening now in Europe is not a natural catastrophe, but a multitude of catastrophic situations,' she began. The death of the seventy-one migrants in the meat truck in Austria the previous week was 'an inconceivable atrocity'.

She spoke of the exhaustion and existential fears and traumas of those who had fled Syria, northern Iraq and Eritrea. These were the three countries the EU was about to introduce relocation quotas for. She stressed the importance of clear, humanitarian principles in dealing with asylum seekers. And she mentioned that the revised estimate of those expected to reach Germany in 2015 was now 800,000.

'We should be proud of the humanitarian principles enshrined in the Basic Law,' she said. 'The second fundamental principle is the principle of human dignity – which is assured in Article 1 of the Basic Law [...] We respect the dignity of each individual.' Germany was not offering automatic asylum to everyone, she explained, but every application would get a fair hearing, based on German law and respect for their humanity.

By that time there had already been 200 attacks on hostels for asylum seekers that year in Germany, and she turned next on those guilty of that violence. 'We will apply the full force of the law against those who verbally or physically attack others, who torch shelters or try to resort to violence. There is zero tolerance for those who call into question the dignity of others.' And she appealed to her fellow Germans to keep away from such protests where people showed 'the hatred in their hearts'. 'The reason so many people dream of a new life in Germany, is that they have suffered persecution, war and despotism in their own.'

'What should Germany do in the face of such a huge challenge?' she asked. More of the same, only better. At a meeting with the prime ministers of the regions in June, the scale of the task facing them was already clear, she said. The solution should be a combination of German thoroughness and flexibility – qualities shown in its handling of German reunification, the Eurozone crisis, the *Wende* – the switchover from nuclear to renewable energy.

More reception centres would be set up. Over the next three weeks, a comprehensive package of measures would be worked out between central and regional government. Asylum procedures would be speeded up. Rapid decisions on repatriation would be needed in cases where applicants stood no prospect of staying in Germany. This referred particularly, but not exclusively, to the tens of thousands of migrants coming from Kosovo and Albania whom I had encountered in Ásotthalom in February. Most were still in Germany, resisting efforts to send them home. Parallel to this, more efforts should be put into integrating those who would be given leave to stay in Germany. More teachers of German would be needed, she said. Then she turned to the European response.

'Europe as a whole must get its act together. The European states must share responsibility for refugees seeking asylum.' Universal civil rights remained the essential European values, she said. Germany and France agreed on what needed to be done next. Consultations would now be held with other countries.

'Merkel the bold,' wrote *The Economist*.[4] 'On refugees, Germany's chancellor is brave, decisive and right.'

> On 31 August Mrs Merkel issued a dramatic call to arms, warning that today's refugee misery will have graver consequences for the future of the EU than the euro mess. 'If Europe fails on the question of refugees,' she said, 'it won't be the Europe we wished for.' She is right. The EU was born after a devastating war, on a promise of solidarity with the persecuted and downtrodden. The biggest displacement of people since 1945 is a test of European values, and of the ability of member states to work together. The refugees from civil wars in Syria and Iraq clearly need help; and European countries can provide it only if they share the task. That means a collective response.
>
> Few other European politicians have had the courage to make such a clear link between Europe's values, its collective self-interest and bold action on refugees . . . Many Eastern European politicians have resorted to xenophobia, refusing to welcome refugees for resettlement even as their citizens enjoy the benefits of borderless travel. No doubt Mrs Merkel is driven, in part, by domestic concerns . . . But a desire to share the burden should not be mistaken for selfishness. In a crisis where Europe has little to be proud of, Mrs Merkel's leadership is a shining exception.

The political debate in Europe about how to handle the influx now had two poles, Angela Merkel and Viktor Orbán. This was a remarkable achievement for the Hungarian prime minister, in an EU dominated by Germany,

France and other rich countries. Orbán put himself forward as the champion, not just of the 'sensible people of East and Central Europe', but of everyone in Western Europe concerned by the arrival of so many people of other cultures. There was just one nod in the Chancellor's ninety-seven-minute press conference towards Hungary. Germany 'greatly appreciates' Hungary's efforts to register all refugees, she said.

Angela Merkel repeatedly used the word refugees (*Flüchtlinge*) in her speeches. Viktor Orbán and his publicity machine insisted on 'illegal immigrants' or simply 'migrants'. And 'migrants' became increasingly pejorative in Hungarian usage as time went by.

In January 2015, during the visit of the Turkish prime minister, Merkel said that 'Islam is part of Europe'. Orbán seemed ignorant of both the extent to which Islam was already part of the continent, and of the rich cultural diversity in many countries. Like others who saw Islam itself as a threat to Christian Europe, he also failed to recognise the great diversity of views among Muslims and the extent to which most European Muslims share the same values as other Europeans.

Merkel based her choice of words, and her welcome to refugees, on data provided by the UNHCR and the International Organization for Migration. This showed that the majority of those reaching Europe were coming from countries where they suffered the effects of war or persecution. Viktor Orbán suggested on the other hand that the 'vast majority' were economic migrants. His ally, the Slovak prime minister Robert Fico put a figure to it: 'Up to 95 per cent are economic migrants,' he claimed. Who was telling the truth? *The Economist* decided to study the figures. Asylum applications from citizens of seven countries had rates of acceptance (of asylum or protected status) of over 50 per cent in the first quarter of 2015 in the EU: Syria, Eritrea, Iraq, Afghanistan, Iran, Somalia and Sudan.

'Put crudely,' wrote *The Economist*, 'citizens of these seven countries obtained protection in the EU over half the time they applied. How many of these people are reaching Europe? The UNHCR says that Syria, Afghanistan and Iraq account for nine in ten of the quarter-million-odd migrants detected arriving in Greece this year.' Meanwhile, on the central Mediterranean route, people from Eritrea, Somalia and Sudan 'comprise 41 per cent of the 119,500 arrivals in Italy, and another 6 per cent come from

Syria. In other words, citizens from countries that usually obtain protection in the EU account for fully 75 per cent of illicit arrivals by sea this year.'

To be fair, *The Economist* added, migration is a complex business, with a wide range of motives. What of those who had already fled war and persecution, had found safety in Turkey, Lebanon, Jordan or even Greece, then decided to travel on to Western Europe in search of a better life? This was the crux of the Hungarian government's argument: the 1951 Refugee Convention said you had a right to safety, but not to choose in which country you would be safe. This was the central point too in the new Hungarian legislation which declared Serbia, Macedonia, Greece and Bulgaria, among others, 'safe countries'. 'Let them stay there then, whoever they are,' was Orbán's line.

'Crunch the numbers further and we find that at least 81 per cent of those migrants entering Greece can expect to receive refugee status or some other form of protection in the EU,' concluded *The Economist*.

As the summer drew to a close, tempers were fraying along the affected borders. On the last weekend of August, 30-kilometre tailbacks developed at the Austrian-Hungarian border at Hegyeshalom, as Austrian police stepped up their vehicle checks. Angry holidaymakers, many of them Turkish Muslims returning to their homes in Germany, stewed in their cars in the heat.

Down at the border near Röszke there was growing frustration both among the migrants and the police who were supposed to be guarding them. There were still no big tents, too few toilets, too few buses, too little water. The UNHCR had been pressing the Hungarian government for months to allow it to provide large tents. The government refused. To allow the UNHCR to pitch large tents would have looked too much like a welcome, while its own policy was one of deterrence.

Over that last weekend in August the Hungarian defence minister Csaba Hende announced that the fence was finished – two days ahead of schedule. It was an optimistic assessment. There was indeed some kind of razor-wire obstacle all along the 175-kilometre border with Serbia. The chief of police, the mild mannered and professional Károly Papp, was sending 3,000 extra police officers, some of them on horseback, backed up with dogs and helicopters at the government's request, to patrol the fence. But the flimsy structure was already decorated in many places with the torn strips of blankets, sleeping bags and clothes left behind by refugees as they crossed through, under or over it. Even this new 'fence-crossing sport' was based on a misunderstanding. No information was provided by either the Serbian or Hungarian authorities to the tens of thousands of migrants pouring north through the Balkans, that there were still crossing points open. Those who did find the openings were informed either by friends and relatives, or by the smugglers. Most had no documents, so they could hardly go to the official road or rail checkpoints. So there was no need to risk injury crossing the fence, there were still plenty of points where the River Tisza or its oxbows, or the railway line, at Röszke or Kelebia, meant that the fence could not be completed. Completing the fence in just six weeks was a logistical achievement, but Viktor Orbán was not impressed. A few days later, the defence minister resigned – the first and only political casualty of the crisis.

On Monday 31 August, while Angela Merkel was addressing the press conference in Berlin, I drove up to Budapest for the first time in more than a week, to see the situation. There were big crowds of refugees around all three main entrances to the east station. As we arrived, the police stood aside briefly to allow hundreds of migrants to board trains bound for Austria and Germany. The police lines soon re-formed, limiting access to anyone who looked like a refugee.

Outside the Thököly street entrance, I photographed a man praying quietly by himself beside his blue tent on a small patch of grass. He wore a black vest and had spread a yellow towel on the grass as his prayer mat. As he knelt to make his prostrations, he glanced sideways, saw my camera, and froze. I felt ashamed, intruding on the privacy of his faith.

A little Syrian girl in a bright pink T-shirt waved at two giant Hungarian policemen. Both had tattoos and close-shaven hair. One softened his hard expression and grinned back, the other frowned his disapproval. Camera crews mingled with the crowd. For the first time since 1989 my country, Hungary, was the centre of the world news.

The technology available to us as journalists helped us bring our listeners and viewers into the square. With a 3G MiFi box in one hand, a laptop and a microphone in the other, I gave one radio report while I was crossing the main road, walking towards the station. I stood on a raised platform giving hourly updates for the television news. Once during a TV live slot, a man stepped into the shot behind me and started shouting and swearing in Hungarian into the camera. I took him firmly by the shoulders, pushed him out of the frame, then carried on answering the question. Police formed lines, some in riot kit but most without, then dispersed, only to re-form. Volunteers were everywhere, carrying food, telephone charging equipment and donations.

The policemen in their maroon caps seemed even younger than the migrants. Many wore green face masks and blue rubber gloves, like surgeons in an operating ward. The pro-government media were brimming with stories of what infectious diseases, from AIDS to hepatitis, the migrants might be carrying. Other police, perhaps more sympathetic to the migrants or at least hoping for easier communication with them, kept their masks in their bags. The giant yellow bearded face of an old man, sculpted above the side door of the station, depicting Father Danube himself, gazed on the scene with amazement, a dark grey pigeon perched on his head.

On the steps at the front of the station, policemen and women in white T-shirts and dark glasses kept the crowds back. One family with three children slept at their feet on a brown blanket, while the children's father searched for his smugglers on his phone or rang his family in Syria. Some of the refugees had managed to get hold of a megaphone. There were occasional demonstrations, groups of fifty to a hundred people moving through the crowd, chanting 'Freedom', or 'Germany', or 'Angela'. One group of men had improvised a large cardboard flag of their country, Afghanistan, and carried the black, red and green tricolour proudly through the crowd. Like poor people the world over, they wore the misspelled copies of expensive brand names on their clothes. The young lad carrying one end of the Afghan flag had the word 'Convease' above a picture of a training shoe, on a blue and white shirt which should have spelt 'Converse.' The riot police in their dark blue, heavily padded uniforms, clutched their helmets and fingered their pepper spray canisters. They stood poker-faced, mostly in wrap-around shades, and tried not to betray any emotions. They appeared to have been chosen for their height. The refugees looked puny and defenceless beside them.

Strange scenes such as these became usual very fast. In the park named after Pope John Paul II nearby, I met a distraught seventeen-year-old Afghan boy who had lost the thirteen-year-old younger brother he was travelling with. Both were on the phone to their mother in Kabul but could not work out where the other was. A word kept coming up which he could not understand, which I realised after a while was 'Nyugati' – the west station.

Suddenly everything was clear. I opened a map and explained to the older boy that his brother must be at the other station. On double checking, via their mother, that proved to be the case, and a much-relieved boy set out with my street map to recover his sibling.

A little Iraqi girl in yellow pyjamas with pink sheep designs played hide and seek with me beneath a bicycle rack.

As the drama developed in Budapest, the BBC rented rooms at a small, modern hotel in Forget-Me-Not street, just to the side of the station. That gave us a base to store camera equipment, recharge phones and batteries, and even rest for a few minutes when it all got too much. In the street outside I met a distressed elderly German man from Bavaria. His mobile phone had completely run down, he had lost the rest of his group, and for several hours he had been trawling the little cafés and restaurants around the station searching in vain for an empty socket where he could charge his phone. As a result, he had lost contact with the rest of his tour group. I took him into our hotel, gave him one of our sockets, and sat him down in the lobby with a large beer. He felt better straight away.

When I asked him what he thought of the refugees, he started crying. 'I feel so sorry for them,' he said. 'I was a refugee too, after the war.'

On 1 September around 2,500 mostly Syrian refugees who had been stranded in Hungary arrived by train in Munich, where they were greeted by cheering crowds with flowers, welcome banners, food and drink. For many in Germany, as well as for the refugees themselves, this was the high point of the crisis, the moment of maximum euphoria, reminiscent of a victorious football team returning to their home town with their latest trophy.

The next day, 2 September, Angela Merkel met Spanish prime minister Mariano Rajoy in Berlin. At the joint press conference afterwards, she answered questions about her 31 August remarks. Syrian refugees arriving in Germany would 'in all probability' be granted asylum, she said, 'which is hardly surprising, given the situation in their country.' Other European countries should do the same, she suggested.

Fabrice Leggeri, the head of Frontex, pondered the potential terrorist threat from the arrival of so many people from war zones in an interview on French radio. The value of Syrian passports had increased, he said, now that Syrians could almost automatically get refugee status in Europe. False Syrian documents were being manufactured in Turkey, but 'there is no evidence at this time . . . that potential terrorists are getting into Europe in this way'.[5]

After Monday's brief respite in the tension at the east station in Budapest, the mood darkened rapidly again, as the police sealed off all entrances to people who looked like refugees. In the streets nearby they carried out identity checks as shopkeepers and smugglers looked on.

On the steps of the station Mohammad Omar Heydari, a seventeen-year-old refugee from Afghanistan showed me the single-page document he had been given in Szeged. Issued by the Csongrad County Police Headquarters, it gave his name and the time and date he had been apprehended in Hungary – 11.10 in the morning on 31 August. Everything on the paper was in Hungarian.

'I acknowledge that I illegally entered Hungary from Serbia,' read the statement. 'I declare that I want to make an asylum claim in Hungary.' Beneath he had circled the IGEN (Yes), rather than the NEM (No) word. The squiggled, illegible signature of an interpreter was below that. Both the migrants and the authorities were still playing out the Dublin fiction. In order to get the twenty-four hours he needed in order to flee Hungary westwards, Mohammed had to pretend he wanted to stay in Hungary and the police and the OIN had to pretend that they wanted him to. At the bottom of the page, in capital letters were the words:

I WARN YOU THAT YOU HAVE 24 HOURS FROM THE RECEIPT OF THIS PAPER TO PRESENT YOURSELF WITHOUT FAIL TO THE REFUGEE CAMP AT SAMSON STREET 149, DEBRECEN.

On the back of the page was a list of contact details for seven NGOs including Amnesty International, and also of the Police Complaints Authority.

Nearby, I watched a small refugee boy escape his mother's attentions and set out to befriend the policemen along the front steps of the station. These were the everyday policemen, not the padded riot police. He was explaining something in his own language with words and hand gestures. One policeman stroked his chin and tried to follow what he meant. Others smiled, then looked awkwardly away.

On the same day a photograph of a small, three-year-old boy in a red T-shirt, dark blue shorts and trainers lying dead, face down in the sand, spread around the world.[6] The picture was taken by the Turkish photographer Nilufer Demir on the Ali Hoca beach near Bodrum on the west coast of Turkey. Alan Kurdi and his family had set out in the darkness a few hours earlier in an overcrowded rubber dinghy to reach the Greek island of Kos, just 4 kilometres away across the water. They must even have been able to see the lights of the island.

It was a journey I had made from Bodrum myself, on a small sailing boat, many years before. But the small dinghy with twelve people on board capsized in high waves just 500 metres out to sea. Alan, his brother Ghalip and mother Reyhan all drowned, despite the efforts of the father, Abdullah Kurdi, to save them. Twelve adults and children from this and another boat, which sank nearby, died in the tragedy.

The family's story, published over the following weeks and months, illustrates the fragile threads on which the lives of so many refugees and migrants hangs. The family were from Kobani on the Syrian-Turkish border, like many of the families I had met in the cornfield at Röszke the previous week. Originally from Damascus, the Kurdi family moved first to Aleppo in 2012, then to Kobani, and finally to Turkey in 2013. They tried returning to Kobani in early 2015 but fled again in June 2015, when IS launched a new offensive to take the strategically important town. After making their way to the west coast of Turkey, with hundreds of thousands of others so far in 2015, they paid a Pakistani smuggler for the crossing. They were trying to reach Canada, where Abdullah's sister Tima worked in Vancouver as a hairdresser. She had made applications for them to join her there, but these had been turned down by the Canadian immigration authorities in June because of missing data. She regularly sent them money, to help them reach Europe anyway. Abdullah accompanied the bodies of his wife and two children back to Kobani for burial. 'I wish I had died with them,' he said.

The next morning, Thursday 3 September, I was in the middle of a live TV broadcast in front of the east station at 7.40 when I heard a commotion behind me. Without warning, the police cordon along the top of the steps simply melted away. There were shouts in the crowd. Everyone started running towards the station. It was mayhem again.

We managed to film the next few minutes, live inside the station, in the middle of a throng of people. On platform 8, a green and yellow German train was labelled the 09.20 departure for Vienna and Munich. Within moments, it was overrun, with every available seat and standing space full, and the door-ways so overcrowded that people looked in danger of being forced back out onto the platform. Each wagon proudly proclaimed fifty-six seats, but there must have been at least 500 people in the four carriages. After trying to persuade the people to get off with loudspeaker announcements, the train finally pulled out of the station, about half an hour behind schedule. There was a mood of euphoria among the crowds of refugees now thronging the station. One train had gone, but there would be more. Surely Hungary wouldn't close the exit again? Many brandished tickets, costing hundreds of euros, they had just queued for and bought, to Munich or beyond. There was a sense of victory in the air – they thought they had overcome the Hungarian government.

Viktor Orbán set out for the airport to fly to Brussels just as the station was reopening to refugees. If he had opened the gates of the station later that day, it might have seemed that he was giving in to pressure from Brussels. As it was, his message seemed to be: 'You want these people? You can have them!' In Brussels, Orbán held talks with all the presidents he could find there – of the European Commission (Jean-Claude Juncker), the European Council (Donald Tusk), the European Parliament (Martin Schultz) and the European People's Party (Joseph Daul). Then he addressed the press.

The migrants were 'a German problem, not a European one,' he told reporters, as the destination country for most of them was Germany. He added that he would not allow them to leave his country without registering. He had come to Brussels because, from 15 September, a new border policing system would be in place in Hungary, he said. The regulations would be passed imminently by the Hungarian Parliament, giving the police and army new powers to stop migrants entering the country. This would be done in full compliance with the rules of Dublin, Schengen and Frontex. Under Schengen, Hungary had not just the right but the duty to defend its own borders and, at the same time, the external Schengen borders of the EU. Hungary had tried to fulfil the requirements until now but had not been successful. Thousands of migrants had crossed the border illegally. This cannot continue. 'I asked all my counterparts today whether they had a better idea than the fence. All replied that they did not, but that they disliked this arrangement. This is also my opinion.'

Later in the same press conference, a German reporter asked him how he would compare his new fence with the old Iron Curtain. 'If we have to compare the two, we must say that the new Iron Curtain is not against us, but for us,' he said bluntly. 'We don't want to live with a large Muslim community – we had that already for 150 years.'[7]

That morning, the *Wall Street Journal* published details of the European Commission's plans to relocate 160,000 asylum seekers across the EU. The sheer scale of the crisis, and the added urgency provoked by images such as those of Alan Kurdi and the 'biblical scenes' at the borders of Serbia and Macedonia, Hungary and Serbia, were finally propelling Europe's sluggish leaders into action. Angela Merkel and François Hollande conferred by telephone and the French president dropped his earlier opposition to the compulsory quota plan, which Juncker would officially unveil on 9 September. Orbán said no concrete numbers had been discussed in his talks with leaders that day, but in any case, he dismissed the plan as a bluff. 'Even its authors know it won't work,' he said.

Back in Hungary, the train with over 500 asylum seekers on board which struggled out of the east station after 10 a.m., got only as far as Bicske, 27 kilometres down the line.[8] There, riot police lined the platforms and the tracks. The refugees were told to disembark to be taken to the refugee camp. They refused and a stand-off developed.

'What do you think of all this,' I asked an elderly local Hungarian woman who was standing among all the TV crews on the far side of the tracks. 'I feel very sorry for them,' she said. Her view was rather unusual among ordinary Hungarians, I suggested. 'That's because our doctor here in Bicske, Dr Ussamah is Syrian, and we love him very much,' she replied.

At that very moment, Dr Ussamah Bourgla was trying to mediate between the police and the men, women and children refusing to leave the train. He told me later:

What I felt that day, I would not wish on my worst enemies. It was like a disaster, everyone set out from the east station with the hope that they would arrive in a peaceful place after three or four years of terrible suffering. Then, after 30 kilometres, everything ended and they stayed without hope, with valid tickets, which they bought from the station.

When I heard from a colleague that the train had arrived in my own town, Bicske, I went down to the station and offered my help to the police. At their request, I translated the commander's words into Arabic.

That they should all leave the train. The refugees wanted to know what would happen to them. The police explained that they would be taken by bus to the comfort and safety of the refugee camp nearby. The refugees refused, insisting that the train continue to Germany, as it was a scheduled train, bound for Germany, and they had tickets to be on it. It was a terrible situation. The people were very angry, they felt they had been tricked.

At this point, the group who had left the train to negotiate with the police tried to get back to it. The police blocked them. In the chaos, a woman clutching a child fell or was pushed by her husband down onto the tracks, and the police tried to pull them up. Some international media initially gave the impression that the incident was an example of police violence. The man crouched over the two of them, sobbing. The incident would later become a favourite example cited by the government spokesman, Zoltán Kovács, of the wickedness of the Western media. In fact it was an example of the fickleness of the Hungarian authorities, who had misled the refugees into thinking they were going to Germany, of the desperation of the refugees when they discovered they had been tricked, and of the awful situation into which the Hungarian police were put, caught in the middle of the conflict between the refugees and their own government.

The other refugees managed to regain the train and the stand-off continued. Some began a hunger strike. I watched as police tried to take them bottles of water. One refugee took the whole case of plastic bottles and smashed it down furiously on the platform. Attempts to take them food met a similar fate. Some refugees lined up in front of the train, separated from the platform where hundreds of TV journalists and photo reporters stood, and held up handmade signs. 'Thank you journalists,' read one. 'No camp, no water, no food, just freedom,' read another. Along the green fuselage of the train a man wrote 'No camp, no Hungary' in large letters with white shaving foam.

The next day, Friday 4 September, the stand-off ended in apparent defeat for the refugees. During an attempted break-out from the train of about a hundred passengers, a fifty-two-year-old Bangladeshi man collapsed, apparently of a heart attack, and died on the spot. Deeply demoralised, the remaining passengers left the train in single file and were escorted by riot police to waiting coaches, which took them to the refugee camp.

Back in Budapest, not everyone tried to board that ill-fated train on the Thursday morning. Many just stood their ground, not daring to board trains, suspecting a trap. Zabihullah Sharifi from Afghanistan was one. He stood with me on platform 7, clutching his one-year-old baby daughter in his arms. She had weighed 12 kilos when they left home, he said, now she weighed only 8. 'This is my love, this is my health.'

He and his family had been waiting at the station for three days. 'We are really sad. We say to Hungary, please don't do it like this. This is very very bad for your country's name. The president of Germany wants to invite these people, and these people know it. There are doctors among us, engineers, educated people. Please Hungary, let us go.'

An educated man wearing a blue shirt and purple pullover, he had left his wife outside in the underpass with their belongings to find out what was happening. He watched the first train leave, then tried to buy a ticket – 'but the ticket office was closed to people like us'. In the meantime, he had heard about the fate of the train which ended up in Bicske and was relieved he and his family were not on it. His plan now was to buy a ticket as soon as the ticket office reopened, and board any train he was sure was really going to Germany. 'We want to respect the law!' He emphasised.

At around one o'clock on Friday afternoon, seeing their hopes of travelling by train dashed, a crowd of about 1,200 migrants set out to walk to Vienna down the motorway.[9] The idea had been bandied about in refugee circles at the station for at least a day. Another factor which possibly influenced their move was fear of violence. Word had spread through the crowds at the station that the Ultras, fanatic supporters of the Hungarian football team, were planning to attack the refugees after the Hungary–Romania match scheduled for that evening.[10]

The marchers set out towards the Danube, and across the Elizabeth Bridge towards the M1 motorway. Filmed by drones from the air, and hundreds of mobile phones from the ground, the march was an astonishing sight, a modern Children's Crusade. People were clutching their knapsacks and plastic bags, pushing prams or wheelchairs, or had small children on their shoulders. The police tried to protect them from the traffic but did not try to stop the march. Perhaps there were just too many of them. The previous day, the police had released a statement which explained the humane approach its top brass were trying to take: 'The police will continue to tackle police tasks related to irregular immigration moderately, taking into account every circumstance, proportionately, legally and professionally.'

As I covered the evolving drama in Bicske, I stayed in contact with Ernö Simon, spokesman of the UNHCR, who was walking with the marchers. By early evening, the column had reached the motorway services at the 23-kilometre mark. I left Bicske to visit them. A long straggling line of refugees snaked along the inside lane and hard shoulder of the motorway, while the police patrolled the middle lane, leaving just one lane for traffic. Hungarian volunteers left their cars on the kerbs of side roads and clambered up the grassy banks of the motorway to bring them food and water.

As darkness fell, the whole scene was lit by the flashes of the press photographers and the top-lights on TV cameras, and by the headlights of police cars and passing traffic. As the wearier fell behind, the crowd of migrants had turned into a long, uneven line stretched along several kilometres of highway. I interviewed several people as they walked, then left my colleagues at a motorway service station to edit and send my report and hitch-hiked back to Budapest. I had to give a talk on a luxury cruise ship on the Danube.

A car with a Slovak registration plate stopped. The woman at the wheel and her teenage son offered me a lift to the capital. They were British and rather hostile to immigrants – despite their kindness in welcoming me, a stranger into their vehicle. As they launched a tirade against all migrants everywhere, my phone buzzed in my pocket. It was a journalist colleague, with the astonishing news that the Hungarian government had just announced it was laying on buses to take the motorway marchers to the Austrian border.

Then my phone buzzed again. It was Haneen, the Syrian girl staying with her family at my friend Viktor's flat near the east station. She was in trouble. In a series of terse, panicky WhatsApp messages, she told me what had happened. She had gone on her own by taxi, against my and Viktor's advice, to a hotel on the road out to the airport, to meet a smuggler. He harassed her. She ran away. I told her to get back to her family in the flat. And I told her that the government were now laying on buses. She and her family needed to get to the motorway services 23 kilometres from Budapest as quickly as possible. Then I rang Viktor. He ordered two taxis in his own name, to pick up Haneen and her family. Because of the threat of prosecution for people-trafficking, it was harder and harder for refugees to get into taxis at all. The taxis took them to the motorway services, where they caught up with the tail end of the march.

Soon after midnight, a fleet of 105 buses picked up around 2,500 people along the motorway, at the services where they were resting, and even those left behind at the east station, and took them to the border. But there were still a few misunderstandings to iron out. The refugees initially refused to trust the government. After what had happened at Bicske, they suspected another trick. So they refused to board the first bus. Just a few people went with it, as a test. It was then driven to the Austria border, from where the passengers rang or texted the others, that the government was keeping its word – they would be allowed to leave the country. Then the others boarded the buses and the convoy set out.

There was one final hurdle. At 3.15 in the morning, Zoltán Kovács, the government spokesman texted me. Now he was asking for help. I rang him back. The Austrians were not letting the people cross, he explained, but the foreign media were blaming the Hungarians! Was I at the border? I wasn't, but several of my BBC colleagues were, on the far side. I gave him their numbers. Soon the misunderstanding was resolved, and everyone on the buses, including those picked up from the motorway and from the east station, walked across the border into Austria.

The next morning, we set out early down the motorway. The trail of litter left by the march was still visible for the first 30 kilometres out of Budapest. Further on, in a parking area, we found five dejected Syrian and Iraqi refugees. They had gone on ahead of the main group, had stopped to sleep sometime in the night, and then had missed the buses. Would we give them a lift to the border? This presented us with a serious dilemma. Until now, anyone in Hungary, including taxi drivers, caught taking migrants even towards the Austrian border, had been arrested for trafficking. But that very night, the Hungarian government had laid on buses to do just that. And these poor souls had been left behind. Either the government had become traffickers or we were helping the government complete their humanitarian quest of the past few hours. We decided to help the government.

Arriving at Hegyeshalom, the border crossing point, we took the old road, which runs parallel to the motorway. Passing the railway station, we saw hundreds more refugees disembarking from the train from Budapest. The Hungarian railway company, MAV, was now allowing refugees to board trains to the border, but not the intercity trains to Vienna and Austria. Word had spread fast, and those regular local trains were now packed to the roof with happy refugees, allowed at last to continue their journeys. We pulled into a side road to let our own passengers join the throng. As we did so, several local people came out of their houses and started photographing us. This must be what it would be like, I thought, remembering my years in János Kádár's Hungary, to live in a police state.

We spent the day at the border crossing, which stretched all the way across both the older crossing point and the newer, five-lane crossing point. Since Hungary joined the Schengen zone on 1 January 2008, there have been no border checks here, but the rusting, empty infrastructure of one of Europe's big borders was still in place. The toilets and offices and antennae, the overgrown verges, the duty-free shops – all empty. Red- and white-striped crash barriers, now preventing nobody from going to nowhere. And the stray dogs, still scavenging.[11]

The Hungarian Red Cross were out in force in their distinctive red reflector jackets, handing out food, water and clothes. The refugees, as ever, were a mixed bag. A woman in black headscarf, blue jeans and sensible shoes, pulling a suitcase on wheels as though she was just rushing for her flight at an airport. Beside her, two little girls in pink and red tights, one clutching a large mauve toy mouse with a long tail and pink ears, giggling with joy. Young lads larking around with carrier bags they swung between them. Fathers with small wild-eyed children clutching their heads. People pushing small children in pushchairs, or older people in wheelchairs. Teenage girls in tight jeans and T-shirts, gazing into my camera with the confidence of youth, conscious of growing up in an age where the image is everything. Several men on crutches, with pained expressions, and legs left behind in the wars they fled from. A group of five young men, one old man and a woman. The old man was white haired and barefoot, limping heavily. They flashed V for victory signs at me as they passed. Nearly everyone was smiling or laughing. Young couples, who'd maybe fallen in love on the journey, like Hungarian freedom fighters on the barricades in 1956, holding hands shyly. There were big puddles from the rain of the past days. Reflected in them, the numbers of refugees seemed to double. Hungary had become, like Serbia, a refugee pipeline to the West. And beside them all, just a few metres away, a steady line of tourist and business traffic, the usual commerce of the world, gazing open-mouthed at the unusual scene.

CHAPTER SIX

THE CLOSING OF THE CURTAIN

In spite of our fragility, our self-perceived weaknesses, today it is Europe that is sought as a place of refuge and exile. It is Europe today that represents a beacon of hope, a haven of stability in the eyes of women and men in the Middle East and in Africa. That is something to be proud of and not something to fear.

Jean-Claude Juncker, President of the European Commission[1]

The political fallout from Viktor Orbán's decision to let the refugees go was enormous. But why did he do it? Orbán tried to ring the Austrian chancellor Werner Faymann several times on the evening of Friday 4 September 2015, and also sent him an official note, but Faymann's staff replied that he would only speak to Orbán after 9 a.m. on Saturday morning. The men would finally speak at 11 p.m. that night, after all the decisions were made.

Through the evening, János Lázár, the minister in charge of the prime minister's office, oversaw a meeting of the National Security Committee in the Parliament building. Shocked by the images from the motorway, the east station, and earlier in the day at Biscske, they knew they had to reestablish control of the situation. Laying on buses to get all these troublesome migrants and refugees out of the country was the logical way to do it. Lázár rang Orbán, who was perched in the VIP box in a Budapest football stadium, waiting for the 20.45 kick-off of the Hungary–Romania match, to pass on the proposal. Orbán made a snap decision: go ahead. Buses should pick up all the people on the motorway and those left behind at the east station and take them to Austria. His treatment of the migrants had made him the butt of criticism for months in the German and Austrian media. If they wanted these people, let them have them.[2]

The decision was communicated to his ambassadors in Berlin and Vienna. The Hungarians suggested there would be 4,000 to 6,000 people in more than 100 buses. 'Hungary is no longer able to guarantee the registration of refugees,' József Czukor, the Hungarian ambassador in Berlin, wrote in an email to Peter Altmaier, Merkel's chief of staff, and Emily Haber, state secretary in charge of refugee issues in the German Interior Ministry. Altmaier rang back immediately.

Back in the stadium, Orbán got on with the real business of the evening: watching the match. Just before half time, the home crowd roared as Ádám Szalai's long-range volley looked set to give Hungary the lead, only to be tipped round the post by the Romanian goalkeeper Ciprian Tătăruşanu. Haneen heard the clamor as her taxi passed the stadium on the way to her dangerous meeting with the smuggler at the Hotel Omnibusz.

At 21.00, János Lázár instructed the Budapest and national transport companies to immediately organise buses and coaches. Then he informed the media about the decision.

Angela Merkel, attending a CDU party gathering in Cologne before flying to Munich, spent a busy evening on the phone to Faymann and her own ministers. Though he was avoiding speaking to Orbán, the Social Democrat chancellor trusted Merkel. Austria would accept the buses – what about Germany? A legal team working for Foreign Minister Franz-Walter Steinmeier told him that under EU law, a country can allow in as many asylum seekers as it wishes. Sigmar Gabriel, the German vice-chancellor, also approved Merkel's decision.

Merkel rang Faymann back: 'Die Balken müssen auf. Wir müssen diesen Menschen helfen,' she told him. 'The barriers must be raised, we must help these people.'[3]

This was a reference to the red and white barriers at the official border crossings. 'Balken' is also the word used in the New Testament for the 'beam' in someone's eye, as in St Matthew's gospel: 'Thou hypocrite, first cast out the beam out of thine own eye; and then shalt thou see clearly to cast the mote out of thy brother's eye.'

'In this emergency situation, we decide that the barriers should be raised. We will not leave people in the lurch,' proclaimed the Austrian chancellor. But he also explained that what they were talking about was not an over-arching solution, but simply a way to solve the dramatic situation of the previous night.

'The police will perform their duties in the framework of the existing laws and with particular attention to proportionality,' read the statement from the Austrian police. 'If an asylum application is submitted, it will be accepted [for consideration],' a spokesman for the Austrian Interior Ministry told *Die Presse*, adding that 'complete control will not be possible'. The authorities in Vienna and at the border post at Nickelsdorf braced themselves for the impact.[4]

The end result was that 18,000 refugees passed through Austria to arrive in Germany over the weekend, of whom 10,000 disembarked at Munich station. There they received a rapturous welcome from well-wishers, who lined the platform to applaud. Many refugees carried crumpled portraits of the German chancellor – their unlikely heroine. The German federal government announced an immediate €3 billion in aid to help the German states accommodate the new arrivals, and another €3 billion to pay for later expenses like social security benefits.[5]

With the gates to Europe wide open, the Austrian chancellor began talking about how to close them. 'The chancellor could not say how long this exceptional situation will last, or how many refugees will travel to or through Austria,' added *Die Presse*, laconically. From 5 September to 16 October, in an act which looks very much like revenge on the German and Austrian governments, Hungary did not register the tens of thousands of new arrivals on its borders with Serbia and Croatia.

The new focus of EU leaders would be quotas. But should they be compulsory or voluntary? After the lukewarm response by national govern-ments to voluntary quotas in the spring of 2015, many leaders felt the time had come for compulsory measures. 'Exceptional circumstances require an exceptional response. Business as usual will not solve the problem,' the UNHCR chief António Guterres said on 4 September. 'Europe cannot go on responding to this crisis with a piecemeal or incremental approach. No country can do it alone, and no country can refuse to do its part.'[6]

Angela Merkel's decision provoked uproar in Germany. 'There is no society that could cope with something like this,' said Bavarian Premier Horst Seehofer, the leader of the Christian Social Union. He had not been informed of the unfolding events on the fateful evening because he was on holiday, and had turned off his mobile phone. Merkel's partners in the Social Democratic Party (SPD) leapt to her defence. SPD Secretary-General Yasmin Fahimi called it 'the only right thing to do'. 'We had to give a strong signal of humanity to show that European values are also valid in difficult times. Hungary's handling of the crisis is unbearable,' Fahimi added. Sunday's *Bild am Sonntag* bore the banner headline 'Merkel ends the shame of Budapest'.[7]

Merkel's move was also widely popular in Germany. Of those asked by the *ZDF Politbarometer* programme, 66 per cent said they agreed with the decision to give refuge to asylum seekers stuck in Hungary while 29 per cent disagreed.[8] Of those polled, 62 per cent believed Germany could cope with arrivals of large numbers of refugees in general, while 35 per cent did not.

Viktor Orbán was busy giving interviews too, over the weekend. *The Times* of London, Associated Press and ORF, the Austrian broadcaster, all got a bite at the cherry – if that is a fair description of the increasingly rotund Hungarian leader. Asked whether his armed forces would be instructed to open fire on refugees, Orbán said no: 'It is not necessary because there will be a fence that cannot be crossed. Whoever wants nevertheless to cross the fence must be arrested and prosecuted. No use of arms will be necessary.'[9] 'We are protecting Europe according to European rules that say borders can be crossed only in certain areas in a controlled way and after registration,' he told ORF.

Hungary now stopped registering new arrivals. Orbán might have lost the battle of the east station, but he was determined to win 'the war on illegal migration'. The next step would be the closing of the remaining gaps in the new Hungarian fence, notably on the railway track between Horgoš and Röszke, and the introduction of a package of measures passed by parliament on 4 September, which were due to come into force on 15 September. Two 'transit zones', were established at Röszke and Kelebia, built into the new fence, where refugees would still be able to apply for asylum in Hungary, nominally fulfilling Hungary's obligations under the 1951 Geneva Convention.

Internationally, the quota issue was the next political challenge – the magic bullet the crisis needed, according to the European Commission, a bullet in the foot or even the brain of the EU, according to the Hungarian leadership: 'If Europe's outer border is not blocked off it makes no sense to speak of quotas. When we have sealed the outer border and thus stopped the illegal migration we can talk about any solution.' Privately, Orbán told my colleagues, Hungary would be open to voluntary quotas. But the German-led rush in Europe was now overwhelmingly in favour of a compulsory solution, imposed on the reluctant East Europeans by a qualified majority. That embittered a Fidesz leadership which often felt it was treated arrogantly by the big European powers.

The numbers for the EU quota system were shaping up. France should take 24,031, Germany 31,443, Spain 14,931, Poland 9,287, Romania 4,646, Hungary 1,294. On 9 September, Juncker made his annual State of the Union address to the European Parliament in Strasbourg. It was long, emotional, and concluded with his proposals to resolve the crisis.[10] He told MEPs:

> It is time to speak frankly about the big issues facing the European Union. Because our European Union is not in a good state. There is not enough Europe in this Union. And there is not enough Union in this Union. We have to change this. And we have to change this now.
>
> We Europeans should remember well that Europe is a continent where nearly everyone has at one time been a refugee. Our common history is marked by millions of Europeans fleeing from religious or political persecution, from war, dictatorship, or oppression.

The nub of the new European Commission proposal was for the 'emergency relocation' across Europe of 160,000 asylum seekers from Greece, Italy and Hungary, in the spirit of solidarity between members. The decision should be taken at the Extraordinary Council of Interior Ministers meeting on 14 September. Parallel to this 'carrot', the 'stick' was to speed up the deportation procedures for those who failed to qualify for asylum. A list of safe countries to which people could be returned should be agreed at the EU level. Such a list should include all candidate countries in the Balkans. More steps should be taken to streamline asylum procedures in all member countries. More joint efforts were also needed to strengthen the outer borders of the EU by reinforcing Frontex. A diplomatic offensive was needed to address the crises in Syria and Libya. And an emergency trust fund, worth €1.8 billion, would be set up to tackle the crises in the Sahel and Lake Chad regions, the Horn of Africa and North Africa.

At the east station in Budapest, the number of refugees camping fell considerably, allowing cleaning staff to hose down the floors. But there were still hundreds of people there, funnelling up from the southern border, or the refugee camps at Kiskunhalas or Debrecen. Now they were resting in Budapest on their way through. For now, there was no further attempt by the Hungarians to stop them leaving.

In the underpass, a man with a Rasta hairstyle and flowery shirt wielded a metal loop with both hands, with a net attached, from which streamed the biggest and most magnificent bubbles. Someone wrote 'Köszönjük Magyarok' – Thank you Hungarians – in chalk on the floor inside a giant pink heart. Girls sat cross-legged on the paving stones with pencils and crayons. One woman handed out flowers. There was a mountain of red, summer apples in one place, handed out from supermarket trolleys, and a great pile of shoes in another. I asked a tall, thin, sad-looking twelve-year-old boy from Syria what he was drawing.

'A new flag for my country.' It was a horizontal tricolour, with blue at the top, white in the middle, green at the bottom. In the middle of the white band were three hearts, each filled with tears. He held it up shyly, to be photographed. *Alam* means flag in Arabic.

The news that Hungary's tough new migrant legislation, approved by parliament on 4 September, might at any moment close the last loophole in the fence, spread down the track at Röszke and put a new urgency into the step of the migrants flooding up through the Balkans. Government commentators might express their dislike for the 'military-style' speed of the migrants, but the truth was that that speed and organisation was provoked by Hungarian government moves. They were running to get in before the portcullis crashed down at the main gate of the Hungarian castle. Likewise, the Hungarian authorities expressed their disgust at a new 'aggression' among the migrants towards them. Presumably the migrants were supposed to embrace them for standing in their way, when Germany had made clear that everyone who applied would get a fair hearing.

Through the first two weeks of September, the numbers coming up the railway track increased each day. On 12 September, a Saturday, 4,000 came in according to police figures, but one had the impression that they were losing count, or at least the will to count. At this eleventh hour, the infrastructure which would have been needed from the first day, was finally taking shape.

The UNHCR at last obtained permission from the government to set up three large tents on the field beside the cornfield. A farmer's hothouse was converted with plastic sheets into a storage facility. More mobile toilets arrived, increasing the number from three to twelve, in a space catering for thousands of new arrivals each day. Greenpeace set up a solar-powered tent where refugees could charge their phones. Official charities like Caritas, the Reformed Church and Baptist groups, the Maltese charity, which had until now been active in official refugee camps but not in official collecting points at the 'point of impact', now miraculously appeared here too, where a week earlier a single MigSol tent stood – among the hundreds of makeshift small tents carried by the refugees themselves. The police finally got enough buses to transport people from the field to the registration point in the famous blue hangar. The UNHCR spokesman told me the government had admitted to him that they had failed to handle the situation here until now.

One morning at dawn near Röszke I asked a large, jovial policeman who had been up all night, what he really thought of his duties. 'It's like Monty Python, isn't it!' he replied, cheerfully. Impressed by his knowledge of British comedy programmes, I asked if he had any particular episode in mind. 'The Ministry of Silly Walks' he replied, without hesitation.[11]

Beside the railway track in early September, I encountered two men in civilian clothes, watching the scene. They had light overcoats with the word 'Police' on them, which they had put to one side. They refused to say which part of the state apparatus they belonged to, or to offer any comment. Unperturbed, I offered to tell them what was going on, and how the Hungarian state was failing the refugees, and putting their own police in a difficult situation. They listened politely and glanced at each other. 'I can agree with a lot of that,' one told me. Now, at least, the infrastructure was being built. Hungary had what could pass as a chaotic, but relatively well-managed refugee camp. The irony was that, within three days, the flow would be stopped.

The situation through the Balkans was volatile, changing every few hours. The Macedonian army and police tried in vain to block 7,000 people, who then broke through their lines. In Hungary, the registration system, painstakingly established over the past months and weeks, had partially collapsed. The quick pre-registration centres, run by the police, were still working at Röszke. These included fingerprinting machines. But the OIN centres, which involved a much longer registration process, at Kiskunhanhalos, Debrecen,

Vámosszabadi and Bicske, appeared to have stopped. The head of OIN, Zsuzsanna Végh, told state radio that 80 per cent of those coming were from Syria, Iraq and Afghanistan, and that 95 per cent of them spent less than two weeks in the country before moving on.

There was still a gaping absence of communication between the authorities and the refugees themselves. Few Hungarian police speak English, and the refugees' English was often merely rudimentary. There were comic moments. A Syrian man came up to me, pleading for help to get his heavily pregnant wife across the road to the doctor's tent on the far side. He was prevented by a cordon of uniformed police, who lined the road in order to try to keep it open for traffic. I explained his predicament to a police officer, who immediately agreed to help. The police line parted to let the man and his wife cross the road. Then, to my horror, thirty more women, children and men proceeded to join them, crossing the road. The police officer started shouting at me – who are all these people? I demanded an explanation from the man. 'They are my family too, they must come with me,' he shouted back. I translated. For a moment it looked as if, by trying to help, I was about to create a major confrontation. Then the police stood aside. The thirty relatives and the man, and his wife, all made it to the police tent. The first joint BBC–ORFK (Országos Rendőr-főkapitanysag, the Hungarian Police) operation of the crisis ended happily.

On 8 September, another incident in the same field won Hungary terrible publicity. A few dozen police had been instructed to stop the thousands of refugees in the field from wandering off before the buses came to take them to be registered. A big group got fed up with this and decided to break out of the field. The police tried to stop them. In the mêlée, Petra László, a young female reporter from N1, a small nationalist TV station, was filmed deliberately trying to trip up refugees as they ran, including Osama Abdul Mohsen, carrying his son, and a young girl. Posted on Twitter by a German journalist, the footage went viral round the world.[12]

N1 made a statement: 'An employee of N1TV today showed unacceptable behaviour at the Röszke collection point. We have terminated the contract of the camera woman with immediate effect today.' A few days later, Petra László publicly apologised: 'I am very sorry for the incident, and as a mother I am especially sorry for the fact that fate pushed a child in my way. I did not see that at that moment. I started to panic and as

I rewatch the film, it seems as if it was not even me.' But the damage had been done.

During the same incident, I also witnessed police running after refugees, tripping them up, and dragging them back to the holding point, using considerably force. One man in particular, who was partly disabled, sobbed violently throughout. It took three policemen to catch him and bring him back. On his T-shirt was a picture of a bear with a 'help' sign, and the words, 'Live with care, save the bear.'

The volunteer groups worked all the time. Mark Kékesi's old brown Mercedes estate was everywhere, bringing supplies from Szeged. Anarchist groups turned up from several countries, distinguishable by their 'No Borders' slogan. A blue banner was hung on the side of a white transit van, with a picture of butterflies, soaring over a fence: 'Ain't no European border high enough – no papers, no fear.'

At the beginning of September, local media had published a screen-shot of instructions from the managers of the state TV, MTVA, asking news teams not to show children – because they aroused too much sympathy in viewers, it seemed.[13] To justify government policies, pro-government media were instructed to emphasise at every opportunity that the vast majority of the 'illegal immigrants' were single men. According to official, EU figures, of the 1.26 million first-time asylum seekers registered in the EU-28 in 2015, 365,000 were under eighteen. In my own, first-hand experience, filming every day at the border, it was hard not to film children – there were simply so many of them.

Huge white clouds billowed across the wide blue skies of the Hungarian plain. I asked a photographer from the Magnum agency what he was going to look for today. 'Just biblical scenes,' he said, in a daze, 'biblical scenes.' There were plenty of those: the headscarved women, the toddlers, the summer heat and dawn chill, and the police playing the role of tall Roman centurions, in their dark blue body armour, green face masks, sunglasses and red caps.

At the Szeged County Court, all criminal cases had been suspended until further notice, in order to prepare for a massive influx of criminal cases, from 15 September. Anyone who so much as laid a finger on the fence would be prosecuted. Crossing illegally into Hungary was about to be transformed from a misdemeanour into a criminal offence. The fence along many sections had grown taller – 3.5 metres, with razor wire along the base and top; 3,800 soldiers had been deployed to help police guard it. More and more dog teams, policemen on horseback, soldiers with semi-automatic rifles, and ever more frequent helicopters appeared each day, to drive home the message. There could be no doubt, a massive crackdown was coming.

14 September was a Monday. I watched men in the pale blue T-shirts of the prison authority, standing on ladders, add new sections to the fence, right up to the railway line, and attach razor wire to the top. More and more police units were visible, many of them with riot helmets clipped to their belts. The soldiers started patrolling in hard helmets. That day, nearly 10,000 refugees entered Hungary, most of them down the railway line.

At dusk, a single, rust-red railway carriage suddenly appeared on the track, pushed up the rails from Röszke by a diesel locomotive. It was a shock to see something resembling a train on the track, we were so used to just seeing people on it. Along the top and sides and bottom of the wagon, razor wire was coiled, like a grotesque decoration. There was even a bit of greenery, like camouflage, as though to conceal the razor wire underneath. Or perhaps it had just caught on the wire, from an overhanging tree. In the brilliant glare of the television lights, the wagon rolled into place, to block the track, and complete the fence. Viktor's new Iron Curtain was complete. Thirty metres down the fence, also on cue, a dove flew up onto the wire and stayed there, silhouetted against the dying light.

On 16 September, Boris Kálnoky, my colleague from *Die Welt*, published his interview with Viktor Orbán.[14] Asked whether he was 'satisfied' with his fence, Orbán replied. 'Satisfaction is for the Rolling Stones. Who would be crazy enough to express satisfaction, when numberless migrants are coming, and one has the thankless task of having to stop them?' Off the record, Orbán told Boris and the other journalists present that Hungary might be willing to accept some kind of quota in future, but only on a voluntary basis. This was a position also echoed by Polish and Czech diplomats in the coming days.

Meanwhile, in Szeged, the first of some 200 people arrested so far for crossing the fence, went on trial. I was in court with Ahmed, aged twenty-one, from Aleppo in Syria, a student from the Mamoun University of Science and Technology. The man seemed stunned. 'I respect the Hungarian law. I did not know it was not permitted to cross.' Aywa Taleb Suadi, from Iraq, was next. 'We saw a hole in the fence and climbed through it. Altogether we were in a group of eight.' The judge was unimpressed. If Hungary had gone to the trouble of building a fence, he suggested, the authorities had clearly not put it there in order for it to be climbed over.

Some of the accused divulged little fragments of their backgrounds which they might not have given away so easily to reporters. Aywa was travelling with his brother. They had received the money for the journey from their parents. 'Three of my brothers were killed in Iraq by Islamic State. One was kidnapped.' At this point, he started crying. The hearing lasted barely an hour and a half, even with the help of a translator. Suddenly, the Hungarian authorities had enough translators – each paid 20,000 forints – €66 an hour – three times more than the prosecution or defence lawyers. The verdict was word perfect, as predicted by a Szeged lawyer friend a few days earlier: deportation, with a one- or two-year interdiction from Hungarian territory.

While Hungary was plugging the last hole in its fence, the rest of the Balkan route, from beginning to end, was in turmoil. The mayor of the Greek island of Lesbos, one of five where migrants were arriving each day in small boats from the Turkish mainland, announced that there were now 30,000 on the island. So far in 2015, 340,000 refugees had already reached Greece across the sea from Turkey.

On the Austrian-Hungarian border at Nickelsdorf, Austrian railways temporarily cancelled all trains in the direction of Vienna. They cited safety reasons – too many refugees were boarding them. Some Austrian trains continued to Germany, packed with refugees, but the line from Salzburg to Munich was temporarily suspended. No trains crossed the Austrian-Hungarian border. The UNHCR announced emergency relief for 65,000 people in Serbia and Macedonia.[15]

When Hungary closed the fence across the track at Röszke, the big question was how the refugees would react. There seemed to be two possibilities. Either to break through what was in most places still a pretty flimsy fence, or simply to avoid that border in future.

The worst incident took place at Röszke the day after the fence closed, on 16 September. This was the old road border between the two countries, just to the east of the motorway crossing point. A crowd of several hundred refugees, diverted there when they could no longer enter Hungary along the railway track, built up through the day. Riot police arrived by the busload on the Hungarian side, including TEK counter-terrorism commandos in full uniform. A series of crash barriers was supposed to prevent the refugees getting through. Offers by the UNHCR, who were present with several Arabic-speaking interpreters, were all rejected by the Hungarian authorities. The government wanted to be certain of winning the Battle of Röszke.

The stand-off continued through the afternoon. 'Open the fence, open the doors,' the refugees chanted. 'No one will make any problem to this country, no one will make any problem to the policeman,' Ahmed Hamed, a man with a megaphone tried to address the closed ranks of riot police. 'You must understand this. Please let us pass.'

In another message to police, he told them they had until 2 p.m. to open the gates, otherwise the crowd would 'take matters into its own hands'. This would later be used at his trial to prove that he was personally threatening the forces of law and order with violence. Several other men in the crowd also used megaphones, sometimes inciting the crowd, sometimes trying to calm them. Tyres were set on fire by the refugees, sending black smoke billowing through the crowd and increasing the doomsday feeling.

At one point, frustrated refugees, unable to advance, threw several projectiles over the barrier at the police. The police responded immediately with a barrage of pepper spray. This was the first unnecessarily violent response. The police were well protected with shields and helmets. There was no need to respond in this way.

In the panic which followed, some refugees including women and children were injured as they tried to flee the spray. Many more projectiles were thrown at the police by the retreating crowd. The police then opened up with water-cannon. Some young men tried to retrieve projectiles. Ahmed Hamed, sitting on the shoulders of another, shouted at them through his megaphone not to throw anything at the police. A group of young men then managed to force open the gate.

Blocked by the police on the Hungarian side, we journalists could only see the rising smoke, and the arrival of more police reinforcements. Journalists covering the events from the Serbian side had easier access. 'I watched one Syrian man come out with a child on his shoulder. The child didn't look too well, so I followed this man all the way up to where the police were standing. He pleaded with the police to take his daughter and give her medical assistance,' said Australian photographer Warren Richardson.[16] Warren, like me, had been at the border for weeks, but while I retreated each evening to the comfort of a hotel in Szeged, he often spent the night at the border, often in an abandoned watchtower, to get the best shots at first light.

The police took the child, then the phalanx of shields closed again. The father of the child now pleaded with the police to let him through to be with his daughter. 'I'm human. Let's be human here. Let's stop this. I come from Syria, a war-torn country. Why is everyone acting like this?' At that moment, according to Warren, the TEK counter-terrorism police attacked the crowd, using the regular police as a shield.

All of a sudden I saw the TEK uniforms running towards the border. And in a matter of seconds, it just kicked off where we were. Everything just went crazy. The police behind us just start pushing us, pushing us and pushing us. It didn't stop.

The TEK guys were just grabbing people, and what they did was place pressure upon the people, squashing them in. All I remember is looking down and seeing that young Syrian girl crying and screaming. I tried to grab hold of her and, just as I tried to grab hold of her, a hand grabbed me by the throat –

On the left-hand side of my body I could feel pain from the baton that was being shoved into my side by an officer. I couldn't make out who the officer was straight away.

Warren was pushed to ground. 'When I turned around and told the officer "I am no threat to you. I'm a journalist." He stopped, looked up and saw his friend. His friend came up behind me and kicked me in the head.' The police then tried to break Warren's cameras before pulling him back towards the Hungarian side of the border.

[The police attack] was well-coordinated. When I was dragged into the Hungarian side, I was able to have a good look at what was going on. There was a photographer on the roof of the Hungarian customs office. At the same time I saw a TEK uniform up there on a higher level of that building. I saw another two officers up there as well. What I noticed with the TEK guys is that they were running two-way radio headsets.

I noticed one Syrian man who looked to be in his sixties. He started convulsing and it looked like he was going into cardiac arrest.

Immediately, I put my cameras down and started CPR. I was told by a TEK officer to 'Get the f*ck away from him!'

He stayed by the man's side and tried to help him. 'He was foaming at the mouth and his heart rate was just pumping, and I knew something was incredibly wrong with him. An officer again told me to "F*ck off!"' Eventually, Warren was detained and taken to the police station in Szeged for questioning. He was later released.

The first 'battle' between refugees and Hungarian police was over. Eleven refugees had been arrested. Twenty police, as well as an uncertain number of refugees, charity workers and journalists were injured. Twelve months later, Ahmed Hamed, the man with the megaphone, was found guilty of 'terrorism' and sentenced to ten years in prison. In April 2017, the Appeals Court over-turned that verdict on the grounds that, as the defence argued, important and contradictory evidence had not been given sufficient weight. A retrial was ordered. In January 2018, he was found guilty of 'assisting an act of terrorism' and sentenced to seven years in prison. Once again, he appealed.

No country in the world would allow a crowd of angry, sometimes violent people, to storm its border. But the use of the anti-terrorist police was clearly intended to reinforce the government message first issued by Viktor Orbán in January, and rammed home in the so-called National Consultation in May, that migrants were synonymous with terrorists. In this sense, the refugees walked into a trap carefully prepared for them by the Hungarian government for publicity purposes.

Two 'transit zones' at Röszke and Kelebia were set up by the OIN. OIN officials told the UNHCR that each of these could process 100 applicants for asylum a day. The one at Röszke, a few hundred metres west of the motorway crossing point, consisted of fifty-four numbered cabins. A steel turnstile allowed access from the Serbian side. But for now, used to travelling fast and impatient to reach Germany, the migrants had little use for such 'bureau-cratic' solutions. Most now rerouted from Serbia towards Croatia. From there, they were taken by bus and train to the Hungarian-Croatian border, where the fence was not yet completed.

The field at Röszke, a major landmark on the journey of some 200,000 refugees to Europe in 2015, was now transformed into a ghostly landscape. The big tents, which had only gone up a few days earlier, were dismantled.

Municipal workers and volunteer activists tried to clear up the worst of the litter. The cornfields where so many people had peed and shat for weeks because of the shortage of toilets, were devastated. Scavengers had a field day. I watched an elderly Hungarian man, on a bicycle, sifting through the piles of clothes, tents and mattresses the refugees left behind, and piling his bicycle high with his treasures.

In the first five days after the closure of Röszke, 30,000 refugees crossed from Serbia into Croatia, defying a plea from the Croatian interior minister Ranko Ostojić to 'stay in refugee centres in Serbia, Macedonia and Greece'. The Croats closed six road crossing points with Serbia, and attempted to create a train and road corridor across the country towards Slovenia. The Slovenian government claimed this was done without any communication with them and they protested loudly. In the meantime, many found a way north from Croatia into Hungary, at Beremend, and further west, along the River Drava, at Gyékényes. For now, Hungary let them in, even as it worked hard to complete its fence on the Croatian border.

On the diplomatic front, the European Commission pressed ahead with its quota solution to the problem. The key day was Tuesday 22 September.[17] Meeting in Brussels, the European Council agreed to Juncker's legally binding plan to relocate 108,000 asylum seekers, overriding the votes of Hungary, Slovakia and the Czech Republic. Poland broke ranks with the Visegrád Four countries to vote in favour. Finland abstained. 'We've reached an agreement with a very big majority, bigger than required by treaty. We would have preferred unanimity, and it's not because we haven't tried,' said Luxembourg foreign minister Jean Asselborn. 'As long as I'm prime minister, mandatory quotas won't be implemented on Slovak territory,' said the Slovak leader, Robert Fico, defiantly. Hungary and Slovakia would take the issue to the European Court of Justice.

*

The next day in Brussels, an emergency summit of EU leaders convened. Details of the failure of most EU states to honour commitments to the World Food Programme (WFP) were made public.[18] The WFP helps feed 1.3 million of more than 4 million Syrian refugees in Turkey, Lebanon, Jordan, Iraq and Egypt. At camps in Jordan alone, the failure of EU countries to fulfil their financial commitments meant an end to the food aid for 229,000 refugees, who were living on handouts of less than half a dollar a day. Hungary gave a total of $339,000 to the WFP in 2015, while Sweden gave $91.2 million. The summit concluded with a short statement.

> Tonight we met to deal with the unprecedented migration and refugee crisis we are facing ... We all recognised that there are no easy solutions and that we can only manage this challenge by working together, in a spirit of solidarity and responsibility. In the meantime we have all to uphold, apply and implement our existing rules, including the Dublin regulation and the Schengen acquis.

An extra $1 billion was pledged to the WFP and UNHCR. Most assistance was pledged to the Balkan countries, ahead of the western Balkan routes conference set for 8 October, and the Valletta conference in Malta scheduled for 11 November.

In order to 'tackle the dramatic situation at our external borders and strengthen controls at those borders' additional resources would be channelled to Frontex, European Asylum Support Office (EASO) and Europol. 'We are all committed to offer sanctuary,' Angela Merkel told the press, adding that building fences was not part of any solution she could see. 'If they don't like the fence, then we can let the migrants though to Austria and Germany,' Viktor Orbán replied. And he did, for three weeks more.

At the summit, EU leaders set themselves a deadline of the end of November to establish so-called hotspots in Greece and Italy. These would be holding camps where asylum seekers could be registered and fingerprinted. From among these, according to the theory, those eligible for asylum would be relocated under the quota scheme to the countries to which they were allotted. Those whose asylum applications were rejected would be sent home. The first hotspot already existed in Catania, Sicily. Four more in Italy, and five in Greece, should now be established, on the five islands, and in the port of Piraeus.[19]

With Röszke closed, I moved to Beremend, south of Pécs on the Hungarian-Croatian border. Each day, coachloads of migrants arrived here and walked through the official crossing point into Hungary. On the Hungarian side, a long line of blue, Budapest buses, transported them to the railway station.

From there they were taken directly either to the Austrian border, or to the train station at Zákány-Gyékényes, from where more refugee trains set out for the border. Near Beremend, I watched Hungarian soldiers and civilians on government work schemes unrolling more razor wire. The landscape was gentler here than the flatlands of Röszke and Mórahalom, less wooded and with rolling fields of harvested wheat and old acacia hedges. The September sun was warm and the soldiers cursed as they cut their bare arms occasionally on the sharp wire. I felt sorry for the soldiers, and for the wildlife, witnessing this barrier rise like a deep scar across their landscape.

Just outside the village of Magyarbóly we stumbled on an identical brown railway wagon to the one that was used to plug the point where the track crossed the fence at Röszke. It was waiting to play a similar function here and was fully decorated already, with razor wire around the edges. Along the tracks, we noticed beautiful large white snail shells with perfect spirals, long abandoned by their owners. To while away the sunny afternoon, we decorated the razor wire with them. A local signalman promised to send me a text as soon as there was any sign of the wagon moving.

Brown-eyed Syrian children arrived by bus with their families at the railway station in Magyarbóly. They waved shyly from the windows, used to seeing reporters on this journey as their allies. They were let onto the train in small groups, past soldiers in camouflage uniforms toting machine-guns.

On a Sunday morning, I asked the local priest in Beremend if we could film inside his church and talk to his parishioners after the service. 'No,' he replied curtly, on the phone, 'stay away from my church.' On the village green in Beremend was a large chunk of limestone rock with a black plaque on it. 'In memory of the inhabitants of Beremend driven from their homes to the Hortobágy plain, on 23rd June 1950.'

Pale-brown army Humvees with heavy machine-guns mounted in the turrets were parked ostentatiously in Beremend, which the refugees would have to walk past on their way into Hungary. The glass in the tops of the turrets was so new, it still had the instructions in English on it: Strike Face This Side Out. With the locals, nonetheless the police and army presence was largely popular. 'We thank you for your sacrifice in our defence,' read a large, hand-drawn sign at Beremend.

We drove to Zákány-Gyékényes, to see the refugees in motion there too. Here, a small gap in the fence which led into the country from Croatia, had been left mysteriously open. The refugees arrived by train from Serbia to the Croatian village of Botovo at irregular intervals, but there was at least one trainload a night, we discovered. As the train disgorged its passengers into the dark, Croatian police and ambulances, their blue lights flashing, showed the refugees the way to Hungary – down the road to a meadow, along a track, and finally to an open field and the gap in the Hungarian fence. By now, Hungary had given up any pretence of checking their identities. They had ten minutes to board trains – hardly enough time for the Hungarian Caritas charity, or volunteers organised by a Hungarian volunteer from Gyöngyös, Babi, and her Syrian husband, to distribute water and food parcels. Then the train set off. Here again, large numbers of Hungarian police and soldiers lined the track – unnecessarily. There were reports in the Hungarian media that the soldiers had been invited in to the village kindergarten, to meet the children. How much more interesting it would have been for those children to meet little Syrian, Iraqi and Afghan children, I thought. At the entrance to Gyékényes was a giant billboard, left over from the 'National Consultation on Immigration and Terrorism' in the spring. The people have decided, the country must be defended.

Back at Magyarbóly, I took an afternoon stroll down to the border at Illocska and fell into step beside an old bloke in a chequered shirt pushing his bicycle, armed with a long pole. He was on his way to a particular clump of walnut trees, he explained. And what did he think of the refugees?

'These people are fleeing war. They should be made welcome and given hospitality here, until it is safe to return to their own countries,' István Mihálovics, 73, told me. He stood outside his house and served them water in the heat of summer, as they trooped through Illocska, he said proudly. He had also offered them some of his very own plum brandy, which, to his chagrin, they refused.

On 30 September, Viktor Orbán addressed the General Assembly of the UN in New York. 'What prevents us from finding an answer, is that there is no consensus about the nature of the challenge. This is not a refugee crisis. This is a mass migratory movement, composed of economic migrants, refugees, asylum seekers and also foreign fighters. This is an uncontrolled and also unregulated process.' An 'unlimited number' of people, he feared, were on their way. They should be 'given back their homes, and their lives' he said, not offered one in Europe.[20]

111

CHAPTER SEVEN

THREE SAVAGE FRONTIERS

My wife and friend, only
so far away. Three savage frontiers. Slowly
it is autumn. Will even autumn forget me here?

Miklós Radnóti[1]

On 30 September 2015 Russian military planes took off from the Khmei-mim airbase on the shore of the eastern Mediterranean, south-east of Latakia. The targets were both IS rebels and Free Syria Army rebels fighting forces loyal to President Bashar Assad. The news went down badly with Syrian refugees trudging the short road from the Croatian station in Botovo, across the border into Hungary.

'The Americans, the British, the French, the Jordanians and the Saudis all bomb us, and say they are doing it to help us,' one man told me, as I walked rapidly at his shoulder, trying to keep up. 'Now the Russians too are bombing us, and they also say it is for our own good!'

The year 2015 was one of fierce battles in Syria, and of major advances for the forces of the so-called Islamic State. In January Kurdish Peshmerga fighters managed to push IS troops out of Kobani, on the Syrian-Turkish border.[2] Kurdish children in the cornfield at Röszke sang me songs about the heroes of Kobani, around their campfires. Their fathers, and sometimes their aunts or older sisters, had stayed behind to fight. The US military provided direct support to ground forces for the first time in the conflict.

In May IS troops captured the ancient city of Palmyra and blew up many of its most beautiful buildings. Khaled Asaad, an eighty-one-year-old scholar and keeper of the antiquities was publicly executed by IS in August.[3] He had cared for the site since 1963. Just before IS troops arrived, he helped with the evacuation of many items from the city to Damascus. 'Their systematic campaign seeks to take us back into prehistory, but they will not succeed,' said his son-in-law Khalil Hariri.

IS didn't destroy everything. Smaller items, dating back centuries before the birth of the Prophet Muhammad, were looted and sold on the international black market. The biggest demand for them was in Western Europe and the United States. They were taken first to Turkey, I was told by one source, and then by ship to Constanta in Romania, or Varna in Bulgaria. And from there by taxi across Romania, and Hungary to Austria. In the other direction, arms flowed into the hands of IS. 'Let's hope there's not a war soon in Croatia,' former Croatian president Stipe Mesić said, 'because we've sold all our weapons to the Iraqis.' Hercules troop carrying planes took off at strange times of the night from the airport in Zagreb, bound for Baghdad. Tens of thousands of Kalashnikovs, left over from the Balkan wars of the early 1990s, were delivered to the Iraqi army, with US mediation. As IS forces advanced, those guns fell into their hands. Barrels which once warmed to the battles in East Slavonia in Croatia or the Krajina in Serbia, next saw action against the Peshmerga around Kobani, Mosul or Sinjar.[4]

Each refugee I met told me their reasons for fleeing their country. Many Syrians said they were escaping from IS, but just as many, probably more, said they were fleeing the brutality of President Bashar Assad. Despite the rhetoric of Barack Obama and David Cameron, who described Assad as an evil man who could not be part of any political solution, there was little awareness in Eastern Europe of him as a dictator who had tried to crush what began as a peaceful revolution. According to Amnesty International, 13,000 Syrians were executed in Syrian jails for opposition to Assad, between 2011 and 2017. Perhaps there would have been more sympathy for Syrians in Hungary if Hungarians had seen the parallels with their own failed revolution of 1956.

Now the Russians had come to his aid, to roll back rebel advances. By the start of 2015, 200,000 Syrians had been killed in four years of civil war. 3.2 million had fled – 1.2 million to Turkey, a similar number to Jordan, and

620,000 to Lebanon.[5] A further 7.6 million were displaced inside their country. The pre-war population of Syria was 23 million, including refugees from other conflicts, especially Iraq. The population of the capital, Damascus, was 1.7 million – about the same population as Budapest. Aleppo, the second city, was numerically larger before the war with 2.1 million people.

During 2015, 100,000 more people died. Syrian government forces still held a wide swathe of land down the Mediterranean coast and along the Lebanese border.[6] The Free Syrian Army, led most effectively by the Al-Nusra Front, held the north-west of the country. IS forces held large areas inland, in what appeared on maps like a skull and cross-bones pattern. Kurdish militias held much of the north, along the border with Turkey, in what they dared hope was part of their future state of Kurdistan. US military and diplomatic support for the Kurds seemed to offer them their greatest opportunity for centuries of achieving their own state. Bitter opposition to that dream by Turkey represented the greatest threat.

June was the bloodiest month of the year, with over 11,000 killed. In July, the number of refugees from Syria passed 4 million, including 1.8 million in Turkey. Due to Russian bombing raids in October, the Syrian forces, backed by Hezbollah fighters from Lebanon and Iran, made major advances. By September 2015, half the Syrian population had been forced to flee their homes, seeking refuge either inside the country, or across the borders.[7]

*

After the Hungarian authorities closed the railway line at Röszke, the refugees were diverted west along the fence towards Croatia. Croatia is shaped like a boomerang, or the arms of the Virgin Mary, hugging Bosnia, the baby Jesus, to her chest. The top arm, resting against Hungary, is about 100 kilometres wide.

The refugees now began funnelling across that border. Croatia was unprepared. Perhaps her politicians quietly hoped the refugees would break through Hungary's defences at Röszke. Or perhaps, just a few months before an election, they were trying not to think about the issue at all.

On 17 September, the Croatian army built a refugee camp at Opatovac, just across the border from the Serbian town of Šid. On the first day, 3,000 arrived; on the second, 11,000. There were 700 beds. Here, as in many places on the route, to be Syrian was gold, any other nationality was suspect. The Afghans, and even the North Africans, tried to pass themselves off as Syrians, to the fury of genuine Syrians. This became one of the main sources of tension between the refugees and there were regular scuffles between them, to add to the general misery of the weeks or months on the road.

This new bottleneck of the crisis was in the lowlands along the Danube and Drava rivers, close to the Croatian cities of Vukovar and Osijek, from which many refugees fled to Hungary in the Balkan wars in the early 1990s. The walls of the refugee camps at that time, in Kiskunhalas, Debrecen, Bicske and Nyírbátor were scarred with a mixture of Arabic and Serbo-Croat graffiti.

During the Bosnian war in 1993, I often took watermelons to a trainload of Bosnian refugees near Čakovec in Croatia. There was one thirteen-year-old girl who acted as the English translator for about 100 people. As we sat drinking coffee with her mother, I asked her what she was reading. *All Quiet on the Western Front*, Erich Maria Remarque's poignant tale of life in the trenches in the First World War. At that time her father was missing somewhere in the quagmire of war in Bosnia, fighting in the Bosnian-Croatian army. Years later, I discovered that he had survived and the family were reunited.

In September 2015 the Croatian government of prime minister Zoran Milanović had two choices: to allow the refugees across his territory to the north into Hungary, or west into Slovenia. He chose Hungary first – to the fury of the Hungarian government.

'Instead of honestly making provision for the immigrants, it sent them straight to Hungary. What kind of European solidarity is this?' Hungarian foreign minister Péter Szijjártó asked rhetorically.

'Your border,' the Croatian prime minister, replied fiercely, 'can only be sealed by killing people. Croatia does not shout, does not build fences, does not send its soldiers to the border. It just does its job,' said Milanović.

In the second half of September 86,000 refugees entered Croatia. Many slept in the fields around the Opatovac refugee camp before being moved on by train and bus to the Hungarian border at Beremend and Zákány. In the chaos, many simply set out on foot across fields of maize and sunflowers, and through the vineyards which dot the famous Ilok wine region. White wines from here were sent to the coronation of Queen Elizabeth in 1953.

All the closure of Röszke had achieved was that exactly the same numbers, about 6,000 a day, were entering Hungary but now through Croatia instead of Serbia. This time, however, the Hungarian authorities showed just how organised they could be if they wanted to. A fleet of blue city buses queued to take them to railway stations nearby, and on to the Austrian border. While the new laws which came into force in Hungary were draconian in many ways towards refugees, there were also elements designed to make the work of the police easier. From now on they could requisition buses and coaches, which meant that the onward transport of refugees to Austria became much easier.

Hungary could have closed that border too at any time but appeared to hesitate. Orbán was in close talks with Slovak, Czech and Polish leaders and seemed determined, this time at least, not to act alone. A consensus already existed among the Visegrád Four countries – Hungary, Slovakia, the Czech Republic and Poland – which fitted his political ambitions well. Orbán now saw his chance to become the leader not just of Hungarians who like him regarded the current influx as a new 'Muslim invasion', but of all 'sensible Europeans' who resented immigration from non-EU countries in general. At talks through the second half of September and the first half of October, Orbán called the Austrian and German bluff: You want these people? Perhaps we should just send them on to you. You want us to stop them? Then please say so publicly, then we won't be blamed so much for doing so.

Orbán was also working hard, with some success, to convince his friends in the German Christian Social Union (CSU) that Angela Merkel was personally to blame for the whole refugee crisis. He gave many interviews to German media in an attempt to persuade German public opinion of this as well. It was a simple narrative, but a false one. Hundreds of thousands of refugees and migrants had already entered Germany by the time Merkel made her comments in late August and early September, cited above. With deteriorations in their physical safety, those then pouring across the borders had made up their minds to leave a wide swath of countries, in the Middle East and beyond, early in 2015 or the previous year. A study published in *Die Zeit*, partly based on Syrians' Google searches of keywords such as 'Germany' throughout the whole of 2015, revealed that there was no increase whatsoever in migrant numbers as a result of Merkel's comments.[8] If the chancellor had been less polite, she could have fairly blamed Orbán's fence for adding to the domino effect, by swaying those who had not yet made up their minds in June.

Orbán did not just offer a simple explanation for what was happening, he offered a simple solution: Germany should close its border. This argument was also based on a false premise: that Germany policed an external border of the EU, which any secondary school geography student could have pointed out was not the case. Those reaching the German border had already crossed five or six European state lines on their way.

If Germany closed her border, as Merkel immediately realised, each country on the Balkan route would face a massive build-up of refugees and migrants, and chaos would result all the way back to Greece in Austria, Slovenia, Croatia, Hungary, Serbia and Macedonia.

Merkel's policy was based on reaching a consensus, while Hungarian policy was based on unilateral action by member states. Meanwhile the European Commission dithered, and its president Jean-Claude Juncker focused on relocation quotas. These would never be popular at an EU level, and would not have affected the current burning issue of the 5,000 souls a day entering the EU. In the absence of leadership from Brussels, Germany was reluctantly leading attempts to find a solution.

*

On 7 October Angela Merkel and French president François Hollande jointly addressed the European Parliament in Strasbourg, the first time the heads of state of the two countries had done so together since Helmut Kohl and François Mitterrand greeted the reunification of Eastern and Western Europe in December 1989.

'We must not succumb to the temptation of falling back into acting in nationalistic terms,' Merkel said. 'National solo efforts are no solution to the refugee crisis.' A plan was needed, and there was already one on hand.[9]

'It all started with a paper we wrote in September,' Gerald Knaus of the Berlin-based European Stability Initiative told me. The ESI report was entitled 'Why People Don't Need to Drown in the Aegean'.[10] 'We made the point that everything depends on Turkey.'

'The situation on the European Union's external borders in the Eastern Mediterranean is out of control,' the report began. 'In the first eight months of 2015, an estimated 433,000 migrants and refugees have reached the EU by sea, most of them – 310,000 – via Greece.' Of this number, 175,000 were Syrian, and therefore almost certain to be granted asylum when they finally reached Western Europe, having risked their lives and been robbed, often several times, by smugglers on the way. There had to be a better solution.

Gerald Knaus had lived in Turkey for seven years, and had excellent contacts with Turkish, German and Dutch diplomats. Crucially, he knew what Turkish politicians most wanted: visa-free access for Turkish citizens to EU countries, and more financial resources to cope with the millions of refugees it was already generously hosting. ESI researchers were themselves influenced by a study-trip to Finland in 2013, along that country's long border with Russia. There they learnt the importance of neighbouring countries in keeping irregular migrant numbers down. Inside Russia, old Soviet-era installations – including two 4-metre-high fences with a track down the middle – and the watchful eye of the FSB, the Russian secret service, kept numbers down. Finland only has a low, largely unmanned fence, mainly to mark the actual border.

The ESI circulated their new proposals to German journalists, who responded enthusiastically, publishing the key elements and carrying long interviews with Knaus. Neither the German (liberal asylum policy) nor the Hungarian (everyone build a fence and shut them all out) approach offered a solution to the ever increasing numbers of Syrian refugees, the ESI argued. Instead, Turkey needed to be recognised as the gatekeeper of the EU and a deal needed to be struck with it – the bare bones of which were, at this stage, that over the next twelve months, Germany, with the organisational assistance of the UNHCR, should take 500,000 asylum seekers directly from Turkey, while Greece should agree to send back all those arriving irregularly in small boats across the Aegean. Order needed to be reimposed on the external border, and in the process, on the internal borders of the EU as well, based on the fair and humanitarian premise that most of those on the road were genuine refugees and deserved the help of Europe on the basis of the 1951 Refugee Convention.

'There was a vacuum at the heart of EU policymaking,' Gerald Knaus told me later. Over the coming months, he toured Western capitals and Ankara, publicly and privately discussing different elements of and objections to the plan. Two Turkish diplomats, the Ambassador to the EU Selim Yenel, and Avni Karsioglu, Turkish Ambassador in Berlin, played a central role in conveying the ideas to Ankara. Contacts inside Angela Merkel's office, and in Foreign Minister Sigmar Gabriel's team, ensured that the proposals received an attentive audience in the German government. As Gabriel and Merkel increasingly referred to it, the German media soon dubbed the ESI proposals 'the Merkel plan'.

*

I went from the Croatian border back to the Serbian one to attend several refugee trials in Szeged. There were two separate courtrooms in use, one in the main county court, on Széchenyi Square, a massive nineteenth-century building painted Habsburg yellow, and a second, more modern one, quickly improvised to serve as a courtroom to reduce the workload. The verdicts were all the same – guilty, deportation. The only variation was in how long people would not be allowed to re-enter Hungary. As if they would ever want to. Earlier in October, the European Commission accused Hungary of contravening the 2013 EU directive on asylum procedures.[11] The letter, written by Director-General of Migration and Home Affairs Matthias Ruete, accused the government of criminalising those who crossed its border, of failing to inform them sufficiently in their own language of the charges against them, of neglecting their rights because of the sheer speed of the procedure, and of failing to make proper provision for the children among them. It also criticised Hungary for refusing to allow human rights organisations into the 'transit zones'.

'A person who wants to apply for asylum has to get access to the territory of the given country, and has to get access to a fair and legal asylum procedure,' Ernö Simon, the UNHCR spokesman told me.

> Now we see that all those people who arrive from Serbia and ask for asylum in Hungary are without exception rejected, just on the grounds that they come from a 'safe' third country, Serbia. The UNHCR does not consider Serbia a safe country. We do not recommend that other countries send asylum seekers back to Serbia, Macedonia, or even Greece. So this is against our official position as well.

After one trial I witnessed a much more mundane, almost ritual humiliation. Following his guilty verdict, a young man in yellow trousers was

119

marched down one of the main boulevards in Szeged, by three large policemen. I followed at a safe distance, taking photographs. His hands were handcuffed behind his back, he struggled to keep his trainers on, because the laces had been removed. All around, the good people of Szeged looked the other way and carried on with their everyday business. Girls with long blonde hair, like dandelions in the autumn sunlight. Young lads pushing bicycles. Parents with children on the back of their bikes, carried on as if everything was normal, as the young man was marched to the headquarters of the Immigration Office on Szeged's very own London Boulevard, which also sported a blue European Union flag on its square yellow exterior.

Samer Kayssoun was an antiques dealer, originally from Homs, Syria's third city. He had been living in Lebanon for two years, then in Turkey for a few months, when he set out to reach Europe. Now he was on trial with his seventeen-year-old nephew, for illegally crossing the fence. 'We were safe in Turkey,' he told the judge, 'but we were not allowed to work there. I left ten family members behind and set out for Europe. It took us ten days to reach Serbia. In Greece I got help from smugglers, they brought us to the Serbia–Hungary border. They pointed out the way. Then we saw the fence.'

He, his nephew and several others climbed over or through the fence, then set out in search of the police, he said. The smugglers had told them the Hungarian police would help them travel on to Austria. Instead, they were immediately arrested and put on trial. Samer cut a strange figure in the court in his large anorak, its hood lined with fake fur, the shoe-laces of his shoes removed, to prevent him hanging himself in his cell. If the smuggler had been a little bit kinder, he would have directed him to join the thousands trudging through the fields in Croatia instead. This knowledge made his current predicament even worse.

I watched the inevitable sentencing, then chatted with the judge. Didn't it disturb him, I asked, that he knew that the sentence he had just delivered could not be carried out? Since Serbia had suspended the mutual deportation agreement between the two countries, very few of the 600 people who had already been sentenced by the court in Szeged, could actually be officially deported. The Hungarian authorities did not know what to do with them. Some ended up in closed asylum detention facilities, some were quietly released and simply continued their journey into Austria. My enquiries at the Vác prison, west of Budapest up the Danube, revealed that there were thirty migrants there, awaiting deportation. The judge in Szeged, on the corridor on his way to his lunch break, said the execution of the sentence had nothing to do with him.

Samer and his nephew were led away to the police cells. We followed them down the corridor of the court house, filming them as far as we could. I assumed they too would spend weeks or months in prison. I discovered, much later, that they only slept one more night in custody before being released into an open camp. Samer rang a friend in Vienna, who drove to Hungary immediately to pick them up by car. Thirty-six hours after his humiliation in the Szeged courtroom he was in a hot shower in a good Viennese hotel. Such were the strange inconsistencies of Hungarian justice. It was like an elaborate theatre performance, designed to give the Hungarian public the illusion of safety and the migrants the illusion of danger.

By the end of October 2015, the Hungarian court system had spent 300 million forints, €1 million, on interpreters alone. It was easy to rack up such charges at €60 an hour. The poor lawyers only got €50 for the three hours they were in court, or were preparing the case. Several Szeged lawyers refused to have anything to do with the whole charade.

*

In Germany, the quarrel intensified between Hans Seehofer, the Bavarian premier whose CSU conference Viktor Orbán blessed with his presence in late September, and Chancellor Merkel. Seehofer wanted Merkel to agree to an upper limit on the number of refugees allowed in each day or each month, or a final total. 'Explicit measures of self-defence to limit immigration are necessary, such as turning back people at the Austrian border,' Seehofer told *Bild Zeitung*. Merkel refused. 'The term self-defence signals that a politician wants to do something that isn't really legal, but which he thinks is necessary,' commented the *Süddeutsche Zeitung*.[12] The CSU youth wing suggested capping refugee numbers at 250,000 a year. The AfD filed criminal charges against Merkel for 'human trafficking.'[13]

'If Bavaria starts turning people away at the border, then it's obvious that Austria will do the same at the Hungarian border,' commented Stephen Dünnwald of the Bavarian Refugee Council. 'And Hungary is already doing that with Serbia. It's a chain reaction and what we call Schengen will break apart very quickly.'[14]

Germany was in turmoil, and each opinion survey seemed to contradict the last. The *Bild Zeitung* claimed that 90 per cent of its readers favoured Seehofer's view that 'we cannot take any more of this', in opposition to Merkel's mantra 'we can cope'. But a poll by the Forsa agency in *Der Spiegel* found that 44 per cent of those asked said they had actively helped refugees in the past year, either by volunteering or with donations.

On 23 October 2015, the European People's Party met in Madrid for its annual congress. Representatives of seventy-five conservative parties from forty countries gathered in what the *Deutsche Welle* correspondent described as 'a windowless concrete bunker near the airport'. Viktor Orbán was photographed raising Angela Merkel's hand towards his mouth to kiss it. The chancellor, in a scarlet jacket with a chunky amber necklace, looked at him suspiciously, as though he was about to bite her hand.[15]

Merkel told the delegates:

Everyone who arrives in Europe has the right to be treated like a human being!

We did not create the Charter of Fundamental Rights so that we could treat people from other places inhumanely.

We must fairly distribute the burden and the tasks among ourselves, with each contributing what they can according to their abilities and their means. It has always been that way in Europe, and that is a formula for success. Therefore, I will not stop fighting, so that we can also master this, perhaps our greatest challenge in decades, in solidarity.

'Today, Europe is rich and weak. That is the most dangerous of combinations,' Orbán replied in his speech. We should not make promises to refugees we cannot keep, he admonished Merkel. Allowing in so many Muslims would 'fundamentally change European society', he said. 'And we don't have a mandate for that.'

Manfred Weber of the CSU, the chairman of the European People's Party group in the European Parliament, leant rather towards Merkel's position, than Orbán's. 'If desperately poor nations like Jordan and Lebanon offer so many Syrians shelter, then Europe has to be able to that as well. That is our primary task, to offer help.' He agreed with Orbán that 'We have to give states back the power to control Europe's external borders.' But this did not mean setting up more borders or fences within Europe, he added.

*

On 15 October, Hungarian minister János Lázár announced that the fence on the Croatian border was now complete. Viktor Orbán announced that it could be closed 'at an hour's notice'. On the morning of Friday 16 October, I watched the ladies from the local Caritas charity, in their short skirts and high-heeled shoes, serve tea to the bus-drivers waiting to transport refugees for the last time. The last few groups of refugees were allowed to cross, twenty at a time. Then at midnight the tall steel barriers clanged shut. The Croatian interior minister announced that migrants would from now on be channelled towards Slovenia.

With no more work to be done at Beremend or Zákány, I moved to Lendava in Slovenia, to watch the refugees arrive there. Meanwhile Angela Merkel held talks in Turkey with President Erdoğan and Prime Minister Davutoğlu.[16]

'We want to create conditions in which refugees can stay nearer to home,' Davutoğlu told her. 'Our priority is to prevent illegal immigration and reduce the number of people crossing our border. In that respect we have had very fruitful negotiations with the EU.' The deal was worth €6 billion to Turkey. Though Merkel was not willing to impose a ceiling on the number of refugees she would accept at home, the other option, now vigorously pursued by the German chancellor, was to persuade Turkey to squeeze them before they set out. One way or another, all European politicians now agreed that the numbers needed to fall.

The tent camp at Lendava was empty when we first arrived – long orderly lines of green army tents in a warehouse area near the middle of town. Overnight, it became a little corner of the Middle East, overflowing with children. Everyone seemed to have lost a family member in the rain and mud of Serbia and Croatia. The main nationalities were Syrians, Iraqis and Afghans. We set up our cameras and people clustered round us, shyly. Standing in our little puddle of technology, our cameras and laptops and satellites and cables, it would have been cruel to refuse to share our communications with the people who needed them most. We lent them our mobile phones. In Croatia in the rain at Opatovac, men had been ordered to board separate buses to women and children. Now everyone was trying to find their families. Many were distraught about their treatment at the hands of the Croats. One man was looking for his pregnant wife and three children. 'Why didn't you stay close to them?' another man wanted to know. 'We were separated by the police,' he explained. Delshan was distraught, looking for her elderly father. A father was trying to reassure his small son that he would see his mother again 'tomorrow'. Always tomorrow. They struggled to grasp that Slovenia, Croatia and Serbia were separate countries, requiring separate telephone codes and SIM cards. They were worn out from a 60-kilometre hike across the fields of Croatia. In the early morning cold, my nose started streaming. A small boy noticed and handed me his little packet of tissues. I took one, hesitantly, from his five. Twenty per cent, perhaps, of his worldly possessions. Islamic hospitality. The bells in a church tower nearby chimed seven.

One evening, back in our hotel in Lendava, an aid worker in Austria called us. Hassan, an Afghan refugee now safely in the Austrian village of Neudorfl, was looking for his mother, aunt and sisters. One of them had used my colleague Orsi's phone to ring him earlier in the day, he thought, but he had missed the call. Hassan sent Orsi a photograph of the women. Orsi went back to the Lendava camp to look for them. All she had was a photograph, and a first name. She went from one cluster of refugees to another. No one recognised the photograph. There was a rapid turnover in the camps, as the efficient Slovenes transported the refugees on to the Austrian border at Šentilj-Spielfeld. She was about to give up, when she heard footsteps, running towards her. She was pulled excitedly into a huddle of women beside a big white tent. The phone was passed round. Hassan's mother, wrapped in a huge blanket, began hugging her. There was an explosion of joy in the chill Slovene night. Orsi took a picture of the family, to send to Hassan. Then there was a moment of sadness, as it turned out that Sediqe, his fifteen-year-old sister, was still missing – the younger woman in the photograph.

We watched an impromptu refugee football match, the goalposts made of rubber tyres. I tried to find out if it was Afghanistan versus Syria, or if the teams were mixed. No one seemed sure. No one even counted the goals. All the tensions and frustrations of their journey flowed out into the tarmac. The goalkeepers hesitated to dive on the hard ground and risk injury after risking so much on their journeys. Many goals were scored that afternoon. The whole refugee crisis for a moment looked to me like a football match. Rich Nations of Europe 2 – Wretched of the Earth 3. But how long would the match last? Can we play in their team, and they in ours? Who's the referee? And what might victory mean, for either side?

In front of his tent, looking into space, I met Elyassin. He was only fifteen, he said, but looked much older. With the help of an interpreter, he told me his story. An Afghan from the Hazara Shi'a minority, his family had fled persecution in Afghanistan to Iran before he was born. When he was fourteen, he was sent to work in a factory. After only a few months there, Revolutionary Guards rounded up the young men like himself, and told them they were being sent to fight in Syria, in one of the Iranian units fighting for President Assad. If they refused to go, their whole families would be deported back to Afghanistan. After a month's rudimentary military training, he was sent straight to the front line, as cannon-fodder. Each morning the boys were injected with heroin before they were sent to the trenches. They fought, out of their minds. After three months of pure hell, they were allowed home to Iran for a few days for a religious holiday. Elyassin fled to Turkey and started on the long trail to Europe. Now he sat in the sunshine in Slovenia, trying to remember how it might feel to be a child. He was now fifteen and no longer knew how to smile.

Children clustered round our cameras, laughing, munching on the huge apples given them by the charity workers. They were happy, safe at last. Under the watchful eye of the Slovene police and army, Red Cross workers and volunteers from ADRA, a humanitarian charity, distributed hot food. No one wore face masks or dark glasses. Had the people somehow become less infectious now the Hungarian authorities were not involved? In contrast to the Hungarian soldiers in their NATO fatigues, bearing big machine-guns, the Slovene soldiers did not carry weapons at all. I watched a small girl in pink trousers, a green stripy top and rubber boots carrying a teddy bear, trudging to and fro, admiring her reflection in the puddles left over by the downpour of the previous night. The food was unpacked from the back of an army truck.

In a large tent at another camp nearby, at Bapska on the Slovene border with Croatia, we found volunteers from Germany, Australia, Argentina and Switzerland chopping vegetables and laughing. They were cooking up a huge cauldron of vegetables for the new arrivals in long white UNHCR tents next door. 'Our common belief is that all borders are ridiculous. We're making a cabbage soup for two border crossings. We never know how many people will be coming, so we just keep cooking hot food to distribute.' These were 'no borders' activists, a cheerful band of anarchists, chopping vegetables and making themselves useful on a very twenty-first-century front line.

Slovenia's approach to the refugee crisis was to allow in as many people as they could register and accommodate. That often created long tailbacks on the Croatian side of the border, as the Slovenes told new groups to wait. While many countries on the Balkan route made efforts to accommodate new arrivals, they were less concerned with those preparing to leave. And the rain had become the biggest problem, drenching refugees, aid workers, police and soldiers alike. The single photocopied papers which refugees waved, with details of registration in Turkey, or Greece, or Serbia, some flimsy official recognition from someone somewhere that they existed, got lost in the mud. People became separated from each other in the crush of trains and buses, in the dark. Efforts by the police and army of one country or another to impose order also meant that men and women could easily be separated.

'There was no food, nothing to drink, no blankets, no Red Cross, just rain,' Mohammed Skerek, a refugee from Syria, remembered the two days he spent at the Croatia–Slovenia border.

It only took an hour for a coach, on the motorway, from Lendava to the Austrian border at Šentilj. Normal passenger rail traffic was temporarily suspended, to make sure trains were available to carry the new arrivals across the country. The authorities were determined to stay in complete control.

'Slovenia is a transit country. We are going to focus even more on safety, security, and order, so our country can function normally,' said Prime Minister Miro Cerar.[17] But there were also preparations for the day when Austria and Germany would say no. 'If the destination countries adopt stricter measures, Slovenia will too.' Each of the countries on the route dreaded the day that the borders 'upriver' would clang shut, on the Hungarian model, and wanted to prevent their own country from turning unto a storage lake of human misery. Everyone on the route was acutely aware of the impending winter. What would happen if these numbers kept coming, in the rain and snow? Over 400,000 refugees reached Germany from Austria between 5 September and 15 October alone.[18]

Each day we drove to Šentilj, to see the refugees entering 'the West'. Two huge white heated tents had been set up at the border crossing between Šentilj and Spielfeld on the Austrian side, with a capacity for 2,000 refugees. As journalists, as at all camps in Slovenia, we were allowed inside to see the conditions. Despite their careful preparations, the Slovenes were now struggling to cope with the large numbers – by now at 8,000 a day. Long queues formed at the crossing point into Austria. They were allowed across into Austria whenever the Austrian authorities said they were ready, day or night, for another group of 150. For once, the authorities on both sides of a European border seemed to be willing and able to coordinate with each other. It was a different story on the Croatia–Slovenia border, where the Croats seemed incapable of telling the Slovenes when the next bus or train would arrive – or unwilling to do so – which resulted in some trains being stopped and the people on board suffering even longer. New border crossings were opened overnight, catching the Slovenes off balance. Slovenia and Austria were, in any case, both members of the Schengen group of countries. In normal times, there were no border controls at Šentilj anyway.

20 October was a Monday. At midnight, we stood in the glare of the spotlights, the roar of a generator, watching more than 2,000 refugees crossing from Šentilj into Spielfeld. The rain of the last forty-eight hours had stopped, but the refugees bore its marks. They were a bedraggled crowd of humanity, wrapped in multi-coloured nylon blankets, clutching their small bags of possessions. Many had not slept for days. The Austrian police were allowing them across to be registered in groups of fifty, as soon as an interpreter became available. 'Farsi' was announced through a loud speaker, and a new group of fifty people shuffled forward. Many of the smaller children were asleep on their parents' shoulders.

Safah was twenty-three, from Syria. She was travelling with her mother and brother. She had already reached Germany once, with her father, she said, but had returned to Turkey, where her family had been living for the past year, to fetch her mother and brother. They had not been living in a camp, but in a house, she said. But she had convinced her family that they should go to Germany.

The last few days, she said, had been 'deadly'. The worst country to cross was Macedonia. 'The Macedonian police treated us in a bad way.' They told her to die, she said. ' "Just stay there and die!" We die over there. We can't

127

even breathe. We have small children, pregnant women with us.' The family had now been travelling for five days and nights, non-stop, she said. Croatia and Slovenia had been better, because 'the authorities cooperated with us'. Though there was sometimes a shortage of blankets.

'It was so cold. We have never seen weather like this before, so rainy, so foggy, so deadly!' Did the weather, and the hardships of the journey make her regret setting out? 'No,' she laughed! 'I want so much to see my father!' Could she imagine ever returning to Syria? Now her voice fell, to almost inaudible. The sound of the generators swelled. The rustling of the anoraks of all the people, shuffling forward, the coughing of children and adults. 'Never,' she said. 'I lost my brother there.' She could hardly speak with grief. 'Now I want to start a new life. The life that we deserve.'

On the far side of the border, the Austrians were getting organised, at both an official and volunteer level. Among the police, men and women with Dolmetscher – interpreter – written on their jackets, moved through the crowds. There were regular loudspeaker announcements in Arabic, Farsi and Pashtu. Buses were being prepared to take them on to the nearest refugee camp in Salzburg. All under the watchful eyes of the Austrian police. One had the impression that Austrian order was being imposed on a weary, huddled mass of people. Everyone was being registered, some for the first time since Turkey. But the priority was humanitarian. They were treated as refugees seeking help, with a right to be here, not economic migrants.

Petra Leschantz was an Arabic-speaking lawyer from Salzburg, who organised a volunteer group called Border Crossing Spielfeld.[19] I met her at Spielfeld on 21 October. 'There are so many stops, so many collecting points on the journey,' she explained, 'it's true many people lost track of each other, but they find each other again. The Red Cross is helping with that a lot.' Over the coming months, Border Crossing Spielfeld became one of the most motivated, best organised groups on the whole route, shepherding people into Austria, keeping track of refugees once they were there, or on the road to Germany, and fighting the push-back in the courts, when Austria started sending refugees back to Slovenia and Croatia. But all that was still to come.

'The grape-harvest is long gone,' I wrote in one report:

But the Balkan grapevine the migrants use to find out where they can go, what they might expect, and even who is bombing their country now, buzzes with news, and rumours. Europe is having second thoughts about accepting more migrants, they realise. They are in a mad rush, before the drawbridges are drawn up in front of the gates of all the castles of Europe. Before the archers appear on the battlements.

It was time to go back to Hungary, for a rest. I had hardly slept a night at home in Budapest since 21 August. Before leaving Slovenia, Gergö Somogyvári, a friend and documentary film-maker with whom I had been working, asked us to record a short video message for his friend Sara, who was about to marry Daniel, a journalist at *Le Monde* newspaper in Paris. We recorded it in the style of a news report, in front of a police station in Maribor, and sent it to the happy couple. That weekend, it was played among many others at their wedding, which Gergö missed because he was working with me.

*

On 25 October, Balkan leaders gathered in Brussels for a mini-summit on the refugee crisis, attended by Austria, Bulgaria, Croatia, Germany, Greece, Hungary, Romania and Slovenia.[20] They agreed a seventeen-point plan of 'operational measures', designed to stop them blaming each other. In numerical terms, big refugee or holding camps were to be set up through the Balkans, administered by the UNHCR. On the eve of the gathering the Bulgarian prime minister Bojko Borisov announced that 'Bulgaria, Romania and Serbia will be ready to close their borders to migrants if Germany and Austria do the same.' On 29 October, the Austrian interior minister announced that a small fence would be built at Spielfeld, either side of the border crossing, to better control those entering the country. On the refugee issue, Chancellor Werner Faymann and Foreign Minister Sebastian Kurz were rapidly moving away from Angela Merkel and closer to the position of Viktor Orbán.

*

13 November was a Friday. At about twenty to ten in the evening, Daniel, the groom for whom we had made our wedding video, was standing by the window of his second-floor flat in Paris, which overlooks the back of the

Bataclan concert venue, when he noticed crowds of people pouring out of the emergency exits, running and shouting. He assumed it must be some kind of fight. Following his journalistic instincts, he started filming them with his mobile phone.[21] Then he heard shooting inside. Outside in the street, some kept running, some collapsed in the narrow street. He saw people coming to the aid of those who were lying on the ground. He shouted from the window – 'What's happening?' But no one replied. He rang a colleague at *Le Monde*, who told him that the Bataclan had been taken over by armed men.

'It was only then that I realised that this is not just a brawl, but something terrible. I went downstairs to open the front door, so people could take refuge. But no one wanted to stop, they just kept running.' The shooting seemed to have stopped. There were several bodies lying in the street. The nearest was a man in a red T-shirt lying face down, groaning. Another man in black clothes went up to him. Daniel and the man in black began to pull the wounded man towards the shelter of the doorway of his block of flats. Once he was inside, Daniel went back to close the door. The street looked deserted now.

'Then I heard what sounded like a firework, explode in my arm. I didn't hear the shot. I realised that I'd been hit. Someone was firing at me, but I couldn't see them. I felt a terrible pain in my arm and blood starting pouring from it.' Thinking back later, he realised that whoever had shot him must have come out from the Bataclan, which is on the first floor, seen two men helping an injured one, and wanted to kill all three of them.

The bullet went right through his upper left arm and lodged itself in the digital doorbell of the house. He tore his shirt, and made a tourniquet above the wound, to slow the flow of blood. Then he attended to the other injured man. The man in black clothes, who had helped him get the other into the doorway, had disappeared. A neighbour helped Daniel and the man in the red T-shirt, who had a bullet in his leg, into the flat. They rang a doctor for advice on how to treat their wounds till the ambulance arrived.

'It took a very long time. The police had blocked off the road. I felt awful, to be in the centre of Paris, bleeding to death, and no one could come to help us.' In the next room, a small child slept through the whole drama. Neighbours tried to make Daniel, and the man in the red shirt, an American called Matthew, more comfortable.

Three heavily armed men had entered the Bataclan venue at 21.30, on either side of the bar, and opened fire indiscriminately into a crowd of about 1,500 young people watching a concert by a California-based band Eagles of Death Metal. The Eagles were a widely respected rock band, while their name was a parody of death metal music. Those whom Daniel encountered managed to escape through the emergency exit to the left of the stage. A video shot by a fan shows guitarist Eden Galindo suddenly stop playing as the bullets crackle through the crowd. A witness watching the concert from the balcony above said the crowd was swept aside 'like a gust of wind through the wheat'. Eighty-nine people died, and hundreds were injured. The three gunmen who carried out the massacre then took a hundred fans hostage. A little after midnight, French anti-terrorist police stormed the venue, and the killers blew up their suicide vests.

The attack at Bataclan was just one of a carefully coordinated series across Paris that night. They began at 21.16 when a suicide bomber, denied entry to the stadium where a French-German international soccer match was taking place, blew himself up outside, killing one person. The plan had been to blow himself up inside the packed football stadium, provoking a stampede to the exits, where two other suicide bombers were waiting.

Three more terrorists opened fire at three different cafés in central Paris, around the same time. The total death toll for the night reached 130, with 368 others injured. It was the highest loss of life in France since the Second World War.

All nine of the perpetrators had fought in Syria.[22] The probable ringleader, Abdelhamid Abaaoud, was a twenty-eight-year-old Belgian-born citizen whose father had emigrated to France from Morocco in 1975. He had been imprisoned three times for violent crime. Saleh Abdeslam, twenty-seven, was also born in Belgium to Moroccan parents who came to France in the 1960s. The two men were friends, who may have first met in prison, living in the predominantly immigrant Molenbeek neighbourhood of Brussels. Abdeslam ran a bar called Les Béguines and was known to be fond of drugs, motorbikes and chasing girls. According to Hungarian and Belgian press reports, published months after the attacks, Abdeslam made two or three trips to Hungary in early and mid-September 2015 in a hired car, to pick up other perpetrators, travelling with false papers up the Balkan route.[23] Omar Mostefai, Samy Amimour and Foued Mohamed-Aggad allegedly stayed in the Grand Park Hotel in the Zugló suburb of Budapest from 9 to 16 September, under the names Jamal Salah, Fooad Moosa and Husein Alkhlf.

Abdeslam arrived in Budapest on 17 September, rested a few hours at the Hotel 30, just down the road from the Grand Park, then at ten that evening set out across Austria and Germany back to Belgium, with the three men.

The story was trumpeted in the Hungarian government media as proof of the close connection between illegal migration and terrorism.[24] The irony was that they travelled undetected because that was the period when Hungary unilaterally suspended registration, in response to the German decision to suspend the Dublin procedures.

Omar Ismail Mostefai was a twenty-nine-year-old French citizen, whose parents came originally from Algeria. He was one of the gunmen at the Bataclan who blew himself up when the anti-terrorist police moved in. Samy Amimour was the second Bataclan attacker, a Frenchman who had fought in Syria. In June 2014 his father visited the country, in a failed attempt to persuade him to leave IS and come home. The third Bataclan attacker, Foued Mohamed-Aggad was also born in France, to Moroccan parents.

A Syrian passport, in the name of Ahmad Al-Mohammed, born in 1990, was found among the bodies. The Greek authorities confirmed that they had registered a man of that name who arrived on a dinghy with 198 others on 3 October. The French justice minister, Christiane Taubira, suggested that the document was either a fake, or a genuine passport issued in a false name. IS conquests in Syria meant that legitimate equipment used to produce passports had fallen into their hands. Smugglers in Turkey also encouraged refugees heading for the coast to surrender their passports, as part of their fare. Many of those passports were then resold, especially since August, and the German announcement that Syrians were likely to get asylum in Germany. The going price in Turkey for a Syrian passport was $2,000. Back in Syria, the Assad regime was selling them to its own citizens for $400 a piece.

Even before the Paris attacks, the intelligence services of several European countries had compiled a list of the serial numbers of 5,000 genuine blank passports from Syria, and 10,000 from Iraq which had gone missing when IS forces occupied the cities where they were stored – Raqqa and Deir al-Zor provinces in Syria, and Anbar, Nineveh and Tikrit in Iraq. One source in the Balkans told me that President Assad's secret services were working closely with German intelligence, with details of IS figures travelling to and from Europe. The list was being constantly updated.

On 20 November, the *New York Times* published profiles of some of the 130 victims.[25] They included Kheir Eddine Sahbi, an Algerian violinist who had been in France for only a year, studying ethnomusicology at the Sorbonne, and Amine Ibnolmobarak, a twenty-nine-year-old Moroccan. Most of the victims were young French men and women. Antoine Leiris's wife Hélène, a make-up artist and mother of their seventeen-month-old son Melvil, died at the Bataclan.[26] He wrote an open letter to her murderers on Facebook:

On Friday evening you stole the life of an exceptional person, the love of my life, the mother of my son, but you will not have my hatred. I don't know who you are and I don't want to know, you are dead souls. If this God for whom you kill blindly made us in his image, every bullet in the body of my wife is a wound in his heart. So no, I will not give you the satisfaction of hating you. You want it, but to respond to hatred with anger would be to give in to the same ignorance that made you what you are. You would like me to be scared, for me to look at my fellow citizens with a suspicious eye, for me to sacrifice my liberty for my security. You have lost. I saw her this morning. At last, after nights and days of waiting. She was as beautiful as when she left on Friday evening, as beautiful as when I fell head over heels in love with her more than 12 years ago. Of course I am devastated with grief, I grant you this small victory, but it will be short-lived. I know she will be with us every day and we will find each other in heaven with free souls which you will never have. Us two, my son and I, we will be stronger than every army in the world. I cannot waste any more time on you as I must go back to my son, who has just woken from his sleep. He is only just 17 months old, he is going to eat his snack just like every other day, then we are going to play like every other day and all his life this little boy will be happy and free. Because you will never have his hatred either.

*

The February morning sunlight shone in through the windows of the Zastava weapons factory in Kragujevac, central Serbia. Ferns and rubber plants were arranged along the window sill. The delicate leaves of one fern framed the serious face of the former Yugoslav leader Josip Broz Tito, in his famous pale suit. In front of one table, where a pretty, dark-haired woman laboured with an AK-47 Kalashnikov, was an icon of the Virgin Mary. Despite the sunlight, a candle burnt on her desk – not for religious reasons, the manager explained, but in order to check for imperfections in the barrels of the guns. All six of the machine-guns used at the Bataclan were made here, he had already confirmed to French investigators, who presented him with their serial numbers. Mostly in the 1980s, just in time to be used in the wars in Croatia, Bosnia and Kosovo. He shrugged – 'We are not responsible for what happens to them after they leave our gates.' Besides, they produce, at the moment, 1,500 Kalashnikovs a day. It is the job of others to trace them, if they can.

In the firing range of the factory, where new models are tested, we were invited to shoot machine-guns, sniper rifles – anything we wanted. We politely declined, so the chief engineer demonstrated them himself, while we filmed and took photographs. We wore headphones, to protect our hearing from the roar of the guns. The tinkling of the spent cartridges on the hard ground was more poignant. I remembered times in Sarajevo, at the beginning of the war, when bullets ricocheted off the wall beside me when a sniper opened fire. A policeman screamed at me to lie down. I did, in a puddle in the pouring rain, a few metres from the safety of the entrance of the Hotel Europa. The Kragujevac factory had the pleasant atmosphere of any craftsman's workshop, with each stage of the weapons' manufacture, the polished wood and gleaming steel, the precision instruments, and the end products, neatly stacked for the next shipment.

Our attempt to trace the guns used in Paris led us to the Serb entity inside Bosnia, known as Republika Srpska. The town of Višegrad on the deep blue Drina River was made famous by the Yugoslav Nobel Prize-winning author Ivo Andrić with his novel *Bridge on the Drina*. The Bosniaks – Bosnian Muslims – were mostly massacred or driven out during the war. It is a miserable city today, for all its physical beauty. The famous Serbian film director Emir Kusturica has tried to inject a bit of Serb nationalist life back into the town, with a series of new buildings along the river, culminating in a brand new Serbian Orthodox church. There are murals glorifying another terrorist, Gavrilo Princip, who assassinated the heir to the Austro-Hungarian throne, the Archduke Ferdinand and his wife Sophie in Sarajevo in June 1914, and sparked the First World War. In a café beside the Drina, we sat down with a

Bosnian Serb army veteran, who admitted to smuggling guns regularly to Western Europe. It was a small-scale trade, he told us. The Serbs always had more guns than the Bosniaks, he explained, and when the war ended in 1995, instead of handing them in as they were required to do under the Dayton Peace Accords, a large number were hidden, under the floorboards of houses, in dusty attics, or buried carefully in oiled cloths in the nearby forests, to be dug up for use in the next war against the Muslims. As the years passed, and the war pensions of the veterans shrank or stagnated, more and more guns were traded on the black market. And the market led to the criminal networks, all with former Yugoslav connections, in Northern and Western Europe. The procedure was simple, he explained. A few guns and grenades in the boot of a car, close to the spare wheel. In more complicated – and expensive operations – built into specially designed compartments. He personally sold Kalashnikovs for €200 each, though he was aware they fetched over €1,000 apiece in France. The route was expensive to organise, and the risk of discovery not minimal. Long prison sentences awaited those who were caught. But what could he do? What could he afford with his pension of €200 a month? It wasn't even enough to pay for firewood in winter.

What would he say if he found out that some of the guns he sold were used by Islamist extremists at the Bataclan, I asked. 'I would shoot myself,' he said, twisting his face into a grimace of pain and fury. Then took another swig of beer.

CHAPTER EIGHT

A WAREHOUSE OF SOULS

Exactly because I am an obstetrician, I am aware how difficult, how strenuous, how expensive, and how many hours it takes to give birth. For this reason I am very angry how many lives are being lost, in war, and at sea, in this flow of migrants.

Yannis Mouzalas, Greek Minister for Migration

A half-moon hung low in the sky over the Balkan mountains, west of the Bulgarian town of Dragoman. Hill paths and tracks wound steeply upwards to the left of the main road, towards the ridge which marks the border with Serbia. Wooden beehives, painted yellow, blue and white, glowed strangely translucent in the gathering dark, beside the old wells in peasant gardens, among the vines. Few houses boasted lights in the windows. The local people have grown old, and their sons and daughters have left for the city, or for Western Europe. They come back for barbecues in the summer, when the hillside wakes up to human voices again. A slight hum of traffic rose from the road below and I could make out a filling station, then the thin necklace of lights of the border crossing point in the valley. The mountains look down onto a corner of the Thracian plain, down towards the Bulgarian capital only 45 kilometres away.

Most of the tracks up the mountain were overlaid with autumn leaves, but after diligent searching, we found one, hugging the contours of the hill, weaving in and out of the cover of pine trees, with the tell-tale signs we were looking for. Litter. Why did refugees and migrants, who had so little, always throw so much away? There were chocolate wrappers and empty cigarette cartons. The proof that these were not from careless Bulgarian youth were the plastic mobile phone cards, the SIM card pushed out of them, with Arabic or Farsi print along the bottom. Thrown to one side in the long grass and carefully cut up, I found one document in the Bulgarian script, issued by the Bulgarian authorities at Elhovo on the Turkish border, on 30 October. Waliullah Mohammed Hashim, born on 1 January 1997 – a sign either of a weary interpreter, or of a migrant who did not know his exact birthday – had recently passed this way. Caught inside Bulgaria after crossing the fence on the Turkish border, or going round it, it had taken him eighteen days to cross Bulgaria. There were also tyre marks in the mud, where the smugglers usually parked their cars.

I was back on the refugee trail – on what might be called the eastern branch of the western Balkan route, across the land border from Turkey into Bulgaria, then from Bulgaria into Serbia, to meet up in Belgrade with the 'western branch', which came up across the Greece–Macedonia border into Serbia. Refugees used Bulgaria in preference to Greece for several reasons. One was the fear of drowning. There were many stories of the dangers of the Aegean. During 2015, 805 people died crossing the short stretch of water in overcrowded dinghies between the Turkish coast and the five closest Greek islands.[1] Another reason why the people came this way was money. It simply cost less to travel through Bulgaria. This meant that there were more Afghans, and fewer Syrians on this route. The Bulgarian smugglers had a derogatory word for them. They called the Afghans 'Taliban'. This was particularly hurtful to people who were actually fleeing the Taliban.

On the Serbian side of the border, at Dimitrovgrad, the police were taking a break at six in the morning when I reached the refugee camp where refugees gather when they walk over the mountains. Ali Khaan had arrived with two friends just half an hour earlier, after a twenty-five-day journey from Afghanistan. He and his friends had reached Bulgaria by swimming across the lake at the point near where the Turkish, Greek and Bulgarian borders meet, probably either the Maritsa or Arda river. In Sofia they were caught sleeping rough by the Bulgarian police, who forced them to hand over €500, their mobile phones and their watches. Dropped by smugglers near this border, they lost their way but were helped by a villager, 'a good guy', to find the right path over the mountain. Once on the Serbian side, a taxi was waiting near a pine wood. They paid the driver to bring them just 3 kilometres to the refugee centre. Volunteers served hot tea and handed out survival blankets. Huddled in gold and silver, they looked like the angels on a Christmas tree, pinned against the camp fence. The containers, laid on for people to rest in, were all full. And the police, who had been working all night to register the new arrivals, were taking a one-hour break. Now the plan was to register, give fingerprints, then take one of the coaches laid on by the Serbian authorities, to Belgrade or to Šid on the Croatian border. The document they received gave them the right to stay in Serbia for seventy-two hours – either to seek asylum there or to leave the country. The vast majority chose to leave. Most spent only three or four hours in Dimitrovgrad. The bus trip to Belgrade cost €25 per person.

Željko Vostić, a local employee of the UNHCR, said many complained of mistreatment by the Bulgarian police. In October, a report by Serbian human rights groups detailed Bulgarian police violence against migrants.[2]

'We're heading for Germany first, probably,' said Ali Khaan. 'Let's see if they accept or deport us, it's up to them. We were kids when the war was on, one war flowed into another. We went to Pakistan as kids, as refugees, to escape the war. Then we came back to our own country.' In Kandahar he worked as transport manager for a company supplying fuel to NATO forces at the airfield. NATO troops first went to Afghanistan in 2003, after the 2001 US invasion.

'I was continuously threatened by the insurgents [Taliban]. Either I should help them or they would kill me and my family.' They wanted to get their hands on his company's trucks. He had to leave very suddenly. Unlike many Afghans I met, he had only positive memories of Western intervention in his country.

They came to rebuild schools, to support female education, brought business, but what I most liked about them, they came to support our culture, our education. We had an educational system only for males before. And they came to help girls go to school too. Once when I was a kid, I read in a book the phrase 'Give me a good mother and I'll give you a good nation.'

He thinks it's from Shakespeare. In fact the words are attributed to Napoleon.[2]

The Taliban are getting back into power, and it's hard to survive there now. So those who can leave, do so. Mostly the young. The government is not able to protect us. So that's a tough and a sad thing. I feel bad about it, but life is more important. You have to live.

Would he ever go home? I asked.

'I can imagine going back one day, as soon as I feel safe there, when my kids can go to school without any fear. Or my sisters can go to school without fear in their hearts, that we're going to be killed, or have acid thrown in their faces.' That was what the religious fundamentalists did to girls who they saw walking to school in the morning, he explained. So his sisters no longer went to school. His parents taught them what they knew at home, but it wasn't the same. He left his parents, his older and younger brother, and his sisters behind in Kandahar. He was afraid they would be targeted by the Taliban, when they heard he had gone.

He had heard fragments of news about the Paris attacks, not the full story, while he was trying to dodge Bulgarian police in Sofia.

I feel bad about what happened. I have my selfie with their flag, that's a sad incident, and it's happening everywhere – what more can I say?

The terrorist does not have any religion. That's the message that I have for everybody. Muslims would love to have peace, our book is all about peace. True Islam teaches us to respect life. We believe that if you kill a human, you kill all humanity, if you save a human you save humanity. I am a modern Muslim, and I follow what our religion says, not what the scholars say, or what the Taliban or the elders say. My family taught us not to follow that. Just follow the book, that's the right thing.

I believe it's true that some of the attackers came with the migrants, because we came all the way here, and nobody searched us. Not once. I also understand that people are afraid of so many refugees in their own country. Among the refugees there are a lot of illiterate people, uneducated people, from different cultures, going to a different environment, and of course they are going to create a mess. We all believe that. But still, I'm thankful to the European community that accepted so many refugees. Everyone is leaving their home and their country because they have to. It's not because people are in a 'mood' to live in Europe, it's because they have to.

Of course there are also people who just wish to live in Europe, to have a good life, and being a human everyone deserves a good life. You can't say, 'I'm a European, so I can have a good life, but you're not European, so you can't.' A good life is for everyone. The thing is, we need to help each other, ignoring religions, and in the meantime respecting religions, still we are humans and we have to have a good humanity between us, a good brotherhood.

That day in Paris, twenty-eight-year-old Abdelhamid Abaaoud was cornered by 110 anti-terrorist police in a flat in the Saint-Denis district. Police had left no stone unturned since the attacks on 13 November. Now, thanks to a tip-off, they surrounded the flat where he was hiding with his cousin Hasna Aitboulachen and several others.[3]

Abaaoud's family came originally from the region of Sous, in south-west Morocco, in the fertile river valley between the High Atlas and Anti-Atlas mountains. The River Sous flows into the Mediterranean near Agadir. Mohammed Awzal, a Sufi poet and author of 'The Ocean of Tears' (died 1749), was the region's most famous son, before Abaaoud.[4] The Sufis have been the first targets of extreme Islamist groups affiliated with Islamic State in many countries, from Afghanistan to Mali. Sufis condemn the jihadists as heretics, because they claim to know the will of God by ordering suicide bombings, for example. The Salafi extremists of IS regard Sufis as heretics because of their mystical attachment to the tombs of their sheikhs, which they destroy where they come to power. Their battles may sometimes look like an attack on the West, but, more often than not, this is actually a war against their fellow Muslims. The West is a sideshow.

Over 5,000 bullets were fired by police in the raid. Abaaoud blew himself up with a suicide vest, and his cousin died in the blast. Eight others were arrested, including the owner of the flat, Jawad Bendaoud. He lent it to two Belgians, he told reporters, as a favour to a friend. When he told them there were no mattresses, they said that was not a problem. They just needed water and a place to pray.

IS claimed responsibility for the Paris attacks, which they said were in retaliation for French airstrikes in Syria and Iraq.

*

Back at Dimitrovgrad, the police were registering new arrivals again. One was Erdhad Tanha Saadat, a radio journalist from Jalalabad in eastern

Afghanistan, on the main road between Kabul and the Pakistani border at the Khyber Pass. While other Afghans suffered at the hands of the Taliban, Jalalabad and the villages around it were increasingly the target of IS. In April 2015, thirty-five people were killed and more than a hundred injured in the city in a suicide bomb attack on a bank where people were queuing to collect their wages. Even the Taliban denounced it.

Da'esh [IS] told me, you must leave journalism and come and work for us. They are not good people, and they want to kill people. They do not want peace in Afghanistan, or anywhere in the whole world. Every day in Nangahar province they kill ten, fifteen, twenty people. I want to go to Europe and Germany, because Germany makes Afghan people welcome. We want to go to Germany because there is peace there, and good people, and good government.

His first experience with Germans at Dimitrovgrad had definitely been positive. Martin was a volunteer who in normal times had his own travelling bakery, driving between the open-air markets of Germany to sell his bread. 'I think it's a kind of duty for me to come here, because in Germany we have a safe life, enough time, and here people are suffering. So I have no choice. My heart made me come here to help.' When the UNHCR and the Serbian Red Cross packed up their stalls at the end of the working day, he and other volunteers stayed up all night, serving hot food and tea to new arrivals like Ali Khaan and Tanha Sadaat.

A month earlier he had been at the Croatian-Serbian border. 'It was a disaster. We were cooking for 2,000 people a day, then the Red Cross arrived and said, "OK, we're taking over now."' They worked for two hours then left, but his group were not allowed to start serving again, so they moved here. He was bitterly critical of all the 'official' charities. 'They're too close to the government,' he said. As we spoke, an elderly local man in a pink cap wheeled his bicycle along the road and stopped to stare at the newcomers. I felt a wariness, not a hostility towards the refugees, from the local population.

Wiebke was another of the German volunteers, handing out clothes from the back of a red van. The clothes came from a huge warehouse in Preševo, the biggest Serbian camp on the Serbia–Macedonia border. Even she became exasperated as everyone crowded round, trying to select trousers, jackets and shoes that might fit them. Some of the refugees arrived barefoot, suffering frostbite. Their flimsy shoes had fallen apart somewhere on the long journey. Wiebke felt sympathy for Angela Merkel's refugee policies, though as a conservative politician she didn't like her. It was true that public opinion was turning against the refugees in Germany, she said, but there was still a lot of solidarity. At Dimitrovgrad at the moment, one German and one Czech group of volunteers were working. At the beginning, most of the volunteers worked in what they called 'wild camps'. Now it had become more organised, and they were also forced to register with the authorities. There was sometimes tension on account of this, as well as because the volunteers tended to work much longer hours.

'For me, every human should have the right to live where he or she wants,' said Wiebke. 'We make all these difficulties in the world. Germany is also an exporter of weapons. One reason we have a good life, is because we keep people elsewhere in the world poor.'

'And Paris?' I asked.

'People say once again that all Arabs are terrorists. Maybe there's one terrorist in a hundred thousand refugees. So for me there is no connection between terrorism and refugees.'

Most of the volunteers were young, pretty women from Germany, always smiling, handing out tea and warm food at all hours of day and night. Most of the refugees here were Afghan men in their late teens or early twenties. The women said they never experienced sexual harassment.

A Serbian bus, with registration plates from the nearby city of Zaječar, started revving its engines to encourage the refugees to take their seats. A Yazidi family, from Sinjar in Iraq, showed me photos on their phone of Sinjar after the IS attack – street after street of homes in ruins. Their journey across Bulgaria had been rough. Five days in police detention near the border. Seventeen people kept by the smugglers in one small room.

In Sofia, Deputy Interior Minister Philip Gunev disputed the picture of Afghanistan descending into chaos which several of the refugees I met at the border depicted.

The reports and intelligence we get from Afghanistan and Iraq, is that there's a sort of frenzy going on right now. That this is a once in a lifetime opportunity to leave and move to Western Europe. Every day, thousands of people from Kabul are trying to get passports and leave. Some even get fake threat letters from the Taliban in order to be able to prove they come from provinces which are eligible for some kind of international protection status.

In Iraq, the situation is slightly different. We've seen about 3 million internally displaced people as a result of the IS offensive over the past year. A great number of these people feel there is a unique opportunity to emigrate to Western Europe.

Turkish airlines have also increased several times the number of their daily flights from Iraq to Turkey. That also results in the change of migratory patterns, an increased number of Iraqi and Afghan refugees.

He was rather defensive about Bulgaria's own record in handling refugees.

We saw a new trend in September, when our asylum centres emptied out. Since August we've seen declining numbers for the first time in two years. Clearly people felt invited to leave towards Western Europe. And nowadays it's very difficult to keep anyone here, even though we offer them international protection, and fingerprint them. We are probably one of the few front-line countries that fingerprints and registers everyone, unlike the entire flow that goes through the western Balkans.

He would have been surprised to hear how diligent the Serbian police I met at Dimitrovgrad were, on the fingerprint front. By now, the fingerprints of one of the Paris bomb suspects, taken on the Greek island of Leros on 7 October, was proof that the Greeks had improved their registration procedures. Mr Gunev denied any systematic violence by the Bulgarian authorities but admitted that there were 'isolated' problems with both corruption and violence in the Bulgarian police force: 'Bulgarian border guards have to follow EU approved training courses. In the past year and a half though, as in other countries, we have had to deploy other police officers who don't have the same level of training. Migrants are being arrested throughout the country.'

Ten times as many migrants had been arrested inside Bulgaria in 2015 than in 2014; 30,000 had applied for asylum. Some officers were working twenty-hour days. The force was stretched to the limits of human endurance. One problem was that the migrants were in such a hurry to leave that they did not report abuses. And even when they did, they didn't want to hang around for months, to testify in court against the officers concerned. Four police officers had been arrested and would now face trial for extortion, he said. 'The excessive use of force in a situation is one thing; allegations of theft are another. We don't need to train officers not to steal!' The death of an Afghan migrant, killed by a ricochet from a bullet when he was trying to evade arrest on 13 October, was an accident he said. And in that case too, all the witnesses had immediately left the country.

I also put the allegations of theft to Nikolai, my contact who until recently served in DANS, the Bulgarian secret service.

In my experience, these are people who have already been robbed by the Turkish security forces. Out of 200 refugees I interviewed, 99 per cent had no papers. Most had already handed most of their money to Turkish traffickers or Turkish police. Out of fifty people, we only found more than €5,000 on one of them. Most are down to their last €500. In Turkey police took everything from them. The traffickers organise everything here. They pay the people who manage the trafficking channels.

Nikolai was equally specific, and critical, of the failure of Western intelligence services to prevent the Paris attacks.

The Turkish authorities said they informed the French that the ringleader, Abdelhamid Abaaoud was no longer in Syria. Yes, but they informed the French after the attacks – not before!

A database exists with all the clues, the needles are all there, in the haystack. But there is a lack of experienced officers to analyse the data, and to concentrate their attention on this one large terrorist cell which we now know had more than twenty people in it.

Was IS using the refugee wave to get people into Europe, or using more traditional ways of switched identities, and roundabout flights to other capitals, I asked.

Both. But now it's easier to use the refugee wave to hide them. Surgical operations, to change faces, and create false identities are very easy. The problem is, they don't only use this channel to send back fighters to their home countries. They also use these channels to traffic the money these people need to perpetrate acts of terror. Because it's very expensive to organise something like the Paris attacks.

The French may claim credit for preventing four attacks in 2015, he said, but they missed the fifth. A 20 per cent failure rate was pretty disastrous. The only way to deal with the refugee problem, and the terror problem, was at the source, he believed. Thirty countries around the world supported IS, including Saudi Arabia – a key Western ally. Even the refugees could have been handled in a better way. If they had been allowed to proceed in a slower way, through four or five different channels, they could all have been properly registered, screened and processed. The lack of coordination between different countries, as they blamed one another, meant that people with bad intentions could easily slip through the net.[5]

*

In mid-December 2015, I travelled to Greece for the first time to cover the refugee situation. Not to the islands, or the border with Macedonia, but to Athens and the port of Piraeus where the big passenger ships arrived from the islands.

For the refugees, there was distressing news from the north. On 23 November, the Macedonian foreign minister Nikola Poposki announced that from then on, only Syrian, Iraqi and Afghan refugees would be allowed to enter his country.[6] A few days later, the Macedonian army began building their first fence at Gevgelija, next to the main road border crossing. Several of the first migrants stranded on the Greek side at Idomeni sewed their lips together in protest. The Macedonian move came in response to similar decisions by the Austrian, Slovenian, Croatian and Serbian governments – a domino effect. That immediately caused a tailback to develop at Idomeni on the Greek side of the border. This was the Vardar River valley, the route since time immemorial for travellers and invaders from Greece to funnel up into the Balkans.

Beside the river, a railway track and a road jostled for space in the narrow, fertile valley which wound northwards towards the cities of Veles and the Macedonian capital, Skopje. The Vardar River empties into the Aegean just to the west of Thessaloniki.

Dressed in early winter sunlight, Athens looked dowdier than I had ever seen her. Many shops were boarded up, and there was graffiti everywhere. There were also many migrants and refugees sleeping in the city's squares, especially in Omonia and Victoria. And almost daily protests against austerity measures, initially opposed, then reluctantly instated by the government of Alexis Tsipras, at the behest of the International Monetary Fund and the European Commission.

The day I arrived, the Greek finance minister Euclid Tsakalotos announced that he had agreed on the reform steps necessary for Greece to receive the next €1 billion tranche of the bailout. The new privatisation fund would generate revenue from the sell-off of state assets. The funds would be used to lower the debt and encourage investment. In particular, the reforms would affect state-owned power generating companies and the electricity distribution grid.

The Taekwondo stadium in the Palaio Faliro district of Athens had seen better times. Opened in 2004, a few days before the Olympic Games were due to begin, it hosted first handball matches, then Taekwondo – a Korean martial art which mixes karate with high and spectacular kicking moves. A report in the *Guardian* newspaper from August 2014 showed it in a gallery of photographs of half-ruined, crumbling venues, ten years after the Games.[7] Now it was a bustle of activity again. Two thousand five hundred refugees had been brought here by bus from the Greece–Macedonia border in the past twenty-four hours alone. In the meantime, two or three ships docked each day at the port of Athens, in Piraeus, from the Greek islands, with up to 700 migrants on each. The decision of the Balkan governments to limit the flow was turning Athens into the latest bottleneck on the Balkan route, or, as the Greek minister for migration put it more poetically, a 'warehouse of souls'.[8]

The Greeks, rather late in the day, tried to accommodate those sent back from the border at the Taekwondo stadium and at Elleniko, the former Athens International Airport – now a derelict, windy space on the edge of nowhere.

Reporters were not allowed into the stadium, but an Iranian refugee filmed conditions inside for me on his mobile phone. Overcrowded corridors, filth and chaos in the bathrooms, not enough mattresses and blankets. At the main gate there were daily protests by refugees. Many of those I spoke to were from Iran, Pakistan and North Africa. They waved signs with slogans like 'Help – we're suffering here!', 'We need solution, we die slow-motion' and 'Open the border, we're human too!' Those queuing for food in a long orderly line across the tarmac were mostly men, but included many women and small children too.

The camp was not closed. Anyone could leave who wanted to, and most chose to do just that, collecting their small rucksacks and clutching black plastic bags with any clothes they had picked up on the way, they walked away up a busy road towards the centre of Athens. A woman wearing an eggshell blue cap and jacket, carrying a clipboard, moved through the crowds, a permanent smile on her face, asking questions. We reporters mounted our cameras outside, or did interview after interview, then sat in a café across the street editing our material and sending it to our editors. The weather was still warm in the day but getting chilly at night. Boys sat wearily on the grass, resting their heads on dark blue UNHCR-issue sleeping bags. Deep in conversation or studying their phones. They had to find a way north, then a way through Macedonia's new defences.

Majid was thirty-eight, from Iran, travelling with his wife and two children. He wanted to weep when the Greek soldiers ordered them onto the bus at Idomeni for the 600-kilometre journey back to Athens. But it would have been too shameful to cry, he told me, as head of the family. They had spent just one night at the stadium, with two blankets between the four of them. Anything was better, the Greek migration minister said, than sleeping in the fields. And he gave those now in Greece, or still arriving at a rate of 3,800 a day, a choice. Apply for asylum there, or accept an offer from the International Organization for Migration, for a plane ticket home. Another Iranian I met had decided it was time to give up and go home.

Hamed was thirty-two. He had left Iran, he said, because he missed freedom to think, freedom to move. And he was fed up with corruption. 'Everything is arranged through contacts, or through money, not through ability. They make us stay inside all the time, smoking drugs. It keeps you passive. You don't do anything.'

In search of a better life, in Sweden, he had flown from Tehran to Istanbul. As an Iranian, he didn't need a visa for Turkey. He had been travelling for a month. He spent four days in Istanbul, then travelled with smugglers to the Turkish coast near Izmir. He crossed by boat at six in the morning, to Mytilene on the island of Lesbos. The journey from Tehran to Athens had cost him €3,000 so far. He was upset to be going back but didn't like the idea of crawling through the ever lengthening barbed wire on the Macedonian border, only to be thrown back again and again till he succeeded. He had already been to the Iranian embassy, to apply for a new passport. There was a queue of over a thousand people there, with the same idea, he said.

Would he be punished for leaving? He had thought this through, too: 'As soon as we arrive, we will be called in for an interrogation which lasts three or four hours. There will be questions. Like where we lost our passports. If you have no police record they will let you out. The Iranian government does not want to appear cruel to people.' His plane left at 9.20 that evening. He was looking forward to seeing his family, but brooding over the failure of his journey, and the loss of so much money.[9]

We were talking downstairs in the recreation room of a former hotel, squatted by Greek anarchists who turned it into a safe house for refugees. It was full to capacity, with people sleeping on the upper storeys on mattresses, several to each room. There was food, water, washing facilities, and medical care, all provided for free. The anarchists were wary of journalists in the house but tolerated our presence for a while.

Another man, Hasan, twenty-eight, said if he went back to Iran he would get, if he was lucky, a prison sentence for life, but more likely he would be hanged. He had worked for PAVA, the General Security and Intelligence Police, most recently 'as a body guard for important people.' As someone who knew state secrets, they would never believe, if he returned, that he had not divulged them. He would be tortured and probably killed. From the careful, contained way he spoke, in Farsi through an interpreter, and from the way other Iranians treated him, with a mixture of fear and respect, his story seemed authentic.

He had got out by applying for a passport to visit Iraq. From there he flew to Turkey. He had left the documents proving his background in the hands of a smuggler he trusted in Istanbul, out of fear that they might be taken off him or get lost on the way. They were his passport to political asylum, somewhere, he hoped. He also had some Iranian documents with him, he said, but as Iranian citizens were not allowed across the border, he was planning to buy forged Iraqi or Syrian documents in Athens.

Victoria Square was already established as the main focus of the many migrant communities passing through Athens. There was a metro stop with trains to and from the port of Piraeus. There were cafés and small restaurants on all sides, and the side roads were riddled with money-changing shops, small travel agents from which smugglers operated, and mobile phone shops. There were also cheap hotels where, for €20 or €30 a night, you could find a small room, if the owners were not already so fed up with the migrant influx that they were turning them all away. In the square, Greek and foreign charities operated. The Dutch-based Boat Rescue Service were especially active. Refugees collected in national groups – mostly Afghans, Pakistanis, Iranians and Moroccans. The children fed stale bread to the pigeons and small boys kicked a deflated football. Clusters of exhausted men gazed at their mobile phones or disappeared into the side-streets to talk to the smugglers again. Middle-aged Greek men, some walking dogs, tried to pick up young migrant men and boys, desperate for money. If they were lucky, they would be paid €10 for sex, usually standing up against a tree in another, more desolate park, a few streets away. Or in the rooms of yet another shabby hotel.

In the middle of the square stood the dramatic bronze statue of Theseus rescuing Hippodamia from the Centaur Eurytion, made by the German sculptor Johannes Pfuhl in 1906.[10] The enraged centaur has one arm around the poor Hippodamia's waist, and wields a rock in his other fist, which he clearly intends to bring down on Theseus's head. Theseus clutches a dagger, in front of the rearing centaur, which he is trying to plunge into the animal's neck. Another of the girls at the wedding feast, half naked, lies swooning on the ground.

In Greek mythology the centaurs – half men, half horses – were invited by Pirithous to his wedding with Hippodamia. The centaurs got blind drunk and tried to abduct both the beautiful bride and her entourage. Theseus and his entourage defended their honour, and thus began the long feud between men and centaurs. Homer invokes the story as a cautionary tale against drinking too much wine. Most of Pfuhl's other sculptures were destroyed in the First or Second World Wars, but his depiction of the German mystic Jakob Boeme still stands in a park in his home town of Gorlitz, the most easterly town of Germany. The sculpture in Victoria Square, frozen in mid-abduction, seemed strangely peaceful among the crowds of refugees, a resting place for the pigeons staining the heads, knees and breasts of the main protagonists white.

Sitting on a bench not far away, I found Hooman, his wife Naghmeh and their six-year-old son Arian, from Tehran. They were converts to Christianity from Islam. There are many Christians in Iran, Hooman explained, but they are not normally persecuted if they shut up about it and don't try to spread the faith. But what the regime cannot tolerate is conversion from Islam to Christianity. Hooman had a good job as a graphic designer, and Naghmeh as a software engineer. They had a large, comfortable flat, and Arian had his own room, full of toys. Then Naghmeh's father found out about their conversion. He was a powerful figure in the Revolutionary Guards and was furious that his own daughter had 'betrayed' him in this way. He broke Hooman's fingers on one occasion. The three of them discussed the situation, and even little Arian agreed that the best thing would be to leave Iran, despite the many dangers they knew awaited them on the journey. A year earlier, they had begun the paperwork to apply for asylum in the United States, but this was known to take three years, and there was no guarantee of success. So they set out, across Turkey, three weeks before I met them. The boat across the Aegean was particularly frightening. 'Arian was singing at the beginning – by the end he was crying, like everyone on that boat.'

There were fifty-two people on board, and it was leaking heavily by the time they saw the coast of Lesbos. 'I tried to do everything for my child, he wore a life jacket, but I couldn't do much, just trust God, and that's all.'

The volunteers on the beach near Mytilene, including several from Manchester, waded out to rescue them. After several days, registering under their correct names and nationalities, they could continue to the mainland. Rather than staying in the stadium, Hooman had found a single room for the three of them near the square for €35 a night. The journey, including flights and smugglers, had cost them $10,000 so far, he said. Now they were down to their last $500, so it was time to go to a refugee camp. As we talked, Arian smiled serenely and hugged the teddy bear he had brought with him all the way from Tehran to his chest. What's his name? I asked. Abri – meaning Tiger in Persian, he said.

Hooman pondered raising more money from somewhere, and paying smugglers again, but decided not to risk it. If he was alone, he might have, but not with his wife and small child. As a graphic designer, he was also skilled in making documents. He said he was tempted to forge them new

Syrian or Iraqi papers, but had decided against that too, because of the risk of prison or worse in Macedonia or Serbia. My Greek colleague rang the refugee camp at Eleonas, which at least had containers in which the family could stay together and have some privacy. To their good fortune, one container was about to become free, that day, in the overcrowded camp. We paid for a taxi to take them there.

Tariq's claim to refugee status, anywhere in Europe, was much flimsier. Aged thirty-seven, a handsome man with a neat beard and moustache, he had a good job as an electrical engineer in Morocco, specialising in water systems and pumps. He had once earned several thousand euros a month working for a big multinational company in several African countries, he said, as we sat sipping tea in a bar not far from Victoria Square. He left Morocco because he found it too repressive. Because there was no real democracy, no freedom of expression. He was an admirer of Europe, and wanted to live there for a while, a few years perhaps, and go back to Morocco on holiday.

On Facebook, he found a site run by smugglers advertising journeys to Europe. He rang the number. Then bought a plane ticket to Istanbul. He and several others were picked up by the smugglers at the airport and taken to a safe house. After a night in Istanbul, they were taken by van the next day, eight of them, to Izmir on the Turkish coast. They waited in the woods near the sea for two hours, before the boat arrived to take them across. The person who steered the boat went free, the smugglers explained. But only an hour out to sea, the 15-horse-power motor stopped, and would not restart. After three and a half hours adrift, they hailed a Turkish fishing boat, which towed them back to the mainland. The next boat too broke down, just 200 metres off the Turkish coast. They travelled back to the safe house in Istanbul. Three days later, they were taken to the coast again, and this time they reached Lesbos, in a convoy of sixty boats. On the way they followed the advice they were given of tearing up their passports and throwing them into the sea. They spent three days on Lesbos, getting registered and finger-printed – 'I gave my real name' – then paid €45 each for the eighteen-hour ferry journey to Piraeus. From Piraeus he paid for a bus straight to Idomeni on the Greek-Macedonian border. There he teamed up with four Moroccan men and a girl, and got advice from a taxi driver about where to cross, at a point where there were no soldiers.

At six in the evening we crossed the border normally. There was no fence, nothing. On the other side we looked for the railway, because if you walk close to the road the police can find you. We walked till four in the morning, then stopped for a brief rest. We slept an hour or two, then continued walking.

At eight o'clock that morning, two men in combat uniform, one of them carrying a rifle, stepped out of the woods and confronted them. They claimed to be police but Tariq said they were not fooled. First they asked for €100 to allow them to go on their way. Finally that dropped to €25, but they still refused to pay, claiming that all their money had been stolen by previous smugglers.

'Then we found a railway station, with many people hiding in the woods around it, waiting to jump aboard. Suddenly the army was there, thirty soldiers. They took away one large group of Pakistanis but they didn't find us. Then we continued walking up the railway line, all night, and crossed the mountain overnight.' When they tried to buy a ticket, at another station, the clerk refused to sell it when they admitted they were from Morocco. So they boarded the train without tickets, only to be thrown off by a policeman on the train, at the next stop. They got as far as Veles.

After crossing the bridge over the Vardar, Tariq went into a filling station with one of his companions, to buy food. The others carried on without them. Once again they were stopped, now just two of them, in the woods by armed men. At gunpoint, the men took most of their remaining money off them. Fortunately, though, they missed his phone.

They finally reached the Macedonian capital, Skopje, only to be caught by police five minutes before their train would have taken them on to the Serbian border. The police took them all the way back to Gevgelija. 'The Macedonian army took us to another point, about a kilometre from the main road crossing point. At this place there were many Moroccans and Pakistanis. Soldiers in uniform beat us with iron cables as we lay on the ground.' Then they were pushed back through the fence, two by two, after another beating. This time they were just kicked and punched. Tariq's first visit to Macedonia lasted six days. He rested at the ever-growing camp at Idomeni. There, early one morning at around six o'clock, they were woken rudely by Greek police and put on a bus back to Athens.

Now he was planning his next attempt on the border. We arranged to meet a few days later, for a beer.

What would he be doing if he was home on a Saturday evening, I asked. 'Much the same,' he smiled. 'Drinking beer, maybe going to a disco later.' Would he ever consider giving up the attempt and going back to Morocco, perhaps with the help of the International Organization for Migration? 'No way. I've spent €3,000, and I'm more than halfway to Germany!' He had €470 left and was trying to get more money wired to him by his cousin in Sweden. But, without proper documents, neither Western Union offices nor MoneyGram would give him access to the money he knew was waiting for him. The only way was to cancel that transaction and get the same person to wire the money to someone who still had a passport – who would then also take a cut of the amount.

'Now I'm looking for people to take us to Europe. For €1,500 they say they will take us by car across Macedonia and Serbia to Austria.' But first he had to find a smuggler he could trust. 'You put your money here, in a locker, and you devise your own [numerical] code. When you reach Austria you ring the man and give him your password, and he gets your money.'

'Who are the smugglers?' I wanted to know.

Normally mafia people from North Africa, Egypt, Algeria, and Syria. They pay the police and take you in open cars. You pay less for a bus, more for a car with only four others in it. At each of the borders, you get out and walk, and the car crosses empty, only to pick you up again at a pre-arranged point near the woods the other side.

As we sat there, he was cheered by a message on WhatsApp from a Moroccan friend who informed him that he had just got as far as Serbia, after paying a similar smuggler. If this man proved reliable, and he could get his hands on the money sent by his relatives, he would try again soon.

On 14 December, the EU announced the creation of a new border and coast guard, a sort of beefed-up Frontex. It would have its own personnel of 1,500 officers.[11] One of the weaknesses of Frontex was that it depended completely on many states who frequently failed to send enough police. Frontex was now lobbying for the power, in exceptional circumstances, to take over control of a country's border. That was a step too far for the Greeks and several other countries.

On 15 December, I interviewed the Greek minister for migration, Yannis Mouzalas. He cut an unusual figure for an employee of the Interior Ministry. In round glasses, slightly unshaven, wearing a beaten-up jacket, he looked as though he had never worn a tie in his life, and could easily have been mistaken for an artist from the left bank of the Seine in Paris, or a Czech dissident. He began by cautiously welcoming the new, stronger international border guard. 'We will have to allow the centre to control some of our sovereignty,' he admitted. But not too much.

Greece stood accused by the EU of only registering and fingerprinting 121,000 of the approximately 500,000 migrants who crossed its territory between 20 July and 30 November. 'The responsibility for this also lies with Europe. Because we were not supplied with fingerprinting machines, even though we kept asking for them. As soon as the machines started coming and as long as they keep coming, we reacted better and our fingerprinting and registration procedures got better and better.' One machine could only record a hundred individuals a day, he explained, and for the first six months they only had ten. Now they had fifty and were asking for a hundred.

The two terrorists posing as refugees, who took part in the Paris attacks were identified by the Greek authorities, he explained.

Shifting to the future, and the strains around the stadium, the disused airport and, above all, to those now stuck at the Macedonian border, he explained the plan in detail: 20,000 people would be housed in private accommodation, either empty flats or with host families. Genuine refugees should be relocated around Europe. Economic migrants should return home, either through voluntary repatriation, or be deported. The stadium and the airport were 'temporary solutions' to prevent people sleeping rough in Athens.

> At the centre of our political approach is that you have to stem the migrant flow on the Turkish coast. Europe should focus now on the resettlement scheme. That means that the refugees should be resettled directly from Turkey, Lebanon and Jordan to Europe. This would prevent the refugees from falling victim to the smugglers, drowning in the Aegean, and end this situation where Europe cannot control the migrant flow.

Some European leaders describe Greece as an open vineyard – meaning our borders are wide open, anyone can just walk in. But our land border with Turkey, on the Evros River, is secure. There is no influx there, only over the sea. The only thing we have to do on a sea border, following the UN rules and the Geneva Convention, and the European and Greek laws, is to save the lives of those at sea. We will not push people back to Turkey, we will not sink the migrant boats.

Mouzalas was an obstetrician, I noted from his biography. Did he feel he was now delivering the baby of a new Europe, I asked, or attending its funeral?

Exactly because I am an obstetrician, I am aware how difficult, how strenuous, how expensive, and how many hours it takes to give birth. For this reason I am very angry how many lives are being lost, in war, at sea, in this flow of migrants. And I am also angry that thousands of children are losing their childhoods in this crisis. This is really tragic. We are witnessing history. No one knows the outcome.

CHAPTER NINE

THE EU–TURKEY DEAL

If possible I would like to become a doctor. My sister told me once that our mother would not have died if she had received proper medical care. I have suffered very much in my life. I would like to lessen the suffering of others.

Eric Özeme, refugee from Democratic Republic of the Congo

On the evening of 31 December 2015, several hundred young men of North African and Middle Eastern origin were among the crowds of revellers who converged on Cologne for the New Year's Eve celebrations. Some had agreed on Facebook in advance to congregate there. Many came with the express aim of groping women. It was a phenomenon known as 'taharrus dzsamaj', and also occurred during the Arab Spring, most notoriously in Tahrir Square in central Cairo, where many local and foreign women were molested.[1]

Some of those who travelled to Cologne were immigrants who already had asylum status in Germany or Belgium. They came from cities including Brussels and Aachen. Others were more recent arrivals, including some who had only been in Germany a few weeks and were living in temporary asylum-seekers hostels in or near the city.

As midnight approached, fuelled by several hours of drinking, the organised assault on women around the main railway station began. Firecrackers were thrown into the crowd, causing panic and confusion and distracting the attention of some 300 police on duty. In the mêlée, the men began surrounding women, corralling them into groups, groping them, and stealing their purses and mobile phones. The victims were mostly German, but also included women from other European countries, and women and girls who were themselves refugees from countries including Afghanistan and Syria. The perpetrators were 'mostly men of North African or Middle Eastern appearance' but included some Germans. Some Syrian men in the crowd, when they saw what was happening, also tried to protect groups of women.

The police were overwhelmed. In the following days and weeks, 1,092 criminal complaints were filed, including 446 cases of sexual assault, and 3 cases of rape. Both the police and mainstream media initially tried to avoid any ethnic stereotyping of the perpetrators. As word spread on social media that they were migrants or immigrants, however, more and more reports appeared stating that the men were overwhelmingly of 'immigrant' appearance. The mayor of Cologne, Henriette Reker, only realised how serious the situation was when Angela Merkel rang her on the evening of 5 January. The events of that night, not only in Cologne but to a lesser extent in eight other German cities, did more damage to the 'welcome culture' towards refugees and migrants than any other single incident.[2] In fact, they dealt a devastating blow to Germany's remarkable willingness to offer a safe haven. In Germany itself, across Europe and the United States, the harshest critics of Angela Merkel's open-door policy cried out with vindictive joy. Now the Germans had got what they deserved, ran the story. How foolish they were to welcome such 'animals' to their country! Even those who had cautiously welcomed refugees until now, had to reconsider their faith that Germany and Europe could integrate the newcomers.

Were those events proof of a genetic weakness in men from non-European cultures? Were they terrorist attacks, as devastating as any use of Kalashnikovs or suicide belts, designed to destroy the goodwill in Germany towards Muslims? Or simply an extreme case of men behaving badly, if they think they can get away with it, and a failure of the police to act in time? IS and Al-Qaeda propaganda has long maintained that Christians are waging a never-ending crusade against Islamic civilisation. The independent investigation carried out by investigators from Nordrhein-Westphalen was published on 7 April 2017.[3]

'The 2015–2016 New Year's Eve attacks could have been prevented, for the most part, if early and resolute action had been taken at the first criminal offences. The overview and the necessary forces were lacking for such a procedure,' the report concluded. The failure of police to intervene early on, according to one expert cited in the report, caused a 'snowball' effect, whereby men thought they could get away with violence. A police decision to reduce the police presence at New Year's Eve celebrations throughout the county was fiercely criticised. The police communications after New Year's Eve, were 'false and misleading'.

The report shed little light, however, on the degree of organisation, or the motives of the perpetrators. One psychologist, Rudolf Egg, who studied more than a thousand of the cases of assault, said he found no evidence of organised criminal activity behind the attacks. He too blamed the police for giving men the impression that they could get away with assault by not intervening in time. Sixteen months after the events, only five men had been arrested, and one sentenced. A twenty-six-year-old Algerian, Hassan T., was sentenced to one year in prison.

*

Savigny-sur-Orge is a small town of 23,000 inhabitants, 19 kilometres south of Paris. Once a collection of homes around a castle, the construction of the railway line in the late nineteenth century turned it first into a suburb of the French capital, then a dormitory town. Now it is home to Eric Ozeme, the refugee from Congo whom I met at Ásotthalom in June 2015. He was waiting for me at the railway station when my train pulled in from the Gare d'Austerlitz. He was wearing the same grey pullover that he wore when he crossed the Serbian border eight months earlier. His face was more relaxed. He liked being in France, and the French had been civil with him, he told me, as we walked the streets from the station to the third floor flat in an apartment block provided for him by the French Red Cross.

His flatmates were all from Africa. The flat was small – a bedroom, a living room/kitchen and a bathroom – sparse, but clean and welcoming. He had the top bunk in the room he shared with the four other asylum seekers. There was ample space. None had sufficient clothes or possessions with which to clutter it up.

From the roadside in Hungary I had a short audio recording of him and some of the group of thirty or so other mostly Congolese with whom he walked much of the way from Athens. But this was my first chance to hear his life story.

Eric was born in Matita, near Kinshasa in October 1995. He never met his father, who died before he was born. His mother, who worked as a small trader, sold coffee and manioc root on the streets of Kinshasa until she died of illness when Eric was seven. He lived with his older sister and brother, went to school for three years, then had to leave at the age of eleven to work on the streets himself, buying and selling small items in order not to starve. In February 2011, when Eric was sixteen, the police burst into his house early in the morning, in the Kinshasa suburb of Ngaba. His friend Jean-Luc had been arrested for plotting to assassinate President Joseph Kabila, they said, and he was suspected as an accomplice. Contemporary news reports make no mention of any plot to assassinate the corrupt Joseph Kabila in 2011. He won his second term as president in December 2011, in an election in which the ballots from 2,000 polling stations, in areas known to favour the rival candidate, went missing.

Congo is one of the richest countries in the world, in mineral deposits. It earns a billion dollars a year from the export of gold alone. It also has rich deposits of copper, cobalt, manganese and diamonds. Its wealth has attracted the greed of the world powers, past and present, and of its African neighbours. It is the second biggest producer of copper in the world after Chile.

A small modern car contains 12 kilos of copper, an expensive model 25 kilos.[4] Because of its excellent conductivity properties, the metal is used in the brakes, the electric driving controls, the gearbox and the heating system. As Eric made his way across Hungary in the summer of 2015, he passed close to factories which manufacture half a million Mercedes, Suzuki and Opel cars each year. Each contains hundreds of metres of copper wiring, which probably originated in his home country. The ruthless exploitation of Africa for its minerals, and the misuse of the proceeds from that wealth by the ruling elite, past and present, is the backdrop to his journey, and that of millions of others over the past decades.

In Hungary and Romania, Bosnia and Bulgaria, France and Spain, I have watched the Roma – Europe's other strangers – push their carts from door to door, collecting scrap metal. Copper is the most prized, above the twisted aluminium and rusting iron. It is paid for by the gram, rather than the kilogram, at the grim recycling centres on the edges of town where the Roma wheel their barrows. Copper offers an interesting interface between wealth and poverty on the capitalist roads of Europe. We look at our faces in copper mirrors, and study the distorted images of ourselves and others, for clues.

Eric, aged sixteen, orphaned and likely to be sentenced to death with his friend Jean-Luc for a crime he did not commit, struck lucky. A prison guard took pity on him. 'Don't you have any friends who have money?' the guard asked him in his cachot, the dank underground cell beneath a police station in the Ngaba district of Kinshasa where he was nervously awaiting his fate. It was nightfall on 28 February 2011. He knew just one man, a friend of his brother's, whom he could ask for money. A human rights activist. The man was called and arrived after dark. A pile of Congolese francs, depicting the stripy zebra-like symbol of Congo, the okapi, on one side and the manioc fruit his mother once sold in the street on the other, changed hands.

With his friend's help Eric fled, first to the Kinshasa district of Masina, then in a pirogue, a narrow dug-out canoe, across the Congo River to Brazzaville. Congo is divided into two states, the Democratic Republic of the Congo, of which Kinshasa is the capital, and the much smaller Republic of the Congo. The two cities, Brazzaville with its 1.4 million inhabitants, and Kinshasa with 11 million, stare uncertainly at each other across the Congo River. They are the two closest capitals on earth and provide a useful refuge for those fleeing one or the other.

Eric hid for three months with the family of his friend Jean-Luc, of whom there was no word. Almost certainly he was killed by the Democratic Republic of the Congo police. In May he got a phone call from the friend who bribed him out of prison. The police were still watching his home, he said. His sister had been imprisoned. His brother Patrique had fled to Angola. He could get him false papers to go to Turkey. He took another pirogue, back across the Congo River. Later the same day he was at the airport, on a flight to Morocco, with his own photograph in his passport, but a false name. In Morocco he changed planes and flew to Istanbul. He arrived there with $200 in his pocket, knowing no one, with nowhere to go.

At Istanbul airport, he befriended a Senegalese man who took him into town to the sprawling Aksaray neighbourhood, where he spent his first few nights in a room with two dozen other African migrants. Aksaray means 'the white palace' in Turkish. It was given this name by migrants from a city of the same name in central Anatolia, who were moved to Istanbul (then called Constantinople) by Sultan Mehmet II, to fill the city after its conquest by the Ottomans in 1453.[5]

Aksaray today is a rough neighbourhood, also notorious for prostitution, especially for women from the former Soviet Union. In Aksaray in the early 2000s, years before Eric reached here, I tried to trace Chechens coming and going from the war in their country against Russia, until I was warned to stop asking questions for my own safety.

Eric scraped a living in Aksaray, collecting plastic bottles from rubbish bins and selling them to be recycled. This paid for his rent, basic food and his bus tickets to Konya, where the Turkish authorities said he should move to a camp – as a minor he was not supposed to be living rough in Istanbul at all. His only official document was a single sheet from the UNHCR office in Ankara in 2011 cited earlier:

> To Whom it May Concern: this is to certify that the above named person has been recognised as a refugee by the United Nations High Commissioner for Refugees, pursuant to its mandate. As a refugee, he is a person of concern to the Office of the High Commissioner for Refugees, and should, in particular, be protected from forcible return to a country where he would face threats to his life or freedom. Any assistance to the above named individual would be most appreciated.

I interpreted this as directed to me personally and took him out to lunch. Meanwhile he told me the rest of his story.

Many of the Syrians and Iraqis crossing Turkey in 2015 also found themselves in Aksaray. From its days as a hub for trafficking women from Eastern Europe to Turkey, there was already a well-established network for smuggling migrants in the other direction, across Eastern to Western Europe. And there was money to be made, hand over fist.

For refugees who decide to stay and come with money in their pockets, Turkey is a relatively easy country in which to integrate, and even a good place to make a business. From 2011 to 2016, 4,000 new businesses were set up by Syrians in Turkey. An article in the *Financial Times* in October 2016 highlights the case of Remo Fouad, a fifty-year-old pastry chef from Aleppo, who started with a small sweet shop and has been expanding his business ever since.[6]

'They didn't like us blacks in Aksaray because they thought we would rape the women,' Eric told me. 'We also had a lot of trouble with Syrians and Kurds. My friend from Brazzaville was shot dead there. Aksaray was too bad. If the police there see a white hit a black, they stand back. But if they think the black is guilty, they shoot you. Blacks have no value in Turkey. I was afraid to live there.'

In October 2013, after his eighteenth birthday, Eric moved to a refugee centre in the Kadikoy district of Istanbul. By the spring of 2015 he was weary of his hand-to-mouth existence. He'd been living on the streets since the age of seven.

I saw Syrians passing through Istanbul with bags on their backs. By then I had saved €400 from collecting materials for recycling from the bins. The Syrians said they were going to Europe. So I went with them to the coast. Others paid €1000, but I was with a Syrian, he accepted €300 from me, and I crossed to [the Greek island of] Kos. The police came and took me to a centre, and gave me refugee papers.

Eric spent a month on Kos because he had no more money. Then another Syrian gave him €50 for the boat fare to Piraeus. In Athens, he survived on the fruit and vegetables thrown away at closing time in the open-air markets. Then he teamed up with other Congolese and a Mauritanian, and set out on the long trek northwards. They walked all the way to the Greek border with Macedonia, 550 kilometres. Then through most of Macedonia, and managed to cross much of Serbia by train and bus, without tickets. Then they walked into Hungary from Subotica.

After I watched him and his companions board the white police bus at Ásotthalom, he was taken to the fingerprinting and registration centre in the blue hangar at Röszke, and the next day to the refugee camp at Bicske. Sitting on his bunkbed in Paris, he showed me his Hungarian ID card, number 135836, dated 1 July 2015. Valid until 14 October 2015 – his twenty-first birthday. But he didn't wait long in Bicske, just a month, figuring out his next move. With a small group of fellow asylum seekers, he caught the train back to Budapest, and boarded the Munich train when the police guarding it were looking the other way. That must have been in early August, before the big crackdown and closure of the station later that month. Miraculously, no one checked the ticket he didn't have, either on the Budapest to Munich or the Munich to Cologne train. In Cologne he banded together with some other refugees, and they travelled by car to Paris, arriving sometime in October 2015.

Eric comes across as a winner, no matter how poor the cards he is dealt. He is serious most of the time, then smiles easily. It's easy to relax in his presence, easy to trust him. He ate a kebab, 'in the Algerian style', in a buffet beside the station, while I sipped a fruit juice. His asylum claim in France had been rejected, but he didn't seem unduly worried, even by the prospect of being deported back to Hungary under the Dublin procedures. He showed me a letter asking him to present himself at the Prefecture, the district council in Essones on 19 February, for deportation to Hungary – the first EU country in which he was registered – where 'your claim for asylum will be processed'. When he turned up obediently on that day, clutching all his possessions in a small knapsack, he was given another paper saying that it had not been possible to return him to Hungary yet because 'no flights were available'. This was an odd explanation, as I had just arrived from the Hungarian capital on one of the four flights between Paris and Budapest each day. Perhaps the French were reluctant to send him back, because of Hungary's poor reputation for handling asylum seekers. German and Swedish judges had publicly proclaimed that asylum seekers could not be returned to Hungary, because they would not receive a fair hearing.

More likely in this case, the Hungarian authorities refused to accept him back – a growing trend. According to the OIN, there were 133 returns under the Dublin regulations in the first three months of 2016, most of them from Germany. The office declined to say how many they had refused. Hungary's hostility to asylum seekers, for once, was working in an asylum seeker's favour.

Eric was given a new date in April to turn up to the Prefecture. In the meantime, I helped him find a good human rights lawyer. He won his appeal and was allowed to stay in France. When he gave me the news, on the phone, just a month later, he sounded overjoyed. 'What are your plans now?' I asked.

'I would like to go back to school, and learn to read and write properly,' he told me, proudly. It was only then that I realised that he was almost illiterate. And then? 'If it is possible, I would like to become a doctor. My sister told me once that mother would not have died if she had received proper medical care. I have suffered very much in my life. I would like to lessen the suffering of others,' Eric told me.

Issa was another of the men in the small group I met at the roadside in Ásotthalom. Now thirty-six, he was a sports instructor and judo teacher in Kinshasa. In 2010 he was recruited, along with other sportsmen, by President Kabila's People's Party for Reconstruction and Democracy (PPRD). He left in 2011, disgusted by orders from the party to violently disrupt anti-government protests. He took part in an anti-Kabila rally in November 2011, on the eve of the election.

> We were in a large crowd of singing people, when I saw a line of police jeeps arrive. At first, I thought they were there to keep order, but then they jumped on us. They knocked me to the ground and dragged me and threw me in the back of a jeep. I was imprisoned in a dungeon, underground, without light, water, food, or toilet. I was tortured and beaten.

Joseph Kabila declared himself the winner of the December 2011 elections, but his rival Etienne Tshisekedi accused Kabila of falsifying the vote to win a second term in office.[7] The bishops of Congo also condemned what they called the 'treachery, lies and terror' of the election. In January 2015 Issa took part in renewed protests against Kabila and was in the crowd when police opened fire with live ammunition, killing and injuring many. The police later came to his home, searching for him, and threatened his father.[8] His partner Fatouma was attacked and raped by police officers when she refused to tell them where he was. He escaped across the Congo River to Brazzaville, where Fatouma joined him. Their first son, five years old, was left behind with relatives. They lay low till April 2015, then took a flight to Istanbul.[9]

After I last saw him, on the border at Ásotthalom, he and Fatouma were registered by police then made their way to Budapest. They managed to board a train from the east station in Budapest and crossed the border into Austria. After being ordered off trains several times across Europe because they had no money for a ticket, they finally reached Brussels a month later. There, they slept in parks as homeless people for the first few weeks, until a Belgian couple took pity on them and offered them a room in their flat, while they applied for asylum. After a while, they felt they would stand a better chance in France. After several months, they were sent to a camp in Béziers on the south coast of France. Their baby daughter Taslimah was born, safe and healthy, despite the traumas of the journey, in January 2016, in the hospital in Carcassonne. Béziers had a mayor from the anti-immigrant Front National. More serious was that the family's application for refugee status was turned down in early 2017 by the French Office for Immigration and Integration (OFII). They moved to a crowded refugee centre in a former hotel in Montpellier. At the time of writing, the family's situation was extremely precarious, as they waited for their appeal to be considered by the National Court of Asylum. The day Taslimah reached eighteen months of age, they were no longer entitled to receive milk formula or nappies under French asylum regulations.

The French Socialist government, like the Conservative British government led by David Cameron, preferred the idea of accepting refugees directly from the camps in Turkey, Lebanon and Jordan, rather than those rushing overland to get into Europe before the gates clanged shut.[10] The idea was that they applied at European embassies in the countries where they were living, were carefully screened and then, if successful, finally invited to travel. Such cases would be given all the help they needed to get established in their new country.

Amena Abomosa, a science teacher in a secondary school in Syria, was one of the successful applicants, described in a report by Angela Charlton and Mirko Krivokapić in the Associated Press in October 2015.[11] She and her family fled Syria to Jordan in 2012, after her husband Abdul was killed outside their home while trying to help an injured child. He was not involved on any side in the war.

Amena, her mother Hanna, her teenage daughters Isra and Reemaz, and twelve-year-old son Muhammad were all issued refugee visas, and flew in style into Charles de Gaulle airport in Paris. They spent two weeks in a transit centre in the suburb of Creteil, then were sent to a small town in Brittany. 'I had to do something. I feel responsible for my family,' Amena told AP. 'They need the important things, food, shelter, a daily life.' She still has deep scars on her stomach from the day Syrian soldiers smashed their way into her flat, and she was injured by flying glass. She would like one day to go home to Syria, she said, but only when it is safe to do so.

On 1 January 2016, the Netherlands took over the rotating presidency of the European Union. With thousands of asylum seekers still streaming over the borders from the south, despite the onset of winter, it was clear that migration would dominate the country's office. The European Commission was still in a state of confusion. 'There was a feeling of the end of the world in Brussels. They were just thinking in terms of giving Turkey a lot of money to stop people travelling on, and quickly sending back economic migrants,' Gerald Knaus told me, having met with European Council president Donald Tusk in early 2016. Tusk remarked that former president of Poland Lech Wałęsa had joked with him that when you want the EU to fall apart, just put a Pole in charge.

Dutch prime minister Mark Rutte took an early interest in the ESI plan, but it was the Dutch Labour Party leader Diderik Samson who adopted it and shepherded it through the European agenda. Samson visited Turkey in December 2015. 'Someone put a copy of our plan in his reading folder. When he read it he decided – let's do this right away, we won't wait for the European Commission,' Gerald Knaus told me.

At a European level, the former 'coalition of the willing' – countries that wanted to seek a solution – had more or less collapsed. Austria had essentially defected to the Hungarian side, Sweden had introduced identity checks on the Øresund Bridge linking it and Denmark in order to reduce the flow of migrants, and Denmark too had introduced controls on its borders.[12] Through the Balkans, Austrian efforts to close their border with Slovenia forced that country as well as Croatia, Serbia and Macedonia to deploy their own militaries. The Schengen system of open borders inside Europe was falling apart. The Germans, Dutch and Turks were left to work out a plan.

'We agree that the pressures causing migration must be reduced. If the Schengen system [of border-free travel] is destroyed, Europe will be seriously endangered – politically and economically. That is why we Europeans have to invest billions in Turkey, Libya, Jordan and other countries in the region as quickly as possible – everybody as much as they can,' German finance minister Wolfgang Schäuble told *Der Spiegel*.[13] Intense discussions began between Angela Merkel and prime minister Ahmet Davutoğlu. There was talk of a 'strategic partnership' between Germany and Turkey. The Turkish government, which had for so long felt neglected and disliked by the European Union, appreciated the attention it was getting. The right deal would both grant Turkey a strategic partnership with Germany and solve the crisis. A key element that would bring all the EU countries on board would be for Turkey to offer to take back those arriving in small boats across the Aegean.

Gerald Knaus travelled to Washington and spoke to Kemal Kirişci, an influential leading Turkish expert on migration, then working at the Brookings Institution. Kirişci then wrote a paper which made the point that even given President Erdoğan's 'illiberal' Turkey, it was important that the EU remain liberal. If the migrant crisis led to the rise of the far right in Europe, and if the Orbán line won on migration, this would be very bad for Turkey too. The time for talking was nearly over. A breakthrough was urgently needed.

Germany, having chosen to accept so many refugees, was also investing large sums in housing, feeding and looking after them. Most of the initial funds came from the €12 billion budget surplus. Schäuble's own idea of a fuel tax, to be paid by all Germans, to accommodate and integrate the refugees, found little support in Germany. He was disappointed. 'At the moment, we are lucky to have a budgetary surplus and don't need such a tax. But Germany cannot handle this task on its own, that much is clear.'[14]

According to a study by the Cologne Institute for Economic Research (IW), €50 billion would be needed to shelter, feed and educate refugees in Germany in 2016 and 2017.[15] Housing, food and welfare would cost €12,000 per refugee per year, with language and integration classes adding another €3,300, making a grand annual total per refugee for each German tax payer of over €15,000. The study estimated possible 2016 first-time asylum requests at 800,000, and 500,000 in 2017. In practice, the numbers proved to be 718,000 in 2016, plunging to 198,000 in 2017.

The IW researchers estimated that 99,000 people in 2016 would be able to afford their own housing and subsistence costs, with that number rising to 276,000 in 2017. These people would still need state subsidies for language and integration classes, however. On the other hand, they would by then also be paying taxes and social security contributions. 'If all goes well, 10 per cent of refugees will find work during their first year,' the director of the

Federal Labour Office (BA) told the *Süddeutsche Zeitung.* 'Fifty per cent will find work after five years here, and 70 per cent after fifteen years.'

*

6 March 2016 was a Sunday. Turkish prime minister Ahmet Davutoğlu sat down with Angela Merkel and Dutch prime minister Mark Rutte in the office of the Turkish ambassador to Berlin Selim Yenel, and reached agreement on all the details. All three governments agreed to what was still in essence the ESI plan.

When the EU–Turkey summit began in the Bergmont palace in Brussels, EU heads of state were astonished to be presented with a fait accompli.[16] They asked for another week to discuss it. Austria and Hungary expressed severe misgivings, arguing that it placed EU security too much at the mercy of Turkey, but the majority were in favour, preferring it to the extreme alternative of closing one border after another.

On 18 March, all twenty-eight prime ministers of EU member states gathered to agree to what became known as the EU–Turkey Statement.[17] It was the most important international agreement in the eighteen months since the influx began in earnest, and was designed to slow, or even stop the influx of migrants and refugees across the Aegean Sea. And to 'destroy the business model of the smugglers' who were bringing them, as politician after politician emphasised.[18]

There were four main points. First, all new 'irregular migrants' crossing from Turkey to the Greek islands would be returned to Turkey. Second, for every Syrian returned to Turkey from the Greek islands, another Syrian would be resettled in the EU. Third, Turkey pledged to prevent new sea or land routes for irregular migration opening from Turkey to the EU. And fourth, once irregular crossings had ended or been substantially reduced, a Voluntary Humanitarian Admission Scheme would be activated.

In exchange, the procedure for Turkish citizens to receive visas to visit EU countries would be rapidly liberalised, meaning that by the end of June 2016, Turkish citizens would no longer need visas at all. The distribution of the €3 billion Turkey had already been promised by the EU to help care for the 2.7 million refugees already in the country, would be speeded up. And a further €3 billion would be given by the end of 2018. The EU also promised to 're-energise' Turkey's accession talks on joining the EU – a process which began in 1963. And Turkey and the EU agreed to work closer together to improve humanitarian conditions inside Syria.

The agreement would come into force at midnight on Saturday 20 March 2016. It could not be termed a legally binding agreement because, as one EU lawyer pointed out two months later, it actually had no legal force. It was rather a 'press communiqué' the unnamed lawyer told MEPs in the Civil Liberties Committee of the European Parliament. No leaders actually signed the document. It was not published in the *Official Journal of the European Union*. In the press photograph, Donald Tusk stands in the centre, with Davutoğlu on his right and Juncker on his left, clutching the document. The three dark-suited men's hands are clenched in a ball of agreement, a triple handshake. Davutoğlu, in yellow tie, is grinning broadly, Tusk in dark blue tie, has the shadow of a smile, while Juncker in the red tie looks unusually serious.

The terminology showed clearly the watershed between those who saw the crisis primarily as humanitarian, and therefore sympathized with the refugees, and referred to them as *irregular migrants* – most in the European Commission – and the governments of hostile countries like Hungary who saw the arrivals primarily as *illegal immigrants*, seeking a better life in Europe. Whatever they called them, the most controversial part of the Action Plan, and the hardest to fulfil, was the return of asylum seekers from the Greek islands to the Turkish mainland. According to the document, 'people who do not have a right to international protection will be immediately returned to Turkey'. There were two obvious problems with this. First, the word 'right' and, second, the word 'immediately'. The new arrivals always argued that they did have to right to protection, and if the Greek asylum authorities ruled against them, they had a right to appeal under both international and EU law. Under the plan, the authors tried to reassure those who criticised the deal on human rights grounds: 'There will be individual interviews, individual assessments and rights of appeal. There will be no blanket and no automatic returns of asylum seekers.' The word 'immediately' thus became difficult to implement. The original assessment, and the inevitable appeals process, would take time.

The plan mentioned two grounds for the inadmissibility of a claim for asylum in Greece. If a person had already been recognised as a refugee in Turkey or enjoyed what was described as 'sufficient protection' there. (The *first country of asylum* principle, Article 35 of the Asylum Procedures Directive of 2013). Or if the person had not yet been granted protection by Turkey, but Turkey was judged able to guarantee effective access to protection (the *safe third country* principle – Article 38 of the Asylum Procedures Directive).

Several other riders were added to the agreement. Belonging to a vulnerable category of refugee, or having relatives already in Europe who pleaded for family reunification, would be possible grounds for acceptance after all, and avoiding the boat trip back to Turkey. All rejections could be appealed. Migrants judged inadmissible, still waiting for a ruling on their appeals, would be held in closed reception centres on the Greek islands, while asylum seekers whose cases had not yet been decided would be held in open camps on the same islands.

In order to carry out the return plan, Frontex would provide eight ships with a capacity of 300–400 passengers each. In order to process all the applications, 200 Greek asylum case workers would be supplemented with 400 asylum experts sent by other EU states. And 1,500 police officers from around the EU would be provided, paid for and organised by Frontex. Containers capable of accommodating 20,000 people, more than tripling the existing 6,000 places, would be set up on the Greek islands. Over the next six months, Greece would also receive €280 million in EU funds to help implement the agreement. This added up to a huge turnaround of the Greek immigration machine. The 'hotspots' on the islands would no longer focus on the registration and screening of new arrivals, ahead of their swift transfer to the mainland, as they had until now. Instead, the new focus would be on implementing returns to Turkey.

The Action Plan got off to a shaky start. On the day it was agreed, there were around 7,000 asylum seekers on the Greek islands, and 36,000 on the mainland. The Turkish government made clear that they would not accept any of these people back, and interpreted the agreement to refer to all *future* arrivals in Greece from Turkey.[19] In future, the Turkish EU minister Volkan Bozkir told the Anadolu News Agency, 'tens of thousands' of refugees would be returned to Turkey, 'but not millions'.

Bulgarian prime minister Boyko Borisov immediately raised the spectre of hundreds of thousands of migrants storming his country's incomplete fence on the border with Turkey if they could no longer take the sea route.

He appealed for Bulgaria to be added to the agreement. As Bulgaria is an EU country bordering on Turkey, Borisov also opposed rapid visa liberalisation with Turkey. Cyprus, an EU member since 2004, also objected to any speeding up of EU accession talks for Turkey until the dispute over the 1974 invasion by Turkish forces and subsequent partition of the island, was resolved. Bulgaria and Cyprus were just two of the five countries to raise serious objections to the plan.[20]

The Hungarian government said it would accept the deal with Turkey only if there were no more relocations. 'Relocations' was the word which referred to EU plans to relocate asylum seekers currently in Greece and Italy to other EU countries under the EU quotas system. The word 'resettlement' referred to the resettling of people from outside the EU, to EU countries. The Hungarian approach drew the wrath of the Italian government of Matteo Renzi. Under the September 2015 Emergency Relocation Plan of the EU, Hungary was asked to accept 1,294 people from Italy and Greece.

France and Spain expressed their fears that the human rights of migrants would be harmed by the Action Plan. 'We interpret it as contrary to the international law, to the Geneva Convention and to the European treaties,' said Spanish foreign minister José Manuel García-Margallo. Many countries expressed the view that the EU was, at best, bribing Turkey to keep refugees on its own territory or, at worst, giving Turkey a 'refugee gun' which it could at any time use against the EU. 'I expect we can make a deal with Turkey, but I have always said we can't put ourselves at the mercy of Turkey,' said Austrian foreign minister Sebastian Kurz.

Human rights groups including Amnesty International and Human Rights Watch bitterly attacked the deal. 'How could refugees be sent back to a country, Turkey, which did not fully respect the Geneva Convention?' they asked. In their view, a cornerstone of the plan, that Turkey could already be regarded as a 'safe third country', was fundamentally flawed.[21]

The European Commission struggled to defend the plan, largely by adding more background explanations. According to a commentary drawn up by Donald Tusk's office, the proposal to resettle one Syrian refugee for each refugee returned to Turkey was 'temporary and extraordinary', and migrants returned to Turkey would be 'protected in accordance with international standards'. In other words, the EU was expecting most asylum seekers to actually stay in Turkey.

In response to this storm of criticism, Turkish officials remained surprisingly cheerful. The Turkish prime minister, Ahmet Davutoğlu played the good guy. His face beamed with happiness in every media photograph. Turkey's all-powerful president, Recep Tayyip Erdoğan barked from Ankara.[22] Unlike certain EU governments, he said, Turkey would not behave hypocritically by closing its borders when faced with a humanitarian catastrophe. That comment did not bode well for Hungarian-Turkish relations. 'We have to accept the people escaping bombs with an open-door policy from now on,' Erdoğan said.

There were two other complications. On 13 March, a car-bomb exploded in Ankara, killing many people, most of them policemen. Also on 13 March, Angela Merkel's governing Christian Democratic Union (CDU)-led coalition suffered serious setbacks in three regional elections, in votes which were interpreted by many as a referendum on her pro-refugee policy. The former CDU stronghold of Baden-Württemberg was won by the Greens (also a pro-migrant party), with the CDU reduced to second place. The right-wing populist, anti-refugee AfD stole the most votes from the CDU there, winning 15 per cent to displace the SPD as the third biggest party. 'We have a very clear position on the refugee issue: we do not want to take in any,' said Alexander Gauland, deputy leader of the AfD.

In Saxony-Anhalt in eastern Germany the CDU hung onto power, but the AfD came second with nearly 25 per cent.[23] In the Rhineland-Palatinate, the AfD also did well, but the CDU and the SPD were well ahead. All in all, the elections left Merkel wounded but not defeated, and as determined as ever not to impose a cap on migrant numbers, which even many in her own party, and the CSU sister party in Bavaria, had long demanded. A cap on numbers would be a 'short-term pseudo-solution', she said. Only a 'concerted European approach' would bring down the numbers, and now the Action Plan offered her what looked like a concerted approach. The AfD, she said, was a 'party that . . . offers no appropriate solutions to problems, but only stokes prejudice and divisions'.

Over the coming months, the success of the EU–Turkey deal would lie not so much in the details – few asylum seekers were actually sent back to Turkey – but rather in its overall deterrent effect, especially on refugees from Syria. To survive, Merkel badly needed the numbers of asylum seekers arriving in her country to drop. Germany needed to be seen to reimpose control. If she refused to introduce a cap herself, if other European states failed to agree to Germany's cautious policy, at least she could count on Turkey.

What began as the ESI plan, and what became the German–Turkish–Dutch plan, pipped the Orbán plan at the post. 'We won the race, but we did not win the narrative battle,' Gerald Knaus told me years later. 'Many people across Europe to this day believe the legend that Angela Merkel could have closed the German border.'[24]

Angela Merkel is widely seen as part of the problem, when in fact she was an important part of the solution.

CHAPTER TEN

THE STREET OF THE FOUR WINDS

Yes, Europe has Christian roots and it is Christianity's responsibility to water those roots. But this must be done in a spirit of service, as in the washing of the feet.

Pope Francis[1]

Just as the deal with Turkey was being announced in Brussels on 18 March, 5 kilometres away across the clustered streets of the Belgian capital, police captured twenty-six-year-old Salah Abdeslam in the rue des Quatre-Vents, the Street of the Four Winds. The place could hardly have been better named. The EU in the spring of 2016 was buffeted by the four winds of climate change, migration, terrorism and populism. For the first time since its foundation, serious voices were doubting its capacity to survive the challenges it now faced from all directions.

Abdeslam was given away by an unusually large order of pizzas and a fingerprint on a glass found at a flat in the Forest district of Brussels three days earlier. Wearing a white hoodie, limping from a bullet wound in the leg, he was dragged from the house by heavily armed policemen, the only one of the ten attackers in Paris the previous November caught alive. His survival, both of the attacks and of the police attempts to arrest him, may not have been accidental, according to a report in the London *Independent*.[2]

The first IS communiqué, claiming responsibility for the Paris attacks, also mentioned an explosion in the 18th arrondissement of the French capital. But there was no terror-related incident there at all. A French police

174

source told John Litchfield of the *Independent* that that was the district from which Abdeslam rang two friends in Brussels, to come and rescue him from the French capital, after dropping off his older brother Ibrahim. Ibrahim detonated his suicide vest outside the Comptoir Voltaire Café, causing only one other injury. According to that report, Abdeslam may have been just as worried about IS killing him in revenge for not carrying out his part in the atrocity as he was about Belgian police catching him. A Belgian website reported him telling a friend four days after the 13 November attacks that they had gone 'too far' and that he regretted taking part in them.

For four months he was the most wanted man in Europe. Until a few weeks before the Paris attacks, he used to enjoy a drink and a smoke in the bar in the rue Etiennes in the Molenbeek district of Brussels he ran with Ibrahim. Hardly the usual profiles of religious fundamentalists.

The big fear in Italy about the Turkey–EU agreement was that the island of Lampedusa and the rugged coast of Sicily would become the main point of entry for migrants to Europe, as the Aegean became too difficult. The fear was realised in so far as this 'central Mediterranean' route did become the most crowded. But the crowds were different. It was not as if a Syrian, fearing for his life in Damascus, would have chosen to travel through Turkey and Greece in 2015, but Libya and Italy in 2016. People fled whichever way they could, and with whichever smugglers they thought they could trust.

The refugees heading across the sea from North Africa to Italy came from the Horn of Africa, especially Eritrea. After them came those from sub-Saharan countries including Mali, Niger, Senegal and Nigeria.

The Africans reaching Libya were taking the dangerous route across the Sahara desert. Large numbers perished on the way.[3] When they reached Libya they were handed on to equally ruthless smugglers in a country torn apart by armed gangs since the removal of Libyan dictator Muammar Gaddafi in 2011. Then they faced the storms of the Mediterranean in poorly built or maintained ships, or large rubber dinghies with up to 150 men, women and children on each. The shortest sea distance between the Libyan coastal town of Sabratha, where most set out from, and the shore of Lampedusa, is 190 kilometres. It was a measure of their despair that, well aware of the dangers, they set out from home in the first place.

On 15 April 2016, the International Organization for Migration released figures which showed that in just three days, 6,000 migrants had crossed from Libya to Italy, compared to only 174 from the Turkish coast to the Greek islands. In the first three weeks after the EU–Turkey deal was signed, 325 migrants were returned from the islands to Turkey, including 10 Syrians, while 79 Syrians from Turkey were resettled in Western Europe. Migrants sent back to Turkey were temporarily housed in a new camp set up under the deal in the town of Kilis.

The Italian prime minister, Matteo Renzi, was quick to reassure his people that the growing number reaching their shores was a temporary, not a permanent, phenomenon.[4] 'There is a problem that concerns our country, but this is not an invasion,' he said. 'The number of boats is barely a few higher compared to last year.' He knew the numbers: that year, 24,000 had crossed the sea to Italy by mid-April, compared to 19,000 for the same period the previous year. On the other hand, in the same period, 154,000 had crossed the Aegean from Turkey before the EU–Turkey deal was signed.

'We have clear ideas about how to deal with it,' said Renzi. The clear idea was to strike deals with North African and sub-Saharan countries to try to keep people at home in the first place. Also to step up naval patrols off Libya, just as NATO ships were to take part in policing Turkish coastal waters. Libyan coastguards were also to be better trained and equipped. That was easier in the Turkish case, as Turkey is a member of NATO. The anarchy in Libya meant that there was no effective government there to strike a deal with, on the Turkish model. There were an estimated 1 million non-Libyan nationals in Libya, according to the International Organization for Migration, some of them migrants, others foreigners working there. If the security situation became even worse, large numbers might try to cross to Italy. In the meantime, the Italian government instructed local authorities to find 15,000 extra beds to deal with the current spike in numbers.[5]

Italians were not just worried about the view to the south. Clouds were gathering along their northern border with Austria too. The increasingly anti-migrant government in Vienna was threatening to close the Brenner pass, the main route into Austria from Italy.

Austria had announced preparations for the introduction of border controls at the pass. The resignation of Austrian chancellor Werner Faymann in May 2016, and his replacement by his Social Democratic Party colleague Christian Kern, ushered in a sharp anti-refugee turn in Austrian government policy. Germany, Denmark and Norway also introduced temporary controls on their borders. The old fault lines between nation state were reappearing across the Schengen zone. 'If the rules are broken, we cannot act as if nothing has happened,' Matteo Renzi warned Vienna.[6]

*

Zoltán Boross was a hard-headed cop with a face of granite and surprisingly vulnerable brown eyes above a tidy moustache. His name card said it all: Department of International Criminality, Illegal Migration Unit. Illegal not irregular. He muttered rather than spoke, mixing the wooden language of state bureaucracy with the passion of a professional devoted to his job. A typical Hungarian law-and-order product of the late Kádár years, at the soft end of state socialism in the 1980s, he started in the border police in 1993 and has never looked back. He sounded obsessed, or at least full of emotion about the bad men and women he pursued.

> They come in all shapes and sizes. In the old days it was just men, but now more and more women are involved. It used to be less educated people, with just primary school education, now there are more and more highly qualified smugglers, with university degrees.

Ten times as many smugglers were active in 2015 as in 2014. The main organisers were in the countries of origin, earning the bulk of the €8,000 it cost, roughly, per person, to get to Europe. Their logistical network stretched all the way across Turkey, up through Eastern Europe and the Balkans to the destination countries. On the way, a cell structure existed, with members of one cell often not knowing the identities of other cells, to minimise the damage of discovery when the police caught the members of one cell. Three systems of payment were used: Western Union, MoneyGram, or other above-board money-transfer systems; the *hawala* system, under which migrants travelled on credit, with various guarantees for the smugglers that they would receive the money through password-protected pigeonholes once a migrant reached the destination; or simply cash in hand, which was the hardest for the police forces to track.

A few days earlier, a twenty-nine-year-old Afghan was arrested in a Budapest bar, allegedly linked to eight Afghans found in a van on the M1 motorway from Budapest to Vienna. 'A typical case. The Afghan smuggler was living in Hungary, probably illegally. The migrants were at the camp in Bicske. They got in touch with a Hungarian woman, she organised the route on.' The Afghan was working with the Hungarian woman. Neither were among the main organisers, and the chain led all the way back to Afghanistan. They were just links near the end of the chain.

International cooperation between police forces was good, but could be much better, Boross said. Hungarian liaison officers work in Turkey. 'Last year we had good and precise data from the Turkish side.' There had also been good cooperation with the Serbian police since 2009 when nineteen Kosovars drowned in the Danube on the Hungarian-Serbian border. On that occasion, the whole network of smugglers was uncovered. Now the Hungarian investigators were focusing on improving collaboration with the Macedonians. There were 110 officers in six units working on illegal migration at the Hungarian National Bureau of Investigations (NNI). The increasing number of cameras, mounted on the fence with Serbia, were not a 'miracle' system, but rather an early warning one, he explained. 'The key question is how fast we can react to the information from the cameras.'

Both at Röszke and at Bácsszentgyörgy in the west, local Hungarian people I spoke to alleged that Hungarian border policemen were bribed to turn a blind eye to smugglers. Did he give any credence to those claims? 'That is an awkward question. There have always been attempts to corrupt border guards. If we come across anything concrete we concentrate all our efforts into tracking down and stopping such practices.' Such cases were not typical, he affirmed, and any found guilty were no longer in the police force.

The hardest period for him and his officers was at the end of August and beginning of September 2015:

It was a very hard time. Next to the larger, professional groups of smugglers, many amateurs were attracted by the big profits. They were charging €150 per person from Röszke to Budapest, or €300 per person to Vienna. They packed them in their vehicles, and sometimes made three trips a day. Private entrepreneurs moved in on the business, from all over the country. There were days we launched four separate cases. And we caught thirty-six gangs. That was a good result.

Overall, I asked, how successful had the fence actually been so far? 'It has a restraining influence. For the past month, it has kept the number entering the country illegally down to about 100 a day.' About 11,000 had been caught in the first four months of the year, after climbing over or cutting through the fence. Some had been put in trial in Szeged. Most had ended up in open camps, from where they quietly continued their journeys to Austria. Once they were safely in the country, how much effort did Hungary actually put into preventing migrants and refugees leaving westwards, to Austria? I asked Boross.

'It is true that every country tries harder to stop people coming in than going out,' he admitted. On the wall above his office was a large colourful map of Central Europe and the Balkans. Hungary was in orange, Serbia, Austria and Ukraine in green, Croatia in purple, Romania in yellow, and Italy in red. Criss-crossing the map black felt-tip lines of notorious smuggling routes had been drawn, some thicker than others to show the volume of the traffic. At the centre of the spider's web, six lines radiated out of Budapest.

As we walked down the stairs to the exit, after an interview which had lasted two and a half hours, I mentioned that we hadn't spoken much about Romania. 'Our impression,' he said carefully, 'is that the Romanians are not telling us the true numbers of those who are passing through their country. Because they want to get into the Schengen zone of countries soon, and that would be harder if they get a reputation as another gateway for illegal immigrants . . .'

So Hungarian investigators had asked their Slovak and Polish counterparts to tell them if the numbers began to rise on their own borders. One new route from Greece, he suspected, was through Bulgaria into Romania, then into Ukraine, and through Ukraine either across the short and mountainous border into Slovakia – 'hard to cross, and full of cameras, which the Slovaks are rather proud of' – and the longer, much more easily negotiable border from Ukraine into Poland.

We stood outside while he lit a cigarette, like a true plain-clothes cop. Other plain-clothes policemen were outside smoking too, lurking at the entrance of an underground carpark. With his long-standing experience of the cruelties inflicted by smugglers and traffickers on those who paid them so much, did he see migrants as victims, or criminals? I asked.

'I see them as *witnesses*,' he said. 'Unfortunately most tell fairy-tales. They think if they give evidence, they will not get help from the smugglers' networks later, to travel on. So we look especially for those who have been cheated by the smugglers, or hurt by them in other ways.'

'Are your actions not pushing more people into the hands of the smugglers?' I asked. 'If you just let people through, or laid on transport, as you did last year, wouldn't that be a more effective way of combatting the trade?'

'The truth lies on both sides,' he said, frankly. The police, like the army, had every reason to be pleased with the Fidesz government. In early May, they were granted an extra $205 million (55.8 billion forints) from the budget, to cover the cost of policing the southern border, and improved communications equipment. The counter-terrorism service, TEK, and other intelligence services received the biggest rise of all.

*

In mid-April, Pope Francis, spiritual leader of 1.2 billion Catholics and the Orthodox Patriarch Bartholomew, spiritual leader of 250 million Orthodox Christians, travelled together to the Greek island of Lesbos with the Greek Archbishop Ieronymous II.[7] The Pope's first trip after becoming pontiff in 2013 was to the island of Lampedusa, and he had often spoken out in sympathy with refugees. As a Catholic from Argentina, who had worked many years with his fellow Jesuits among the poor in the shanty towns of Buenos Aires, he had a strong sympathy for the poor and oppressed. Lesbos, even more than the other islands, was the Greek bottleneck of the refugee influx, with 850,000 passing through in 2015 – ten times the permanent population of the island. Before aid agencies and volunteers arrived and got organised, the local Greek population did most of the rescuing and caring for the weary and bedraggled, clambering up the beaches.[8]

'On remote Greek islands, grandmothers have sung terrified little babies to sleep, while teachers, pensioners and students have spent months offering food, shelter, clothing and comfort to refugees who have risked their lives to flee war and terror,' read the petition organised by a group of academics, who nominated the people of the Greek islands for the Nobel Peace Prize for their efforts to help refugees.[9]

1 Afghan boys by the roadside near Ásotthalom, June 2015. *The eyes of the Afghans lit up as I unpacked the big fruit. Do you have a knife? One of the boys asked. No? He shrugged, lifted the fat green cylindrical melon into the air, and let it crash onto the tarmac at his feet* (p. 56).

2 Eric Özeme, from the Democratic Republic of the Congo, at our first meeting on the roadside near Ásotthalom, June 2015. *What did you know about Hungary before you came? What did you expect? I asked. 'C'est la paix, quoi' – it's a country at peace! – he replied, and that was quite enough* (p. 53).

3 Refugees queue for the buses at the Röszke cornfield that will take them to a registration centre, September 2015. *Each morning I drove down to the cornfield at Röszke to do my early reports for the BBC beside the railway track as the sun came up, and long lines of asylum seekers appeared from the fields of maize and sunflowers (p. 63).*

4 A field of tents at Röszke, September 2015. *Most of the refugees carried a single rucksack with as many things as they could squeeze into it, but some carried two or three tied together, helping weaker members of their group. There were still just two or three mobile toilets in the police collecting point in the cornfield at Röszke (p. 73).*

5 A Syrian boy holds up his new design for the flag of his country, East Station, Budapest, September 2015. *It was a horizontal tricolour, with blue at the top, white in the middle, green at the bottom. In the middle of the white band were three hearts, each filled with tears (p. 99).*

6 Hungarian police, East Station, Budapest, September 2015. *After Monday's brief respite in the tension … the mood darkened rapidly again, as the police sealed off all entrances to people who looked like refugees. In the streets nearby they carried out identity checks as shopkeepers and smugglers looked on (p. 85).*

7 Yazidi refugees, Dimitrovgrad, Serbia, November 2015. *A Yazidi family, from Sinjar in Iraq, showed me photos on their phone of Sinjar after the IS attack – street after street of homes in ruins. Their journey across Bulgaria had been rough. Five days in police detention near the border. Seventeen people kept by the smugglers in one small room (p. 142).*

8 A volunteer serves food to Afghan refugees beside the police registration point at Dimitrovgrad, Serbia, November 2015. *Most of the volunteers were young, pretty women from Germany, always smiling, handing out tea and warm food at all hours of day and night. Most of the refugees here were Afghan men in their late teens or early twenties. The women said they never experienced sexual harassment (p. 142).*

9 A sister and brother at the One Stop Centre refugee camp, Subotica, Serbia, September 2016. *When I had finished asking my questions, she said she wanted to tell me something. She wanted, through me, to thank all the people around the world who help the poor people who have no land, and no country now, she said (p. 219).*

10 Refugee women cooking supper on the Serbian side of the Hungarian border at Kelebia, September 2016. '*Women will fight for their children's sake. They don't need to eat, they don't need to sleep, so long as they feel they are taking their children to a place where they will be safe, where they might even be able to go to school*' (p. 219).

11 Women at the water tap, Horgoš illegal encampment, Serbia, September 2016. *All day women and children filled bowls and water bottles here. Men and women washed their hair, and children played. The two taps remained legally on Hungarian territory ... The first 2 metres inside the camp were Hungarian soil (p. 202).*

12 Lunchtime at the Horgoš illegal encampment, Serbia, September 2016. *Some refugees were heating up tins of tuna on their fires, others roasted sweetcorn they had picked from neighbouring fields or bought in the shop in Horgoš. Everywhere tea was being brewed in blackened tin or enamel mugs (p. 202).*

13 A young Somali at Adaševci, with the lists of those queuing to get into the Hungarian transit zones, September 2016. *The lists gave the impression of a long queue of people, all jostling to move forwards, some overtaking others, others getting left behind. A young Somali man let me take his photograph in front of the lists. Then he ran his finger up and down the rows in vain. He could not find his own name (p. 216).*

14 A Hungarian soldier on guard duty at the Röszke transit zone, September 2016. *Along the top of the cabins, police and soldiers patrolled. Life must have become excruciatingly boring for them, after 4 July, with so few migrants to catch. Only a few dozen attempted to get through the 175-kilometre long fence each night. They faced an army of up to 10,000 police and soldiers (p. 202).*

15 Haneen on the train from Lübeck to Bargteheide, June 2017. *Even now she sometimes notices children staring at her headscarf. But she has not considered giving it up. 'It's part of who I am.' She likes many things in Germany but she needs to stay herself and the scarf is part of that (p. 271).*

16 Safaa outside the hospital in Szeged, Hungary, March 2018. *Thanks to the mediation of the UNHCR and the goodwill of the Hungarian Immigration Office, Safaa and Hali were placed in Hungary's last open refugee camp, at Vámosszabadi, while their family reunification request was considered by the German authorities (p. 257).*

17 Aidi beside the River Danube in Regensburg, Germany, March 2018. *'First I will go to school, to learn German. Then I will go to university. Because I have one dream. I want to work in an office. I would love so much to work in an office. That's my dream!' (p. 263).*

The situation of migrants on Lesbos deteriorated sharply with the EU–Turkey deal. The three main aid organisations – International Rescue Committee, Norwegian Refugee Council and Oxfam – which had been active until then, all decided to leave rather than be associated with a policy of mass expulsions. The camp at Moria turned from being an open place where refugees could rest after the sea journey and prepare for to travel onwards on large passenger ferries, into little better than a prison camp. An atmosphere of gloom and despair had descended on the inmates. Another positive aspect of the Pope's visit was that the camp was given a spring clean. Walls were whitewashed, showers repaired and clean clothes distributed, before the religious leaders arrived.

'Does Europe have the capacity to accept so many migrants now?' the pontiff was asked by a reporter from the French Catholic magazine, *La Croix*, a few days after his visit.[10]

That is a fair and responsible question because one cannot open the gates wide unreasonably. However, the deeper question is why there are so many migrants now . . . The initial problems are the wars in the Middle East and in Africa as well as the underdevelopment of the African continent, which causes hunger. If there are wars, it is because there exist arms manufacturers – which can be justified for defensive purposes – and above all arms traffickers. If there is so much unemployment, it is because of a lack of investment capable of providing employment, of which Africa has such a great need. More generally, this raises the question of a world economic system that has descended into the idolatry of money. The great majority of humanity's wealth has fallen into the hands of a minority of the population.

Coming back to the migrant issue, the worst form of welcome is to 'ghettoize' them. On the contrary, it's necessary to integrate them. In Brussels, the terrorists were Belgians, children of migrants, but they grew up in a ghetto. In London, the new mayor [Sadiq Khan, a Muslim] took his oath of office in a cathedral and will undoubtedly meet the queen. This illustrates the need for Europe to rediscover its capacity to integrate.

The religious leaders visited Moria, a camp where 3,000 migrants were now detained, awaiting deportation to Turkey if their asylum applications failed. They spent five hours on the island, touring the camp and talking to the migrants.

> I am here to tell you, you are not alone . . . The Greek people have gener-
> ously responded to your needs despite their own difficulties. Yes, so
> much more needs to be done but let us thank God that in our suffering
> he never leaves us alone.
>
> We hope that the world will heed these scenes of tragic and indeed
> desperate need, and respond in a way worthy of our common humanity.

The religious leaders said prayers for all those who had died on the journey there, then the Pope took three families of twelve Syrian refugees back to the Vatican with him. Six were children, and all were threatened with deportation, though they had arrived on the island before the deal came into effect. In Italy, they would be cared for by the Sant' Egidio charity.

For the thousands left behind, the picture looked bleak. After weeks or months of waiting for an interview with the EASO officer, asylum seekers were no longer asked about the conditions in their home countries, or why they fled in the first place.[11] Interviewers were suddenly only interested in conditions in Turkey. If they had been tolerable, now that Turkey had been declared a 'safe country' by the EU, they were considered suitable for sending back. The only remaining safeguard was a comparatively strenuous appeals procedure. In the year from 20 March 2016 to 20 March 2017, only 916 people were actually deported from the Greek islands to Turkey. Being on appeal in the Moria camp was a mixed blessing. Migrants were clinging by their fingernails to their fragile position on the inside edge of the EU. But their situation was neither stable, nor comfortable.

Another criticism of the EU–Turkey Statement came from the Hungarian-born financier and philanthropist George Soros.[12] In an article in the *New York Review of Books* published in April 2016, he identified four main flaws. That it was a German plan, imposed on the EU, rather than a common European approach. It was underfunded. It imposed quotas, which many member states opposed, requiring refugees to live in countries where they didn't want to be. And, finally, it transformed Greece into a holding pen for refugees.

The EU–Turkey deal could, nevertheless, be made to work, Soros suggested, if enough funding was thrown at it. What was needed was what he called 'surge funding' – large sums, made available at the moment of need, deliberately targeted – rather than the current EU policy of putting in too little money, continuously.

> Most of the building blocks for an effective asylum system are available; they only need to be assembled into a comprehensive and coherent policy. Critically, refugees and the countries that contain them in the Middle East must receive enough financial support to make their lives there viable, allowing them to work and to send their children to school. That would help to keep the inflow of refugees to a level that Europe can absorb. This can be accomplished by establishing a firm and reliable target for the number of refugee arrivals: between 300,000 and 500,000 per year.

These refugees would be coming to Europe by invitation, not wasting their frugal resources on the smugglers who exploited them, often brutally, at the moment. 'This number is large enough to give refugees the assurance that many of them can eventually seek refuge in Europe, yet small enough to be accommodated by European governments even in the current unfavorable political climate,' Soros continued.

> There are established techniques for the voluntary balancing of supply and demand in other fields, such as with matching students to schools and junior doctors to hospitals. In this case, people determined to go to a particular destination would have to wait longer than those who accept the destination allotted to them. The asylum seekers could then be required to await their turn where they are currently located. This would be much cheaper and less painful than the current chaos, in which the migrants are the main victims. Those who jump the line would lose their place and have to start all over again.

He calculated that €30 billion a year would be needed to make the scheme work and suggested that the sum be borrowed on the financial markets, exploiting for the first time the EU's triple A credit rating. The sum should be enough to help Turkey and other front-line states improve their facilities for refugees, for the funding of an efficient EU asylum agency and security force, tasked with protecting the external borders, and establishing common standards across the EU for the reception and integration of refugees, he wrote. It might sound expensive, but it would certainly be cheaper than allowing the Schengen system of free trade to collapse. The cost of that had been estimated by the Bertelsmann Foundation and the French government as potentially more than €100 billion a year, in lost GDP.

*

Mazen was from Damascus. He was living in a makeshift shelter, half-tent, half-branches, with UNHCR blankets stretched between them at Horgoš, a few metres from the Hungarian border. Only a few metres of razor wire and a few thousand Hungarian police and soldiers separated him from the rest of his family. He and his two daughters, aged fifteen and twenty, had reached Serbia from Bulgaria fifteen days earlier, he said, and had been at Horgoš for two days. His wife and two sons had travelled ahead of them and had already been in Hanover in Germany for nine months. Why did he come to this border, exactly?

'As you know, crossing borders illegally, and paying smugglers is prohibited. So I have to come the legal way. I have to take these young ladies to their mother. I don't have any other way to reach there.' So he had joined the ever lengthening queue of refugees and migrants trying to enter Hungary legally through the transit zones at Röszke and Kelebia.

Mazen worked as an IT engineer in Syria. Daily life in Damascus had become too dangerous he said. 'Syria has been torn up into many pieces. We don't have a country anymore . . . There are so many mad people there, Assad, his security police, IS, it's a disaster.' As the head of the family, he felt he had to take his daughters to safety. 'I cannot play the role of mother to them,' he explained a little forlornly, man to man. His wife had looked into the possibility of asking the German authorities for family reunification, so they could get a visa for Germany, but it might take several years.

There were sixty or seventy people in the camp, under the watchful eye of Hungarian police and soldiers, walking up and down the roof of the transit zone, raising binoculars to their eyes. The Serbian police were less efficient, and less well equipped. It was a long walk on the Serbian side to the village of Horgoš. When the police were there, men were sometimes refused permission to leave the camp and go to the village to buy food or cigarettes. The worst aspect of life here, and at the other transit zone at Tompa, was the uncertainty. No one knew when they would be let into Hungary. The most vulnerable had priority, in theory, but sometimes that would lead to families being divided, so migrants would rather wait longer, in order to be able to carry on together. At this time, twenty to thirty people a day were being let into the transit zones at Horgoš-Röszke, and a similar number at Tompa. After registration, families would then be allowed to continue to the open camps at Bicske or Vámosszabadi. Single men were usually held much longer, up to thirty days in the transit zones. There was room for fifty in each, in small containers, but rarely more than a couple of dozen there at any one time. From the Hungarian side, it was easy to look through the wire, and follow the pace of life inside. It moved at a snail's pace. There were very few Hungarian immigration officers. Those there were seemed sluggish, and certainly unfriendly to the media. It was as if they were trying to work as slowly as possible. So much for the fast-track procedure, promised under various Hungarian laws and legal amendments.

As I talked with refugees at Horgoš, officials of the UNHCR, the Serbian Refugee Council and Doctors Without Borders moved through the camp, distributing food, offering medical help. A couple of refugees asked them for rubber gloves, so they could clear away the rubbish.

Goran Makić was an employee of Médecins Sans Frontières.

We offer basic medical care to all these people, especially to the most vulnerable, pregnant women, small children, families. There are chronic illnesses, people with diabetes and other complaints they brought with them from home. There are people deeply traumatised by war. And there are people with just the everyday complaints of those who have walked long distances in inappropriate footwear, with irregular food, and only rare possibilities for personal hygiene.

Médecins Sans Frontières also provided medical help to the 150 migrants arriving each night at the bus station in Subotica, 20 kilometres down the motorway, or across the fields. The numbers were well down from the previous September or October when a thousand people were in this camp, but still substantial at about 250, he explained. As it was an unofficial camp, different organisations coordinated their work with one another. The main problem was that the Hungarian authorities let through so few people, he said. Those – mostly young men, travelling alone – who got in, then were rejected, were the most forlorn. Some tried to climb the fence, further away from the camp, and were often caught and pushed back. Some went back to Belgrade, as they realised the only way to proceed was with smugglers. The fence was forcing all but the lucky few who were accepted by Hungary, straight into the hands of the smugglers.

> It's difficult to follow the new routes, but it's not a secret that people are coming through Bulgaria now. There are also still a lot of people in the camps in Serbia, at Šid, Adaševci, Principovac, Preševo. A small number, like these here, are trying the legal way into Hungary. People are exhausted. It's already 24 degrees today. It will be terrible here when it gets hot again. These are improvised shelters. You get four or five days of high temperatures, then wind and rain.

By the end of April, 3,500 had entered Hungary legally, through the transit zones, since the start of the year.

At around ten in the morning, there was a sudden commotion over at the fence, at the steel turnstile which led into the transit zone. Mazen heard his name called out. He scooped up his daughters, a couple of bags, and they started running. With a screech and a groan, the turnstile turned, police walkie-talkies crackled, and they disappeared into the first container. Three of the fifteen people allowed into Röszke that day.

On the forecourt of the first filling station on the motorway on the Serbian side of the border, I stopped to talk to a young Iranian couple holding hands, Said and Fatima. They were Christian converts from the city of Mashhad, they said.[13] She was twenty-six, he was thirty. They had spent about thirty days in Turkey. Their original plan to cross to the Greek islands was scuppered by the EU–Turkey agreement, so they walked for four days to cross the Turkish-Bulgarian border. No, they were not married yet, they smiled, shyly. And they were fed up with eating tuna fish. At some point, the UNHCR, who supplied much of the food to the camp at Horgoš, ordered a vast number of tins of tuna fish, to satisfy the no-pork sensibilities of the Muslims. They ate it cold, straight from the tins, or cooked it up for a change on the metal rods they fixed over the fire holes they dug in the sandy soil. This was the same soil so well suited to growing sweet potatoes, not far away in Ásotthalom, the 'sweet-potato capital' of Hungary. I gave the young Iranians the cheese sandwiches I had carefully prepared for my own lunch, from home-made bread, that morning in Budapest. They could hardly have thanked me more if I had handed them a wad of euros.

Mashhad, their home in Iran, is the second largest place of pilgrimage in the world, after Mecca, with 20 million visitors a year. Shi'ite Muslims go there to visit the shrine of Imam Reza, the eighth Shi'ite imam. There are an estimated 3 million Afghan refugees in Iran, and of these, 300,000 live in Mashhad, which is close to the Afghan border. The city is also famous for its jewellery, especially of the precious stone turquoise, and for the production of a particularly valued carpet, known as the Mashhad turkbâf, made with a special Turkish knotting technique by immigrants who came from Tabriz in the nineteenth century.

'Fewer Hungarians from Hungary are going abroad to work now, but more Hungarians are going from Vojvodina. I think that's because of the growing xenophobia here,' Ilona Kulcov told me. We were sitting in her small, tidy office in Szeged, from which she organised work for Hungarians in Britain. Across the border in Serbia, in the city of Subotica which has a significant Hungarian population, she ran a similar office. There was a big difference, she explained. In Vojvodina, the large province in northern Serbia with important cities like Subotica and Novi Sad, many different cultural and linguistic groups mingle, and live side by side. Most of the bakers are Albanians from Kosovo. This was once part of Austro-Hungary, and there are many Hungarians. There are also Germans, Croats, Jews, Roma and Romanians, and other nationalities, not to mention the Serb and Roma refugees from the Krajina and from Kosovo.

'When Hungarians from Subotica go to Britain, they have no problems living in a multicultural society. Hungarians from Hungary are more shocked, and find it harder to settle down,' she told me. 'They're used to living in a mono-cultural society. To have neighbours from different cultures, especially children of Asian and African and Caribbean origin sitting next to their children at school, was quite a shock.'

I visited the Hungarian refugee camps at Bicske, and at Vámosszabadi – or rather, the main gate, as journalists in Hungary, unlike in Serbia or Bulgaria, are never allowed inside. Just down the road from the Bicske camp, in the entrance hall of a Tesco supermarket, furtive-looking Afghan migrants queued at a Western Union money-transfer office. The Hungarian men behind the counter were bored, dispensed money grudgingly, or refused it because of the misspelling of a name. Hungarian shoppers and security guards watched the scene suspiciously. Two local teenagers tried, unsuccessfully, to sell a tablet with a broken screen to the Afghans.

*

In early May 2016 the European Commission published its proposals to overhaul European Asylum Policy.[14] The cornerstone was the idea of shared responsibility, as outlined in all the treaties EU members signed when they joined the EU. Each of the twenty-eight EU members would be asked to take a fair quota of migrants, corresponding to their size and wealth. The actual number, and who exactly was sent, would be decided by a computer, based at EASO headquarters in Malta. To encourage asylum seekers to stay where they were sent, welfare, housing, education and other social and integration services would only be available for each in the country she or he was sent to. This was designed to solve a previous objection to quota schemes, especially from the East Europeans, that it was 'impossible' to keep an asylum seeker in the country to which they were assigned against their will. Countries could refuse to take their fair share of asylum seekers but would be required to pay a 'solidarity tax' of €250,000 per person. That would add up to €1.5 billion for Poland, if it refused to accept all 6,200 refugees it was allocated, and €300 million for Hungary.

On the day the plan was announced, the foreign ministers of Hungary, Poland, Slovakia and the Czech Republic were meeting for a Visegrád Four summit in Prague. Their outrage was immediate.[15] 'This is blackmail,' grumbled Hungarian foreign minister Péter Szijjártó. 'The quota concept is a dead-end street and I would like to ask the commission not to run into this dead-end street any more.' 'It sounds like an idea announced during April Fool's Day,' said Polish foreign minister Witold Waszczykowski. Czech foreign minister Lubomir Zaoralek said he was 'unpleasantly surprised': 'The commission is returning to a proposal upon which there is no agreement. It should not propose something that divides us.'

The East Europeans had overestimated their weight in the new Europe. As one country after another reimposed border controls and – with the stubborn exception of Germany – began capping migrant numbers, East European governments had convinced themselves that they were 'winning the argument'. In fact, changes to policy were a reluctant acknowledgement by member states that there were limits to their own generosity – limits that were closely related to performances in elections. But that didn't mean that they had now embraced the demographic or security or cultural arguments advanced by the anti-refugee governments in Budapest, Bratislava, Prague or later Warsaw. Such views remained in the minority, identified as at best ungenerous and at worst racist, across the twenty-eight-member block. 'We either face this challenge together or we give up on facing it at all, with dire consequences for all,' said Frans Timmermans, the vice-president of the commission.[16]

In an adaptation of the existing Dublin procedures, migrants would still be required to request asylum in either the EU member country where they first arrived, or in the country in which they now live. 'If a country receives more than 150 per cent of its "fair share" of asylum seekers in a year – a level calculated on the basis of population and national income – then it triggers a system to redistribute claimants around Europe,' explained the *Financial Times*.[17] Alongside this proposal were less controversial suggestions to expand the EU database of fingerprints, EURODAC. EASO would be expanded to become the 'nerve centre' of the new EU asylum system, with 500 asylum experts available to be posted to any future refugee front lines. Finally, those countries – including Germany, Austria, Sweden, Denmark and Norway – that had introduced temporary border controls to cope with the sheer number of migrants arriving, were allowed to extend those controls for a further six months.

'The most sensible course of action for the EU would be to use this opportunity to find more lasting solutions to the migrant crisis,' wrote the *Financial Times*:

> The bloc needs to strengthen its external borders so as to manage new arrivals in the future. It should put in place measures to share out asylum seekers among member states. And if it is to stop the growing flow of migrants coming across the Mediterranean towards Italy, it needs to deepen relations with the countries of North Africa, strengthening their security and economic development.

*

189

In late May I heard from Bulgaria that a smuggler I had been trying to track down was finally willing to talk to me. It had been a long negotiation, through a network of contacts, up and down the River Danube. This was also a time of persistent reports of Bulgarian vigilantes taking the law into their own hands and catching and mistreating migrants, either those trying to enter the country from Turkey or leave it through Serbia.

The smuggler, let's call him Vlado, met me at the café outside the hotel I had chosen to stay in because of its reputation as a haunt for smugglers, overlooking the Lion's Bridge in Sofia. All around us migrants and refugees from Afghanistan, Pakistan, Iran, the Middle East and many African countries waited in small groups, studied the screen of their phones, or gazed forlornly into space. It was getting harder to get into Europe, and they were painfully aware that it would only get harder still. They were tortured by the thought that they had missed the boat. Their best hope was still people like Vlado.

We found a quieter bar, a few streets away, in a slightly more touristed area, to appear less conspicuous. He was younger than I expected, about twenty-eight, with the brash confidence of a film star, rather than a member of a criminal fraternity. I didn't record anything on tape but took copious notes.

He picked his clients up near the Turkish border, he explained, especially in the easternmost section, below the city of Burgas, where the fence was not yet complete. From there they were taken to Burgas, then from Burgas to Sofia. Why not avoid the capital? I asked, and stay close to the Danube, if you are taking them to the north-west of the country anyway. He shook his head. Because our organisations were created in Sofia, he explained. And there too, he and his men had their best contacts with the Bulgarian police.

In 2015, Vlado said, he earnt €200,000 in three months, transporting sixty to eighty refugees a day across Bulgaria, from the Turkish to the Serbian border. Half of that money went on paying off middlemen, his drivers, and the police. The other half went into his pocket. In 2015, 30,000 migrants registered with the authorities in Bulgaria, I knew. What did he think was the true number, who transited the country? He told me there were five or six other smuggling bands like his own, though his was the biggest. We calculated the numbers on the back of an envelope. That figure represented between a quarter and a half of those who actually crossed the country, he suggested. So somewhere between 60,000 and 120,000 people.

The convoys worked like this. The police knew they should always stop the first vehicle in the convoy. There was always just a driver in that one. The second vehicle was always waved through the police checkpoint. Then a third and final car followed the second, watching the back of the convoy, to make sure no rogue policemen, who hadn't been paid off, didn't try to interfere with the plan.

Who picks the migrants up on the far side of the border? I asked 'We have the honour,' he said, 'to be in contact with Serbian people who do this.'

As we stood up to leave, I handed him my map of north-west Bulgaria. He studied it carefully, then marked three small 'x's on it, along the border with Serbia, where he and his people normally took people across. 'But you won't find anyone there!' He laughed. 'If we're any good at our job!'

We drove to Vidin on the River Danube, a town which has seen more prosperous days but still possesses a certain riverside charm. And from there we followed our map, down to the Timok River, a tributary of the Danube which forms a small section of the border with Serbia. Vlado was right – all we found were fields of sunflowers, ankle deep. A wild quince tree, its fruit still small and hard, but full of promise. And a black mulberry, just ripe, a feast for the birds, and the children on this Bulgarian-Serbian frontier. In one clearing, near a village where he drew a small *x* on my map, I found the remains of fireplaces, biscuit wrappers, baby-wipes and cigarette butts – a place where groups of people whiled away the twilight, waiting for darkness to fall before they slipped away through the vineyards into Serbia.

In Vidin I went for a run along the river-shore, early one morning, and befriended Samet, the imam of the local mosque, pottering around in the beautiful rose gardens of his house of prayer. Built in 1801, when Bulgaria was still just a rosebush in the increasingly overgrown Ottoman garden, the mosque boasts a heart instead of a crescent moon on the peak of its minaret – the only one in the Muslim world with that distinction. The architect put the heart there, Samet explained, in honour of his parents. That word 'honour' again, I thought.

In honour of the architect and filial love, we flew our camera-drone around his mosque, above the tree tops. It filmed the Danube, stretching away like a silver ribbon below, and the city of Vidin, and beyond, the flat lands all the way to the Serbian border. We sent the delighted imam a copy of the film, a bird's eye view of his own corner of paradise – a God's eye view, I almost wrote.

Back in Sofia, I met Philip Gunev, the deputy interior minister. He confirmed many details of my smuggler's tale, including the extent of corruption in the police force. Even rather high up. He told one recent story of an officer found with €5,000 in his pocket. Polygraph tests – better-known as lie detectors – would soon be introduced in the police, he said, despite resistance from the police trade unions. Back in my hotel, I looked up the polygraph, and stumbled on this quotation: 'We discovered there were some Eastern Europeans who could defeat the polygraph at any time. Americans are not very good at it, because we are raised to tell the truth . . .' said Richard Helms, former director of the CIA. That could be bad news for the Bulgarian authorities.

Philip Gunev was rather relaxed about the numbers now passing through Bulgaria, compared to a year before: 50 to 100 a day, he estimated. That was the figure he supplied to the weekly video conference call with the interior ministers of other countries on the Balkan route. At that call, the other interior ministers and their representatives seemed relaxed about the numbers too. Only the Hungarians believed that it was necessary, or even possible, to reduce the number to zero.

Greece has a 1,000-kilometre land border with Bulgaria and Macedonia and Albania, and Bulgaria has an additional 300-kilometre border with Turkey. So it's natural that some people will manage to go through, it's impossible to seal the borders.

I don't think anyone is trying to really do this. Even the Hungarians realised that building a fence doesn't solve the problem. The fence is just one of the instruments to try to keep things in a manageable condition. It's an instrument which reduces the need for such a large number of border guards to control a very long border.

According to the weekly video conference meetings of the interior ministers and Frontex, he said, 200 to 400 migrants were currently reaching Austria each day. About half these came through the Balkan route, the other half up from Italy. Of these around fifty a day went through his country, from Turkey, he believed, and another hundred or more through Serbia from Greece. What that added up to was about a tenfold reduction in the numbers of just one year earlier.

Realistically it will be very difficult to bring the numbers any further down, because organised crime over the past several years now has developed significant networks.

We have so far constructed about 140 kilometres of border fence. This fence has helped us to reduce the number of officers we had to send from around the country to help the border guards on that Turkish border. But it's only an instrument! People can cut through or climb through or dig under fences. Fences are just another instrument to help control border areas.

CHAPTER ELEVEN

KEEP CALM AND THINK OF ENGLAND

> The decision is yours, but I would like you to know that Hungary is
> proud to stand with you as a member of the European Union.
> Viktor Orbán, paid advertisement in the *Daily Mail*, 21 June 2016[1]

The British people voted to leave the EU on Thursday 23 June 2016. The
result was clear by 4.30 Hungarian time on Friday morning. Viktor Orbán,
though known to be an early riser, didn't have much time to absorb the
shock before he was live on air on the Kossuth radio morning programme at
7.30. For once, he sounded genuinely shaken. A few days earlier he had
appealed to the people of Britain, through a full-page political advertisement in the *Daily Mail*, not to leave.

'The decision is yours, but I would like you to know that Hungary is
proud to stand with you as a member of the European Union,' Mr Orbán
wrote. The words were white capitals on a square blue background, rather
like the 'Keep calm' series appearing on coffee mugs, postcards and T-shirts
across Europe at that time. The dark blue square was superimposed on a
Hungarian tricolour, fluttering in the wind on a pale blue sky, through
which drifted large white unthreatening cumulus clouds. But his words, like
those of more moderate leaders across Europe, fell on the stony hearts of
the 17.4 million Britons who voted to leave. Hungary, like the other East
European countries, wanted Britain to stay in the EU, as a necessary counter-
weight to the federalist dreams of French, Belgian, German, Italian and
Scandinavian leaders. They liked the quirky British defence of their own

sovereignty, the mockery of the uniformity which 'the bureaucrats in Brussels' constantly seemed to be trying to impose – according to the British tabloids at least. Without Britain, Hungary was going to be a lot lonelier at the long EU table. And further down towards the end.

'The key issue . . . was immigration,' Mr Orbán said on public radio, as he struggled to explain to the people of Hungary what had happened in the Brexit vote.[2] He failed to add, however, that the word 'immigrants' in Britain means mostly East Europeans, and increasingly among them, the Hungarians. David Cameron had visited Hungary in January, in one of his last-ditch efforts to win concessions from EU countries to reduce immigration to the UK to below 100,000 a year, from the over 300,000 where it currently stood.

The key to that, he believed, was to reduce or eradicate benefits for fly-by-night East Europeans, including Hungarians, whom the *Daily Mail* and the *Daily Express* claimed were only drawn to the UK in the first place by the possibility of cheating the British state. That was pure rubbish, of course. Hundreds of thousands of hard-working Poles, Lithuanians, Hungarians and Romanians did work in Britain, often in jobs for which they were hopelessly overqualified, earning the minimum wage, living in overcrowded and often uncomfortable accommodation in order to pay off their debts or save for their future. And in doing so, they paid of lot of National Insurance contributions and taxes to the British state. But the British Conservative Party was driven by the United Kingdom Independence Party (UKIP) agenda. And now UKIP, a party that couldn't win a parliamentary election, had achieved all they ever wanted anyway – to drag my island kicking and screaming away from its European mother.

The shock in Britain about what the British had done with the vote was amplified across Europe. On the grim, industrial battlefields of eastern Ukraine, young men were dying for the right to fly the dark blue European flag from a pole in front of their local council offices. In Serbia, Bosnia and Macedonia, the hope of EU membership, perhaps as soon as 2020, was the main argument of ordinary people to restrain the block-headed nationalists who were eager to start new conflicts. With one country, Britain, now set to leave the EU, it seemed unlikely that it would ever expand again. Croatia would be the last allowed in. It was a dark day for young people who felt a budding European identity, alongside their national and other senses of belonging.

Geert Wilders disagreed. The leader of the Dutch Freedom Party was in an excellent mood when I met him, later on the morning of the Brexit result, in the hallway of the Gellért Hotel in Budapest.

'Britain is again in charge of its own country, and I congratulate the British people on their excellent choice,' he told me, as we sat at the end of the smart, old-fashioned café, and the waitresses tried to work out who this dashing young man (Wilders) was, with his almost comical quiff, and little posse of bodyguards. He was on a private visit to Budapest, he explained, because his wife is Hungarian. He watched with disdain as I constructed a makeshift tripod for my small digital camera out of a pile of trays and saucers. I came completely unprepared for this encounter and decided the plates would make a marginally more stable base than the hotel's excellent cheese scones.

The Netherlands would follow Britain out of the EU, Wilders predicted, provided he won the elections scheduled for early 2017, as opinion polls were suggesting. How soon could they leave? I asked. A referendum could be arranged 'within twelve months', he explained. Although it would not be binding under Dutch law, he was confident that such a plebiscite to leave would be irresistible. And that it would be followed soon after by a similar decision by France if Marine Le Pen and her Front National won the presidency.

> It is too late to reform the EU. The end of the European Union is just a matter of time, and not such a long time . . . The EU is more or less dead. It's just that a lot of politicians can't get used to that idea . . . We separatists did not kill it, they did it themselves, by making an economic project into a political project, and by ignoring the people.

What would he say to all those, like myself, who fear conflict in Europe without the EU?

> I would say, don't be afraid. It was not because we had no political body like the EU that it came to war in the past. It happened in the 1930s when certain countries lost democracy. That was the danger that was not

KEEP CALM AND THINK OF ENGLAND

tackled. I believe on the contrary that democracy needs the nation state. Democracy means you have a nation state, that you have an identity, that you rally around the national flag, that you have national sovereignty and that you have national decisions. And if all European countries had that, they would benefit from working with one another, when it comes to free trade, to economic cooperation, to fighting terrorism ... The problem is that we are not ruled by Thatchers, but by Camerons and Merkels and Ruttes, by people not fighting for their country but who are transferring away more sovereign rights, day in and day out.

As European countries reeled from the shock of the British referendum result, Slovakia prepared to take over the helm of the EU for six months from 1 July. Like Hungary, Slovakia was not a fan of refugees, even though very few had even tried to enter the country. In a nod to Austria, a small camp was allowed at Gabčikovo, in the shadow of the ugly hydroelectric project opened in 1992. It was to be for migrants waiting for their asylum claims to be considered in neighbouring Austria. But even here the government insisted that only Christians be hosted, not Muslims.

Slovakia, like Hungary, also launched a legal challenge to the September 2015 plan of the European Commission to redistribute refugees more fairly among EU member states. There was no sign yet of a verdict in those cases, and Slovakia had no intention of dropping that legal challenge to the body it was about to lead.

Speaking at a press conference with Jean-Claude Juncker in Bratislava, Prime Minister Robert Fico sounded somewhat conciliatory. A 'flexible' approach would be needed to migration, which would allow EU member states to make their own proposals. As the summer progressed, the word 'flexible' recurred more and more often in the communications of Visegrád Four leaders, leading up to the proclamation of 'flexible solidarity' at the summit in mid-October. Juncker and like-minded leaders dug in their heels and said member states had to abide by the EU treaties they had signed and could not cherry-pick between them. Fico, Orbán, Zeman and Tusk emphasised the need to shore up the borders of the European Fortress, rather than wasting precious time discussing how to redistribute those who had already got into the castle, when the gates were still ajar.

'My name is Rohullah Hassan, I'm from Kabul city, Afghanistan. And I'm a refugee in an illegal camp in Serbia.' I found the entrance to the makeshift camp at Horgoš, just on the Serbian side of the border with Hungary at Röszke, with some difficulty. First you have to cross the border on the old road to Horgoš. Then visit the little, first-floor police station, surrounded by pine trees, where friendly Serbian policemen and women check that the Interior Ministry in Belgrade has approved your visit. Then you drive in a big loop through the village of Horgoš, back onto the main Belgrade to Budapest motorway, and drive almost right up to the motorway border crossing. Then you do a U-turn of dubious legality, narrowly missing a red-and white-painted crash barrier, to get onto the motorway heading back towards Belgrade. But even before you reach the first bridge over the motorway, you turn onto the hard shoulder, and drive through a gap in the fence and turn right along a rough, sandy track, back towards the border. On your right, a line of trucks leaving Hungary. On your left, apple orchards and maize stripped bare while still unripe by hungry refugees from distant zones of war or hunger or dissent. Straight ahead, a jumble of bright tent tops, makeshift shelters made of branches and blankets, home to an ever-changing population of Afghans, Iranians and Africans. The Arabic speakers tended to make their way to another makeshift, illegal camp at Kelebia, 30 kilometres to the west – like this one, hunched up against the Hungarian border fence.

Rohullah was travelling with his wife and four children. He had crossed each border he had reached illegally until now, he told me. Into Iran, Turkey, Bulgaria and Serbia. He was grateful, he said, that Hungary was finally going to give his family a chance to cross its border legally – however long that took. The 'transit zone' at Röszke was a long line of fifty cabins, painted dark blue and topped with razor wire, to form this section of Hungary's border barrier. The difference was that at the eastern end of the zone, there was a steel turnstile, which reminded me of the entry point from Israel into Gaza. Once a day, at around ten in the morning, fifteen asylum seekers, fourteen from families and one single man, were allowed to enter through the turn-stile into the cabins. There, their asylum claims were registered. Families were then sent on to the refugee camps at either Bicske or Vámosszabadi.

The single men were normally kept in the cabins for a month, before it was decided whether or not they would be allowed to travel on.

On the Hungarian side everything happened slowly. No journalists were allowed inside the transit zones, but it was possible to watch through the fence. Occasionally, an official from OIN, stirred himself to get up off his chair and go into a cabin, casting a backward scowl at the journalist photographing him through the wire. When the two zones – one at Horgoš, the other at Kelebia – were set up in September 2015, OIN informed the UNHCR that they could process 100 asylum seekers a day. A go-slow process was clearly taking place, in which the government instructed the OIN to deal at a snail's pace with the applications, in order to avoid any impression that the asylum seekers might be welcome. But the sheer determination of people like Rohullah Hassan and his family won through in the end. They would wait forever, if need be, to move up the long list. And eventually they did get in. Like hundreds of thousands before them, they would then go through the charade of applying for asylum in a country where they do not want to be, and which would not accept them, even if they wanted to stay. Then they would quietly slip away across the border into Austria, and beyond. Before the fences got even thicker, and the natives even more hostile.

There were around 700 people living in the camp at Horgoš when I visited. The number had shot up since 4 July, when a new Hungarian law came into effect, allowing the police to immediately deport any migrant found within 8 kilometres of the fence. That was the rough distance between this section of the border fence and Route 55, which runs westwards from Szeged all the way to Baja on the Danube. But several people in the camp told me they had already been deported from deeper inside Hungary. A man from Eritrea said he had talked to fellow Africans who were picked up in Budapest, and pushed back through the fence, at night, when no one was watching.

The camp at Horgoš was rife with reports of Hungarian police violence when I visited. One young man said the police kicked him as he lay on the ground, not resisting arrest. And that as they were pushing him back through one of the gates in the fence, they squirted pepper spray in his eyes, to discourage him from ever trying to climb over the fence again. As such reports multiplied, the Hungarian Helsinki Committee, Human Rights Watch, Médecins Sans Frontières, and the Jesuit Refugee Service began to take testimony, backed up with medical and photographic evidence.[3]

Heavy bruises, in the shape of police batons, and dog bites, were especially frequent, though the dogs should have been muzzled. Frontex at that time had fifty-one officers deployed in the Balkans in their 'Flexible' mission, of whom three Austrian officers were on duty on the Hungarian-Serbian border, when a reporter from the French newspaper *Libération* stumbled across them. The role of Frontex on the Hungarian stage was 'awkward' the reporter suggested. Their code of conduct was to strictly respect the rights of migrants. Had they witnessed any interventions from the Hungarian side which failed to live up to that code, which Hungarian laws also insisted on, the French reporter wanted to know.

'We do not have the mandate to supervise the work of national border guards,' said Izabella Cooper, the Frontex spokesperson, in Warsaw. 'If an officer deployed by Frontex came across an asylum seeker, his task was simply to refer to the local police authorities.'

Momčilo Djurdjević, a Médecins Sans Frontières doctor, related first-hand evidence of excessive force used by Hungarian police against those who crossed the fence illegally:

> We have witnessed a lot of cases intentional trauma that can be related to excessive use of force. And from the testimonies that we collected from the refugees we have evidence that they have been mistreated in some way by the Hungarian police. And not only by the Hungarian police. We have also had people from other borders and other regions who were clearly the victims of mistreatment by the local authorities. Bruises, cuts, dog bites, police stick-shaped bruises on their bodies. I would stress, we have never witnessed the beatings live ourselves. We only have testimonies and medical evidence.

The Jesuit Refugee Service had posted pictures of the injuries he described. The Hungarian police rejected all accusations of using excessive force. Most of Momčilo's work here was primary health care.

> Medical needs here at Horgoš are closely related to the conditions people are in every day here, poor hygiene, poor diet, the sun, limited access to clean water. Most of the land is dry and sandy as you can see, and temperatures here can rise to sub-Saharan ones on some days. All of

that combined contributes to respiratory infections, diarrhoea and skin rashes. And, of course, a lot of people who make their journey even by foot all the way from Macedonia have all kinds of accidental trauma on their feet or on their bodies. So they are already exhausted when they reach this place, and as hygiene and basic shelter are really of such low quality, this all contributes to worsen their condition.

The other thing which angered Momčilo after nearly twelve months working with refugees, he said, was that the Hungarian authorities were to blame for this situation. Just two weeks earlier, there were only 200 refugees at Horgoš, he explained. Thanks to the Hungarian police crackdown, and the 8-kilometre rule, Horgoš was turning into a big bottleneck. There were now more than 800 people there. What would be the solution, if someone in power would be willing to listen to him, I asked.

There is a need for some kind of unified strategy between different countries on this route, some kind of agreement that will increase the quality of the people at this site and give some kind of information. Because the mental situation, the psychology of these people is very tense now. They are extremely anxious, when can they leave, what's going to happen, is the border going to open, or not. With these increased push-backs, a lot of rumours are spreading, and they are getting more anxious and desperate.

What does Momčilo say to those in Europe, especially in Hungary, who think that most of those coming are economic migrants, not genuine refugees? 'It is very hard to prove if someone is actually an economic migrant. From my perspective as a doctor, those I treat are mostly families, the very young and older people, with chronic diseases. And a lot of them, the vast majority are coming from war-torn countries.' As he had been working with the refugees for nearly a year, since September 2015, I asked him what had changed.

The main change since last September has been in the numbers. But as the number of refugees decreased, their vulnerability increased. When large numbers passed swiftly through Serbia, bus transportation was available. Now a lot of people are here for a month or more. In these conditions, more people get ill.

One kindness from the Hungarian side which made a great difference to the refugees trapped at Horgoš, especially in the baking July heat with temperatures reaching as high as 37 degrees Celsius, was the provision of clean running water. A single pipe ran from one of the blue cabins of the transit zone, leading to two taps. All day women and children filled bowls and water bottles here. Men and women washed their hair, and children played. The two taps remained legally on Hungarian territory, as the white posts showed. The first 2 metres inside the camp were Hungarian soil. The refugees, under the 1951 Refugee Convention, had only to stand there, in the pool of mud spreading beside the taps, and call across to the other side to claim asylum.

Along the top of the cabins, police and soldiers patrolled. Life must have become excruciatingly boring for them, after 4 July, with so few migrants to catch. Only a few dozen attempted to get through the 175-kilometre long fence each night. They faced an army of up to 10,000 police and soldiers.[4] While on the Hungarian side I had the impression of a whole countryside mobilised for a war against illegal migration, on the Serbian side police patrolled occasionally in old Lada Nivas, rather like those used by László Toroczkai's 'field rangers' in Ásotthalom. The Serbian police appeared to want a quiet life, and probably didn't have enough diesel money to waste too much time looking for refugees.

In the camp at Horgoš, some refugees were heating up tins of tuna on their fires, others roasted sweetcorn they had picked from neighbouring fields or bought in the shop in Horgoš. Everywhere tea was being brewed in blackened tin or enamel mugs. Wherever I went, I was welcomed, and invited into the tent encampment – an open area between the tents where mats had been laid out, and blankets or pieces of awning strung up between poles of acacia, cut from the bushes nearby to create a bit of shade. Visitors carefully removed their shoes before entering and sat cross-legged. Some listened to music on radios or phones to while away the time. Many people had Indian-made chargers, which looked like giant egg-timers or small drums, to generate enough energy to charge a phone or a dim light against the evening dark.

'We need safer areas, more food, and more toilets,' Rohullah explained. Sometimes the Serbian police prevented them from walking the 3 or 4 kilo-metres to the market in Horgoš. They felt trapped here, between two countries, on the long journey to Europe.

I went to see a small pond near the encampment where, three days before I came to Horgoš, a small Afghan boy of seven or eight years old drowned. It was overgrown with reeds, and even after the tragedy, several children were playing there in the treacherous mud, with no adults to look after them. The dead child's mother was pointed out to me, walking past in deep conversation with a UNHCR official. The UN agency was trying to negotiate with the local authorities for the child to be buried in a village cemetery. The mother was insisting that she would like to take his body with her, into Hungary. In the meantime, her son lay in the morgue in Subotica.

Sitting on the white-painted border-stone I met Heydels Mohammed, aged seventeen, from Somalia. He wore a clean white T-shirt, and his curly hair was dyed yellow along the top. He had been here five days, and, like any teenager, was getting impatient. His name was on the list to enter Hungary, he said, but as a single male travelling alone his chances of getting in anytime soon were very low.

> I don't know what to do now. I don't want to do anything illegal, because if I cross the fence the Hungarian soldiers will beat me, and make pepper spray, so it's dangerous.
>
> My father died in Somalia. My mother and sister and brother are still there. There are too many problems. With Al-Shabab, with Al-Qaida, with the government. If you work for the government, Al-Shabab kills you, if you join Al-Shabab, the government kills you![5]

Somalia, like Congo, gained independence in 1960, the year I was born, and has had rough years of alternating drought, civil war and foreign invasions ever since. In 2006 radical Islamists known as the Islamic Courts Union seized much of central and southern Somalia, including the capital Mogadishu, and declared Shariah law. Ethiopian troops invaded, and in January 2007 the Islamists lost the town. In the meantime, a radical offshoot of the movement, known as Al-Shabab ('the youth') was formed. (The

Taliban means 'the students' in Pashtu). Between 2010 and 2012, 260,000 people are estimated to have died in the famine in Somalia.

Kenyan forces first entered Somalia to fight Al-Shabab in 2011. Al-Shabab merged with Al-Qaeda in 2012. While Al-Shabab have to a great extent been suppressed militarily, the group still launches regular attacks across the border in Kenya, including a suicide attack in Nairobi which killed sixty in September 2013. In April 2017, 147 students were killed by Al-Shabab militants at Garissa University in northern Kenya. Christians were singled out and shot in cold blood.

In the open space in front of another tent, closer to the border fence I met Faisal, aged eighteen, from Afghanistan. He was travelling with his mother and father, four sisters, and another couple with two children:

> We had a hard way from Greece to here, it was so hard to cross Macedonia because there are so many police there. We tried to cross four or five times but each time we were caught and the police took us back to Greece. On the sixth attempt we made it. A smuggler in Belgrade said he could get us into Hungary illegally, but my father turned him down. We just want to be patient.

They had been camping at Horgoš for fifteen days.

> Today I asked a Hungarian soldier, in English, through the fence, why don't you allow refugees to pass? He said that the European Union, Germany, and other countries asked them to close the border. I told him there are good and bad people everywhere. How do I know you are a good person? he asked. I will be patient and prove to you I am a good person, I told him. He wished me good luck!

The previous day, a fire had broken out at the camp, which threatened to get out of hand. It could have been an accident, but in the dry, parched grass, many suspected it was started deliberately. The refugees beat it out themselves with branches.

Both here and at Kelebia, informal lists were drawn up by leaders chosen by the refugees at each camp. These were handed or emailed to the Hungarian immigration authorities, with the mediation of the Serbian Commissariat for Refugees.

From Horgoš I drove east through Subotica to Sombor, another formerly Hungarian town, close to the River Danube in the north-west corner of Serbia. I had received a tip-off that on one recent Saturday evening eighteen taxis full of refugees drove to the Hungarian border in a convoy, and somehow managed to cross. Aid workers had told me that they believed smugglers were active in the camp at Horgoš, but everyone I asked there denied this. They said they had met smugglers often, but that trips were organised from Belgrade. It would be logical to avoid the too well-known Röszke–Horgoš–Kelebia–Tompa crossing points, and funnel people quietly through at a place where fewer police were watching and where journalists rarely trod.

In Sombor, the fact that refugees were smuggled across the border from here into Hungary was an open secret. Certain local organised crime bosses, known to the police but too powerful to touch, had switched to migrant-trafficking from drugs, I was told, because there was more money in it. One of the routes taken, was between the small Serbian village of Rastina (Hadikfalva) and the Hungarian village of Bácsszentgyörgy. The police on both sides of the border were involved in the business, my source said.

As the sun set to my left, I drove the straight road between fields of tall maize, freshly harvested wheat, and sunflowers taller than a man, anxious to reach Rastina before dark. In Rastina men sitting at an outdoor bar watched my car crawling past with interest. At the end of the road, where a track led to the Hungarian fence, a Serbian police car was parked. I turned right along Radomir Putnik street until it petered out, at the foot of a small hill with an old, Cold War era watchtower on the top. General Putnik was Chief of the Serbian General Staff in the First World War, and the Balkan wars which preceded it.[6] He gave the order for the final, desperate retreat of his army through the mountains of Montenegro and Albania in the winter of 1916. Seriously ill and exhausted, he had to be carried in a chair through the treacherous mountain passes. He survived the journey but died the following year in France.

The hill gave a perfect vantage point to survey the fence, stretching as far as the eye could see across the low rolling hills, in the last light of a balmy summer evening. Two men were planting something in the rich black soil near the border. There was a row of blue, green and brown painted beehives almost touching the fence. Through the coils of razor wire, the Hungarian policemen patrolling the fence in pairs on the far side were clearly visible. There was also what looked like an army tent on the Hungarian side, and a ruined house with its roof caved in on the Serbian side. The pale-yellow Catholic church in Bácsszentgyörgy was clearly visible across the fields.

I slept in Sombor and crossed the next day to Hungary, for a closer look. The road crossing from Bezdan towards Baja was relaxed. The Serbian police officers seemed bored, the Hungarians eager. There was also a lot of military activity on the Hungarian side, soldiers were climbing down from a lorry, replacing the overnight patrol. I drove north, then turned right at Csatálja. On the wall of the primary school, a fresco painted in 1930 showed a young man dressed all in white, his left hand lightly touching a curling Hungarian flag, held by a soldier in modern uniform, while he held out his right hand in benediction to a group of children and their mother. The front child held up the coat of arms of Hungary towards him. The scene took place beneath the spreading arms of an ancient tree. In the background was a church with twin towers, and to the right a man in ancient headdress and tunic, holding two horses. On closer inspection, the long haired, saintly youth had a halo around his head. It must have been St Stephen, the king who founded modern Hungary in the year 1000, the man responsible for converting the Hungarians to Christianity. According to the village website, this Bácska region was ravaged by war and illness during the century and a half of Ottoman occupation from 1541 to 1686. In the eight-eenth century it was reinhabited by German Swabians, encouraged by the Austrian Empress Maria Theresa to migrate to Hungary to repopulate the country. They arrived in their long wooden boats down the Danube from Ulm.

On the village war memorial were the names of the 86 men from this village who fell in the First World War, and the 138 who fell in the Second.[7] By 1941 the village only had six Jews, who were deported with 20,000 others from the wider region in June 1944 to be killed in Auschwitz. Almost the whole village, 2,200 Germans, were forced to leave in 1946–7, in the wave of expulsions after the Second World War. They emigrated to West Germany. Their places were taken partly by Hungarian Szeklers from Bukovina, deep inside Romania, and partly by Hungarians forced to leave their homes in southern Bácska, when it reverted to Yugoslav control.

On the outskirts of Bácsszentgyörgy the road led directly towards Rastina on the Serbian side. The tump with the watchtower where I had stood the previous evening was clearly visible. The road was blocked by the fence, and a group of soldiers in camouflage uniform watched my approach suspiciously. There was also an old stone cross with the figure of Christ spreadeagled in agony across it, his face turned towards the fence, as though he was looking at it, and a bowed figure of Mary at the base. A field of tall sunflowers, their heads bowed like a congregation at prayer, stretched all the way to the church.

The officer in charge asked me politely to leave, as this was an area of security operations. I asked if I could take pictures. Only back into Hungary, he said. Surely I could take pictures of Christ on the Cross. No way. I tried to make idle conversation and he softened a little. A tiny, brightly feathered bee-eater flew constantly in and out of Hungary, to a steep sandy bank on one side of the blocked road on the Hungarian side, where it disappeared into a labyrinth of holes. The officer confided that this was one of the few pleasures of his job, watching this particular bird crossing the border he was supposed to be defending. I remembered Viktor Orbán's comment that not even a bird could enter Hungary now without permission.

In the village shop I bought a bottle of water and struck up a conversation with the proprietor. He told me that you could see migrants every day on the streets of the village, who had somehow crossed the fence, and that 'locals' were also involved in the business. He spoke disparagingly of Muslims, and Islam in general.

Outside the church the legend of St Dominic was recorded. It tells how a heretic challenged him to an ordeal of fire. Each wrote down their faith on paper, and threw it, one after the other onto the fire. The heretic's words were reduced immediately to ashes, while those of St Dominic remained un-singed, not once, but twice, when they repeated the experiment. Outside the shop, a cardboard cut-out of a policeman, Rudolf Sipos, held open a range of recruiting leaflets.

Back in Subotica, I bought five pairs of shoes for Faisal and his brothers and sisters. They wrote their sizes down in the back of my notebook. Their own footwear had worn out on the long journey from Afghanistan. I also bought notebooks and crayons for the children, and coffee, tea and dates. They were rather surprised, and very happy to see me again. The shoes were more or less the right sizes.

Almost as soon as I arrived at the camp, a big Serbian Red Cross Mitsubishi turned up, to hand out bread. A long queue formed. Away from the queue, a woman in a yellow and white dress, purple headscarf and pink flip-flops started sobbing, stumbling towards the transit zone. She sat down on the ground beside the steel turnstiles. Other women gathered around her, trying to calm her down. Her patience had snapped. Soon the camp 'commander', a pleasant twenty-five-year-old Afghan doctor arrived, and eventually succeeded in soothing her. Her companions led her back to her tent, still sobbing.

Saboor Nadem, twenty-five, was a radio and TV journalist from the Ghur region of Afghanistan. He also worked as the secretary in the local library. The last straw was when both the Taliban and local government officials started ringing him and threatening his life if he didn't write stories favourable to them. 'I cannot do that, I am not allowed as a journalist to favour either side,' he told them. He moved his mother and sister to Herat, then set out for Europe. He had heard from friends who had made the journey before him that he could live and work in safety here. He crossed the Aegean to the island of Lesbos in a small rubber dinghy on 28 February, just days before the Turkey–EU agreement came into force. From Athens, he paid a smuggler €2,500 to get him as far as Serbia. 'I do not like them, but we cannot get anywhere without them.' The journey had been far harder than he imagined. Once he rang his mother and asked her if he should return. She wept on the phone, and pleaded with him not to, because he would surely be killed.

Now the smuggler was ringing again, offering to get him to the place above all where he would like to go – the United Kingdom. But it would cost another €2,500, he was told – through Italy, Switzerland, Denmark and Norway. Just to Germany from Horgoš would cost him €1,500.

For now at least, he wanted to try the legal way, on the long waiting list into Hungary. If he could just make it to Budapest, he would simply take the train.

The back of the dark blue transit zone faced the camp. A yellowing poster from the Hungarian Red Cross decorated one of the panels: I am looking for my . . . brother, son, family, mother, husband. Each of the sixteen photographs was accompanied by a number, not a name. So many people lost or mislaid or separated on the long journey to Europe.[8]

*

On Friday, 15 July, the Turkish president Recep Tayyip Erdoğan was on holiday with his family in the coastal resort of Marmaris. At about five thirty in the afternoon, his brother-in-law rang from Istanbul, slightly perturbed. Why were all those tanks blocking the Bosphorus bridges? Presumably it was just an exercise?[9]

Erdoğan rang his intelligence chief, just to check. No reply. Then he rang the chief-of-staff of the armed forces. No reply. Only then did he begin to panic. Later that evening, soldiers loyal to the coup plotters descended from helicopters by rope onto his hotel. He had already left. He asked his pilot to fly him to Ankara. His bodyguard convinced him Istanbul was a better idea, because he had been mayor there for a long time and could be sure of greater loyalty.

Erdoğan accepted that advice. On the flight to Istanbul, an F16 fighter from the plotters' airbase at Akinci, north-west of Ankara locked onto Erdoğan's plane. Whoever on the plane was supposed to pull the trigger, changed his mind, and Erdoğan survived. The Turkish president then went live on CNN-Turk, via the FaceTime app on the stunned reporter's phone, to tell the nation he was still in charge. Erdoğan also appealed to loyal Muslims to gather at their local mosques to defend the legally elected government. Troops hesitated, then sided with the regime, against the plotters. By three in the morning, Erdoğan was back in full control, and mass retribution began against those who had been so bold as to try to overthrow him.

The airports of Istanbul and Ankara were closed from Friday evening to early Sunday morning. I reached Sofia on Saturday evening, then flew in with a small BBC team on one of the first flights. President Erdoğan had survived assassination and the overthrow of his thirteen-year-old government by a whisker. Even liberal friends of mine in Turkey, sworn opponents of Erdoğan, were relieved. If the coup had succeeded, they told me, 'there would have been a civil war here'.

A week later, a forty-page, de-encrypted translation of the discussions between the coup plotters on their own WhatsApp group showed just how close they had come to toppling the government, and how ruthlessly. I stayed for two weeks in Turkey, partly in Ankara, mostly in Istanbul, reporting on the daily outpouring of joy and indignation by supporters of Erdoğan's AK Party (Justice and Development party). Governments around Europe and in North America were a little slow to congratulate Erdoğan on his remarkable survival. And quick to condemn him for the crackdown which followed.

One of the key questions on many minds was: how would the failed putsch and its aftermath affect the conflict in Syria and Iraq? How would it affect Turkey's conflict with the Kurds, and their aspirations to finally carve out an independent Kurdistan, including segments of Turkey, Iraq, Syria and Iran? And above all, for the purposes of this book, how would it affect the EU–Turkey deal on slowing the flow of refugees to Europe?

Milat was twenty, from Afghanistan. He had been in Istanbul for nearly six months, trapped by the EU–Turkey agreement. Like most other Afghans in Turkey who reach Istanbul, he had gravitated to the Zeytinburnu district. Zeytinburnu, which means 'the cape of olive trees', slopes steeply down towards the sea, its main street decorated with shops and banks and restaurants, tailing off at the bottom in a sprawl of new building around the unfinished motorway out to the airport. Beyond that was the park, with its tall poplar trees and weekend crowds. When Milat's money ran out he moved down the hill to live in the park. As military jets screamed overhead on the fateful Friday night, he and his friends huddled under the flyover. The town was rife with rumours that a curfew was coming into force, and all foreigners would be caught and deported. One of his friends, sitting on the grass nearby, listening to our conversation, said he was afraid that the war they had escaped in Afghanistan was now following them here. All expressed relief that the coup had failed. They also spoke of their gratitude to Turkey, and to Erdoğan personally, for 'tolerating' their presence in the country. But also of their frustration that they remained invisible and illegal here, with no official recognition of their plight. Syrians were the 'first-class' refugees, they said. Afghans came a poor second on the refugee ladder.

Mohammed, nineteen, from Panshir province agreed. 'There are lots of problems in Afghanistan, that's why we are here. Neither the government nor the UN care about us.' 'There was a family living here under the bridge, and one of them was very ill. No one could help. Without a residence card, the doctors will not treat you. Finally another Afghan took him to hospital.' Most likely the stranger paid for the treatment from his own pocket. Likewise, without a residence card, they were not allowed to work.

Why don't they just carry on to Europe? I asked, hearing Viktor Orbán curse me over my shoulder as I spoke.

The sea route is closed. We can get to the Bulgarian border easily. The Turkish police let us go. But we know we will be caught three, four, five times by the Bulgarian police, and thrown back. And each time we will be beaten. Maybe the fifth time we will get through. We will pay all our money to the smugglers, who will also abuse us. Then we will be caught and beaten many more times by the police in other countries. Only the bravest young men attempt this. Instead we will wait here, hoping that Europe will open its borders again.

Mustafa from Kabul had already reached Bulgaria twice. 'We crossed the border and spent five days hiding in the jungle. Then the police caught us. They were very rough with us. They hit us, then put us in prison for a month. Some days there was no food at all.' He had decided not to try again through Bulgaria. 'I might die on the way.' He too had decided to stay in Istanbul and 'wait for Europe to open the gates again'. I didn't have the heart to tell him that Europe never would.

A small boy, perhaps ten years old, in a pale grey tunic, was weaving his way through the weekend crowds in the park beside the Marmara Sea. Freight ships lay lazily at anchor offshore, waiting for their place in the long line of marine traffic down the Bosphorus to the Black Sea. Bold young men swam off the rocks, perhaps toughening themselves up for the long hard trek ahead through the Balkans. Local Turks and Afghans, to my untrained eye almost indistinguishable from each other, fanned little fires into life, to cook their food. There was the smell of meat cooking, and smoke drifting across the afternoon. On one side of the park a ring of onlookers formed around two men wrestling. A little girl on a tricycle rode past, flying a cluster of pink balloons above her, like candy-floss.

The boy was called Yunus, and had the sweetest, most innocent smile. His tunic was clean and ironed, and he carried in his hands a green plastic basket covered with a cloth. He could recognise the Afghans in the park easily, he said. He wove from one cluster to the next, selling the flatbreads for one Turkish lira apiece, which his mother made every night. Would he take me to her? Yes, but only when his entire pile of breads was sold, and he had only just begun.

We walked up into Zeytinburnu. Mohammed Zaman was living in a two-room apartment with his daughter-in-law, her two sons, and Mohammed's four nephews. He was separated at the Iranian-Turkish border from his wife and four other sons when the Iranian police opened fire on them. Half the family made it across the border and got as far as Munich, while he and the others were forced back. Initially they went back all the way to Afghanistan. Now they were trying to reach Germany again – but the EU–Turkish deal had blocked their way. He had run out of money, and the landlord was threatening to evict them. He was turning to one relative after another – in Afghanistan – to ask if they could send him money. He was a plain-clothes policeman at home, and was threatened by the Taliban for that reason, he said.

'My wife is sick in Germany in hospital. The children have been given a flat to live in, but she is sick with worry. We feel as if a kind of Berlin Wall separates us from the rest of our family.'

I asked about attacks in Germany in which fellow Afghans had been implicated. How did he feel towards the perpetrators?

'There are good and bad people everywhere. People who carry out such attacks have no sense of humanity, of compassion. And they create such a big problem for people like us. For the refugees.'

Perhaps they were not really Afghans, he added. Some of the Pakistanis and Iranians who have gone to Germany registered as Afghans, because they thought that would increase their chances of getting asylum. 'You can buy fake documents very cheaply in Afghanistan, and unfortunately the Germans don't check these as well as they should ... Long ago when I was young, British, German and American tourists came to our country. They cherished our hospitality. We are not bad people. But politics destroyed all this.'

Mujeeb was twenty-six, recently married, and working in an Afghan restaurant in Zeytinburnu. He came here not as a refugee, but to work. The restaurant was run by his wife's uncle. His plan was to stay in Turkey and raise his family. I asked him about the Afghan flags waved at rallies in support of the president, since the failed coup.

President Erdoğan is very famous in Afghanistan for two reasons. First, we are actually the same race and speak similar languages, Uzbek and Turkmen. Second, some support him because they regard him as a very good Muslim, because of the solidarity he expresses for his fellow Muslims. They say he is the best, or even the only good Muslim leader in the world.

CHAPTER TWELVE

THE WOMEN OF ADAŠEVCI

People who have just economic problems don't want to come any more, but those who have political or security problems are moving, they have no other choice. No one wants to leave their own homeland without any reason.

Ali Sadat, Afghan refugee

This crisis is a test of our common humanity – whether we give in to suspicion and fear and build walls, or whether we see ourselves in one another.

Barack Obama, UN Summit on Refugees, September 2016[1]

The Adaševci refugee camp sits awkwardly in a motorway service station on the Belgrade to Zagreb highway, just before the Croatian border. On the far side of the motorway, underneath a MOL petrol sign, a board reads: Preševo 480 kilometres. Most refugees in Serbia crossed from Macedonia near Preševo. The refugee camp in Preševo, on the site of a former tobacco factory, is where they first claim asylum in Serbia. The sign is a reminder of how far they have come and how far they still have to go. For now, they are stuck in Serbia, up to ten thousand of them in thirteen camps or sleeping rough, stopped or delayed in their tracks by the Hungarian fence.[2]

Men and women asylum seekers milled around in front of the former motel, now the central building of the camp, under a sky of dark grey clouds, threatening rain. Only a hundred metres away, long-distance motorists filled up their fuel tanks, and dawdled over a coffee and a pastry, a punctuation mark on their own, easier journeys. Few refugees had the money to buy anything there.

Katan, a middle-aged Yazidi woman from Iraq, sat with her three children on a bunk bed in a giant white UNHCR tent, just behind the main building. She was ill, with asthma and high blood pressure. They were on their way to Germany, she explained, to join up with her husband who went ahead of them. Other Yazidi women helped them get this far. I imagined how hard it was for this woman, who could only walk slowly and painfully, to make the long trek across the Turkish-Bulgarian border, dodging Turkish and Bulgarian police, and Bulgarian vigilantes. I asked if I could take her photograph – she refused, shyly, ashamed of her appearance, of the lines of worry etched onto her face, of her charity clothes. 'Please, photograph my children, but not me.' So her children sat on the triple bunk bed, with green metal frames and grey blankets, to gaze into my camera. Neither of the boys smiled. They looked with big brown eyes full of hope deep into my lens. The boy on the right clutched a toy jeep. The little girl wore a grey stripy sweatshirt with the number 32 in stars, and a white skirt with pink blobs over her red trousers. They posed again for me in the doorway of the tent, as the rain started to fall heavily again. More children joined them, and the visit of this stranger started to get more fun, so they began to smile. In the background, their mothers or older sisters appeared, clutching mineral water bottles or mobile phones.

In the dining room in the main building there was a great hubbub of Arabic, Persian and other languages. The main subject of conversation was the suicide of a young Afghan man the day before. Only twenty-one, he hanged himself in the woods on the far side of the motorway, because he couldn't bear the months of waiting for the chance to enter Hungary legally, through the transit zones.

On the walls of the dining room were twenty sheets of names, followed by nationality, language and the number of children travelling with them, if any. Twenty-five names on each, 500 adults, plus children – the current population of Adaševci. This was also my first glimpse of the lists of people waiting to enter the Hungarian transit zones. Single men had to wait longest, many months. The most vulnerable women and children should wait the shortest time. But this was not an exact science. The lists were torn, and barely legible in places. Sometimes a nationality or a language was crossed out, or replaced by another. The lists gave the impression of a long queue of people, all jostling to move forwards, some overtaking others, others getting left behind. A young Somali man let me take his photograph in front of the lists. Then he ran his finger up and down the rows in vain. He could not find his own name.

I had heard that many women and children were travelling the Balkan route alone, and I wanted to know why. Zahra Husainy was in her late twenties, a handsome, dignified, determined woman from the Hazara tribe in Afghanistan. She was born in exile in Iran and married a fellow Afghan there. Her husband then ran away with another woman to Europe, in 2015. His family demanded that she and the children move in with them. She refused, borrowed money from her own parents, and set out to Europe with the children, a girl aged thirteen and a boy aged four. As she talked, in a relatively comfortable room upstairs in the ex-motel, her son and I rolled a ball to and fro across the floor.

'When we started the journey we were alone, but on the route good people accompanied us. In the boat from Turkey to Greece we fell into the sea, but were rescued from the water. The second time we tried to cross, we succeeded.' The family spent four months in Greece, received more money from her parents, then carried on north.

The worst part of the journey was crossing from Greece to Macedonia, she said. They had to walk and run through the woods for sixteen hours, as the Afghan smugglers acting as their guides threatened to hit them if they did not go faster. 'We will beat you all the way to Serbia,' they told her. Her daughter was ill and she herself was fainting with hunger. They lost their last possessions, the few things they had managed to keep with them all the way from Iran, on the railway track in Macedonia. They came the rest of the way with nothing but the clothes on their backs.

She did not want to talk about sexual violence. Two single men had travelled the last part of the way with her to Serbia. Originally they seemed kind and helpful, she said, but now they were threatening her. They wanted her to tell the Hungarian authorities that they were her relatives. She refused, but they had somehow managed to get their names on the list next to hers. She told the Serbian authorities. They told her that they could do nothing, but she should tell the Hungarian authorities when she reached the transit zone. If she did, the men threatened to harm her and her children. They had already beaten her, and pulled her hair, she said. She was desperate. There were many similar stories. The Hungarian fence was turning northern Serbia into a pressure cooker, where the refugees fought each other for a place in the queue. Refugees also tried to bribe the Serbian authorities to move their names up the list. I heard many allegations that the bribes were both solicited and accepted.

Because single men had to wait so long to get a place in the Hungarian transit zone, they tried to persuade, or force women and children to pretend they were family members, in order to get into Hungary quicker. What were her plans when she reached Germany, I asked. Would she try to find her ex-husband, the father of her children? 'I don't know anybody in Germany,' she said. 'I have no more contact with him because he had bad relations with another lady.'

Ali Sadat, an Afghan refugee confirmed her story. Why didn't people travel with smugglers through Croatia, as the camp was so close to the Croatian, rather than the Hungarian border? I asked. Some did, he confirmed, but 'every day the borders are getting harder to cross. The fences are not the problem, the problem is the dogs and the police who turn their dogs on you.' In his experience, the Bulgarian and the Hungarian police were the worst.

Ali spoke Arabic, English, Urdu, Hindi, Pashtu, Farsi and Russian – some of which he had learnt on the journey – 'the refugee trail is a great university!' He laughed. Because of his language skills, he was much in demand by the Serbian Refugee Secretariat, and the NGOs and charities in the camp. With his cheerful manner and boundless energy, he was also popular with the other refugees. Using UN blankets, he built a rough volleyball court to help fill the empty hours in the camp.

Ali was travelling with his four sisters, and had come from Greece through Albania and Kosovo – the first refugee I had met who used that route. The mountains of Albania were the only place on the route where he regretted ever starting his journey. They walked in a group of fifteen people, without a guide, following the maps on his mobile phone. Others who tried to cross Albania were not so lucky, he said; some ended up in prison for six months.

Why were so many women on the journey pregnant? I asked. 'Many get pregnant before they set out, because they think that if their children are born in Europe, the family will have more chance to stay,' he said. But the long delays at country after country and the hardships of the journey meant many women gave birth on the way, often in poor conditions. 'It's not fair that some countries opened the route then closed it again, because many people were encouraged to set out.'

The message of just how hard the route had become was getting back. 'People who have just economic problems don't want to come any more, but those who have political or security problems are moving, they have no other choice. No one wants to leave their own homeland without any reason.' On the screen above his head in the crowded dining area, Arsenal were leading Hull one-nil.

Outside, I met Fasal Amin, a young Afghan who had already reached Germany successfully once. There, he found out that his wife, parents, and three children had all been killed by a roadside bomb near Kabul. The German authorities gave him the €700 he needed for the flight back. He spent a month there, buried his loved ones, then set out for Germany again, distraught and deeply traumatised. There was nothing, and no one left for him in his own country. He spoke sometimes loudly, waving his hands around, then suddenly quietly, almost a whisper against the buzz of trucks, passing on the highway. Could such a man ever be happy again, after all he had been through? Only adrenalin kept him going, and the constant roar of his own grief.

From Adaševci I went to the official refugee camp or One Stop Centre in Subotica. At fifty-eight, Dalal Hasan was one of the older women I met on the route. She was travelling with her two grandchildren, aged seven and four, and her daughter-in-law, who was thirty. Her husband, a taxi driver, was killed in 2014 in an airstrike, trying to rescue other children who were injured in the street in Aleppo. They crossed the Evros River from Turkey to Greece in a small boat. She had set out with no money whatsoever. Other refugees paid the smugglers for them, she said.

'We are poor people from Syria. A simple and honest and good-hearted family. Everyone wants to help us.' The last straw which made them flee Aleppo was hunger. 'There was so much bombing. We were afraid of everything. We were sick and had no money to buy something to eat.'

Smugglers in Macedonia locked them in a room in the mountains, broke the windows, and threatened to kill them if each family did not produce more money. They refused them even water. They were so thirsty, their skin turned yellow, she said. When I had finished asking my questions, she said she wanted to tell me something. She wanted, through me, to thank all the people around the world who help the poor people who have no land, and no country now, she said.

I walked her back to the room where she slept. Babies were crying, refugees were treading silently on still-wet concrete. Rita Belić, the camp doctor, said she had attended the births of three babies at Adaševci. Dalal Hasan was wearing the pink, plastic sandals she received from volunteers in Belgrade. She had lost the shoes she had come all the way from Aleppo in.

At Kelebia, Gordana worked for Care International, helping refugees on their way to Hungary at a small roadside camp. She was a Serbian refugee herself – from Croatia – kicked out of her own home by the Croatian military in the summer of 1995. Many of the volunteers in Serbia were refugees like her, she said. They understood what it was like.[3]

The NGOs in Kelebia rented a small patch of ground, to provide a safe play area for children, a distribution point for food and tea and clothes to those living nearby, in a cluster of shacks beside the Hungarian fence, hoping to enter the transit zone into Hungary. Was the Balkan route now more or less over? I asked.

People in need are like water. They will always find ways forward. Fences cannot stop them, but they can reduce their numbers. This will stop only if there is an end to the wars in their countries. People always look for a way to survive, and there will always be people who keep trying.

The children give their mothers the energy to try. Women will fight for their children's sake. They don't need to eat, they don't need to sleep, so long as they feel they are taking their children to a place where they will be safe, where they might even be able to go to school.

*

After the British referendum in June, a second European plebiscite loomed in October 2016 – the anti-quota referendum in Hungary.

Do you want the European Union to be able to mandate the obligatory resettlement of non-Hungarian citizens into Hungary even without the approval of the National Assembly?

Like the questions included in the 'National Consultation' questionnaire in the spring of 2015, the referendum question was heavily loaded to favour the government's own interpretation.

It was not clear whether the European Commission still believed in the compulsory quota idea. Apart from Italy and Greece, the two countries which would have benefited from the relocation of asylum seekers, no EU country appeared very enthusiastic. By September 2016, only around 20,000 of the 100,000 supposed to be relocated had in fact arrived at their destination. Many countries were struggling to cope with the volume of people who had arrived uninvited. Nevertheless, the quota idea was a useful publicity weapon for the Hungarian government in its 'war' with Brussels. The government used it to maintain the public's worries about immigrants, even though relatively few had come through the country since the fences were erected on the Serbian and Croatian borders, and even fewer of them either wanted, or were considered eligible, to stay in Hungary.

From March to September 2016, giant roadside billboards, and television, radio and online advertisements rammed home the government's message. We have defended our front door, now the European Commission wants to smuggle illegal economic migrants into our country by the back door, they suggested. The campaign reached a particular intensity during the Rio Olympics in August. Short advertisements appeared on state television every half an hour, urging the public that it was their patriotic duty to take part in the referendum. There was also controversy over TV coverage of one of the swimming heats, where an eighteen-year-old Syrian swimmer, Yusra Mardini, one of the ten-member Refugee Team competing in the Olympics, came first. The TV commentator listed all the other names, except hers. He later said this was due to a technical fault and was not intentional. Yusra Mardini reached Germany in the summer of 2015. When the outboard motor on her overcrowded dinghy broke down in the Aegean, she and other refugees swam for three hours, to propel it to the shore of a Greek island.

Most opposition parties urged a boycott of the referendum, while the far-right Jobbik party offered lukewarm support. Only the satirical Twin-Tailed

Dog Party (TTDP) dared mock the government. Through crowd-funding, advertised on social media, the party raised €100,000. Their rival billboards and city light posters mocked the government's messages, in both style and content. There were twenty-seven versions, modelled on the government's '*Did you know . . .*' question. These included:

> *Did you know that there's a war in Syria?*
> *Did you know that the average Hungarian has seen more UFOs than migrants?*
> *Did you know that the main rivals of Hungarian athletes in the Rio Olympics were foreigners?*
> *Did you know that one million Hungarians want to emigrate to Europe?*

'We can't do anything about all the people who spend their days hating migrants,' TTDP leader Gergely Kovács told me, 'people who have probably seen more aliens from other planets in their lives than immigrants. What we can do is appeal to the millions in Hungary who are upset by the government campaign. We want them to know they are not alone.'

The government defended both its referendum, and the campaign. 'I don't believe that common sense can be called xenophobia,' said government spokesman Zoltán Kovács. 'People all over the EU sense that something wrong is happening with migration. What is happening is out of control. We need to regain our ability to reinforce law and order at the borders of the European Union.'

Polling agencies recorded a shift in public attitudes towards refugees and migrants. While there was a lot of sympathy towards refugees the previous summer, when many Hungarians had everyday experience of actually encountering them, the absence of migrants and the omnipresence of the government campaign swayed the hesitant.

'In September 2015 two-thirds of Hungarians we asked were in favour of helping the migrants, one year on two-thirds are against,' András Pulai, director of the Publicus Institute told me. 'In September 2016 only 21 per cent of those asked had any sympathy or solidarity towards them, and 78 per cent said they didn't want any refugees settled in Hungary – even those fleeing war or persecution.'

Gergely Kovács said such figures gave a wrong picture of the hard-heartedness of Hungarians: 'It's really important for us to show that Hungary and the Hungarian people are much more friendly and normal than you would imagine if you just see the government posters. There are millions here who don't agree with this campaign.' His party urged people not to boycott the vote, as some opposition parties did, but instead to spoil their ballots.

*

A series of high-level summits in September offered European and world leaders a chance to propose or repeat their visions of a solution to the refugee crisis. Slovakia took over the rotating presidency of the EU on 1 July. Like Viktor Orbán, Slovak prime minister Robert Fico was implacably opposed to accepting asylum seekers. EU leaders met in Bratislava in an atmosphere of strained politeness – and confusion over whether the quota idea was still alive.[4] The Hungarian government needed it to be, in order for their expensive referendum to still seem relevant. Other EU governments, including the Slovaks, were trying to sound more reasonable, and tone down the language of dispute.

Angela Merkel contributed to the search for more inclusive language by admitting that she had made mistakes in her handling of the refugee issue.[5] She told reporters that she would like to 'turn back the clock by many, many years, to better prepare [herself] and the whole government and all those in positions of responsibility for the situation that caught us unprepared in the late summer of 2015'. It was not the admission of so many people to Germany that was the mistake, nor the absence of a cap on numbers ever since, she explained, but the lack of preparation, and the lack of explanation to other countries – this she should have done differently, she said.

> The state of the EU in general and particularly the refugee crisis is not good at all. In Europe, we still don't have a common understanding to acknowl-edge the flight of so many people for what it actually is, a global and moral challenge . . . It weighs on me, too, that we haven't succeeded in that.

Her confession was provoked by another poor electoral result for her CDU, this time in her home state of Mecklenburg-Vorpommern. The SPD won comfortably, but the AfD came second, with the CDU slipping to third place – for the first time in its history. The main issue in the campaign was immigration, even though there were relatively few in Germany – 23,000 were accepted in 2015. The result was another warning to the German chancellor.

The Bratislava summit was the first official summit after the Brexit vote in June, at which EU leaders could spell out their vision of the future without Britain. In the warm-up, Viktor Orbán was characteristically blunt: 'The moment is now; a cultural counter-revolution is possible,' he announced in Krynica, a resort in the Carpathian mountains in southern Poland, where a regional economic gathering took place in early September.[6] 'People don't change, national and religious identity still have their place . . . There is no European identity that could replace them.'

Warming to his theme, he explained that the problem in Europe was now the arrogance and ideology of European elites. The elites had insisted that 'it wasn't modern to be a Pole, a Hungarian, a Czech, a Christian or other believer; they proposed a new identity – the European identity . . . but Britons have said "No", they want to be British.' The answer, Orbán and his friend Jaroslav Kaczynski, leader of the governing Law and Justice (PiS) party in Poland insisted, was a major overhaul of the EU to give national parliaments a stronger voice. Federalism should be abandoned. Kaczynski also laid into the 'hegemony' of Germany in EU affairs. The diversity of Europe was being wiped out by the rise of what he called 'pop culture, American culture'.

At the Bratislava summit, Orbán suggested that the answer was to put the waves of migrants in huge camps or 'hotspots' outside the EU, for example in Libya. In one of his traditional volte-faces, he also suddenly backed the idea of a European army – without explaining how this squared with his constant appeals to increase and defend national sovereignty. His vision of migration as primarily a security issue seemed to have persuaded him to change his mind. One task of the new army, he argued, would be to defend the outer borders of the EU. The conservative Luxembourg prime minister, Jean Asselborn, contributed to the warlike atmosphere by suggesting that Hungary be excluded from the EU, or at least have its membership suspended, for the government's 'disgraceful' conduct over the refugee crisis.

In the end, the final declaration in Bratislava, and the road-map for the future agreed there, was a compromise. The Visegrád countries arrived

THE ROAD BEFORE ME WEEPS

there with a declaration of their own, calling for 'flexible solidarity'. This would mean that those countries that do not accept the relocation of asylum seekers could contribute in other ways, for example by strengthening or patrolling the outer borders of the EU, or providing equipment. The 'potential and experience' of each country should be taken into account. The Visegrád proposal was broadly welcomed as constructive by former critics of the Visegrád countries, including Angela Merkel and Martin Schulz.

In the final document, the Visegrád countries won a growing commitment from the others to strengthen the outer borders of the EU. There should be no return to the chaos of the previous year, all agreed. There was also a commitment to strengthen consensus and solidarity among member states, after the terrible squabbles between them. A broader consensus would be needed on a long-term policy on immigration, 'including on how to apply the principles of responsibility and solidarity in the future'. The peoples of Europe needed to feel a greater sense of security.

The success of the summit created another problem for the Hungarian government. If 'the compulsory quota idea is now dead' as Slovak prime minister Robert Fico announced triumphantly, why were the Hungarians still holding a referendum to oppose it?[7]

On 19 September in New York, the United Nations General Assembly convened the first ever summit devoted to refugees and migrants.[8] There were an estimated 21.3 million refugees in the world: 84 per cent were temporarily sheltered in poor countries, only 16 per cent in rich ones. It was a statistic worthy of a giant roadside billboard in Hungary, but there was no one to pay for that one. Governments had been slow to respond to the increasingly desperate appeals by UN agencies for funding. Only 19 per cent of the target had been contributed to the UN appeal for South Sudan, 22 per cent to the appeal for Yemen, and 49 per cent to the appeal for Syria. Russia accepted no refugees for resettlement, and nor did the Gulf States, although many people from conflict-torn states worked there. Saudi Arabia said it had suspended the deportation of thousands of Syrians who had over-stayed their visas.[9]

Foreign Minister Péter Szijjártó attended the New York summit for Hungary and struck the usual defiant note.[10] He told the Assembly:

We have protected our borders so far and we will not allow mass violation of our borders in the future either. We have to make clear that in the meantime there are migratory polices all around the world which have failed. Migratory policies which consider all migrants as refugees have failed. Migratory policies which want to force countries to receive thousands of migrants against the will of their own citizens have failed.

US president Barack Obama's speech was rather different in content and tone:[11]

We are here because, right now, there are mothers separated from their children – like the woman in a camp in Greece, who held on to her family photographs, heard her children cry on the phone, and who said 'my breath is my children ... every day I am dying 10, 20, 30 times.' We're here because there are fathers who simply want to build a new life and provide for their families – like Refaai Hamo, from Syria, who lost his wife and daughter in the war, who we welcomed to America, and who says, 'I still think I have a chance to make a difference in the world.' [...]

If we were to turn refugees away simply because of their background or religion or, for example, because they are Muslim, then we would be reinforcing terrorist propaganda that nations like my own are somehow opposed to Islam, which is an ugly lie that must be rejected in all of our countries by upholding the values of pluralism and diversity. And finally, this crisis is a test of our common humanity – whether we give in to suspicion and fear and build walls, or whether we see ourselves in one another.

The New York Declaration for Refugees and Migrants was signed by representatives of all 193 countries present. The signatories agreed that 'protecting those who are forced to flee and supporting the countries that shelter them are shared international responsibilities that must be borne more equitably and predictably'.

The British charity Oxfam was disappointed.[12] 'The world had the chance to come up with a more humane approach, but for now governments gave us a half-hearted response. We cannot continue to accept it,' wrote Josephine Liebl an Oxfam official who specialises in Africa.

The most important result of the summit, was to task the UNHCR with developing a Global Compact for Refugees, and a separate Global Compact for Safe, Regular and Orderly Migration.[13] The first committees for both would meet in early 2018. The leaders of countries on the western Balkan route, plus Donald Tusk, Angela Merkel, Austrian chancellor Christian Kern and Hungary's Viktor Orbán met in Vienna for the final summit of the month on 24 September 2016.

'We need to confirm – politically and in practice – that the western Balkan route of irregular migration is closed for good,' said Tusk. Kern called for 'massive improvement' of the EU's external borders. Viktor Orbán went further, calling for the establishment of what he called 'a giant refugee city', on the Libyan coast. European Migration Commissioner Dimitris Avramopoulos reminded participants that any solution to the EU's migration wave should be based on humanity and dignity. 'Solidarity is not à la carte,' he said. The day before the summit began, more than 160 migrants drowned when their boat sank off Libya.

In an interview in the Austrian daily *Der Standard* Chancellor Christian Kern praised Hungary's contribution to slowing the refugee influx:

> We are ourselves beneficiaries of this policy of [Hungarian prime minister] Orbán, as a result of which far fewer refugees are reaching Austria and Germany. This means that we also share the responsibility of addressing the negative consequences of this measure. Some time, these people are going to set out on their own account, so that the problem will shift to a different European border.[14]

Austria would spend around €2 billion accommodating and integrating refugees in 2016, he said. Kern might understand, even praise Hungary on one level, but he also warned Hungary, like all other countries, to accept its quota of asylum seekers:

> Unless we are able to resolve this problem, then the entire European project, rooted as it is in solidarity and commonality, will be at stake. Such is the scale of the problem, that no one has any right to shirk his responsibility. In the long term, this would not be acceptable.

*

Back in Hungary, already in August, the government had launched recruitment for a new unit of 'border-hunters' in the police. The name was unfortunate, coming at a time of numerous allegations of Hungarian police brutality against migrants. My sources in the police insisted that there was no policy of brutality, and that the top brass were doing all they could to ensure human rights standards were respected, and to avoid recruiting new officers with racist views.

Three thousand border-hunters, who would also be full police officers, were needed to reinforce the southern border. It was to be the most modern recruitment campaign ever launched by the police. Posters appeared across the country, on Facebook, and on the police.hu website. Three smiling police officers, one tall, one short and one female, in dark red caps, looking into the camera. Applicants should be over eighteen, Hungarian citizens with A-levels, be physically fit, and will have to pass a psychological test to make sure they are suitable. Pay would be €484 a month for the first two months, increasing to €710 from then on. The new recruits, like existing officers, would be armed with pistols, pepper spray, truncheons, handcuffs and protective equipment. They would be deployed after six months' training, from May 2017.

The number of migrants and refugees reaching the Hungarian border though the western Balkan route had fallen to less than 200 a day since the start of the year. Thirty were allowed into Hungary each day through the transit zones, fifteen at Röszke, fifteen at Kelebia. The Balkan route, despite Donald Tusk's words, was still open, but just a crack.

During the early summer of 2016, in May, June and the first half of July, fifty to sixty refugees on average managed to reach the nearest Greek islands from the Turkish coast in their small boats. After the failed coup in Turkey on 15 July, that number doubled to 112 a day, and stayed at that level through August and September. The Turkish police had other things on their mind – rounding up suspected coup plotters, or themselves falling under suspicion, as President Erdoğan purged the state administration of anyone suspected of 'Gulenist' allegiance. The EU–Turkey agreement, in force since 20 May, was beginning to stumble. There was also a suspicion in some, West European quarters, that the Turkish government eased the police presence on the west coast to warn the EU that the 'refugee weapon' could still be activated.

The newcomers were mostly stranded on the islands in leaky detention camps where they were held while the Greek Asylum Service assessed their claims. By September, there were around 14,000 on the five islands, compared to 8,450 in mid-June. They could easily leave the camps through holes in the fence to visit local villages, but as there was nowhere else to go they returned to their overcrowded camps through the same holes. There were no more ferryloads of migrants to Piraeus. Around 3,000 refugees, nevertheless, managed to reach the mainland on scheduled ferries during those three summer months – an average of just over thirty a day.

Comparisons had begun to be made between Greece and the Pacific island of Nauru, where Australia sends all migrants attempting to reach her shores by sea, for their claims to be assessed. It was also clear that while the EU–Turkey agreement still had a strong braking effect on the migration of people between the Middle East and Western Europe, many aspects of the agreement were not working. In their September assessment of the agreement, the ESI wrote that 9,250 people reached Greece from Turkey by boat during the summer months, and only 116 of these were returned.[15] These formed one part of the 578 asylum seekers returned from the Greek islands to the Turkish mainland from mid-March till the end of September.

In September, the European Commission published an upbeat update on the success of their agreement with Turkey. But it did admit some weaknesses. The Greek Asylum Service was working too slowly, the authors grumbled. Human rights lawyers in Greece argued that Turkey was still not a 'safe' country to return refugees to. Almost all of those sentenced to return from the islands appealed, and most won cases brought to the newly established Greek Appeals Authority.[16]

'The Greek Asylum Service can take two kinds of decisions,' the ESI wrote:

Firstly, on admissibility. In this case it concludes that since Turkey is safe for an applicant, no asylum decision is required in Greece. The application in Greece would be found inadmissible and the applicant could be returned to Turkey. If the applicant is a Syrian, he or she would get temporary protection in Turkey. If the applicant is a non-Syrian, he or she should submit an asylum claim there. Alternatively, the Greek Asylum Service could conduct a full asylum procedure in Greece. In that

case the applicant can only be returned to Turkey, as an illegal immigrant, if protection is denied.

The Greek Asylum Service does not even conduct admissibility
procedures with non-Syrians such as Afghans, Iraqis and Pakistanis
since it does not consider Turkey a safe third country for non-Syrian
refugees.

Over the six months of the operation of the EU–Turkey agreement, the ESI
concluded scathingly, only six asylum claims had been judged inadmissible
on the Greek islands. A total of sixteen Greek asylum workers were now
present on the islands, the study found, together with forty-one asylum
experts drafted in from other EU countries:

> At the heart of the EU–Turkey agreement is the goal to discourage irreg-
> ular crossings by returning most of those who arrive on Greek islands to
> Turkey following a credible assessment of their asylum claims. It is hard
> to explain why there is no more serious discussion in the [EU] report on
> why this is not happening.

The growing numbers on the islands were leading to growing tensions
between locals and migrants, especially on Lesbos and Chios. On 14
September, a march by residents protesting against what they saw as the
takeover of their island by asylum seekers ended in violence as police used
teargas to prevent them reaching the camp.

On 19 September, a fire broke out at the overcrowded Moria camp on
Lesbos. Fifty prefabricated homes burnt down, and more than 5,000 people
living in the camp fled into the surrounding fields. In the chaos which
followed, local people and police tried to send the migrants back towards
their burning camp.

How could the situation be solved? While the ESI report's authors
preferred the proper implementation of an agreement which they themselves had proposed, the more likely conclusion, they feared, was that the
Greek authorities would simply restart the big ferries – and ship migrants
from the overcrowded islands to the overcrowded mainland. If that
happened, the pressure on the Greek-Macedonian border would grow to
breaking point again, and if large columns of refugees starting winding their

way up through the Balkans in the rains of autumn and the snows of winter, this would 'provide a boost to leaders such as Viktor Orbán, who have long argued that in order to control its external borders the EU ought to be prepared to set aside human rights concerns, treating migrants as an "invading army" and suspending the application of the refugee convention'. It could also help further disintegrate the EU, with elections ahead in France, the Netherlands and Germany in 2017. All of this would add to the 'political momentum of the anti-refugee, populist far-right'.

Up to a hundred refugees a day continued to make it through the Turkish-Bulgarian border, despite the ever-lengthening fence and the tough reputation of the Bulgarian border guards. Of the 60,000 refugees trapped on the Greek mainland, up to a hundred more managed to make it through Macedonia to Serbia each day too. This added up to about 200 people a day reaching Belgrade. There they surfaced for a while, like fish coming up for air. In Belgrade, they slept first in makeshift camps near the railway and bus stations. Then they gravitated to one of the thirteen camps around the country set up by the Serbian Commissariat for Refugees.

The ESI published its own proposals. The EU should acknowledge the genuine concerns of both the Greeks and the Turks, and offer credible support to both, to help the few thousand most vulnerable asylum claimants. The EU should recognise what the Greek Asylum Service had been arguing for months, that Turkey is not yet a safe country. Finally, an EU social envoy should be appointed, to oversee the agreement and maintain contact with Turkish officials.

> The Turkish government does not want to fight smugglers in a fruitless battle along its Aegean coast, nor have more dead children washed up on its shores. Turkey also has a strong national interest in not wanting anti-refugee, anti-Muslim forces to get even stronger in 2017 in key EU member states.

Above all, Turkey needed to do much more, with EU help, to prove that it is a safe third country to which the Greeks need have no qualms in returning migrants. If that was done, the EU should have no hesitation in fulfilling its side of the bargain – to allow visa-free travel for Turkish citizens in the Schengen group of countries.

If these ideas were not implemented, the authors warned, chaos might result:

The Macedonian reception and asylum system would collapse within weeks if more people were to cross the border. Serbia would face a similar crisis. As winter sets in, the western Balkans would turn into a battleground between migrants, smugglers, border guards, soldiers and vigilante groups, destabilising an already fragile region. And ever larger numbers of people would begin to cross again into Central Europe.

*

In Hungary, the referendum campaign entered its final week. In parliament, Gábor Vona, leader of the increasingly centrist but still nationalist Jobbik party, addressed Viktor Orbán across the floor of the house.

We are glad you have joined us to support a Europe of Nations. [. . .] In Western Europe multiculturalism is now the reality. It is not a question there of whether to live in a multicultural society or not, but how to live there. While here in Central East Europe, we still have the chance to decide. And I believe we should vote not to.

The referendum was, after all, originally a Jobbik idea, so Jobbik could hardly not back it now. But, Vona argued, if it failed to be valid by not reaching the required 50 per cent, it would give Brussels a stick with which to beat Hungary. Instead, Vona argued, it would have been much simpler, and cheaper, to simply change the constitution to make it impossible to accept quotas. He called on Orbán to resign if turnout did not reach 50 per cent. He went on:

You have used the theme of the flood of migrants like an Arabian magic carpet, which flies away among the clouds, in order to avoid seeing the Hungarian reality. And if the carpet lands somewhere, you sweep the problems under the carpet! The problems of education, of health, of corruption. Because what is the reality here? Prime Minister, the reality is that while you play Jean de Savoy in Brussels, your foot-soldiers are stealing the country at home!

231

Jean de Savoy was the Habsburg general famed for his battles with Ottoman forces in the seventeenth century, and for burning much of the beautiful city of Sarajevo to the ground. 'There will be no legal consequences of the referendum, because the referendum question is not within the competence of the Hungarian Parliament,' commented Robert László of the leftist Political Capital think tank. 'On the political level, however, there could be consequences, because Viktor Orbán wants to be a really heavyweight European politician. He wants to be leading figure of the strengthening nation-states within Europe.'

Referendum day was 2 October, a Sunday. I visited voting stations in several parts of Budapest, finishing in Újlipótváros, the increasingly gentrified district between the Danube and the west railway station, and the only one in the city still controlled by the Socialists. There was a steady turnout of mainly older people, vehement Fidesz supporters. But younger people mostly refused to take part.

Everything hinged on turnout. By early evening, it was clear that the 50 per cent hurdle, necessary to make the result valid, would not be reached. The final figures showed 39.8 per cent voted, while a further 6 per cent spoilt their ballots – an unprecedentedly high number in Hungary.[17]

Journalists gathered to hear Orbán's reaction in the 'Whale', a converted warehouse on the Danube shore in Pest. Only cameramen and women were allowed upstairs to the second floor, where Orbán made a brief, carefully rehearsed statement: 'Brussels or Budapest. That was the question, and we have decided that the right to decide [who Hungarians want to live with] lies solely with Budapest.' The constitution would be amended accordingly, Orbán said, to 'reflect the will of the people'. 'The weapon will be strong enough in Brussels too. Brussels cannot force its will on Hungary.'[18]

An ally of the prime minister told me that he was initially devastated by the failure of the referendum.[19] His spin-doctors reassured him that he could portray the result as a victory, as 98 per cent of those who cast a valid vote voted 'No' to allowing the EU to 'mandate the obligatory resettlement of non-Hungarian citizens into Hungary even without the approval of the National Assembly'. To make sure this interpretation became widespread, the Fidesz media, especially the tabloids, echoed references to this great victory for weeks on end. And more giant billboards appeared all over the country. The Hungarian people 'had spoken'.

That message was met with incredulity by all the Hungarians who had voted with their feet to boycott the referendum, and across Europe. 'The Hungarians are more European than their government,' said Luxembourg foreign minister Jean Asselborn. 'This is a bad day for Viktor Orbán and good day for Hungary and the European Union.' The government had spent €48 million asking people to vote 'no' who would have voted 'no' anyway, and stirred up even more xenophobia in a country treated to a monotonous diet of xenophobia by the government since January 2015.[20]

CHAPTER THIRTEEN

A SLOW AND PAINFUL EUROPE

Yes, Europe is slow. It is painful. It has deep cuts like the withdrawal of a member state. And, yes, Europe should focus on what it can really do better than the nation state . . .

But where Europe – in global competition, in protecting our external borders or migration – faces issues together, it must find answers together. No matter how arduous and tough that is.

Angela Merkel, 1 January 2017[1]

In mid-December 2016, Hungary's 'best' refugee camp at Bicske was closed after thirty-six years, partly because it was unpopular in the Fidesz-run town, and because very few refugees were actually crossing into Hungary any more – despite the continuous scaremongering. The last residents were moved out at only an hour's notice.

The last sixty residents of the camp were scattered to the four winds. Some to the camp in Balassagyarmat, some to Vámosszabadi, and three to the homeless shelter in Grassalkovich street in Budapest, run by a Baptist charity. Antal Grassalkovich was a Hungarian noble, born in 1694 in Ürmény, now in southern Slovakia. He was famous for his work helping German immigrants settle in Hungary during the reign of the Empress Maria Theresa.

Those sent to Körmend were in the worst situation. The tents where they were rehoused had wooden floors and rudimentary wood-burning stoves in the middle, but there was no insulation of any kind. A local Catholic priest,

Zoltán Németh invited the asylum seekers from their cold tents to his warm guest house instead. His gesture made national news, because of its rarity.[2] The only parallel anyone could remember was when Asztrik Várszegi, arch-abbot of the Pannonhalma monastery, welcomed Syrian asylum seekers in September 2015, contradicting a statement from Archbishop Péter Erdö that churches should not open their doors, as that would be tantamount to helping smugglers.

A press conference was set for 11 a.m. Father Németh introduced me to Gabriella Sári, from the Sant'Egidio foundation, a Catholic social-workers charity which had been active at Bicske. She had spent several months in Syria, restoring icons in churches before the war, and got to know some of those transferred to Körmend through her work. She contacted Father Németh, and he immediately offered them shelter.

One of the men, Thomas, talked to me in the kitchen of the guest block of the parish. He was from west Cameroon and had been in Hungary for three years, first in the camp in Debrecen, which the government closed at the end of 2015, then in Bicske. It seemed that he was running out of places to go.

He left Cameroon for Kenya in 2013, he explained, on a scholarship to study there. In Nairobi he applied for and received a visa to visit Hungary, and flew to Budapest. He was arrested in Hungary when his visa ran out and had been moved since then from camp to camp. The only reason he would be granted asylum in Hungary as a Cameroonian citizen, he was told privately by an employee of the Immigration Office, was if he was gay.

Even last week on the BBC there were reports of people being slaugh-tered and killed because they were protesting. Officials here say my application for asylum is delayed because I have contradicted myself in the six interviews I have had so far. But I have proved that I was suffering persecution again and again, but nothing has changed.

According to the BBC website, riots had indeed broken out in the city of Bamenda in the north-west of the country in November, after the authori-ties tried to impose French-speaking teachers and court officials in predom-inantly English-speaking areas.[3] Cameroon was a German colony, divided into British and French areas after the First World War. English is still the main language in the southwest and northwest regions along the border with Nigeria. All the other eight regions are Francophone. One protester claimed that the 10 million English-speaking citizens of the country had been marginalised for fifty years. All English-speaking schools had temporarily been shut because of the troubles. I wondered how much the immigration officials keep up with shifting events in the countries of origin.

Thomas went on:

The main problem in the camp where we were taken here in Körmend was not the heating. The main problem is that we humans are not comfortable living outside, and a tent is like living outside, you sleep and the wind blows. No matter the intensity of heat from the stove, you always feel cold at night because the tent cannot conserve the heat. You keep putting more wood on the fire, every two hours, but it changes nothing because you never feel warm inside.

What would he most like to do? I asked. 'To resume my studies in Chemical Engineering. We hope for a better future in every sense. I would like to be helpful in society.' He felt inspired by the 'Moonshot' initiative for cancer research, announced by President Obama in his State of the Union address in January 2016.[4] While in Bicske, he had started learning German at the Goethe Institute in Budapest. Now he couldn't continue his classes.

I hope to find peace here. There's propaganda that immigrants are this or that but fortunately some people have found out that immigrants are not bad!

My dad is a Baptist, my mum is Catholic, and I went to Baptist secondary school. But the message is the same. Jesus Christ died on the cross, assisting as he did. We shouldn't segregate Muslims from Christians, like the government does. We should accommodate all people in spite of our differences. We should bring our similarities . . . to forge ahead together.

Standing beside him in the kitchen was Abdul, aged twenty-one, from Afghanistan. He had reached Europe through Greece, Macedonia and

Serbia, he said, and had even got as far as Germany once, stowing away on a cargo train. But the German police had caught him and deported him to Hungary, as the place where he was first registered under the Dublin procedures. Now he simply didn't know where to go.

Afghanistan in the autumn of 2016 was descending deeper into violence, just as EU countries led by Germany stepped up the repatriation of Afghans.[5] According to EASO, an equal number of civilian casualties was caused by government and insurgent forces. The last places of peace and stability in the country were certain districts of Kabul. Nevertheless, on 4 October, the EU–Afghanistan Joint Way Forward plan was launched, under which EU states would be able to charter flights to take home Afghans who refused to leave voluntarily.[6] Germany deported the first group of thirty-four in December and a second group of twenty-six in January 2017. German interior minister Thomas de Maizière announced that Germany would send back up to 11,800 Afghans.[7]

'Young Afghans don't see any future in Afghanistan and most are stuck in Kabul because they can't travel to the provinces,' Abdul Ghafoor, a refugee rights activist deported from Norway in 2013, told the EUobserver website.[8] With little or no help once they reached home, many attempted, once again, to reach Europe. There were at least 2.7 million Afghan refugees in Pakistan and Iran. In 2015, 178,000 – nearly one in five – of the asylum seekers who reached Europe were from Afghanistan.

At the press conference, Father Németh defended his decision to give the refugees shelter. Neither the church council nor the police had objected. The migrants were simply obliged to report once a day to the camp, which they did. On the first night eight had stayed, on the second night five. They had facilities to wash and to cook here. And he was planning to serve them a big Christmas dinner.

Why had Körmend alone of all the Christian parishes in Hungary followed Pope Francis's appeal and offered help to refugees? I asked.

We are not unique. I think every priest would do the same, if he found himself in this situation, on the border . . . Many are helping today in the country, as individuals.

Pope Francis made his appeal on 6 September last year in his Sunday sermon, and many people scratched their heads about what to do. Here in Körmend I called together the church advisory council on 9 September so we could discuss how to respond. The majority of those present rejected the Pope's words. Their reaction was, 'We do not need to take this seriously anyway, because there won't be any refugees here.' But on exactly the same day the government started building a refugee reception centre here.

For several days after the Hungarian-Serbian border was closed in October 2015, refugees were brought to Körmend from Beremend on the Croatian border. Father Németh and his parishioners helped them at the roadside, day and night, before the flood was diverted to Szentgotthard, south-west of Körmend.

I don't know how many 'terrorists' there were among them. What I do know is that we met many grateful people, struggling with very difficult circumstances.

I must admit there is not a very positive image of us Hungarians in the West. A few weeks ago I spoke to a Benedictine abbot who told me that Hungary has a reputation as haters of refugees. Of course, I tried to soften that image. I told him that Hungarians do not hate strangers. Perhaps we are just afraid or concerned about big waves of them. In the past day I have received many emails and messages from people who support what we are doing here, and offering help. All those people gave their full names and addresses. Those who express doubt or scepticism in the media usually express their hatred anonymously.

His parish was most definitely not trying to replace the work of the state, he said. But as far as he knew, he was not breaking any laws by showing Christian charity.

From Körmend I crossed the Austrian border towards Gussing. There were no border controls on the Hungarian side, just a temporary cabin on the Austrian side where a friendly policeman waved me through with the most cursory glance into the car.

It's a two-hour drive from Körmend to Traiskirchen, first through pretty Austrian villages, then up the A2 motorway north, towards Vienna. On the car radio, I listened to the latest news about deportations from Germany.[9]

The refugee camp was an important stopping place for Hungarian refugees in 1956. On the site of a former Austro-Hungarian cavalry barracks, the tall buildings and low wall around it reminded me of the castle at Gödöllö. There were big white UNHCR tents in the courtyard, where the horses were once put through their paces, and a Caritas van parked on the pavement outside where volunteers were serving hot drinks. I last saw Ali Sadat at the Adaševci motel camp in September. Aged twenty-eight, he had a company in Afghanistan importing telecommunications towers from Russia. The company still exists, but he was forced to leave by the threats of violence against him and his family – by both sides, he says – if he didn't pay protection money. He decided to flee with his four sisters, who are all older than him. All have university degrees. Once they are safely settled in Austria, Ali plans to go back to Afghanistan, close down his company, and start a similar business in Europe. Ali was working when I got to Traiskirchen, looking after three small children who were travelling alone, so I set out to explore the town – the small fifteenth-century church of St Nicholas, a good bookshop, a couple of cafés, an Indian restaurant and a pizzeria. Not much else. The white Austrian winter was closing in on the foothills which ran all the way to Vienna.

The asylum seekers in the camp were free to come and go, and were prominent on the streets around the camp, but hardly visible in the centre of town. There was a man selling Christmas trees in the main square.

Ali greeted me enthusiastically at the main gate, flashing his laminated pass at the night-watchman to get out. It was only 5.30 p.m. but already dark and wintry in the streets outside. We drove into town for a pizza. He was more dynamic here than in Serbia. He had finally reached the goal of his journey, and his phone rang every few minutes, as he helped organise the lives of all around him. His journey here from Serbia across Hungary illustrates the different fates of so many migrants on this route, and how a little charm and good luck can radically improve one's journey. Ali was spotted by the BBC in Kabul even before he set out, and filmed much of his journey on the Go-Pro camera my colleagues there gave him. He featured in the BBC documentary *Exodus*.[10]

At the camp in Adaševci, he made himself so useful to the camp administrators that he was soon 'promoted' to be the camp commander at Horgoš, the liaison person between the Serbian and Hungarian refugee authorities, finalising who would be let into the transit zones. He spent twenty-eight days at Horgoš as camp leader, while his sisters waited in the refugee reception centre in Subotica. He was upset by the cold and lack of basic facilities at Horgoš, and the constant rain, but managed to negotiate better food, blankets and, most important of all, smoother passage into Hungary for dozens of refugees while he was there. 'It was like a desert,' he remembers. He also surprised me with tales of just how many refugees were managing to get through the Hungarian fence and not get caught, despite the massive police and army presence. One in three got through, he reckoned. The fence was easy to cut, and the smugglers went with them. If they were caught they just pretended to be fellow migrants. Some were returned every night. 'The smugglers, the criminals are always one step ahead of the police, and they are very clever.'

Like other refugees I spoke to, he related tales of Hungarian police brutality. But they were kind to him and his sisters, for which he was grateful, he told me. They were only kept for four hours in the transit zone, then transferred by bus to the open camp in Vámosszabadi near Győr. 'I think the Hungarian authorities would have liked me to apply for asylum, because they thought I could be useful to them,' he said. But he had no intention of staying long. 'So few people are granted asylum in Hungary, we stood little chance. And anyway, Hungary does not show respect to refugees. I wanted to reach a country where they are kind to asylum seekers.'

After a few days in Vámosszabadi, he and his sisters took the bus into Győr and bought train tickets to Vienna. When the police saw them on the station, they checked their camp documents and said they could not board the train. They feigned resignation, left the station, then ran back on to the platform when the train arrived. This time no one tried to stop them. The Hungarian border police on the train left them in peace. When the train was already on Austrian territory, the Austrian police noticed that one of his sisters did not have the right documents. 'Then we all surrendered,' he told me. 'The Austrians were the first friendly police we met on the whole journey from Afghanistan.'

They spent a night in a police cell, then were taken to Traiskirchen. This was normally a transit camp but Ali and his sisters were allowed to stay longer because he had a lung problem which needed medical attention. He too had heard that Germany was stepping up deportations of Afghans. 'It's ironic that the first country to make us welcome is also the first to start sending us back,' he said bitterly. 'The situation in Afghanistan is even worse now than it was a year ago and is getting worse still. They are sending some of those people back to their deaths.'

I asked about the young German girl raped and murdered in Freiburg by a seventeen-year-old Afghan asylum seeker in October.[11]

'I think first I should say how sorry we are to the family of that lady. We are also all nervous because of this. But I hope people will remember that not all fingers on a hand are the same, not all people are the same, not all Afghans are like that.'

Ali had done some research on the perpetrator, who had grown up in Iran: 'People in Afghanistan, especially educated people, are very respectful of women. But we have a lot of cruel people too, who sell and buy women like animals. I just feel sorry about what happened in Freiburg. It was very bad what he did, and we want the court to punish that guy.'

What was his advice to European policy makers?

'To gain something we should also lose something. In some cases, Europe is right to deport people. But the EU also needs physical workers and carers to work here, whose work benefits these countries.'

In any case, the mess in the Middle East and in his own country was caused by Europeans interfering, he said. The wars fought in Afghanistan were turf-wars for control of the lucrative European and US drug trade. NATO was strong enough to stop the war there, and defeat Da'esh and the Taliban. They must have some reason for not doing so.

Back in Budapest, with Christmas coming, I interviewed Balázs Orbán, head of the Migration Research Institute set up by the Századvég think tank in September 2015 to advise the government. How much had his institute been able to find out in the first fourteen months of its existence, about who exactly the asylum seekers, migrants or refugees were, and why they were coming, I asked.

The vast majority of Hungarians think that those arriving at the Hungarian-Serbian border right now are economic migrants rather than refugees. They think the countries they come from are stable. They know there are serious conflicts around Europe, the Middle East, in sub-Saharan

Africa, in Asia, but they don't think the migrants are escaping direct persecution.

Had that view changed over time? I asked.

The official starting point of my institute and my personal view is that while the attitudes of migrants are extremely complex [. . .] we in Europe do not differentiate between those who actually need international protection and those who do not.

The language and the practice of the 1951 Refugee Convention were both outdated, he explained, and in need of reform. The existing rules forced those arriving to claim asylum, often in countries where they didn't want to be anyway.

Balázs also attempted to shed light on why Hungarians appeared so hostile to migrants. According to a public opinion survey carried out by his institute at the beginning of 2016, a quarter of those asked said they had had personal contacts with migrants, on the streets, or trains, or railway stations. And of these, 75 per cent said that contact was rather negative than positive. 'My analysis is that this was because of the irregular way people are crossing borders and walking across the country without permission. This is true for the population in every country. So it's not true that the majority of Hungarians do not like these people.' They just had negative experiences of them.

So the huge Hungarian billboard campaigns, the constant anti-migrant propaganda of the government had had no effect? I asked, a little incredulously.

Not really. The Tárki survey in September 2015 showed that when the numbers were highest, people's sympathy with them was also at its highest. Hungarians are motivated by pragmatism, not ideology or xenophobia.

Sympathy towards them changed when people witnessed the way migration happened. When they saw what happened at the east station, when they saw migrants marching along the highways. Hungarians like law and order, and that story was about something else. That is why attitudes changed from positive to negative.

From the government perspective, this situation caused serious tensions in hosting or transit countries. People had valid concerns, and in this situation it does matter how the government reacts.

While in Hungary in 2015 the government took public concerns seriously, Balázs explained, in Austria the government did not, and this neglect of the grassroots concerns of Austrian voters caused serious tensions in society. 'Voters were radicalised. They wanted to express their opinion in a much harsher way. This didn't happen in Hungary. We haven't had any demonstrations against migrants here. The government's communication has calmed down public opinion, not radicalised it.' His view contrasted strongly with my own observation that the Hungarian government was radicalising the public with its ceaseless campaigns and turning them against genuine refugees.

According to statistics released the same month by the Hungarian Helsinki Committee, based on figures from the OIN and the UNHCR, 69 per cent of the 28,000 people who sought asylum in Hungary between January and October 2016 were from zones of war or terror: Syria, Afghanistan, Iraq or Somalia.[12] If the Hungarian public didn't know that, it was because someone had misinformed them.

There is a minority in the Hungarian population, not a growing number but the same number as in past years, who do not like any foreigners. That is the radical right. While the majority of the population thinks that those people are different from us and we should help them because they are in trouble. But it is not a solution to let them in, because that would not be good for them or for us.

A majority of Hungarians also say we should put more money into projects which help their countries of origin. But we don't think we should host them and offer them a new life here, because these people do not want to live our life and we don't want to live their life.

The people who do not like migrants are the same as those before who didn't like Gypsies or Jews. They are typically radical right-wing radical xenophobic people.

And you don't think their narrative has spread in society? I asked.

No, I don't think so. The only thing you could experience is that they are a bit harsher in communication, they are much more visible. There's also a sociological principle that in these situations these people can be louder, much more visible, but not in the long term. It will disappear.

I arranged to see Ussamah Bourgla, the Syrian doctor I first met in Bicske in September 2015. I had heard from colleagues that he and his family were leaving Hungary. He had a rather different perspective on xenophobia to Balázs Orbán.

We sat in his daughter Amira's flat in the 8th district of Budapest. Ussamah is a gentle-mannered man, in his mid-fifties. He has five children in all, four daughters and a son, just like Viktor Orbán. He even met Orbán once, in around 2008 when he was leader of the opposition. Ussamah was the manager of the football team in Bicske, and his son was in the team. Orbán's son Gáspar was playing in the same tournament. They chatted for a few moments during the match, and Ussamah found him charming. He was from Tall, a small town near Damascus, and came to Hungary as a medical student in the early 1980s. 'I was sent here by the Socialist government of the older Assad, Hafiz. I had taken part as a young student in the earlier revolution in Syria, from 1978 to 81, to defend Assad. I believed in that regime then. It was only later I found out what terrible things it did.'

In Hungary he started his medical studies in Budapest and finished them in Szeged. Budapest was too crowded. He fell in love with his future wife and moved as a GP first to Ózd then to Bicske in 1992. Their four children followed in quick succession. He always loved Hungary and the Hungarians, he said. 'I joined the Socialist Party in 2009, out of solidarity with it, just when everyone else was leaving it. Social justice is an important idea for me.'

Ussamah listened to Viktor Orbán's comments on the *Charlie Hebdo* terror attack in Paris in January 2015, with dismay.

Everyone went to Paris to mourn the dead, but Orbán went to declare his movement against refugees, against Islam. A few weeks later I took part in a TV discussion on ATV, when I tried to explain the danger of Orbán's speech, where it might lead. When I heard him I knew: we will have to leave Hungary.

I still love this country. I feel like I am at home, so it was a very difficult decision but we have to make it because we didn't feel comfortable
here after that speech. We have foreign names, we felt like we didn't feel
at home any more here, so we decided to look for some place to live
peacefully.

I am a respected doctor in my town, but elsewhere no one knows who
I am. They just notice that I am a foreigner like any other refugee they
have been forced to hate.

Neither he nor his children had been the victims of physical violence
since Orbán's ominous speech, he said, but they had been exposed to verbal
abuse. One of his daughters worked at the reception desk of a company, and
on several occasions when she answered the phone, the person on the other
end asked to speak to 'a Hungarian'. Amira, aged 22, had just got a degree as
a food scientist. She also had a part-time job as manager of a café in a business district in downtown Budapest.

Some customers were quite rude. At the start it was not a big deal, and I
didn't pay it much attention. But when all those posters were put up by
the government, people became more rude day by day. The first one I
clearly remember, I had a name badge with my full name on it, like all of
the staff. A customer started asking me where I come from, and why I
speak Hungarian so perfectly. I told him I was born here.

'No, I was asking where you come from,' he said, really aggressively.

'I was born here, so I think I'm Hungarian,' I told him. 'I'm the
manager here.' Then he accused me of stealing the job from Hungarians.
And so on.

Me and my workmates joked about it at first. But the second one was
meaner. We made different sizes of coffees. I asked a customer whether
he wanted a medium or large cappuccino, and he said in a horrible voice
he wants a Hungarian cappuccino, and that I should understand that
because I am in Hungary right now, I should learn how to make a
Hungarian cappuccino.

After that, such comments became an almost everyday occurrence, so she
left. 'The most surprising part is that most of them were working in nearby

offices, they were considered smart, well-educated, not poorly educated people.'

Wasn't she afraid the same thing might happen in post-Brexit Britain? I asked.

Not at all. It's an absolutely different world, I've worked there for six months, everyone is so nice. They accepted the fact that I come from another country and I am there to serve them, so they were really kind and polite, even when sometimes I didn't understand the Manchester accent. But they were really helpful, everyone. I can't think of one time when someone was rude to me.

'There's a big difference between what the government and the people think,' her father added. 'Of course, there are people in every country who dislike strangers, but the big problem here in Hungary is that the government itself distributes the hatred.' His wife and the other four children were already working in England, Ussamah said. He just needed to finish his English language exams, then he too would be gone.

*

The year 2016 ended with a truck attack on a Christmas market in Berlin, and a shooting in an Istanbul nightclub. The perpetrator of the Berlin atrocity was a Tunisian asylum seeker who had been rejected and then disappeared before he could be deported.

On 11 January 2017, Barack Obama gave his last speech as president, a bid to console supporters appalled by the victory of Donald Trump. His speech was also a challenge to 'autocrats' including Viktor Orbán.

A faith in reason, and enterprise, and the primacy of right over might allowed the United States to resist the lure of fascism and tyranny during the Great Depression, and build a post-World War II order with other democracies. That order is now being challenged. First by violent fanatics who claim to speak for Islam; more recently by autocrats in foreign capitals who see free markets, open democracies, and civil society itself as a threat to their power. The peril each poses to our democracy is more far-reaching than a car-bomb or a missile.

On 20 January, as Donald Trump was sworn in, he received a letter from Pope Francis, suggesting the new president should not forget the great tradition of US compassion for the downtrodden: 'Under your leadership, may America's stature continue to be measured above all by its concern for the poor, the outcast and those in need who, like Lazarus, stand before our door.'[13]

In the Balkans, those standing at the door had to endure the coldest winter for many years.[14] Six thousand people squeezed into overcrowded official camps, while up to two thousand lived rough, in an abandoned warehouse behind the railway station in Belgrade, in the ruined brick factory on the outskirts of Subotica, in the makeshift camps at Horgoš and Kelebia. Médecins Sans Frontières, Doctors of the World, and a loose network of NGOs and volunteers like Fresh Response did their best to care for them, treating frequent cases of frostbite, of burns from the open fires the refugees tried to keep warm beside and cook over, and of dog bites and truncheon injuries from Bulgarian and Hungarian police.

'For months we have called on the EU, UNHCR and Serbian authorities to put in place long-term solutions to avoid this catastrophic situation,' said Stephane Moissaing, head of Médecins Sans Frontières in Serbia.

> The collective failure of these institutions has left even the most basic needs uncovered, exposing already vulnerable people to even more suffering. Several people have already died of hypothermia at the borders of Serbia and Bulgaria, we cannot simply sit and update the number of those who die during the dangerous border crossings or fall victim to violence since the closure of the Balkan route.

CHAPTER FOURTEEN

BORDERLANDS

I will sing of the mercies of the Lord forever: with my mouth will I make
known thy faithfulness to all generations. For I have said, Mercy shall be.

Psalm 89

Ildikó Farkas drove the big 4×4 with confidence through the snow and
deeply rutted tracks of the *Tánya világ* – the world of poor, isolated farmsteads around Mórahalom. For fourteen years she had been taking food to
the elderly and disabled in these flatlands, scattered along the Hungarian-
Serbian border. She could navigate each track and clump of trees, each
tumble-down farm with her eyes shut.

In the back of her pick-up were nine sets of tupperware dishes, with the
name of each recipient written in capitals on the handles – István, István,
András, Edit. There was a slice of pork in one, kohlrabi stew in the second,
meat soup in the third. The food came from the kitchens of the old people's
home in Mórahalom. The lunches cost $2 a day, five days a week – $40 a
month. Those people on the farms living on under $100 a month got them
for half-price – $1 a day.

Ildikó also delivered firewood and took children to school. The farms
she visited were all close to the fence, and her customers had some experience of the refugee crisis.

András felt sorry for the refugees. He used the word *refugees,* not
migrants. Hundreds passed his farm in the summer of 2015. Some he found
sleeping in his barn. He gave them cool water from his well in the summer

heat. He still lives in the same small house where he was born in the bitterly cold winter of 1947. The midwife who delivered him, 'and it was a hard birth, for my poor mother', ended up staying with them for several days.

Several tracks away in the snow, eighty-four-year-old István lived on his own too. He had no sympathy for the migrants. He'd had a hard life, he told me, an orphan, adopted by a well-off peasant whose lands were taken away by the Communists after the Second World War. His punishment for being the adopted son of a 'kulak', as the better-off farmers were called, was to be sent to work in the coal mines. He fully supported Viktor Orbán and his fence-building endeavours. Nothing endeared the newcomers to him: 'They left a trail of plastic bottles and rubbish wherever they went.'

He saw no parallel between his own suffering, and theirs. 'I survived everything that happened here, and stayed.' As they filed down the track next to his house, he exchanged not a single word with them. They were folk from another planet, 'like ants', he explained. Thin and agile despite his years, he cooked up coffee for us in his humble kitchen, glowing from the heat thrown out by an old Vesta wood-burning stove.

We drove on, past dogs on chains and piles of scrap machinery, sheds with gaping holes where pigs were once kept, a lone donkey marching up and down on too short a tether, and two cats curled up together on a short plank to keep warm.

In one house a lady of ninety-one asked when the cold weather would end. I counted ten packets of pills beside her on the bed. Wherever we looked we saw grinding poverty and broken health. One man explained how much the government's €33 Christmas bonus meant to him. Another complained that the 1.6 per cent yearly increase in his pension was a joke. In one of the better-kept farms, a cockerel welcomed us loudly. There were certificates on the wall in recognition of the bravery and dedication with which local people helped their community in the terrible flood in the Tisza valley in 1970.

Tompa was half an hour's drive west on Route 55. The road was resurfaced just before the refugee influx, and now functioned as the main supply road for police and army vehicles patrolling the border. We met Sándor in front of the town hall in Tompa, for a guided tour of the old defences. Long before the refugees, these peaceful villages braced themselves to defend their land and honour from a 'Yugoslav invasion'. Tito's Yugoslavia, unlike the Eastern Bloc, was not subservient to Moscow, and young Hungarian conscripts spent their military training preparing for a Third World War fought on the southern, as well as the western, borders.

Tompa, Sándor explained, was a product of the 1920 Trianon Treaty. The village grew originally as the 'garden district' of Subotica, 12 kilometres to the south in Serbia, an important, multicultural cathedral city of the Austro-Hungarian empire. When Subotica was swallowed up in the new Kingdom of Serbs, Croats and Slovenes in 1918, Tompa was left with just a line of houses and no zone of attraction, no local heart to reach out to.

Sándor drove us through the streets, pointing out concrete bunkers built in the early 1950s, when the Hungarian Communist Party quarrelled with Josip Tito's Yugoslav Communist Party. The border fence is not a solution, he said, just a stop-gap measure. 'If a big group of determined migrants wanted to break through it, they could – unless the border guards could use live rounds – and then what an international scandal there would be!' Migrants from the Arab world could certainly not integrate in Europe, he believed.

'Look at our own Gypsies! Though I've got nothing against people of a darker skin colour . . .'

We drove up to the border crossing. On either side of the road were small restaurants, petrol stations with forecourts full of broken vehicles, trading companies either closed or in a state of permanent decline. During the Yugoslav wars, this had been a great place for smugglers. Many of them were local men, he said proudly.

*

Tibor Varga is a Protestant priest who has a reputation in Subotica as a man who helps everyone in need. He has a small office down some steps just off one of the main boulevards. As I arrived to meet him, an elderly Roma woman dropped by to ask if he had any spare blankets – or bananas, she added hopefully. She didn't leave empty handed. The office was stacked with provisions. Tibor is a pastor for the Golgotha Christian community, an offshoot of the American Calvary Hill Church. He's a big man, driven by his faith, his enormous energy, and his firm conviction that he is doing God's work on earth. In the past three years most of his energies have been spent on helping the refugees who live in the woods and the abandoned buildings around Subotica. He collects and spends about €500 a week on them. The gifts come not from him, he explains carefully to everyone he meets, but from God.

We went shopping together in one of the large supermarkets on the edge of the city. He bought the cheapest of everything – great sacks of potatoes, onions, garlic, bags of rice and flour, litres of milk, twelve packs of sunflower oil, 25-kilo sacks of dried beans, kilo bags of sugar and vast numbers of teabags – he had €200 in his pocket, and at least 200 hungry refugees to feed. The only 'luxuries' were a dozen whole chickens which the refugees would cook on their open fires, and packets of turmeric, ginger, spicy paprika and curry powder. If he had more money, he said, he would simply buy more, not different products. Many refugees suffer from bad shoes and a lack of clothes as the weather gets colder. Sometimes he can help, from donations. But mostly he just supplies the basic necessities of life.

'What I admire most about the refugees is their determination, their stamina,' he said, as we pushed an ever heavier trolley between the aisles of the supermarket.

Another thing is that, unlike the Roma, they only take what they need, and say no to items they don't have an immediate use for. The Roma scoop up everything they can.

These people are outside the system, away from the camps. In any case, if everyone went to the camps, they would be overcrowded, and they would be sent back to Preševo – on the Macedonian border. People don't want that. They don't want to lose the progress they feel they've made on their journeys. They would rather put up with hardship in the woods.

You don't need so much money to make people happy. In summer I love to see their faces when I bring them watermelons. Watermelons are so cheap here then. I take a lot of them.

They have often invited him to share their meal and, no matter how much of a hurry he is in, he cannot resist such expressions of gratitude.

By the autumn of 2017, the second layer of the fence on the Hungarian-Serbian border was finished, with a service road down the middle restricted to Hungarian police and army vehicles. There were cameras with night-vision equipment fixed every few hundred metres along the outer fence.

The second fence was electrified, like the old Iron Curtain, but not with sufficient voltage to harm anyone, just to send a signal to the security forces.

Refugees calculated that they had about three minutes, from the moment they cut through the outer fence and began to scramble over the second, before the soldiers and police arrived in force. The only way to succeed, they learned through hard experience, was to arrive at the fence in groups of about fifteen. They cut through, then divided into five groups of three, running in all directions. Then they lay low. This worked relatively well during the summer months, when there was still foliage on the trees and bushes, and crops in the fields. Some told me that after crossing, they lay still for as long as five days, not moving, without food or water, before they dared to carry on. And all the while the Hungarian police were searching for them, with dogs and sometimes helicopter support. They called this 'gaming'.

Those who were caught said they were often kicked and beaten by the police, as they lay on the ground. They only felt safe when German or Austrian police, deployed as part of the Frontex mission, were present. Then the Hungarians were on their best behaviour, they said.

First stop with Tibor was a derelict building in Palić, just off the main road, close to the once beautiful lake and tourist resort. As our car came bumping down the dirt track, we saw sudden movement in the bushes, as people tried to run away. They came back, sheepishly, when they saw it was Tibor. Furtive, thin, haggard Bangladeshi and Pakistan men hugged the Hungarian evangelical priest like a long-lost uncle. He knew many of them by name.

Hasan was from Bangladesh and had once got as far as Győr in western Hungary before he was caught and pushed back into Serbia. The Hungarian police had a rather liberal interpretation of the 8-kilometre rule which came into force in July 2016. Hasan had crossed the fence so many times he had become an expert. He even knew some of the Hungarian police on the other side of the border by name. He had a host of anecdotes about his experiences in Hungary. Once, when he was on the metro in Budapest, he heard the announcement, in Hungarian and English, 'next stop, Astoria'. For one marvellous moment, he thought the announcer said: 'Next stop, Austria.'

Tibor opened the back door of his truck, asked how many people were living in the ruined building, and distributed food accordingly. It should last them three or four days, until he or another NGO helping the refugees, called BelgrAID, visited them again. On metal sheets over an outside fire, we could see traces of the flat breads they had eaten earlier that day and the remains of a pot of curried beans. Inside the building were pitiful little piles of blankets in the dust and broken glass. The doors and window fittings, the wiring and plumbing had been ripped out by previous raiders.

As the nights grew colder what the men really needed was sleeping bags, they explained. Tibor replied patiently that he did not have such funds. Perhaps next time. The men nodded stoically. They did not complain if their requests could not be met. They just asked, in case. On the floor of one of the rooms, I found a faded postcard, written in Hungarian in a sloping, old-fashioned hand, to the former owners of the house, with Easter greetings. I could just make out the date: April 1964.

Hasan had crossed the Hungarian fence twenty-five times, he said, and had had enough of it. Now he was waiting for relatives in Bangladesh to send him more funds via the Western Union. This time he was going to try to reach Italy through Croatia and Slovenia. There was no fence there, but the River Danube was a big obstacle and there were many police and army patrols. The going rate with smugglers to Western Europe was €3,000.

Unexpectedly, for a man who is doing so much to help Muslim refugees reach Western Europe, Tibor Varga shared some of the Hungarian prime minister's views. 'This clash of civilisations is hard,' he explained. I challenged him on this. Doesn't Samuel Huntington's theory ignore the overlap of civilisations, how much different civilisations have contributed to and shared with each other over the course of history? Doesn't the theory suggest, on nebulous grounds, a permanent war, or inevitable conflict?

There are many misunderstandings between civilisations. Mistaken presumptions about what the other side is doing, or thinking. Those people not able to integrate, to get into the society they arrive in, will form their own parallel societies. Those who don't mingle are very dangerous. They could have an effect on Europe like a cancer in the body.

We are a humanitarian organisation, but we have Christian principles. So our aim is not just to help physically and materially, but to communicate our spirituality. To communicate to them that there is salvation only through Jesus Christ. No other religion can save them. You might say that message is too harsh. But Jesus too could be harsh. He said: no one can reach the Father, except through me. We know that people who embrace other religions are lost. But we show them love, the love that comes from God.

Some of his own happiest moments are when he has baptised formerly Muslim and atheist refugees. He holds church services, for Iranians in particular, in abandoned buildings and, when the weather permits, in the open air. 'We have witnesses who told us of people who wanted to become Christians, who met people on the way who were Christians. As a result of such charity, they converted. 'In Europe, people lost their Christian perspective, and live according to a very liberal way of life which does not respect our roots. Europe lost its Christian identity. We are not just doing a job, we are living it. We help not just refugees, but everyone who needs help.'

The refugees in Palić were frightened of the Serbian police. One showed me a shaky video, taken on a mobile phone by a man hiding in the bushes, of a recent raid by plainclothes police on the building. Burly, short-haired men wandered casually between the buildings, smashing cooking utensils, cutting plastic water containers with knives, and doing everything they could to destroy the fragile means of subsistence eked out here. It was just another of the many 'acts of deterrence' along the route, to send a message to them that they are not welcome – the opposite of Tibor's Christian charity.

From the ruined building we set out again in his minivan, crossing the main Belgrade to Budapest motorway, then turned off the road onto the sandy tracks lined with apple trees close to the Hungarian border. Tibor pointed to a line of darker fir trees, already inside Hungary. Between them, hidden by the apple trees, was the Hungarian fence.

The opening words of Psalm 89, cited at the beginning of this chapter, were written out by hand, in capital letters, on a piece of paper on the dashboard of the van. Tibor stopped abruptly next to a clump of bushes. We waited a couple of minutes, then three men appeared. More warm embraces. These refugees, two of Afghan appearance, one from Africa, didn't even have a ruin to shelter in. They were part of a group of a dozen or so at this place, sleeping in tents or makeshift structures they built in the bushes, waiting for the right time to make yet another attempt on the fence. If it wasn't for Tibor and BelgrAID they would starve.

As we drove away after unloading more provisions, we stopped for a moment to taste the sweet red apples which still hung from the low-lying branches of the trees, long after all the leaves had fallen. Local people in Serbia often help the refugees, with water, or food, Tibor explained. But they didn't like it if aid organisations or journalists started visiting regularly, churning up the mud, and drawing the attention of the police.

The final stop on this distribution trip was an open field, next to the ruins of what was once a substantial brick storehouse, on the grounds of a manor house. A sign beside the track flagged a region of outstanding natural beauty and value because of certain rare grasses and plants. About fifty men and women were waiting – the largest group I had seen in a long time. Tibor had messaged them on WhatsApp, so they were expecting him. More embraces. He joked with some, pretended to be stern with others. Some of the men helped him unload the remaining provisions. One of the women asked if he had any nappies and sanitary pads. Not this time, but he would try to bring some on the next visit. Some of those present, hearing we were from Hungary, were genuinely curious as to why Hungarians, compared to all the other peoples on their route, seem so determined to stop them in their tracks. I tried to explain – with examples from history, fear, the government. Not an easy task, standing in this desolate field, on the wrong side of the fence.

*

By the autumn of 2017, the men in the bushes told me, it had become well nigh impossible to cross the Hungarian fence. One option now for the trickle of migrants coming up through Vojvodina, the northernmost province, was to veer right – eastwards – into Romania. The Hungary–Romania border is 448 kilometres long. There is no fence, though Hungarian officials sometimes threaten that they are going to build one. With the Hungary–Serbia border hermetically sealed, smugglers developed a new route from the western Romanian city of Timișoara, across central Hungary into Slovakia, and from there through the Czech Republic and across into Germany over the 815-kilometre long Czech-German border. As Hungary, Slovakia, the Czech Republic and Germany are all part of the Schengen group of countries, there are no border controls between them. And while Hungary went to great lengths to stop refugees and migrants entering its territory, there wasn't much concern about those who did get in, leaving again, as Zoltán Boross admitted to me in an earlier chapter. Those caught entering from Romania, however, were pushed back where they came from.

On Sunday, 1 October 2017, eighteen refugees crossed the open fields on the Romania–Hungary border, about 100 kilometres east of Subotica. Fifteen were Yazidis, two Kurds, and one Arabic speaker, all from northern Iraq. They included five children, Sachem and Pasha, twins aged nine, a twelve-year-old girl Horia, Sonja aged five and Aiman, nine. There is no fence on the border here but frequent police patrols. They walked for two nights and slept during the day. A Tunisian smuggler came for them at 01.30 on the morning of 3 October, in a minivan with an Italian registration plate. The refugees squeezed in, and sat on the floor next to each other.

'After only a few minutes, we saw the flashing lights of a police car behind us,' Safaa, aged twenty-one, told me. 'The driver shouted at us, in Arabic, to get down, and keep out of sight. Then he drove faster and faster.' The next thing he knew, Safaa was lying in the wet grass next to the twisted wreckage of the van. He heard the crackle of police walkie-talkies and saw the blue lights of many ambulances. 'I could hear Sonja crying, so I knew she was alright, but my mum was just lying there, as though she was dead. Then the medics took her away.' The van had rolled down the embankment of the M43 motorway. Footage from a local television station, taken within hours of the crash, shows debris scattered across the road and at the foot of the slope. The chalk marks on the road where the driver fell from the moving vehicle. A line of police cars and ambulances, in a river of blue flashing lights. And the wreck of the black van.

Baran, the mother of the twins, died in the accident. The driver, a Tunisian aged forty-five, died later the same day in hospital. Hali, Safaa's mother, was one of those with the worst injuries. Her skull was cracked, and she suffered brain damage, a broken pelvis and broken legs. The children escaped largely unscathed, but all the adults were injured, some badly.

Three months after the accident I visited Hali with Safaa in the hospital in Szeged. She could open her eyes and move her hands slightly, and spoke a few words to her son. She spoke only of the past, of Iraq. She did not understand where she was or remember the accident. Safaa spent all his days at her bedside. There is a shortage of doctors and nurses in Hungarian hospitals as so many have gone to Western Europe to work. So Safaa was a welcome addition to the ward, giving his mother sips of water from a tube, feeding her, mopping her brow.

His young sister Sonja, just five years old, was only lightly injured in the crash and was fetched from Hungary by relatives, who took her to Germany. Thanks to the many operations and excellent medical care she received, Hali's condition was stable. By April 2018 she could speak a little more, and recognise other people, but she could hardly move. Safaa's family paid the hospital for her care, and for his stay in Hungary – $10,000 for the first five months. Most of the money came from his older brother in Munich. But the family's funds ran out.

The family hoped to get Safaa and his mother to Munich, and that the whole family could be reunited there. But Germany had enough refugees already and was not looking for any more – certainly not in Bavaria, the bastion of Horst Seehofer's CSU. Applying for family reunification could take years. The doctors at the Szeged hospital told Safaa that there was nothing more they could do for his mother. I went with him to meet Dr Endre Varga, the traumatologist overseeing his case. What his mother needed now, he explained, was constant attention from family members, backed up by an expert medical team. She needed the stimulus of words and music, food and water, and all the attention which her children could best provide, to help her regain her memory. And she would need active daily physiotherapy, to help her regain the ability to walk.

Safaa faced a difficult choice. If he applied for asylum in Hungary, he and his mother would probably be transferred to the prison-like conditions of a transit zone for many months while their applications were considered. They would probably be separated. If she came with him there, in a wheel-chair, he was concerned that she would not receive the constant care she needed in such an enclosure, behind barbed wire. If she stayed in a hospital which his family could no longer afford to pay for, who would attend to her? Yet if they did not ask for asylum in Hungary, both of them would be deported back to Romania. In early summer 2018 their case took a sudden turn for the better. Thanks to the mediation of the UNHCR and the good-will of the Hungarian Immigration Office, Safaa and Hali were placed in Hungary's last open refugee camp, at Vámosszabadi, while their family reunification request was considered by the German authorities. Hali's condition continued to improve, slowly, and she could recognise and converse with visiting UNHCR officials and thank them for all their help.

Just across the Romanian border in Timişoara, I went looking for other victims of the crash. Samir, aged twenty-five, from Mosul in Iraq, came slowly down the road towards me on crutches. The refugee camp, known as the Emergency Transit Centre, is on the northern fringe of Timişoara, next to a large shopping mall. There are 200 places for people already granted refugee status, awaiting resettlement mostly in the UK and the US. And there are a further fifty places for asylum seekers, those who have recently crossed illegally from Serbia to Romania.

Samir was in pain as he moved, especially when swivelling round to sit down. We went into the shopping mall, to a café where the waitresses are known to be kind to refugees. They let them recharge their phones here, and sit in the warm for hours on end, even if they don't drink anything. Sometimes they even bring them free sandwiches or cups of tea.

Samir wore a dark hoodie pullover with an orange lining. He had a short beard and dark brown eyes. Goran, a Kurdish refugee from the camp, who has also applied for asylum in Romania, translated for us, from Arabic to English. Samir has two sisters and three brothers left, after another brother was killed by Shi'a militia. But he has had no news from any of them, or from his mother and father, for a long time. He doesn't even know if they are still alive. His father served in the Iraqi army when Saddam Hussein was in power before the 2003 US-led invasion. After Saddam was toppled, the US disbanded that army, a move generally accepted now as a disaster, as many of its best trained soldiers ended up joining the forces of the so-called Islamic State; as troops with battle experience they played a central role in making IS such an effective fighting force.

Samir's father fled over the border into Turkey. When IS occupied Mosul in July 2014, Samir's Kurdish mother hid him in their house. After Mosul was recaptured by Iraqi forces in July 2017, he was regarded as suspect by the new authorities. He went to Turkey, then returned to Iraq when he thought it was safe. He was caught by an armed Shi'a group, the same one that killed his brother, who put him in prison and tortured him – presumably as a suspected collaborator. When he was released, he escaped to Turkey again, and from there, reached Romania through Bulgaria and Serbia.

The medical care he received in Hungary after the accident was good, he said, but the police were constantly asking when he would be well enough to be deported. Two police officers were constantly present in the Hungarian hospital, though Samir was hardly in any condition to run away. The doctors allowed them to take him away too soon. In Romania, the condition of his leg worsened, his scar opened, and he got an infection. Now he was uncertain where to go. He applied for asylum in Romania but continued to look for chances to move on. Through Facebook, he stayed in contact with others who had passed through the camp, and had then reached France, Italy or Germany with the help of smugglers. They offered to help him. He was torn. 'I don't want to go to any more countries. I'm tired of crossing borders. Germany, Romania, they are all the same to me because I have never been to Europe before.'

Samir was a keen footballer before the accident, but because of his injuries would probably never play again. As he was good at fixing mobile phones and computers, he hoped to find that kind of work. Or as a social worker. 'So many people have helped me on this journey. I would like to help refugees too, in future.'

First, though, he would need to finish his schooling, which was cut short by the US invasion in 2003, when he was ten. When I asked if he had any possessions that he brought with him from Iraq, he reached for his collar, and turned it back to reveal a thin silver necklace from his father. On his left wrist was a thicker, silver bracelet from his sister. Another bracelet, from his mother, which he wore on his right wrist, was lost during the accident.

Murat, his wife Khose and nine-year-old son, Aiman, Yazidis from a village near Sinjar, were also injured in the crash. Aiman was playing table tennis with other Kurds in the camp when I arrived. Later that morning I visited his Romanian language class. There were just three pupils, practising the peculiar vowels and syllables of a strange alphabet, in a country where they did not want to stay any longer than absolutely necessary. But at least learning Romanian eased the boredom of waiting.

Aiman took me to see his mother and father, across the yard. All three were deported from Hungary in December. They spent many hours waiting at the border, in pain, for the officials to complete the paperwork. Khose's injuries – to her spine and legs – worsened, and she had to spend two more months in hospital in Timişoara. Goran, my interpreter, shook with fury as he told me their story. He showed me photos on his phone of how he had to clean the infected wounds of the deportees himself, because they couldn't be admitted to hospital in time.

Aiman spent most of his time helping his injured parents, cooking food, washing the dishes and the clothes and changing the bedsheets, his mother told me proudly.

Murat described the drama of his family's escape from Sinjar, when IS forces entered. He was the only person in his family with a car. He drove his wife and child and as many relatives as would fit in, up the mountain to escape. But when he tried to go back for his wife's family, it was too late – the city had fallen. Nine family members are still missing, including several girls and children. Two years have passed, with no word from them. He fears they are all dead.

Could he ever imagine going back to Sinjar? I remembered the scenes of utter devastation, street after street of rubble, which other Yazidi refugees showed me, in Dimitrovgrad in Serbia in November 2015.

'What should I go back to?' Murat replied, quietly. 'I will see on one side of my house those whom IS killed, and on the other side I will see the gap where my missing relatives used to live. I will miss them every day. So where should I go back to? I cannot go back to a town with so many problems.'

'The most important thing now is for my wife to recover. In my heart we all still want to go to Germany, and for the four children I left behind in Iraq to come and join us there, and for us to live together as a family again. We cannot stay here.'

Aidi was twenty, a serious, determined Yazidi girl, who stayed behind in Iraq to attend a Business Studies course at Dohuk University when her mother and six brothers and sisters set out for Europe in 2016. Her father had moved to Germany several years earlier. In September 2017 she set out alone to join them in Munich. She teamed up with another girl in Romania, then was involved in the same crash in Hungary. She ended up in the hospital in Orosháza, east of Szeged, with serious leg injuries. In the hospital she was befriended by Noémi Nikodém, a local Baptist pastor.

I thought the doctor would have to amputate my legs, and that I would never walk again. But Doctor Zoltán said to me: Aidi, do not be afraid. You will walk again. The doctors and nurses were very kind, everyone in Hungary was very kind to me, and I am so grateful to them.

Noémi's mother and other family members came to visit her in the hospital. Then Aidi too was deported to Timişoara. In the camp kitchen, she sang softly under her breath as she washed the dishes.

*

In 2016, only 1,900 people applied for asylum in Romania. In 2017 the number rose to 4,600, as more people tried to transit Romania on their way to Western Europe.[1] Most passed through Timişoara. Resettlement was a different issue – a glimpse of good practice in the often frustrating international refugee system: 126,000 refugees were resettled by the UNHCR from the countries where they first fled, and which were deemed unsafe, to other countries around the world. The Emergency Transit Centre in Timişoara acts as a halfway house for those already accepted for resettlement.[2] There they attend courses and complete the final paperwork before they are flown to their destination countries. Since the camp was established by the Romanian Immigration and Asylum Office (IGI), the UNHCR and the International Organization for Migration (IOM) in 2008, 2,500 refugees have passed through it.

On the afternoon I arrived, twenty-nine refugees from Afghanistan, Somalia, Iraq and Eritrea, all of whom were living in Syria when the war broke out, were packing for their journey to the UK the next day. They had all applied for asylum in Britain, while still in Syria. The process had taken several years but had ultimately been successful. Now they were very excited.

Ruqia was from Somalia, travelling with her son and two teenage daughters Ahlam and Yasmin. They sat on the beds in their bright yellow and orange African clothes, like butterflies in the grey Romanian winter. They grinned from ear to ear, leaning back on suitcases packed for their early morning departure to Manchester, via Munich, on Lufthansa flights. They already knew the addresses of the flats they had been allocated in Bradford, in north-east England. The last years in Syria had been hell, Ruqia told me, and the family constantly in danger.

The next morning at 3.30 I met them again at Timişoara airport, weary from lack of sleep. Officials from the IOM helped them unpack their bags from the bus, then lined up the bags at the check-in gate, as the airline staff were not yet there for the 05.50 flight. The IOM people went outside for a coffee and a smoke. At this point a Lufthansa check-in official approached me, presumably because I was wearing a jacket which gave me an air of authority. The bags were in the wrong line, in front of Business Class, she explained, indignantly. They should be moved at once, in order not to discomfort her Business Class passengers. The thought of moving fifty-eight bags even a short distance seemed daunting. I started to wake up some of the men to help me, then was overcome by a wave of indignation.

'Don't you realise these people have come from war zones?' I asked her. 'They have endured war, shelling, bombing, rape and imprisonment, and you are now concerned that they are standing 3 metres to the right of where they should be?' Couldn't she just swap the signs for Business and Economy class? Fortunately, the IOM officials returned at this point and resolved the situation in a matter of seconds, in a hurricane of Romanian. Then the families disappeared through the gates. Their plane would fly high over the Hungarian fence, to Manchester with a stopover in Munich. Then they would start a new life in Hull and Leeds, in the north of England.

The camp was strangely empty after their departure. Commander Vasilescu was proud of both sides of his camp's work, with refugees and with irregular migrants. 'When I see families with children I feel compassion for them because I have a family too. Maybe if I was in the same position as them I would do the same.' He was well aware that most were just resting under his care, while they looked for smugglers in Timişoara, to take them on to Western Europe. 'Even if they don't respect our rules, we try to understand. Perhaps they were not fortunate enough to go to school, maybe they have a different religion or culture. We try to respect them and to provide them with the information they need to respect us.'

On the wall of one of the UNHCR rooms in the camp was a child's painting of a little girl in a blue dress, offering a bunch of flowers to a soldier in camouflage uniform, kneeling in the grass in front of her. A yellow butterfly, perched on his finger, was inspecting the flowers. Bullets dropped from the soldier's left hand. Outside in the playground, a little Iraqi girl in a brown anorak swung to and fro on a red and blue swing in the morning sunlight, her eyes tight shut.

In the weeks after I met them there, all the victims of the crash left Romania with the help of smugglers.[3] Samir reached Italy. Murat, Khose and Aiman were hidden in a truck when they were discovered by police in the Czech Republic. After two months in an asylum detention camp there, they were released and finally made it to Hanover to their relatives.

Aidi was smuggled by car across the Hungarian border in February 2018, hidden under a blanket in the back. Quite probably the border guards were bribed, as each car is checked rather thoroughly. After a twenty-hour journey from Timişoara, the smuggler dropped her off outside the flat where her parents, brother and sister live, in Munich.

'I hugged them, and we all cried so much.' She hadn't seen them for more than eighteen months. The authorities placed her in a refugee reception centre in Regensburg, where I went to visit her the following month. We sat on the shore of the Danube, close to the ancient stone bridge, with the medieval towers of the city reflecting in the river and the church bells ringing out the quarter hours across the water. She was so happy, and she spelt out her plans. 'First I will go to school, to learn German. Then I will go to university. Because I have one dream. I want to work in an office. I would so much love to work in an office. That's my dream!'

First of all, though, she had to get asylum in Germany. In April 2018 she was told that her application for asylum had been turned down. For a while it seemed she would be deported back to Romania. After everything she had suffered on the journey, the crash in Hungary, the deportation to Romania, the new journey to Germany, and her joy at being reunited with her family, her world appeared about to unravel once again. Then, on appeal, her application was granted after all. She sent her Hungarian friend, Noémi, photos of the big family picnic her father organised in her honour in a park in Munich to celebrate.

Two hours' drive to the north in the East German city of Gotha, I met Akhir, another of the survivors of the crash in Hungary. Like most of the others, he was also deported by the Hungarian authorities to Romania and spent several weeks in the refugee camp in Timişoara. From there, still on crutches, he was smuggled in a lorry through Hungary to Germany.

The smuggler told us the journey would only take four to six hours. In fact, it took thirty-seven hours. We had no food, just water. It was also very cold – January 2018. Then the lorry stopped and we were told to get out and hide in a forest at the roadside. We waited many hours, then a van picked us up and took us to another place. Finally we were transferred to a car. After a while the driver said: 'You are now in Germany.'

We spoke in his room in the rather dilapidated camp on the outskirts of Gotha. He lifted his shirt to show me his scars from the accident – down his shoulder, on his arm and across his abdomen. He was very glad to have reached Germany safely but desperately lonely. His wife and children rang while we were talking. 'Take me to you now,' his three-year-old son asked, as though he could reach out and pluck him through the phone.

I went with Akhir to meet Sigrid Ansorg, a youth integration officer of the Evangelical Church Community in Gotha. She explained patiently to him that even before he got asylum, he could start a German language course. The more efforts he made to start integration – he had been in Germany two months when we met, and still hardly spoke a word of the language – the more chance he stood of getting asylum. Then, in the best case scenario, his wife and children could follow him to Germany on family unification grounds, about a year after his own request was accepted – if it was accepted. She introduced him to another Kurdish man, who promised to take him to meet his father. 'It is important you integrate in your own community, as well as integrating in Germany,' she explained. The camp was full of lonely people, far from home, isolated, spending hours on the internet with their distant families, but hardly in contact even with other camp inmates. The challenge facing Germany, how to cope with so many lonely people, is daunting. Through his window, beyond the bicycles of the camp staff, stretched an open field with a row of solid German oak trees.

In 2015, 890,000 asylum claims were made in Germany, 280,000 in 2016 and 190,000 in 2017.[4] The steep fall helped Germany to cope, but the family reunification issue was a thorny one, especially at a time of coalition negotiations. Through the autumn of 2017, Germany's Green party held out for maximum family reunifications, while the Bavarian CSU refused to accept that. Aidi's situation appeared to hinge on a Green party success – but those coalition talks broke down, and the new German government eventually resembled the former CDU–CSU–SPD grand coalition, albeit a weaker one than before.

My research in Hungary led me to the two nine-year-old boys, Hachem and Pasha, whose mother was killed in the crash. They were looked after in the SOS Children's Village in Fót, near Budapest, with a twelve-year-old girl, Horia, who was travelling on her own. The UNHCR helped the Hungarian authorities and the Red Cross trace relatives of the three children in Western Europe. After several months in Fót, they were finally reunited with their relatives in Austria and Germany. By May 2018, fifteen of the seventeen survivors of the crash had reached Germany. One, Omar, had been deported back to Romania under the Dublin procedures. Only Safaa and his mother Hali were left behind in Hungary.

CHAPTER FIFTEEN

WISH YOU WERE HERE

As a nation, we have become fearful. And fear is dangerous, both to others and to ourselves. It causes us to lash out, stop thinking, lose our perspicacity, and bury our analytic capabilities. [...] And why have we become fearful? Because fear is easier to deal with than discomfort. Discomfort is too demanding.

Adam Seligman, University of Boston[1]

Berlin, June 2017

Nawras Ali lives in the Moabit district of Berlin. I last saw him at the east station in Budapest in late August 2015, taking part in a protest against the Hungarian government's decision to stop refugees travelling on. He is settled now in the German capital with a good job, a nice flat and plenty of friends, both German and Syrian. He has been granted asylum. He has already passed his B1-level language exam and is working towards the C1. The language exam system starts with A1, for beginners, and finishes at C2 which is interpreter standard. All refugees are required to reach at least level B1. Germany is taking the integration of its new arrivals very seriously. Most importantly, Nawras has found work, as an editor at a German-Syrian video centre helping documentary film makers in the Middle East. His office is a few minutes' walk from the metro stop at Turmstrasse.

The street is bustling in the early summer, lined with food shops whose outdoor shelves boast all the shapes and colours and varieties of the fruit and vegetable kingdom. He's waiting for me on the pavement in front of his office, lightly bearded, brown-eyed, twenty-six years old. In Damascus he was a poet and a translator, with a degree in hotel management. He left Syria to avoid the draft.

> I decided to leave my country because it's not my war. Should I risk my life for somebody to stay president? Or for somebody else to become president? It's a war over chairs. Why should I die for such a thing?
>
> I left everything behind. Imagine that you've left your family, all the places, all the memories, all the people that you've ever loved, all your friends. You only now have your name – but the new people you meet cannot even say your name properly! So you've also left your name behind as well.

On the Greek island of Kos, having lost all his possessions overboard from the crowded, leaking dinghy during the sea-crossing from Turkey, he bought a small wooden disc with the peace symbol on it, which he still wears around his neck – the peace he came to Europe to find.

The hospitality and welcome he has received in Germany began in Macedonia. 'When we were walking across the border from Macedonia towards Serbia we met a German soldier. He asked us: are you going to Germany? We said yes, and he said to us: then you should learn to say "Guten Morgen!" And he was really nice, and that was my first impression.'

When he reached Germany in September 2015 he spent the first twelve months at a refugee camp in Morbach in the south. Without knowing a word before he came, he learned almost fluent German, and gave Arabic lessons. In Berlin, we sit at a long wooden table upstairs in his office, speaking in hushed tones, so as not to disturb his colleagues in the editing suites which open off the corridor.

Does he feel free now, in Europe, after escaping the war at home? I ask. A melancholy smile passes over his face. He quotes Pink Floyd: 'Did they get you to trade your heroes for ghosts? Hot ashes for trees? Hot air for a cool breeze?' 'It's not a freedom of course . . . but what other options do we have? It's not right, but the world is not right.'

Later he shows me the flat he shares with another refugee. He's earning enough now to pay his own rent, national insurance and tax, so he's already contributing to the German economy after less than two years in the country. The flat is modern and tidy, with a small balcony. Through the window, the wind is blasting across the flat plains of north-east Germany. Hot air for a cool breeze . . .

Many people were welcoming from the start and they are still welcoming. But other people are not racist, they are simply afraid, they are being cautious and simply trying to have a more decent understanding of what's happening here. Who are those people? Are we going to have a good life if they are part of our society, or not? I completely understand this.

He has watched with concern the series of incidents involving asylum seekers – starting with the 2015 New Year's Eve attacks on women in Cologne.

What happened in Cologne affected everybody. First of all the women who had to suffer those terrible events. And it affected a lot of people who had nothing to do with those things, who came here because of war or other bad situations in their countries.

How was it possible that 1,000 men – like a small army – got together and decided to molest and harass and even rape a group of ladies in such a terrible way?

If even 1 per cent of the 1 million refugees who came to Europe were terrorists, that would add up to 10,000. We should have had 10,000 terrorist attacks through the last two years. And how many were there? Five or six? So what should we understand from this? Maybe some of those guys were sent by terrorist organisations. But I also think that some of them were mentally ill. Leaving your country, going through terrible things there or on your journey, then staying alone in a completely different culture, harms you.

Even in my own experience, I went for two or three months when I hardly spoke to anyone. It's easy to lose your mind.

Nawras mentions the case of the German citizen of Turkish origin who ran amok in a Munich shopping mall in September 2016.

He had an identity crisis. He always wanted to be regarded as a German, but felt he was always seen as Turkish, as an immigrant. Finally, he exploded inside and staged this terrorist action. Look at the USA and you can see a lot of similar incidents, in schools or wherever, when people have been bullied or psychologically tormented, and they do such terrible things.

The incidents made him even more determined to integrate and prove he can be trusted. 'When you have been given an opportunity to start a new life, you have an even bigger obligation, to respect the place and the people who helped you and prevent others from hurting people or hurting this beautiful society.'

There is no such thing as collective guilt, he says. All refugees should not be blamed, though he knows they always would be. If he ever overheard anyone plotting anything bad against Germany, or even expressing extreme views, he would turn straight to the police, without hesitation.

Would he ever become completely German? Would Germans ever really accept him, a stranger in their midst?

You know it's funny, somehow I think about this question every single day. When I was in Morbach I met a guy from Syria who had lived here in Germany for forty years. He told me: if you want to spend your life here, you need to kill a lot of things inside yourself. You need to die and come back to life with another personality, another attitude. If you think any more about your own country, you will just torment yourself, torn between this completely Western society, and your completely Eastern society, and you will be nobody anymore, neither Syrian nor German, just a guy who comes from somewhere else and stays here. I don't know the answer, but what other options do we have?

That evening he takes me to a bar called Neu Nachbarschaft, new neighbourliness. It's a typical German place, with a long table called a Stammtisch, a table for regulars. But instead of heavy beer drinking, bottles slammed on the table and youth the worse for wear from the effects of alcohol and drugs, most people are sipping tea and chatting cheerfully. He takes me round and introduces me to his friends, German and Syrian, women and men. He drinks hot ginger, I drink beer. Yann, a postgraduate student from Zurich, explains the philosophy of the place. Anyone who wants to learn German and meet Germans, refugee or not, can come here. Young Germans who want to meet foreigners come here to teach, or just chat, and party. In the hubbub, I have to almost shout to make myself heard. Would Nawras ever consider going back to Syria?

I remember the night when I was leaving Damascus. It must have been nearly 2 a.m. I was going to the place where the buses stop, to catch a bus to Beirut airport in Lebanon. As the car was driving outside the house of my sister, I looked everywhere. I saw the old citadel of Damascus, the cars, the streets, even the garbage cans. I was trying to memorise everything, even the smells. Damascus is special. It is not just another city. It is the oldest capital on earth. Whenever you go in the old city you have that feeling that you are seeing and smelling things that are 10,000 years old. All those civilisations, all those people that ever lived there, reliving their lives. As I left Damascus, I said to myself: I will go back, one more time.

Bargteheide, Schleswig-Holstein

Haneen meets me at the railway station in the small town where she now lives with her father, Bashar. I know from her Facebook photos that she wears a hijab, a headscarf covering her hair. She has an oval, pretty face, with very exact eyebrows, and a serious, self-confident manner which alternates with an easy laugh. We walk through Bargteheide in bright sunlight, with rain clouds building quickly in a chill wind. These are the plains of northern Europe and I can already hear seagulls and smell the salt of the North Sea on the breeze. No one stares at her, a girl in a hijab, or at us, a European man and a Middle Eastern woman. There's a small-town friendliness. We exchange greetings with people as we pass.

The flat where she lives with her father is fifteen minutes' walk from the station, on the second floor of a redbrick building, with bicycles in the hallway and flowers on the window sills. It's all spick and span, radiating provincial German middle-class order. Most of the names on the doorbells are German and slippers are arranged neatly beside welcome mats. Her dad is out at his German classes. He's at beginner's level A1, learning the alphabet and basic grammar, which he will need before he can restart his profession as carpenter and tailor. Haneen has already completed her B2 language exam. When we met in Hungary, we spoke English. Now she would prefer to speak German. She finds the two languages confusingly similar, after her native Arabic.

Her mother Maha is still in Damascus with her older sister Ranim, twenty-three, and younger brother Nour, thirteen. She misses them hugely and hopes they will soon be able to join them in Germany. But Germany no longer has an embassy in Damascus, so, in order to apply for a visa to join her husband and Haneen in Germany, Maha must travel to either Lebanon or Jordan. Both countries, already overwhelmed by Syrian refugees, make travel difficult. Maha has an appointment soon in Amman at the German embassy, but it is not yet clear if she will get permission from the Jordanian authorities to go. If she does, and her application for a family reunion is successful, the process will take another six months. It would be easier to travel to Beirut by car from Damascus, but the queue for an appointment at the German embassy there is much longer. She has still not received a reply to her letter sent five months earlier. Judging by the experience of other refugees, her mother and younger brother will get permission to come, eventually. It's just a matter of time, patience, Bashar tells me later, when he gets back from his German course.

Together, we look at photographs I took of her and their group in the cornfield at Röszke, on the Hungary–Serbia border. She points out other people she recognises from the group she was travelling with. Her friend Rama was given refugee status in France, after many months on the island of Corsica. She is still hoping to go to England, to visit her aunt.

Haneen's uncle, her father's brother, is also here in Bargteheide, in a flat on the other side of town. A young Palestinian man and his father are living in Hamburg – they're still in touch, occasionally. And that Syrian woman, travelling alone, she last saw in the transit camp in Dresden.

Haneen is grateful to Germany for their flat, and a room of her own which she has painted in white, pink and purple. She and her father were recognised as refugees in February 2016 – just five months after they arrived in Germany. They get €360 each a month, which is just enough to live on, as the Job Centre – the German institution which manages asylum seekers – also pays their rent.[2]

Bashar's carpentry workshop in the Zamalka suburb of Damascus was completely destroyed in an airstrike in 2014.[3] She remembers running for cover as she walked home from the school where her mother teaches religion. After her father lost his livelihood, his business and all his tools, the family first moved to another flat, nearer the centre. Then they decided that Bashar and Haneen should go ahead to Europe, and the others would follow. Two things discouraged them from travelling together – the cost, and the danger of the journey.

The worst part of the journey was the nine-hour trip in a hopelessly over-crowded rubber dinghy from the Turkish coast to the Greek island of Samos. The engine failed, and the boat was sinking when a Chinese cargo ship spotted them and alerted the Greek coastguard. A police launch took the soaking refugees aboard. Four days later, after only two nights of sleep, and a final 30-kilometre walk from Serbia into Hungary, they reached Röszke.

After Damascus, she's a little bored of Bargteheide, she confesses, so we take the train to Lübeck. She loves window-shopping there, strolling through the old town, looking at its old churches and municipal buildings with their spikey Hanseatic spires. The ancientness of the place reminds her a little of Damascus.

She wants to study architecture at the university in Lübeck. Even before she left Syria, she dreamt of becoming an architect. It's Ramadan, so she and her father are not eating or drinking anything till the sun goes down. We sit by the river in the sunshine. The language is the hardest thing for her to get used to. Most of her friends are fellow refugees, for the time being. There's still a loose network of Syrians and Iraqis she got to know in various camps. She's impatient for the day when she can meet young Germans too. She finds them friendly and welcoming, but reserved.

The only time she experienced fear or hostility was when she was in eastern Germany, in a camp in a basketball stadium in Dresden. Even now she sometimes notices children staring at her headscarf. But she has not considered giving it up. 'It's part of who I am.' She likes many things in Germany but she needs to stay herself and the scarf is part of that. 'Germans accept that. They have no problems with people from another culture. There are people who don't like the refugees but most accept us.'

Walking back to the railway station in Lübeck we pass a statue of Otto von Bismarck on his horse, the bronze turned green by the salt in the north German rain. Who was Bismarck? she asks. A predecessor of Angela Merkel,

271

I say, and of Helmut Kohl. This figure with his spiked war helmet and bushy moustache. The unifier of the German states through war and diplomacy. The man who created a Germany large and strong enough to help so many refugees today. And the absurd thought crossed my mind that, today, in the early twenty-first century, Bismarck would be a great name for a dog. A servant wiser than his master.

In Haneen's room in Bargteheide there's an array of the little pins she uses to pin her scarf up, and a small arsenal of perfumes and lipsticks. Pictures of her fellow students, and of her German teacher, Anna, her first friend in Germany, line the walls. She's reading an American thriller, *Dead Girls Don't Lie*, and the Turkish author Elif Shafak's novel *The Forty Rules of Love*.

Are Germans interested in her, for who she is, or are they just waiting for her to become like them? She finds the question amusing.

'I'd just like to be like me. I can't just decide to be German. I don't think anyone can be another person! Nobody can be someone that they are not, but there are many good things we could learn from this culture, like their attention to time. They are so . . .' – she struggles for the word – 'pünktlich. Punctual. I think that's great.'

On the radio she mostly listens to rock music. Her favourite station is Radio Hamburg. 'Just music, no news. I don't like news.' While we were out, her father was preparing the Ramadan meal for us. They share the cooking and the housework, depending on which of them has German lessons that day. Bashar has cooked flat Arab breads with sour cream, grated cheese, dotted with black cumin seeds, a large salad, and a cucumber and yogurt salad with garlic and mint, like a Greek tzatziki. It's all vegetarian, out of respect for me, their guest. There is also a large bottle of brown liquid, mixed by Bashar from water and tamarind, a traditional drink for the breaking of the fast.

Bashar says a short prayer, thanking God for his bounty, his help to people in need, and the sacrifice they have made to him, by not eating during his holy month. We slowly chew on our dates, then tuck into the main course.

Cologne

Tariq is late for our meeting at the main station because he has an appointment with his bank-manager. It's not easy having a bank account under a false name, but life for him in Germany is easier that way.

His real name has become a burden because he first registered as an asylum seeker in Austria and gave his fingerprints there. When he reached Germany, he applied for asylum again, under his real name. But Moroccans stand little chance of getting asylum in the EU because Morocco is classified as a 'safe' country. The only chance, unless they can prove persecution, is to say they come from the western Sahara districts, close to the border with Mauritania, where a territorial dispute still flares up occasionally. In fact Tariq is not a refugee at all. He's an electrical engineer with a degree from the University of Marrakesh, specialising in building power plants, and he came to Europe to seek his fortune. Under the rules in force, there was little chance for him to apply for work in his own profession. So he had to go through the performance of claiming asylum even though he's not running away from anything – apart from low wages, few prospects and boredom in his home town in western Morocco.

The square in front of the station looks the same as it did in the photographs from New Year's Eve, 2015. The dark cathedral, rearing up like a horse, the lenses in the second-hand camera shop at its foot, the faces of the policemen in their booths in front of the station entrance all brood on the same questions: what does it mean to be German today? And was it wise to let so many non-Germans shelter beneath our huge Aquiline wings?

Tariq arrives, wearing a flowery black and white shirt, and mirror sunglasses. His hair is longer than when I last saw him, curling black over his collar. He's too thin, I think, starved by the years of illegality, but handsome with it. When he takes off his sunglasses, his brown eyes are surprising gentle and vulnerable. He would need a good dentist, and then he could apply for any job, hold his own with any official.

We walk down to the shore of the Rhine to talk. The day is hot, scantily clad girls sunbathe on the grass, while the tourists sip away the summer afternoon at a row of expensive cafés. Poorer or freer souls like us, sit in the shade of the trees and watch the world go by, with our bottles of fizzy apple juice.

'If you come to Germany and ask for asylum the government gives you a place to sleep, and pocket money,' Tariq explains. He gets €287 a month, plus a free bed in the former classroom he shares with twelve others in a school in the Cologne suburb of Troisdorf. 'With this money you can survive but you cannot make anything for your future. You can also get work on the black market.' He does this too, one day a week, for €5 or €6 an hour – well

273

below the minimum wage. Washing up in a restaurant, working on a building site, some painting and decorating. He knows people who have done this for years. He's a comparative newcomer to the game.

There were a lot of other North Africans who came at the same time as him, in 2015 or 2016, he says. Moroccans, Algerians, Tunisians, Egyptians. Some of them were already in Europe, in Spain or Portugal or Italy, working illegally. Others were new, like him. The refugee crisis gave them another strategy to survive in the EU, the asylum card. The hard thing for illegals, is their illegality. The danger of being stopped by the police without papers, of going to prison, of being deported. The refugee crisis gave them a way to apply for papers and find a free place to stay. To get just legal enough to survive a few more months, then disappear with another name.

If you look at this from the point of view of the police, in a time of terrorism, it's a nightmare, I suggested to Tariq. He scratched his head. He wasn't exactly used to looking at things from a police perspective. He saw the issue more in terms of poor travellers struggling for survival in an often hostile Europe.

'You can give any name you want. But it also says on your ID card that it is not based on original documents. So it's easy. I know some people who used five names. Sometimes they ask you, which is your correct name? So you can choose any name.' Such uncertainty about their identity worked in their favour, he explained. If you had genuine documents, and the police knew for certain who you were, they could prove this to the authorities of your own country and arrange for your deportation there.

Each asylum seeker also gives his fingerprints, so the authorities can identify him with all the other people he has tried to be. They just don't know which of the names he has used, if any, is the real one. He did know Algerians and Tunisians who had been deported, however. The police came for them at two o'clock in the morning and took them straight to the airport in Frankfurt. A few hours later they were home. And a few months or years later, one way or another, they were back in Europe. There was less pressure on Moroccans.

'Without a passport they don't believe you anyway. Even if I give my correct name.' He tore up his own passport on a small boat crossing the Aegean, when he first saw the lights of Mytilene on Lesbos. But no sooner had he thrown the bits of paper in the water than the outboard motor broke down. They were rescued by the Turkish coastguard and towed back to the Turkish coast. So then he was in Turkey with no documents. On the third attempt to cross to the Greek islands, he succeeded.

He was still in Athens when the Cologne events of New Year's Eve 2015 happened, but as a North African living in Cologne, he feels 'the Cologne effect.' If he goes into a supermarket, the security guards follow him. If he heard a fellow immigrant talking about how much he hates Germany, or even planning an attack, what would he do? 'First I would sit down and talk with him, like a friend. But if he didn't listen to me, I would go to the police. I would lose a friend, but I would save many people – children, women, the elderly.'

We take a train together to Troisdorf, the quiet suburb of Cologne where he lives in a former primary school with a shifting population of around fifty fellow asylum seekers. Troisdorf is twenty-five minutes from the city centre, a strange mixture of middle-class German inhabitants and many waves of migrants. There are Russian shops, Asian supermarkets, Turkish cafés and Iranian taxi drivers.

Tariq is not a strict Muslim – we drank beer together in Athens – but many of his fellow asylum seekers are, so he invites me to share the Ramadan meal together with him and his room-mates that evening. First we go shopping together. I buy the ingredients: frozen pizzas, feta cheese, yogurt, falafel, cucumbers and tomatoes. He already has a chicken in the fridge. The supermarket is full of fellow Muslims with similar plans, families of head-scarved women, bearded men followed by a gaggle of children, the grown-ups a little strained after not eating or drinking all day, the children playful in the luxury of not having yet reached the age where fasting is encouraged. I've hardly eaten or drunk all day either, in order to better understand the people I will spend the evening with.

The playground of the school is still decorated with wall paintings of underwater scenes – giant octopuses, sharks, rainbow fish, with crazy divers and small ships resting on the surface.

In the middle of the playground are three large concrete table-tennis tables. Some people are sitting in doorways, some are already hard at work in the former kitchen. Tariq shows me to his room, a former classroom which still has the words 'Frau Pieper, Klasse 9–10' on a little piece of paper next to the door. The room is divided into several living spaces with blan-

275

kets and metal rods. There are three beds in his corner, with small, messy piles of possessions; men living alone, in limbo. Other classrooms, where families with children are living, are more homely. Many are from African countries, Guinea, Nigeria and Eritrea. The Eritreans have a good chance of asylum, the others little chance, but they are all cooking together, laughing together in the kitchen, preparing to eat for the first time that day. One of the Guineans is cooking fish, he tells me. Sea fish or river fish? River fish! He laughs, as though the idea of sea fish were ridiculous. Another Moroccan wires up his phone to a loudspeaker and starts blasting out what sounds like a North African rap artist. Onions and minced meat sizzle in one pan, our falafel in another. Two Algerian men chop potatoes. Most of the cooks here are men, and there's a loose camaraderie, linked by their Islamic culture. As I chop the cucumber and garlic, and mix it with the yogurt for a salad, I want to taste whether it has enough salt, then suddenly remember no one is allowed to eat today till 21.45.

The last hour passes very slowly. Everyone is putting the finishing touches to their meals. Finally, the time comes. I sit down with a man from Eritrea who has been here eight months. He was born in Somalia, to parents who had already fled Eritrea. He has never seen his own country. Another Moroccan, Ahmed, says he has been in Europe thirteen years. He started in Italy, and has only been deported once, from Belgium, last year. Then he made his way back to Germany. Each time he applies for asylum, in order to get the papers needed to stay temporarily. He lives off his allowance, and like Tariq, a day's work here and there, in the kitchen of a Turkish restaurant, or picking fruit on a rural farm where no one cares too much where the labourers come from, so long as they work hard and don't need to be paid too much.

These are people on the edge of a world, in transit. Some are registered elsewhere in Germany and have just come for a visit. Some have been living here in the school more than a year. Two security guards in black shirts, an Iranian and a Kazakh, patrol the corridors, but there is no order to keep. The Iranian laughs and jokes with everyone, asking about the ingredients, the herbs and spices in each dish. The Kazakh is burlier, unfriendlier, hardly blinks when I smile at him. Tariq tells me he was a refugee himself and has been in Germany for fourteen years. He lived many years in a small room with ten people, Tariq says, and suffered a lot in his life, that's why he never laughs, but he's not a bad man.

Tariq is waiting for news from his cousin in Sweden, from whom he got money on the journey, when his own ran out. His cousin will come by car to fetch him in the next few months, he hopes. He has heard that the police checks on the Øresund bridge from Denmark to Sweden, introduced in 2015, have been stopped. Trains and railway stations attract the police, but the motorways of Europe are the best way to travel, he knows. There he can fit in more easily with the crowd. If he makes it to Sweden, he won't apply for asylum there. He'll just live quietly with his cousin, who can find him work in the black economy. Sweden was, after all, the original goal of his journey. He walks me part of the way up the street, towards my hotel. At thirty-six, he's older than most of the immigrants I've met. What does he miss most about Morocco? He grins, shyly. 'My Mum.'

Ansbach

The railway line from Cologne to Ansbach leads through peaceful, hilly countryside, glides past orderly German towns and villages. The roofs of long medieval German barns slope sharply down towards the track, from an earlier era when winters were still winters. After the flat north, and the industrial faces of Cologne, I feel as though I'm in the Shire in Tolkien's classic *The Hobbit* or *The Lord of the Rings*.

Further down my carriage, a group of young women have decorated their space with balloons and party bunting, and play awful disco music from a cheap loudspeaker. They're drinking a bright yellow liquid from little glasses that must be quite strong, judging from the rising level of jollity. In the next carriage there's what seems to be a sports club, in which all the men wear orange T-shirts and drink beer and sing loudly, though it's only ten in the morning. I start to miss my gentle, sober Muslims.

At each station, the intercity train gets more crowded. People with reservations fight their way down the aisles, but it is all rather good humoured. The ticket inspector is a young woman with a kind word for everyone, who has a calming effect on the travellers. Soon most people have a seat or at least a suitcase to sit on. The train is immaculately clean, even the toilets. This vast network of trains, all running like clockwork, exactly on time. A million more people have arrived? No problem, we just reopen disused buildings, set up container camps, give them an allowance, set them to learning German. No national consultations, no official campaign to warn people how dangerous they might be. Just one party, the AfD, campaigning against them, but all the mainstream parties sitting down to work out how to integrate the newcomers and set them to useful tasks, not how to keep them out. This is a tolerant, thoughtful country.

Omar is waiting for me at the Herrieder Tor in Ansbach, with his girl-friend Carolina, her nine-year-old daughter, her sister, her brother-in-law and their children. He stands out as a tall, self-confident Iraqi in a friendly cluster of Germans. We walk together, all of us, through the narrow, cobbled streets of the old city in Ansbach. It's a feast day in this pretty Bavarian town, there are stands with games for children, fast food stalls selling vegetarian flammkuchen and wok-burgers, barrel organs and ice creams. There are also many refugees here, Kurdish, Syrian, Iraqi and Somali, mingling with East European immigrants from Romania and Albania. There are shops selling shisha water-pipes next to traditional beer-cellars and sausage stalls. The meat stands mention delicacies like lamb and beef alongside the more traditional pork, as a gesture to Muslim customers. It's still very Bavarian, but with an international, Middle Eastern twist, adding to the general frivolity of a day off in mid-week. And each quarter, the bells toll from the many churches, reminding all and sundry that everyone owes their freedom from work to the Christian roots of this community.

Omar has had several girlfriends since he came here eighteen months ago, he tells me, but now he has found Carolina and is in love. She's a Bavarian village girl, blonde and vivacious, who was teased when she first came to the town because of her village accent. The father of her daughter was a Somali asylum seeker who left her when he got his refugee status.

She had a low opinion of Arab men before she met Omar, she says. She thought they mistreat their wives, that they were dirty, uneducated. But all that has changed now, and she finds him very 'attentive, romantic and reliable'.

He has learnt German quickly, has already passed his B1 exam and is studying hard for his B2. When he has passed that, he can take his driving licence. From the autumn, he will study computer engineering. He had just qualified as an English teacher when he had to flee Mosul, on the day in August 2015 when IS took over the city, but he's been told there's not so much demand in Germany for English teachers.

'I'm so happy. I'm doing my language courses, I found the vocational course that I like, which I didn't have the chance to do in Iraq. Germany has been good to me. People are nice, and I'm grateful to them. I'm making progress.'

We sit together in the park while Carolina takes her daughter and cousins to a playground. The birds are loud, joggers pass, and young Germans on bikes. Is everything in Germany perfect then? I ask. Not quite, he admits.

I'm sorry to say this, but the Germans sometimes seem like machines. They look straight ahead, not left or right, they work all the time and don't have any time for themselves. Then at the weekend they just sleep or go to the swimming pool or something. A person needs some time for himself, to enjoy life too. Maybe this comes from the history. They had to rebuild their country after the Second World War. And they did rebuild it, as the strongest economy in Europe. But work here takes over everything.

Another thing is the relationships. I've noticed people don't have great contacts with one another. Let's say the daughter lives in Bavaria and her parents are in Hamburg. Maybe they speak on the phone every two months. Or send a text. And that's it!

He worries that if he settles down here, and starts a German family of his own, he would be expected to behave like that too, and he wouldn't like that. The family is very important in Iraqi culture, he explains.

My brother is in the UK, my family is in Iraq, and we are in contact every two or three days. If someone is sick we go to him, if someone needs money we send it to him. For example, my brother in the UK gave me the money to come to Europe. He did so much for me, and he called his friends to see if they can help me too.

Another thing which drives him crazy is the paperwork. None of his qualifications from Iraq, not even his driving licence, are recognised here, so he has to do everything again. 'Even to go to the supermarket here, you need a paper!' He exaggerates. 'And the internet is so bad. When I talk to my family in Iraq, and the signal is so weak, they can hardly believe that I'm really in Germany!'

There are also strange anomalies in the system for asylum seekers, administered by the BAMF. He has noticed that more educated refugees get sent to the villages, while less educated ones are put in the cities. He has also witnessed with his own eyes how some asylum seekers cheat the system.

I knew one man who was actually from Egypt, who managed to pass himself off as a Syrian. He was given refugee status for three years. But he was lying! I told them only the truth, and I was only given permission to stay for one year. I'm grateful for that of course, but still . . .

The refugees who come here need to work hard on themselves. They have to learn this language, they need to do many things, to integrate. But it's also true that whatever you do, you will never quite reach the level you wanted. There are some areas that the Germans reserve just for themselves. You will never be fully accepted as one of them.

Omar stays with Carolina in Ansbach sometimes, but his official place of residence is in a refugee camp in Schopfloch, a village 40 kilometres away. He shares accommodation with Kurdish Iraqis, with Afghans, Somalis and Eritreans. It's a very diverse group, he says, but with a common responsibility.

We are guests here and we need to give the best we have. In our country it's the same. If you are foreign and come into another country, you need to be polite, to be on your best behaviour.

Some people here don't like refugees, but they don't like Italians, or Spanish people, or foreigners in general either. People are waiting for what we are going to do, so we just have to do our best.

That evening Omar, Carolina and I meet Magda, an official in the local council in Schopfloch whom Omar regards as his protectrice, his 'German mother'. We sit at an outdoor café. He eats ice cream, I drink beer, the girls drink fresh lemonade. The town is buzzing with yet another Bavarian religious festival – nowadays it seems, a chance for the locals to eat sausages and consume vast amounts of beer. Magda tells us her story.

I grew up in a refugee family too – my father came from the Sudetenland, in what is now North Bohemia, in the Czech Republic. I was born in

Germany after the war, but he told us as children many stories about his old home, and what it was like to flee. That's why I help refugees today.[4]

Nevertheless, when we first heard in 2015 that 130 asylum seekers would be placed in our village it was very difficult. People were very fearful. No one could really imagine it. And up to a point that is still the case today. Many people have not taken the trouble to get to know these people better. If they had, they would not entertain such fears any longer. Although everything has calmed down, it has been very peaceful here, nothing at all has happened to disturb that.

Not in Schopfloch, that is, but the first suicide bombing in Germany took place just a few hundred metres from where we are sitting, in July 2016. Mohammad Daleel was a twenty-seven-year-old Syrian who arrived in Germany in August 2014.[5] His first request for asylum was turned down, and he was supposed to be deported to Bulgaria, the first country where he registered. Bulgaria automatically granted him asylum, and under the Dublin procedures, the German court argued that that was therefore where he ought to be. According to German media reports, he tried to kill himself twice, and was given psychiatric treatment. He appealed against the deportation decision, but in early July 2016 was told that his appeal had been rejected, and he must return to Bulgaria.

Just when he became radicalised is still not clear. He began to assemble the ingredients for a homemade bomb in the refugee hostel in Ansbach. July 26th was a Sunday, and a music festival was scheduled in the town centre. Following a knife attack a few days earlier in Munich, the police presence in Ansbach too had been strengthened. Daleel carried a rucksack, and either because of this, or because he had no ticket, he was refused entry to the concert, which was attended by 2,500 people in a closed space. He sat down outside Eugene's wine bar at 22.22, leant forward, and his backpack exploded – possibly by accident. His last internet contact that evening was with a person in Saudi Arabia. He died on the spot. Fifteen bystanders were injured, four of them seriously. On his mobile phone, a video was found of him pledging allegiance to IS, which also claimed him, in a communiqué several days later, as one of their 'soldiers'. The evidence made public so far suggests that he was in fact a 'lone wolf' whose mind snapped during the loneliness of exile and because of the failure of his asylum claim, rather than a so-called 'sleeper', sent from the Middle East to attack soft targets when the time was right.[6]

With Magda, Carolina and Omar, we visit the scene of the attack. 'These were people who had already been living for a long time in Germany,' said Magda, referring not just to Daleel but to the perpetrators of other recent attacks.

They were not newly arrived refugees. The media exaggerated so much. I still don't know exactly what really happened in Cologne. I just don't believe that those involved were normal young men. None of those I have got to know here were there.

People who live in ghettoes, whatever their ethnic origin, are more likely to turn to crime. Some may join IS, others will organise themselves in gangs or whatever. And then such atrocities are the result. So these are individual acts. The media and the politicians exaggerate their importance. I'm often alone with them, in the evenings to eat, I have never had reason for fear.

This is also what happened in Germany with Hitler. He said to them, 'Come with us, and everything will be better and different.' They can catch people like that. But when people integrate well it's totally different. Omar could never be caught like that. Because he is well-integrated, because he can see where his life is going, where his path leads. That's the answer – we should work harder to make sure people don't end up in ghettoes. So they learn German even better, so they find work, and such problems don't arise.

Bruchsal

Marah, twenty-two, from Aleppo in Syria, comes to meet me with her sister Rama, twenty. She can't remember exactly where she first met me, but it must have been either in front of the east station in Budapest or on the hard shoulder of the motorway, during the long march towards Vienna on 4 September. 'I gave so many interviews that day!'

Their father died before the war started in Syria. They travelled to Europe with their mother, Mouna, forty-four, and their brothers Hamze, fifteen, and Faisal, sixteen. Marah has long blonde hair, her sister a slightly darker shade. Both could pass as Germans – almost. They are observing Ramadan, though neither covers their hair with a scarf.

'Perhaps I will wear a headscarf later, perhaps not,' explains Marah. At this time in her life, as a refugee in Germany, she chooses not to. But the decision is not so much to do with what the locals think of her, rather about her relationship to her faith, she says. Right now, it is important to her to keep the fast, but not to cover her hair.

The three of us sit at a café in the pedestrian zone in Bruchsal. The waitress brings a menu. I order coffee and water. The girls say nothing for them, thank you. A flicker of recognition appears in the waitress's eyes. With so many Turkish Muslims, and so many refugees in Bruchsal, she is well aware that it is Ramadan. Her Neckar valley sense of hospitality nonetheless ensures that she brings a large bottle of water, and extra glasses for the girls – 'just in case'. As temptations go it is a rather innocent one, but the girls resist it easily.

During the first eight months, we were waiting to be able to start language classes. Then we were waiting to find out own flat. My brothers could go to a normal German school, so in a way it was easier for them. They could make friends really fast. Before that they went to a preparatory school but that wasn't so useful, mostly drawing and playing.

We don't have a lot of German contacts, but we have got to know some people. We meet in the street or in cafés or in the language school, but not really true friends, I think we should go to university or work to really get to know people and have a strong relation to them.

Marah has found part-time work though, first in a bakery, now in a home-goods store, thirty-eight hours a week. She likes it there and the other staff are friendly. She started playing the violin, but had to give it up because she doesn't have time at the moment, with the language classes and her work, and helping her mother at home. Soon her German will be good enough to go to university, she hopes, to study telecommunication engineering. Rama plans to move to Cologne, to finish her language courses. Then she would like to study bio-engineering, she thinks.

Marah likes the cosmopolitan feel in Bruchsal, and the whole country: 'That's what's I find so beautiful in Germany. It's always nice to see a mixture of people and that makes a country like an international country, like USA.

There's people here from the whole world and I think it's very good . . . we can learn from each other, and like this, life is not boring.'[7]

News of terrorist incidents in Germany and other countries made the girls sad, they say.

> Because people got hurt, and also because we are afraid that the people will turn against us, against all immigrants. Though I don't think they have here. I always trying to explain that the people are different in every country, and there are bad Syrians too. That doesn't mean we're all bad. I think the situation will get better. Because the longer we spend here, the more Germans will get to know us, and understand us.

There's no 'Syrian community', or community of immigrants from other countries here, that she knows of. 'Syrians here don't like to meet each other so often, we all want to get to know Germans, learn the language from them, and learn their way of life. The better contacts you have, the more likely you can find work, or an apartment.'

The main regret they have here, is that it has been very hard for their mother to get used to Germany. She's learnt the alphabet and she has the basic words, but it's proving hard for her to make progress with German. She's rather lonely and says she would go home to Syrian immediately, were it not for her children. But she knows it's better for the children, and far less dangerous, so she stays. They all stay. And life goes on. Back in Aleppo, their old flat is in any case in an area now controlled by snipers. There is still no electricity or water supply. There will be no going back for any of them for a long time, the girls think. They follow developments closely, mostly through friends' posts on Facebook or Twitter.

After they have gone home to help their mother prepare the Ramadan feast, I visit a bookshop and chat with the owner. She welcomes the refugees but says their arrival has laid bare the division between the former East and West Germany – a division she had hoped had been at least partly over-come. She is upset about the hostility shown to the refugees by many in eastern Germany. It's like in the rest of Eastern Europe, she says. People are afraid of what they don't know, yet they don't want to get to know it. Their politicians manipulate their fear, and certain politicians know how to push the buttons which bring those fears to the fore. Nevertheless, she is cautiously optimistic. After everything Germany has been through in the last century, she is hopeful that the people can see through the machinations of those who push such buttons.

I find the street where Marah and her family live, near the railway tracks. It's an old house, several storeys high, with a good wooden staircase up to their second floor flat. All the flats have Middle Eastern-sounding names outside. They were found for them by the Job Centre. It's still hard to persuade local people to rent out their flats to refugees, Marah told me earlier. They never say that is the reason, but she feels it. They say usually say someone applied just before them.

The kitchen is all a bustle. Her mother, Mouna, offers me her wrist as her hands are wet. Both sisters and brothers are hard at work cooking, there are small pastries frying in one pan, parsley chopped on a board with tomatoes and bulgur for the tabbouleh salad, and wonderful scents wafting through the room. There's also a soft undertow of laughter, given a sharper edge by the hunger, the anticipation of everyone in the room – only ninety minutes to go to the breaking of the fast. My own contribution is a bowl of green and black olives, from a stall in the market, and some peaches. Where do you come from, originally? I asked the young man selling them, his dark curly hair and beard suggesting the Middle East. 'I'm German, I was born in Germany,' he told me, somewhat resentful of the question. If his parents came here from Turkey, he implies, that is their problem.

I'm shown through to the living room to meet Ludwig. He's a cheerful, gentle fellow in his mid-sixties who has become a personal friend of the Al-Saaed family. He was an English teacher for thirty-five years here in Bruchsal, and when all the refugees arrived in his town, he volunteered immediately to help.

'When I saw the pictures from Munich, of all the welcome banners and crowds on the railways station in September 2015, I thought: this is all very well, but this is where the hard work begins,' he tells me. It's a pattern which has been repeated all over Germany, which has proven central to the integration process – local citizens of all ages, but especially those with time on their hands, stepping forward to adopt, mentor or guide the immigrants. While the local authorities can organise a certain amount, through the Job Centres, in terms of funding, studying and finding a flat, it is these personal relationships which really help the refugees most.

Ludwig and I sip fruit juice in the living room, which Marah insists that we drink in the hot evening, though we weakly protest that we ought, like her, to keep the fast for another hour. Ludwig tells me about a new citizens' initiative in the town, against the refugees. A friend of his came to ask if he would like to be involved in a rival citizens' initiative, made up of people who actively support the refugees, but Ludwig said no. He doesn't want to get mixed up in the politics, he says. It's enough for him to help a family like Marah's on a daily basis. That's what he would like his contribution to be. He would take part in such a group, however, 'if it comes to that.' And will it? I ask. It could go either way, he concludes.

The food arrives, dispelling all fears, real or imagined. Little pastries like Indian samosas, but with spinach and soft cheese in them. A great spaghetti bake, in a tomato sauce with cheese on the top, and all kinds of European and Middle Eastern salads.

Mulhouse, France

The train from Freiburg to Mulhouse crosses the Rhine. There are slim German cyclists, like spiders in their tight rubber cycling gear, nursing their expensive, lightweight machines and brilliant fluorescent helmets. Two elderly couples, also German, loudly lament the attitudes of modern youth.

The journey into France only takes twenty minutes. Mujeeb is waiting for me at the station, wearing what looks like the same black waiter's shirt he wore for his job in the Afghan restaurant in Istanbul in July 2016. He helped translate for the Afghan refugees living in the park on the shore of the Sea of Marmara, or in their cheap rooms in the Zeytinburnu district, sloping down steeply to the water's edge.

A few months after I left Istanbul, the Taliban rang him. He saw on his phone that it was an Afghan number, and answered it thinking that it must be a friend or relative. 'We know where you live,' said the voice. The voice told him his own address, where he was living peacefully with his wife and two small children, after fleeing the Taliban in 2015. In Turkey, unlike most other refugees, Mujeeb had money in his pocket, a Turkish visa and residency papers, and a steady job. With his father-in-law, he set up the restaurant in a district where many Afghans live, and it soon became a successful business and a focal point for the local Afghan as well as the Turkish community. That proved to be a mistake. He was too visible, and soon the Taliban tracked him down.

The root of all his and his family's problems was his brother Hasib's work as a journalist for French NATO troops at the Kapisa airbase in western Afghanistan from 2009 to 2012. Radio Omid FM was no ordinary radio station. It was a controversial propaganda tool in the war NATO was fighting against the Taliban. The public were encouraged to contact the station to inform on fellow Afghans working for the insurgents. The French soldiers in Task Force La Fayette, with their fleet of attack helicopters, killed many Taliban commanders and foot-soldiers.[8] As a presenter, Hasib's voice became well known on the airwaves, and the threats against his life and those of the other staff at the radio multiplied. When the French forces pulled out in 2012, they took Hasib with them, and gave him refugee status in France. But they left his father, mother, two brothers and sister behind. They became the subject of almost daily threats. The message was always the same: persuade Hasib to return to face Taliban 'justice' for collaborating with the enemy, or face Taliban revenge themselves, in his place.

At first the family hoped they were bluffing. Then in September 2014 Mujeeb was just arriving home to his flat when four armed and masked men seized him, and bundled him into a waiting car. His head was forced down between his knees, so he couldn't see where they were taking him. One of his captors hit him on the back of the head with the butt of his gun. He was saved by a police checkpoint. He was suddenly pushed out of the car, and his captors fled.

The incident shocked the family. Mujeeb, his wife and their baby daughter were sent to Istanbul. The other family members moved house again. Everything appeared to be going well, till that phone call. 'Your brother's actions resulted in the deaths of many of our men. You must persuade him to return to Afghanistan. Tell him his father is sick.' Mujeeb refused. The calls continued. 'Do not think we cannot harm you in Istanbul. We have our people there too. If you do not send your brother home, we will kill you.'

Mujeeb consulted with his family, and they agreed that he should follow his brother to France and seek asylum there. In the meantime, his wife and children should change their address and follow Mujeeb as soon as possible.

As a legal resident in Turkey, it was not difficult to get a forty-five-day visa for the Schengen group of countries. He flew to Germany then took the train to the town in France where his brother lives. His brother's daughter is seriously ill and the family is often with her in hospital. That particular town was full of refugees. Mujeeb decided to try Mulhouse, thinking that his chances would be greater. He could not have known that, after clearing the 'jungle' camp in Calais of several thousand asylum seekers in late 2016 and early 2017, the French authorities sent many of the refugees from Calais to Mulhouse.

'The first interview, at the regional capital in Colmar, was awful,' Mujeeb explains. 'They didn't believe my story, shouted at me, accused me of lying, of withholding information that they had not even asked for. The man told me he was fed up with 'lying immigrants'. But what I told him was simply the truth.'

Mujeeb and I sit in a cybernet café and try to find more about Radio Omid to strengthen his case. There's an article in the daily *Libération* about the French military's war of attrition against the Taliban. Unconfirmed sources told the reporter that the French troops based at Kapisa killed around 150 Taliban insurgents over the twelve months leading to October 2009, including nearly half in the valley of Alassaï. 'Such results allowed the French military contingent to reestablish their credibility with the US commanders,' concluded the reporter.

Most importantly for Mujeeb, there's an interview with a French journalist, Raphael Krafft, who visited the base at Kapisa and witnessed the operation of the radio station first-hand. We write to the journalist on Facebook, and within minutes he replies. We start printing out documents to strengthen Mujeeb's case.[9]

His immediate concern was shelter. Apart from staying at his brother's place, he has rented a cheap room above a restaurant. His room is at the end of a long, gloomy corridor, and the doors are padded, like in a brothel or a Communist-era ministry in Eastern Europe. But there are gashes in the padding, as though someone has attacked the doors with a knife. Mujeeb's room has the musty smell of unwashed laundry, and a view of the street. He's got about €500 left of the €2,000 he came to Europe with. He's trying to save every penny.

We sit at a café in the square in front of the cathedral. He is fasting, so I can't even buy him a sandwich. A choir of Frenchmen suddenly assemble and start singing patriotic songs. Tourists start photographing them. The bells of the cathedral chime every fifteen minutes.

I always try to be optimistic. Coming to France now is my last and only opportunity to escape from the Taliban. I must just do my best and hope I can get refugee status for myself and my family.

You cannot live with something very bad in your mind, that maybe you will be killed tomorrow or the next day, you cannot plan your life in this way.

To make matters worse, he has lost his passport. He took a late-night bus from his brother's town back to Mulhouse, which involved changing buses. He thinks he left the passport in a café while he was waiting for the next bus, but he's not sure. A stranger in a strange land, he asked his brother's advice. 'Forget the passport,' he told him, 'you won't need it now anyway.' I disagree. After meeting so many people who destroyed or threw away their papers, I know how hard it is for them that they simply cannot prove who they really are. I suggest he contacts the café, and then the police. He has nothing to lose. He will think about it, he says.

He spends a lot of time, worrying about his wife and children. What will he do if France rejects his asylum request? I ask.

'I have no other plan. If I get rejected its really the start of another big disaster in my life.' His children don't understand where he is, and why he never comes home. 'It's so hard when they always ask me, when are you coming home?'

It's very hard, when you had a very lovely life in your own country, and then you have to leave everything, your family, your friends, all your material things, your furniture, your car. But you leave everything behind and move to another country, and work so hard to make another life. And then you have to leave that too.

We make a plan to meet some other asylum seekers to go to the mosque together. Each evening during Ramadan, the Turkish Al Aksa mosque in Mulhouse provides free food – a godsend for poor refugees like Mujeeb. It's a long walk through the town, but they never waste money on public transport.

Omar Farhad from Laghman province in Afghanistan is one of our small group, winding our way through the French streets to the long-awaited meal. There's no point in hurrying though, as food will not be served until after the sun goes down. So we talk.

'I was hoping to go to England, but I got stuck in the Jungle at Calais for six months,' Omar explains. Thanks to all the publicity about it, when it was closed down in December 2016, the French interior minister promised that all those moved from there would be treated well.[10] And he kept his promise. Omar was given a place in a pleasant, shared flat in Mulhouse, with a shower, kitchen, a TV, a fridge, 'everything', he says happily. And pocket money. Unlike in Germany, asylum seekers in France have to pay their own rent from the €330 they receive a month. That leaves Omar with €220 to live on a month. The office in charge of immigration in France is called the OFII.[11] After the initial interview, it can take six months to a year to get the second, decisive interview. If your application is turned down at that point, you can appeal – which takes another six months to a year. In the meantime, you are living in limbo.

'It's hard to make a long-term plan, all we can hope for is to live in security and good conditions. I have made friends here, who came here long ago. I just hope one day I can live like them,' says Omar.

Two weeks after I left Mulhouse, I get a cheerful message from Mujeeb. The OFII have recognised that he is a genuine asylum seeker, and have given him a room of his own and some money to live on in another town. He sends photographs. A bed with clean white sheets. A peaceful, rural scene outside his window.

Luzern, Switzerland

The train from Mulhouse takes me south to Basel, where I change for Zurich, then again for Luzern. Switzerland seems even more affluent, more picture perfect than Germany, a soap opera landscape where everyone has perfect teeth and appears to be wearing new clothes.

I first met Saboor, a journalist from Afghanistan, at the camp at Horgoš on the Serbian border, in June 2016. He lived there for four months. Several weeks after we met he cut through the fence into Hungary. He was caught, beaten and pepper-sprayed by the police, then put in prison for a month. Then he was sent to the open camp at Vámosszabadi, near Győr. A man there gave him a number for a smuggler. Which country would you like to go to? The man asked. 'Any country where I will be safe,' he answered. They settled on Switzerland.

He was put in the back of a lorry – alone. Three days later he climbed out, in Basel, and went in search of the nearest police station. It was 30 August 2016. 'For the first eight days I was imprisoned in a basement in the Klausenberg camp in Sarnen canton. It was a crazy place – everyone there complained. The food was not good, the behaviour of the staff was not good, there were no facilities and the governor told us she hated refugees.' Klausenberg is one of six 'reception and processing' centres, run by SEM, the State Secretariat for Migration.[12] It was on a mountainside, far from everywhere – a frequent complaint of asylum seekers in Switzerland. 'I felt like I was a criminal. I came to Europe and found myself in a prison for refugees! When I was in Afghanistan I was in danger from the Taliban and IS and other groups who searched for me to kill me. But here in Europe life is not good. I feel like I'm being killed every day.'

After three months he was transferred to another camp called Sonnenhof, in Luzern canton. Under Swiss asylum law, the cantons (there are twenty-six in Switzerland) take over responsibility for the care of each applicant. Luzern has a particular problem at the moment, as a tax-break for companies failed to provide the expected level of new investment. Tax incomes for the canton fell sharply, and asylum seekers were among the first to suffer from a fall in the available budget.

Asylum rules have also become more draconian in the country in recent years, under pressure from the governing right-wing Schweizerische Volkspartei (Swiss People's Party), the SVP. It became the strongest political party in Switzerland at the 2015 elections, with 29 per cent of the vote and 65 seats in the 199 seat Parliament.[13] The cold shoulder Saboor felt was largely due to the rise of the SVP and its anti-immigrant stance. What he didn't know was that at least as an Afghan he had a chance of getting status. Applicants from Balkan countries were usually rejected within forty-eight hours, and from certain African countries within two weeks, under the 'accelerated expulsion procedure' pushed through by the SVP and approved at a referendum in June 2016.

Conditions at the Sonnenhof camp were somewhat better, Saboor told me. It was an open camp, he could come and go, there was even a shop nearby where could buy small things like biscuits. In each camp there was a system of minor punishments which he found unnecessarily oppressive.

When you left the camp you had to check out and in again on your return with the chip-card you were given. If you forgot, money was taken off your monthly allowance. And there was a string of other slight breaches of camp rules which he said were interpreted over-zealously by the camp authorities. However hard anyone tried, each ended up losing 20 to 30 francs of their precious 280 francs allowance each month. And the sanctions regime put each inmate in a permanent state of tension with the authorities, Saboor explained. They were treated as naughty children, not adult asylum seekers with wounded self-esteem. Certain inmates also received preferential treatment on the basis of skin colour or language, he suggested. In due course he was transferred from there to his current home, half an hour by train from Luzern. I had no opportunity to put his views to the SEM, but according to an overview of asylum practices in each country, published by the pro-immigration European Council for Refugees and Exiles: 'The interests of the asylum seekers are hardly taken into account in the allocation system . . . This system is problematic, as it fails to seize opportunities that would facilitate integration, such as language or further family ties.'

It would have been easier to bear the little indignities if time was not passing so slowly, Saboor told me. He had already spent nine months in the new camp, and there was no news about his asylum request. According to SEM statistics, Saboor was one of 3,229 Afghans who applied for asylum in 2016, while 7,479 applications from Afghans were still under consideration from the previous year. According to the decisions of first instance, 13.8 per cent were granted asylum, 75.6 per cent were granted temporary protection, and 10.6 per cent were rejected.[14]

I try to cheer Saboor up, but he is glum and frustrated and homesick. We sit at a table overlooking the lake. Swans sail by like East European monarchs in exile, ducklings follow their mothers, tourists take selfies of themselves on the famous wooden Chapel Bridge, and the Swiss clocks in the church towers of the city chime each fifteen minutes, their bells made crisper by the strange sharpening effect that water has sound. In the distance, the Pilatus mountain peaks, once famed for their dragons, and the Rigi mountains stood aloof, quietly contributing their waters to the River Reuss, which flows into the lake. The Rigi was the subject of several beautiful watercolour paintings by the British landscape artist J.M.W. Turner, and was also visited by the American author Mark Twain.

Later we take the train to his accommodation, about half an hour from Luzern. It's like a hostel, close to the railway station, with a reception office downstairs, run by a smiley young woman who's not only polite, but also very friendly. Upstairs on the first floor, a man is playing a mournful guitar in the living room. Saboor's room is on the top floor, right under the attic. It's clean and tidy, with three bunkbeds and a common table. One of his fellow Afghans is working with a set of tools to try to repair his bed, which creaks at every movement, waking his room-mates up in the night. We sit at the table in the middle. It's still Ramadan, so there's no comfort food available for Saboor. He insists I eat from his packet of dried figs, nonetheless. What will he do if his asylum request is rejected? I ask.

'Maybe I'll go back to Afghanistan and join the Taliban,' he says. 'I could be their spokesman!' He's joking, of course, but there's a bitterness in his voice he cannot hide. Europe, so far, has fallen far short of his expectations.

SEVEN LEVELS OF DESPAIR

> There are seven levels of despair – one for each day of the week . . . Any strategy planned by political leaders to whom such despair is unimaginable will fail, and will recruit more and more enemies.
>
> John Berger[1]

The western Balkans have always acted as a gateway to Central and Northern Europe for refugees, migrants, traders, soldiers and adventurers. The flow of humanity along that route from 2014 to 2016 was simply noticeably larger, and reported on in much more, dramatic detail. By 2018 it had been reduced to its usual steady trickle. Confronted by the new reality of the Hungarian fence, asylum seekers branch west through Albania and Bosnia, or east through Romania, with all the potential dangers depicted in chapter 14.

The traffic on the other main entry point into Europe from the south, the central Mediterranean route across the sea from North Africa to Italy, also diminished considerably. Future migration can be expected to follow a similar pattern – a slow, steady influx, interrupted by sudden surges provoked by man-made disasters like war and climate change. As one route closes, another opens.

In its attempts to impose more control over that process, Europe has become more of a fortress, and will continue to bolster its defences. In June 2018, the European Commission announced that it would triple its annual budget for combatting illegal migration to €5 billion in the next seven-year budget period (2021–8).[2] The funding, the Commission declared, would be aimed at 'ensuring proper control of borders, not closing them. The commission has never financed fences and will not do so under the new EU budget either.' The money will be spent largely on continuing the transformation of Frontex into a 10,000-strong standing police force along the land and sea borders of the bloc, and on all the technical gadgetry that force and the twenty-seven national police forces would need.

In the summer of 2018, one could almost speak about a 'lull' in migration in Europe. The deals struck between the EU and the Turkish government, and the EU and the Libyan warlords, were relatively effective. Only 1,000 Africans a month attempted the desperate journey north across the Sahara from the city of Agadez in Niger, compared to more than 10,000 a month in 2016.[3]

Politicians across the political spectrum, from far right to left, agreed that sudden mass movements of people should be prevented at source. Money is being ploughed into sub-Saharan countries in Africa. At best, this will help create work and better conditions, so fewer people feel the necessity to leave. At its worst, it will function as little more than a bribe to the governments of the region, to build their own fences to keep their people in and line their own pockets. Three rival governments in Libya, and up to a thousand militias, control the fate of up to a million migrants who have crossed the Sahara. Around one-fifth of these attempt the journey across the Mediterranean, while the majority try to find work in Libya.

International diplomacy failed to prevent or stop a spate of wars in the Middle East and has so far failed to find a solution in Libya. Europe remains an attractive place of refuge, despite its internal problems, which have been exacerbated by the impact of asylum seekers.

The much-maligned Iron Curtain served the interests of democratic West Europeans, as well as dictatorial East European ones. It conveniently cut off the poorer, more quarrelsome cousins in the east, and allowed Western Europe to develop faster. The new Iron Curtains are designed to defend Europe from the 'impoverished' other arriving from the south – or his or her cartoon image. The irony is that Western Europe would not grow richer without immigrants, it would undoubtedly grow poorer.

The tens of thousands of refugees stuck in Greece and the thousands stranded in the Balkans are resting, nursing their wounds. Turkey's 828 kilometre wall on the Syrian border is nearly complete.[4]

The war in Syria goes on. Of a pre-war population of 23 million, 6 million Syrians are still displaced inside their country, 5 million are refugees in the neighbouring countries of Turkey, Jordan and Lebanon, while around 1 million Syrians have reached Europe. That leaves a further 11 million Syrians still living in their own homes. Syrians constitute about a third of those who came to Europe in the years covered by my book. Half of them, according to one estimate, have a university education, and will be sorely missed if they do not return home, one day, when the war is over.

With the military defeat of IS in Syria and Iraq, some people have bravely attempted to go home – but face an uncertain future in towns and cities without water, electricity and jobs, alongside the danger of unexploded devices. If they return too soon, they may have to flee again.[5]

The war in both countries continues to uproot more people, while Lebanon, Jordan and Turkey are impatient for the refugees they have generously hosted so far, to go home. The war in Afghanistan is close to its fortieth anniversary. It began when I was a second-year student at university. I fear it will still be under way when I retire.

The war in Yemen, in fact a proxy war between Saudi Arabia and Iran, takes a heavy toll of human life and inflicts misery every day. The world, as ever, is in a sorry state.

Even as the numbers of new arrivals shrink, the political backlash provoked by the newcomers is growing. The peoples of Europe, confused by the impact of technology and globalisation, are looking around for someone to blame. The 'liberal elites' are one target, the migrants and asylum seekers the elites are accused of allowing into Europe are another.

According to one estimate, new fences stretching around 1,200 kilometres have been erected along the borders of Europe.[6] Populist, nationalist and nativist parties are growing in influence. According to one definition: 'Populism is not a deep ideology but rather a logic of political organisation. At its core lies a sharp distinction between friend and enemy, in which populists' supporters are portrayed as the legitimate people, and all opposition is painted as illegitimate.'

In Germany in September 2017, Angela Merkel's CDU won a third consecutive election victory, with 12.5 million votes, 27 per cent of the electorate.[7] Her party were down 2.5 million votes compared to the previous federal election in 2013. The number of CDU seats in the federal parliament fell from 254 to 200. Together with the CSU, the CDU's sister party in Bavaria, the two parties won 33 per cent. The Social Democrats were a distant second with 20 per cent, followed by the far-right, anti-immigration party, the AfD with 12.6 per cent. Close behind the AfD were the liberal FDP, the Left and the Greens.

Immigration, and Angela Merkel's handling of the refugee influx into Germany, was the single biggest issue. Her victory, though smaller than before, gave her a fourth consecutive term in office – she has ruled her country since 2005. Her open-door policy to refugees was partially vindicated. More than 87 per cent of the German electorate – all except the AfD voters – expressed their support for controlled immigration.

In the post-election period, as the chancellor struggled to find coalition partners, she finally accepted the need to cap the number of asylum seekers Germany could accept at between 180,000 and 200,000 a year. This corresponded closely to the number who actually sought asylum in Germany in 2017 – 189,000, an average of 548 a day. In the first few months of 2018, 333 new asylum seekers were registered a day, suggesting another decrease for 2018. The new interior minister was Horst Seehofer, leader of the CSU in Bavaria, and a sharp critic of Angela Merkel's immigration policies.

A few weeks after her election victory, Angela Merkel met Viktor Orbán at an EU summit. 'Viktor, help me, I have a problem!' she joked, according to one Hungarian government source. 'The CSU want to admit 200,000 refugees a year. What shall I do?' The joke illustrates the distance that still exists between East European governments which refuse to take in any asylum seekers from Italy and Greece, and those who continue to take in many, while insisting that European solidarity means sharing that burden. When, in the spring of 2018, Horst Seehofer provoked a crisis in the German coalition government by threatening Angela Merkel with a deadline to close the German-Austrian border, she called his bluff.

The argument of the Visegrád Four countries, that 'solidarity' includes building fences to strengthen the external borders, is not accepted in Europe. Viktor Orbán may have been among the first to loudly proclaim that external borders need to be strengthened. But this is seen across Europe as a law and order issue, to preserve the Schengen system, separate from the political question of EU solidarity, and the moral necessity to help fellow human beings in distress.

In Austria, thirty-one-year-old Sebastian Kurz led his Austrian Peoples' Party to victory in the November 2017 elections with 32 per cent of the vote, and immediately forged an alliance with the far-right Freedom Party of Heinz-Christian Strache, which won 26 per cent. Strache became vice-chancellor. Strache's anti-Islamic sentiments are summed up in his catch-phrase *Pummerin statt Muezzin*. The Pummerin is the name of the main bell in St Stephen's Cathedral in Vienna. Sebastian Kurz rose to the top in Austria by promising to close the Balkan route. In June 2016, still as foreign minister, Kurz was quoted in *Der Spiegel*:

> We in Austria have always had lots of immigration. But when one starts, as happened in Europe last year, to open the borders and to transport people northwards as fast as possible, then of course it's not just Syrians who come. People from all around the world then see their chance to quickly come to Europe.
>
> It is we in Europe, and not the human traffickers, who decide whom we take in. Whoever wants to enter illegally has forfeited their chance.
>
> At the same time, countries like Austria and Germany declare themselves willing to bring some of the poorest of the poor to Europe through resettlement programs. The decision cannot merely benefit the young men who are fit enough to withstand the journey.[8]

Seehofer's scheme to close the border between Bavaria and Austria collapsed in June 2018, just as it had in September 2015 when the Austrian government declared that they would not accept failed asylum seekers back from Germany.

Italy granted 120,000 asylum requests from 2014 to 2017. At the end of 2017, a further 200,000 were living in camps and shelters, awaiting a response.[9] They have proved a heavy burden on Italian society. Many Italians feel let down both by their politicians, for allowing this to happen, and by the failure of many countries, especially in Eastern Europe, to show their solidarity by accepting some of them. These would not have been 'illegal immigrants' as some governments have alleged, but vulnerable people pre-screened before departure, and rescreened by the host country before they were accepted. By EU and UNHCR criteria, they should stand a good chance of getting international protection.

In March 2018, in the Italian general election, two populist, anti-immigrant parties, Matteo Salvini's League and the Five Star movement of Luigi di Maio came first and second, with a combined total of 23 million votes, compared to 7 million for the centre left alliance led by Matteo Renzi.[10] In June 2018, they formed a coalition government, led by a fifty-three-year-old lawyer, Giuseppe Conte.[11]

The new hard-line governments in Western Europe teamed up with old hard-line governments in Eastern Europe, to devise new policies to limit irregular migration. A central plank of their policies will be to actually carry out the deportation of those whose asylum requests have been rejected. Each theft, rape, or murder is blamed on the whole refugee community. 'Gypsy crime' has been replaced by 'migrant crime' in the slogans of far-right leaders and the tabloid media they foster. This happens at a time when crime figures in Germany are falling steadily, including the number of crimes carried out by those granted or applying for some degree of protection.

In June 2018, the Italian government refused to allow the *Aquarius*, a ship run by the French NGO SOS Méditerranée with 629 migrants rescued off the coast of Libya on board, to dock in Sicily. Nevertheless, Prime Minister Conte was at pains to emphasise how many migrants Italy had already taken in, and the fact that the country would continue to accept more. To illustrate his point, another ship with over 700 souls on board could dock the next day. A week later, the *Aquarius* and two others landed in Valencia in Spain, courtesy of the new Spanish Socialist prime minister Pedro Sánchez. Meanwhile the French president Emmanuel Macron offered to accept those on board who wished to continue to France.[12]

'This offer shows that this is the framework of cooperation with which Europe must respond, with a spirit of European solidarity and real content,' Sánchez wrote to Macron. But the happy resolution of the highly symbolic *Aquarius* affair highlighted the general lack of agreement on all future boats. For many people in Africa, a journey to Europe, despite all the risks, still appears the main hope of a better life.

As Bulgarian political scientist Ivan Krastev wrote:

For a growing number of people the idea of change signifies changing one's country, not one's government. The problem with the migration revolution – as in any revolution, really – is that it contains within itself the capacity to inspire counter-revolution. In this case, the revolution has inspired the rise of threatened majorities as a major force in European politics. These anxious majorities fear that foreigners are taking over their countries and jeopardising their way of life, and they are convinced that the current crisis is brought on by a conspiracy between cosmopolitan-minded elites and tribal-minded immigrants.[13]

But perhaps the situation is not so dire. One backlash inspires another. To continue Krastev's analogy, the counter-revolution is already provoking a revolution. The danger of Brexit reminded many Britons, especially among the young, how 'European' they actually feel. And by the summer of 2018, the national mood had swung back, in favour of measured, controlled immigration. In Germany, public alarm about criminal acts committed by immigrants rose, even as the statistics showed a clear fall.[14]

The new nationalists in Europe may delight in one another's attempts to paint the 'foreign devils' on the walls, but they provoke ordinary decent citizens to stand up for an open, tolerant Europe. And nationalists, by definition, are opposed to one another. The glory of the Hungarian national myth sits uncomfortably with the glorious myths of the Slovaks, Croats and Romanians. And the memory of the meltdown caused by German and Italian nationalism in the 1930s is still fresh enough to warn people away from a new nationalist experiment. A more nationalist Western Europe will mean less money in structural and cohesion funds for Eastern Europe. Politicians in Budapest, Bratislava, Prague and Warsaw may yet rue the spread of their own rhetoric.

What has been learnt in the past four years? How can the refugee and migration issues facing the European continent be resolved? Are we any the wiser?

First, we have a moral duty and legal obligation to help genuine refugees. This principle remains true, despite the strains caused by the arrival of between 1 and 2 million genuine refugees, and despite the attempts of populist politicians to turn public sentiment against them. And despite the fear and dislocation caused by a small number of fanatics, who besmirch the good name of Islam with acts of terror. The temporary care of so many traumatised people, or their permanent integration, will be a massive challenge.

Second, the flow of refugees and migrants must be controlled, and the public reassured that this is indeed the case. The media share an enormous responsibility for this. Work visa programmes should be expanded, as should resettlement programmes.

The current self-selection process, whereby mainly the better-off or toughest people reach Europe, should change in favour of the more vulnerable.

Third, the EU needs to reach broad agreement on the reform of its asylum system, in particular to ease the burden on front-line states like Greece and Italy. A system for the relocation of asylum seekers should be established, which is neither compulsory nor voluntary, but automatic. Only in this way can it be depoliticised. If certain countries choose to opt out of that system, let them contribute more in other ways. Future East European governments may finally realise the value of immigration too.

Fourth, there is an urgent need to expand our concept of who exactly a refugee is, to include environmental refugees. The rich North, which caused climate change with its profligate use of carbon fuels, has a moral duty to help its victims in the poor South – just as much as the former slave states and colonial powers had a duty to help the descendants of their former subjects. As Pope Francis wrote in his 2015 encyclical *Laudato Si' – On care for our common home*:

> There has been a tragic rise in the number of migrants seeking to flee from the growing poverty caused by environmental degradation. They are not recognized by international conventions as refugees; they bear the loss of the lives they have left behind, without enjoying any legal protection whatsoever.[15]

Fifth, European countries continue to need the energy and skills of migrants. It is intolerable that migrants should continue to depend on the expensive, life-threatening services of criminal gangs. Much more efficient and fairer forms of legal migration, including circular migration, which allows people to go home safely after a time, need to be found.

Sixth, refugees need to be recognised as a development issue, as well as a humanitarian one. Ways must be found to integrate them into local economies and help them find more permanent accommodation, work and education. This is one of the cornerstones of the UN Compacts on Migration and

Refugees. Working groups are edging towards agreement on both definitions and solutions, based on international good practice. An important part of this recognition is long-term thinking which prepares refugees to return home. Most of the Syrians I met while researching this book told me they would be willing to return home to rebuild their country when they felt safe to do so. There is a contradiction between the efforts of countries, led by Germany, to 'integrate' the newcomers, and the newcomers' own daydreams of return. But the resolution of that contradiction should not be beyond our intelligence and organising skills.

Finally, seven decades of immigration to Europe have changed the continent, but they have also enriched it. National cultures are surprisingly resilient and we should beware of politicians who exaggerate their fragility for their own electoral gain.

I have tried in this book to refute the arguments of those who, either accidentally or on purpose, muddle Islam and terrorism. I hear the arguments of those who raise the spectre of the 'submission' of Europe to a young and vigorous Islamic minority, but I believe there is a far greater danger of that minority being scapegoated by right-wing extremists than of them 'taking over'. We have already seen many incidents in West European cities, of blind acts of hatred against Muslims. Islamophobia comes from the same wellsprings as anti-Semitism. At the same time, there is no excuse for anti-Semitism among the new immigrants. European values cannot be cherry-picked by newcomers any more than they can by already established communities.

'I have disputed the thesis that Europe is in the throes of a "clash of civilisations",' wrote Jytte Klausen.[16]

> Certainly there are strains and conflicts as states accommodate large numbers of Muslims, who are a relatively recent presence in Western Europe. However, the difficulty is not that Muslims are generally anti-democratic. The challenge is rather that they seek integration in European societies and claim a voice in European institutions, while insisting on equitable treatment for their communal organisations.

She speaks of a four-way conflict, between secular, sometimes anti-clerical Christians and Muslims on the one hand, and religious Christians and

Muslims on the other. 'European governments have the means to resolve these conflicts in a way that promotes integration,' she writes, 'but only if they act together with a broad spectrum of Muslim representatives.'

The next few years may be difficult ones in Europe. There is a danger of conflict: between the haves and have-nots, and between newcomers and native peoples. But the strengths of Europe which attracted so many immigrants here in the first place, the basic common sense of ordinary people, and the universal Christian heritage of the continent, point in a different direction. To a continent, and a union of peoples, able to respect one another's differences and cooperate in defence of common values. The weeping of the road may yet console the men, women and children walking down it.

NOTES

Introduction

1. *The Book of Sir Thomas More*: Shakespeare's only surviving literary manuscript, https://www.bl.uk/collection-items/shakespeares-handwriting-inthe-book-of-sir-thomas-more; Ian McKellen performing St Thomas More's Refugee Speech by Shakespeare, https://www.youtube.com/watch?v=afK_bXD7pMo; 'The banned 400-year-old Shakespearean speech', http://www.huffingtonpost.com/entry/shakespearean-speech-used-to-support-refugees_us_57e2b0b7e4b0e80b1b9f8ad7?

2. John Berger, *Hold Everything Dear: Dispatches on Survival and Resistance* (Verso, 2007).

3. 'Hungarian Folka Archive: The road before me weeps, the path is sorrowful' (Népzenetár – 'Sir az út elöttem bánkodik as osveny'), http://nepzenetar.hu/dalszoveg/4355/Sir-az-ut-elottem-bankodik-azosveny

4. Sándor Sára documentary, 1987, https://www.youtube.com/watch?v=SknxqpaF6zE

5. Vízöntö, 'The Road Before Me Weeps' (music video), 1998: https://www.youtube.com/watch?v=aQxFPdTh3d0

6. Website on Lajtha László (1892–1963), http://lajtha.heritagehouse.hu

7. For a full account, see Michael R. Marrus, *The Unwanted: European Refugees from the First World War Through the Cold War* (Oxford University Press, 1985).

8. Adrian Edwards, 'Forced displacement at record 68.5 million', 19 June 2018, http://www.unhcr.org/news/stories/2018/6/5b222c494/forced-displacement-record-685-million.html

9. Henry Fountain, 'Researchers link Syrian conflict to a drought made worse by climate change', 2 March 2015, https://www.nytimes.com/2015/03/03/science/earth/study-links-syria-conflict-to-drought-caused-by-climate-change.html. The role of climate change has also been challenged, see Jan Selby et al., 'Climate change and the Syrian civil war revisited', September 2017, https://www.sciencedirect.com/science/article/pii/S0962629816301822

10. Michael Ignatieff, *The Ordinary Virtues: Moral Order in a Divided World* (Harvard University Press, 2017).

11. Alexander Betts and Paul Collier, *Refuge: Transforming a Broken Refugee System* (Allen Lane, 2017).

12. Philip Faigle et al., 'It really wasn't Merkel', 11 October 2016, http://www.zeit.de/politik/ausland/2016-10/angela-merkel-influence-refugees-open-borders-balkan-route

13. Eurostat, 'Asylum statistics', 16 March 2018 and 18 April 2018, http://ec.europa.eu/eurostat/statistics-explained/index.php/Asylum_statistics. See also Phillip Connor, 'Still in limbo . . ', 20 September 2017, http://www.pewglobal.org/2017/09/20/a-million-asylum-

seekers-await-word-on-whether-they-can-call-europe-home/; 'EU asylum applications drop off drastically in 2017', 30 December 2017, http://www.dw.com/en/eu-asylum-applications-drop-off-drastically-in-2017/a-41976192; Eurostat, 15 June 2018, 'Asylum quarterly report', http://ec.europa.eu/eurostat/statistics-explained/index.php/Asylum_quarterly_report; '202,834 Asylträge im Jahr 2014', 14 January 2015, https://www.bmi.bund.de/SharedDocs/pressemitteilungen/DE/2015/01/asylzahlen_2014.html

14. For a useful overview of EU policy developments, see: European Parliament, *Migration and Asylum: A Challenge for Europe* (Fact Sheets on the EU), June 2018, http://www.europarl.europa.eu/RegData/etudes/PERI/2017/600414/IPOL_PERI(2017)600414_EN.pdf;

15. 'Turkey–Syria border wall to be completed by spring', 18 December 2017, http://www.hurriyetdailynews.com/turkey-syria-border-wall-to-be-completed-by-spring-124303

16. For analysis of the relative costs and benefits of asylum seekers in Europe, see, inter alia: https://www.loc.gov/law/help/refugee-law/europeanunion.php; https://www.oecd.org/els/mig/migration-policy-debates-13.pdf; https://www.economist.com/international/2018/04/21/european-countries-should-make-it-easier-for-refugees-to-work; https://voxeu.org/article/fiscal-cost-refugees-europe; https://www.politico.eu/article/refugee-crisis-cost-germany-over-e20-billion-in-2016/; http://www.amnesty.eu/content/assets/Reports/EUR_050012014 Fortress_Europe_complete_web_EN.pdf

17. Smugglers earnings in 2015, https://www.ft.com/content/9b00f2ce-e9d7-30c4-a490-532a59a35c55

18. http://www.spiegel.de/international/germany/germany-and-immigration-the-changing-face-of-the-country-a-1203143.html; https://en.wikipedia.org/wiki/Immigration_to_Germany

19. https://ec.europa.eu/eurostat/statistics-explained/index.php/Migration_and_migrant_population_statistics

20. 'Language of human rights often conflicts with local virtues, Ignatieff tells U of T audience', University of Toronto News, 4 October 2016, https://www.utoronto.ca/news/human-rights-ignatieff

1 The Year of the Migrant

1. John Berger, *And Our Faces, My Heart, Brief as Photos* (Pantheon Books, 1984).

2. 'Welcome refugees and reject racism – Merkel says after rallies', 31 December 2014, https://www.reuters.com/article/us-germany-merkel-idUSKBN0K90GL20141231

3. 'Anti-Islam "Pegida" march in German city of Dresden', 16 December 2014, https://www.bbc.com/news/world-europe-30478321.

4. Yaşar Aydın, *The Germany–Turkey Migration Corridor: Refitting Policies for a Transnational Age* (Migration Policy Institute, 2016); M. Bartsch et al., 'Turkish immigration to Germany: a sorry history of self-deception and wasted opportunities', 7 September 2010, http://www.spiegel.de/international/germany/turkish-immigration-to-germany-a-sorry-history-of-self-deception-and-wasted-opportunities-a-716067.html.

5. 'Immigration to France', https://en.wikipedia.org/wiki/Immigration_to_France, last edited 21 June 2018; K. Hamilton et al., 'The challenge of French diversity', 1 November 2004, https://www.migrationpolicy.org/article/challenge-french-diversity.

6. 'History of the Jews in France', https://en.wikipedia.org/wiki/History_of_the_Jews_in_France, last updated 22 June 2018; 'Attacks in France on Muslims, Jews and churches soar', 20 January 2016, http://www.thelocal.fr/20160120/france-sees-scores-of-attacksagainst-jews-muslims-and-churches.

7. 'Policeman Ahmed Merabet mourned after death in Charlie Hebdo attack', 8 January 2015, https://www.theguardian.com/world/2015/jan/08/ahmed-merabet-mourned-charlie-hebdo-paris-attack; 'Ahmed Merabet, "français, policier, musulman", tué par les frères Kouachi', 13 Janaury 2015, http://www.liberation.fr/societe/2015/01/13/ahmed-merabet-francais-policier-musulman-tue-par-les-freres-kouachi_1179546.

8. 'Orbán: 'We will not give asylum to economic migrants', 11 January 2015,https://index.hu/belfold/2015/01/11/orban_gazdasagi_bevandorloknak_nem_adunk_menedeket/
9. 'Worldwide displacement hits all-time high as war and persecution increase', 18 June 2015, http://www.unhcr.org/news/latest/2015/6/558193896/worldwide-displacement-hits-all-time-high-war-persecution-increase.html.
10. 'Orbán to the BBC: "It's part of life"', 30 January 2015, https://www.youtube.com/watch?v–UQfRhiTDrY.
11. 'Immigrants are flooding our country: 90 percent are Muslims', 14 January 2015, http://valasz.hu/itthon/ozonlenek-a-bevandorlok-magyarorszagra-a-90-szazalekuk-muszlim-108474.
12. Al Jazeera Balkans, Avni Ahmetaj report, 'Migration crisis in Kosovo', 3 February 2015, https://www.youtube.com/watch?v=cPAhKEDTZf0.
13. 'UNHCR saddened by death of baby Kosovar asylum-seeker in Hungary', 26 February 2015, http://www.unhcr.org/ceu/8646-unhcr-saddened-by-death-of-baby-kosovar-asylum-seeker-in-hungary.html.
14. 'UNHCR calls on Hungary to protect, not persecute, refugees', 8 May 2015, http://www.unhcr.org/news/press/2015/5/554cc16e9/unhcr-calls-hungary-protect-persecute-refugees.html.

2 A Time of Fear

1. Written answers from former inmate to the author's questions, June 2015
2. 'Charlie Hebdo: Bulgaria extradites terror suspect', 29 January 2015, http://www.bbc.com/news/world-europe-31047020
3. Turkey National Intelligence Organization website, https://www.mit.gov.tr/eng/
4. 'British jihadist Imran Khawaja jailed for 12 years', 6 February 2015, http://www.bbc.com/news/uk-31166062
5. Prime Minister's Office, 'National consultation on immigration to begin', 24 April 2015, http://www.kormany.hu/en/prime-minister-s-office/news/national-consultation-on-immigration-to-begin
6. 'UNHCR calls on Hungary to protect, not persecute, refugees', 8 May 2015, http://www.unhcr.org/news/press/2015/5/554cc16e9/unhcr-calls-hungary-protect-persecute-refugees.html?query—ontserrat%20Feixas%20Vihé
7. Hungarian government portal on Riga statement, 4 February 2015, http://www.kormany.hu/hu/igazsagugyi-miniszterium/europai-unios-es-nemzetkozi-igazsagugyi-egyuttmukodesert-felelos-allamtitkarsag/hirek/berke-barna-kepviselte-magyarorszagot-a-bel-es-igazsagugyi-tanacs-rigai-ulesen-2015-02-04
8. EU Terrorism Situation and Trend Report (TE-SAT) 2016, https://www.europol.europa.eu/activities-services/main-reports/european-union-terrorism-situation-and-trend-report-te-sat-2016
9. Number of migrants caught, by date, March 2015, http://www.police.hu/hu/hirek-es-informaciok/hatarinfo/elfogott-migransok-szama-lekerdezes?created%5Bmin%5D=2018-06-01&created%5Bmax%5D=2018-07-01&created%5Bmin_year%5D=2015&created%5Bmin_month%5D=03; 'Number of migrants caught, by date', April 2015, http://www.police.hu/hu/hirek-es-informaciok/hatarinfo/elfogott-migransok-szama-lekerdezes?created%5Bmin%5D=2018-06-01&created%5Bmax%5D=2018-07-01&created%5Bmin_year%5D=2015&created%5Bmin_month%5D=04 (April)
10. 'Pope Francis and his Hungarian critics', 13 August 2016, http://hungarianspectrum.org/tag/laszlo-rigo-kiss/
11. 'UNHCR billboards in Hungary celebrate contributions by refugees', 19 June 2015, http://www.unhcr.org/news/latest/2015/6/5583d1466/unhcr-billboards-hungary-celebrate-contributions-refugees.html
12. A Traveller's Guide to East Macedonia and Thrace: www.jti-rhodope.eu

13. Giovanni Cocco, 'Moving Walls' photos, December 2014; http://www.eurozine.com/articles/2014-12-03-cocco-en.html

14. N. Nielsen, 'Fortress Europe: a Greek wall close up', 21 December 2012, https://euobserver.com/fortress-eu/118565;

15. 'Evros – Long way to Europe', October 2014: http://stopevroswall.blogspot.hu/2014_10_01_archive.html

16. *Greece as a Country of Asylum: UNHCR Observations on the Current Situation of Asylum in Greece*, December 2014, http://www.refworld.org/docid/54cb3af34.html

17. B. Cheshirkov, 'Bulgarians urged to "see refugees through new eyes" in media campaign', 24 November 2014, http://www.unhcr.org/news/latest/2014/11/547355546/bulgarians-urged-refugees-new-eyes-media-campaign.html

18. Facebook group of Harmanli Playschool, established November 2014: https://www.facebook.com/groups/HarmanliRefugeeCampPlaySchool/

19. 'Battle of al-Hasakah (2015)', https://en.wikipedia.org/wiki/Battle_of_al-Hasakah_(2015), last updated 28 March 2018.

20. A. Ammirati, 'What is the Dublin Regulation', 8 December 2015, http://openmigration.org/en/analyses/what-is-the-dublin-regulation/

21. Bulgarian Helsinki Committee, Statistics Bulgaria, http://www.asylumineurope.org/reports/country/bulgaria/statistics

3 Viktor Orbán's Jihad

1. 'Jihad: a misunderstood concept from Islam', http://islamicsupremecouncil.org/understanding-islam/legal-rulings/5-jihad-a-misunderstood-concept-from-islam.html?start=9

2. 'Worldwide displacement hits all-time high as war and persecution increase', 18 June 2015, http://www.unhcr.org/news/latest/2015/6/558193896/worldwide-displacement-hits-all-time-high-war-persecution-increase.html

3. Viktor Orbán 'We are considering every possibility' 12 June 2015: http://www.kormany.hu/hu/a-miniszterelnok/beszedek-publikaciok-interjuk/minden-lehetoseget-szamba-kell-venni-a-bevandorlok-kerdeseben

4. Hungarian Helsinki Committee, *Building a Legal Fence: Changes to Hungarian Asylum Law Jeopardise Access to Protection in Hungary*, 7 August 2015, https://helsinki.hu/wp-content/uploads/HHC-HU-asylum-law-amendment-2015-August-info-note.pdf

5. 'New UNHCR report warns against returning asylum-seekers to Greece', 30 January 2015, http://www.unhcr.org/news/briefing/2015/1/54cb698d9/new-unhcr-report-warns-against-returning-asylum-seekers-greece.html

6. *Bulgaria as a Country of Asylum: UNHCR Observations on the Current Situation of Asylum in Bulgaria*, April 2014, http://www.unhcr.org/protection/operations/53198b489/unhcr-observations-situation-asylum-bulgaria.html

7. Amnesty International, *Europe's Borderlands: Violations against Refugees and Migrants in Macedonia, Serbia and Hungary*, 2015, https://www.amnesty.org/en/documents/eur70/1579/2015/en/

8. 'Worldwide displacement hits all-time high as war and persecution increase', 18 June 2015, http://www.unhcr.org/news/latest/2015/6/558193896/worldwide-displacement-hits-all-time-high-war-persecution-increase.html

9. 'Every day 40–60 buses full of migrants arrivee in Kanizsa from Belgrade', Délmagyarország (South Hungary) Daily, 28 August 2015 http://www.delmagyar.hu/szeged_hirek/naponta_40-60_migranssal_teli_busz_erkezik_belgradbol_magyarkanizsara/2443278/

10. 'Mauritania: water crisis in Nouakchott', 22 July 2014, http://www.euronews.com/2014/07/22/mauritania-water-crisis-in-nouakchott

11. László Magyar, African explorer: https://hu.wikipedia.org/wiki/Magyar_László_(Afrika-kutató)

4 The Dog's Breakfast

1. *Financial Times*, leader, 31 December 2015.
2. 'Calais migrant crisis: Cameron warns UK is "no safe haven"', 30 July 2015, http://www.bbc.com/news/uk-33713268
3. Hungarian Helsinki Committee, *Building a Legal Fence: Changes to Hunharian Asylum Law Jeopardise Access to Protection in Hungary*, 7 August 2015, https://helsinki.hu/wp-content/uploads/HHC-HU-asylum-law-amendment-2015-August-info-note.pdf
4. Article on Gyálarét, Hungarian wikipedia: https://hu.wikipedia.org/wiki/Gyálarét
5. For a useful overview of arrivals in Hungary from 2014–2018, and the low rate of asylum or protection granted, see: IOM, 'Migration issues in Hungary', http://www.iom.hu/migration-issues-hungary, last updated 29 June 2018.
6. *Wall Street Journal*, 'Obscure German tweet helped spur migrant march from Hungary', 6 July 2018, https://www.wsj.com/articles/obscure-german-tweet-help-spur-migrant-march-from-hungary-1441901563; A. Dernbach, 'Germany suspends Dublin agreement for Syrian refugees', 26 August 2015, http://www.euractiv.com/section/migrations/news/germanysuspends-dublin-agreement-for-syrian-refugees/
7. On 20 July 2015, the Justice and Home Affairs Council of the EU agreed on the 'temporary and exceptional' relocation of persons 'in clear need of international protection' from Greece and Turkey. This would later be expanded into the relocation quota system: Justice and Home Affairs Council meeting, 20 July 2015, http://www.consilium.europa.eu/en/meetings/jha/2015/07/20/
8. Asylum Information Database, Dublin procedures, Germany, http://www.asylumineurope.org/reports/country/germany/asylum-procedure/procedures/dublin
9. I. Coles and S. Nasralia, 'The migrant truck tragedy: "I feel really bad about what happened"', 12 November 2015, https://www.reuters.com/investigates/special-report/europe-migrants-truck/
10. 'Hungarian police arrest driver of lorry that had 71 dead migrants inside', 28 August 2015, https://www.theguardian.com/world/2015/aug/28/more-than-70-dead-austria-migrant-truck-tragedy
11. 'Migrant crisis: Merkel warns of EU failure', 31 August 2015, http://www.bbc.com/news/world-europe-34108224
12. '11 charged in migrant death truck incident', BAON Bács-Kiskun news portal, 4 May 2017: https://www.baon.hu/bacs-kiskun/kek-hirek-bulvar-bacs-kiskun/11-embercsempesz-ellen-emeltek-vadat-a-halalkamion-ugyeben-724004/
13. UN Convention on the Law of the Sea of 10 December 1982, http://www.un.org/depts/los/convention_agreements/convention_overview_convention.htm; International Convention on Maritime Search and Rescue, http://www.imo.org/en/About/Conventions/ListOfConventions/Pages/International-Convention-on-Maritime-Search-and-Rescue-(SAR).aspx; SOLAS Convention (International Convention for the Safety of Life at Sea), https://en.wikipedia.org/wiki/SOLAS_Convention
14. Hungarian Helsinki Committee, https://www.helsinki.hu/en/
15. Menedék, Hungarian Association for Migrants, https://menedek.hu/en
16. Kalunba charity, http://kalunba.org
17. Migration Aid, http://www.migrationaid.net/csoport/
18. *Le Monde*, 'Crise migratoire: le ton monte entre la France et la Hongrie', 30 August 2018, http://www.lemonde.fr/international/article/2015/08/30/laurent-fabius-denonce-l-attitude-scandaleuse-de-la-hongrie-dans-la-crise-des-migrants_4740538_3210.html
19. 'Szijjártó hits back at French Foreign Minister', Magyar Nemzet daily, 31 August 2015, https://mno.hu/belfold/szijjarto-visszavagott-a-francia-kulugyminiszternek-1302397
20. 'Together, bravely' opinion piece by Jean-Claude Juncker in Népszabadság daily, 27 August 2015: http://nol.hu/velemeny/egyutt-batran-1559435

5 A Refugee Victory

1. Angela Merkel on refugee policy: 'Flexibility is called for now', 31 August 2015, https://www.bundesregierung.de/Content/EN/Artikel/2015/08_en/2015-08-31-sommer-pk-der-kanzlerin_en.html; 'Merkel in der Bundespressekonferenz', 31 August 2015, https://www.youtube.com/watch?v=UdVjH0JEbJ4

2. 'This is also an Iron Curtain, but this one is for us not against us', Viktor Orbán, 3 September 2015, https://444.hu/2015/09/03/orban-ez-is-egy-vasfuggony-csak-ez-most-ertunk-van/

3. 'Migrant crisis "a German problem"', 3 September 2015, http://www.bbc.com/news/world-europe-34136823

4. Economist leader comment on 'Merkel the bold', 3 September 2015, https://www.economist.com/news/leaders/21663228-refugees-germanys-chancellor-brave-decisive-and-right-merkel-bold

5. 'Migrants: Frontex signale un traffic de faux passeports syriens', 1 September 2015, http://www.europe1.fr/international/migrants-frontex-signale-un-trafic-de-faux-passeports-syriens-2508147

6. 'Death of Alan Kurdi', https://en.wikipedia.org/wiki/Death_of_Alan_Kurdi, last updated 4 July 2018.

7. For a summary of comments by Viktor Orbán and his ministers on Islam, see: 'Orbán's double standards on Islam' Népszava daily, 2 October 2015, http://nepszava.hu/cikk/1071820-orban-ketkulacsos-muszlimbaratsaga

8. 'They tricked the refugees' Népszabadság daily, 3 September 2015, http://nol.hu/belfold/atvertek-a-menekulteket-pattanasig-feszult-a-helyzet-bicsken-1560817; 'Refugee scandal at Bicske station' 3 September 2015, http://www.blikk.hu/aktualis/politika/menekultek-botrany-a-bicskei-vasutallomason/ggshr73

9. 'Refugees set out with tents and sleeping bags' Index news portal, 4 September 2015, https://index.hu/video/2015/09/04/vonulas_menekultek_menekultvalsag/

10. 'Clashes erupt between refugees, football hooligans in Budapest (video, photos), 4 September 2015, https://www.rt.com/news/314459-clashes-refugees-football-hungary/

11. N. Thorpe, 'Tired migrants finally cross into Austria', 5 September 2015, http://www.bbc.com/news/world-europe-34166115

6 The Closing of the Curtain

1. http://europa.eu/rapid/press-release_IP-15-5700_en.htm

2. For an excellent, blow-by-blow reconstruction of the events of that night, see: 'The night Germany lost control', 30 August 2016, http://www.zeit.de/gesellschaft/2016-08/refugees-open-border-policy-september-2015-angela-merkel

3. B. Bayrhammer, 'Faymann: EU–Lösung oder Friedensnobelpreis abgeben', 5 September 2015, http://diepresse.com/home/innenpolitik/4814407/Faymann_EULoesung-oder-Friedensnobelpreis-abgeben?

4. P. Bognar and E. Kocina, 'Refugees may go to Austria' Die Presse 4 September 2015: http://diepresse.com/home/ausland/eu/4813926/Fluechtlingeduerfen-nach-Oesterreich?from=suche.intern.portal

5. N. Nielsen, 'Germany sets example on EU migrants', 7 September 2015, https://euobserver.com/migration/130130

6. J. Clayton, 'UNHCR chief issues key guidelines for dealing with Europe's refugee crisis', 4 September 2015, http://www.unhcr.org/55e9793b6.html#_ga=1.74185362.1633667661.1453992302

7. Ralf Schuler, 'Will the Refugee crisis destroy the Union?', 6 September 2015, https://www.bild.de/politik/inland/grosse-koalition/zerreisst-fluechtlingskrise-union-42470310.bild.html

8. ZDF-Political Barometer, 11 September 2015, https://presseportal.zdf.de/pressemitteilung/mitteilung/zdf-politbarometer-september-2015/

9. 'We must keep Europe Christian says Hungarian PM', 17 September 2015, https://www.thetimes.co.uk/article/we-must-keep-europe-christian-says-hungarian-pm-fjwnmlzcv07

10. http://europa.eu/rapid/press-release_SPEECH-15-5614_en.htm

11. Monty Python: Ministry of Silly Walks sketch, https://www.youtube.com/watch?v=iV2ViNJFZC8

12. 'N1 sacked the camerawoman who kicked the refugee child' kasnyikm, 444, 8 September 2015 https://444.hu/2015/09/08/ime-a-menekult-kisgyerekeket-rugdoso-n1-operatorno

13. 'Internal instruction from editors: no refugee children on public service TV', 25 August 2015, https://444.hu/2015/08/25/belso-szerkesztoi-utasitasra-nem-szerepelhetnek-gyerekek-a-kozszolgalati-teve-menekultes-anyagaiban/

14. B. Kálnoky, 'In the end there will be more Muslims than us', 16 September 2015, https://www.welt.de/politik/ausland/article146497225/Am-Ende-werden-die-Muslime-mehr-sein-als-wir.html

15. M. Fleming, 'UNHCR outlines proposals to manage refugee and migration crisis in Europe ahead of EU Summit', 22 September 2015, http://www.unhcr.org/news/latest/2015/9/56015ba86/unhcr-outlines-proposals-manage-refugee-migration-crisis-europe-ahead-eu.html

16. B. Novak, 'Counter-terrorism police racheted up violence at Röszke says photographer', September 21 2015, https://budapestbeacon.com/counter-terrorism-police-ratcheted-up-violence-at-roszke-says-photographer/; R. Field, 'What really happened at Röszke?', 22 September 2015, http://budapestbeacon.com/public-policy/what-really-happened-at-Röszke/27850; 'Witnesses recount chaos at Röszke following border closure at trial of Ahmed H.', 24 September 2016, http://budapestbeacon.com/public-policy/witnesses-recount-chaos-at-Röszke-following-border-closure-at-trial-of-ahmed-h/ 39821

17. Informal meeting of EU heads of state or government on migration, 23 September 2015: http://www.consilium.europa.eu/en/press/press-releases/2015/09/23-statement-informal-meeting/; N. Nielsen and E. Zalan, 'EU forces "voluntary" migrant relocation on eastern states', 22 September 2015, https://euobserver.com/migration/130374; 'Migrant crisis: opponents furious over new EU quotas', 22 September 2015, http://www.bbc.com/news/world-europe-34331126

18. World Food Programme, Annual Performance Report for 2015, https://docs.wfp.org/api/documents/213317f2-2843-4208-bf57-74208bf23bcf/download/

19. Statewatch, 'Explanatory note on the "Hotspot" approach': http://www.statewatch.org/news/2015/jul/eu-com-hotsposts.pdf

20. Statement by H.E. Viktor Orbán: http://www.un.org/en/development/desa/population/migration/events/ga/2015/docs/statements/HUNGARY.pdf

7 Three Savage Frontiers

1. 'Letter to my wife' Miklós Radnóti, Lager Heidenau, August–September 1944: http://radnoti.mtak.hu/hu/04-07.htm

2. 'Battle for Kobane', 25 June 2015, https://www.bbc.com/news/world-middle-east-29688108

3. 'Beheaded Syrian scholar refused to lead Isis to hidden Palmyra antiquities', 19 August 2015, https://www.theguardian.com/world/2015/aug/18/isis-beheads-archaeologist-syria

4. Readers' comments on 'Ask not from whom the AK-47s flow', April 2016, https://www.economist.com/news/europe/21697019-answer-often-serbia-croatia-or-bulgaria-ask-not-whom-ak-47s-flow

5. 'Conflict timeline 2015', http://www.iamsyria.org/2015.html

6. 'Casualties of the Syrian civil war', https://en.wikipedia.org/wiki/Casualties_of_the_Syrian_Civil_War, last updated 7 July 2018.

7. 'Global trends: forced displacement in 2016', http://www.unhcr.org/globaltrends2016/

8. Philip Faigle et al., 'It really wasn't Merkel', 11 October 2016, http://www.zeit.de/politik/ausland/2016-10/angela-merkel-influence-refugees-open-borders-balkan-route

9. 'François Hollande and Angela Merkel face MEPs', 7 October 2015, http://www.europarl.europa.eu/news/en/press-room/20150929IPR94921/francois-hollande-and-angela-merkel-face-meps

10. 'Why people don't need to drown in the Aegean', a policy proposal, ESI, 17 September 2015: https://www.esiweb.org/pdf/ESI%20-%20Why%20people%20drown%20in%20the%20Aegean%20-%2017%20September%202015.pdf

11. 'Letter from European Commission to Hungarian government', 6 October 2015, http://www.statewatch.org/news/2015/oct/eu-com-letter-hungary.pdf

12. Stefan Braun, 'Refugees will decide Merkel's fate', 7 October 2015: http://www.sueddeutsche.de/politik/asylpolitik-die-fluechtlinge-werden-merkels-schicksal-1.2681500

13. 'Seehofer's explosive self-defence speech': http://www.spiegel.de/kultur/gesellschaft/horst-seehofer-brisantes-notwehr-gerede-a-1057081.html

14. 'Seehofer widens rift with Merkel over refugee policy' 9 October 2015, Deutsche Welle: https://www.dw.com/en/seehofer-widens-rift-with-merkel-over-refugee-policy/a-18773458

15. ' "We are in deep trouble": Orbán stares down Merkel on migration . . ', 22 October 2015, https://www.politico.eu/article/orban-refugees-hungary-we-are-in-deep-trouble/ (Madrid)

16. T. Arango, 'Merkel links Turkey's E.U. hopes to stemming flow of refugees', 18 October 2015, https://www.nytimes.com/2015/10/19/world/merkel-links-turkeys-eu-hopes-to-stemming-flow-of-refugees.html

17. 'Migrant crisis: Thousands enter Slovenia after Hungary closes border', 18 October 2015: https://www.bbc.com/news/world-europe-34564830

18. 'Still the refugees are coming, but in Europe the barriers are rising', 31 October 2015, https://www.theguardian.com/world/2015/oct/31/austria-fence-slovenia-wire-europe-refugees

19. Border Crossing Spielfeld website, https://bordercrossingspielfeld.org

20. 'Meeting on the Western Balkans Migration Route: Leaders agree on 17-point plan of action', Brussels, 25 October 2015: http://europa.eu/rapid/press-release_IP-15-5904_en.htm

21. G. van Kote, 'Daniel Psenny: "La balle, on ne l'entend pas arriver" ', 19 November 2015, http://www.lemonde.fr/attaques-a-paris/article/2015/11/19/daniel-psenny-la-balle-on-ne-l-entend-pas-arriver_4813686_4809495.html

22. 'Here's what we know about the Paris attackers', 15 November 2015, Updated 4 January 2017: https://www.huffingtonpost.com/entry/paris-attackers_us_56488d01e4b0603773496f39?c4gnl8fr

23. M. McPhee and B. Ross, 'US Intel: ISIS may have passport printing machine, blank passports', 10 December 2015, http://abcnews.go.com/International/us-intel-isis passport-printing-machine-blank-passports/story?id=35700681

24. 'The mass murderers of Paris planned and waited in Budapest', 27 September 2016, https://magyaridok.hu/belfold/budapesten-szervezkedtek-es-varakoztak-parizsi-tomeggyilkosok-1038598/

25. 'Paris victims, remembered', 20 November 2015, https://www.nytimes.com/interactive/2015/11/20/world/europe/Paris-terror-victims-list.html

26. ' "You will not have my hate": Antoine Leiris on losing his wife in the Paris attacks', 16 October 2016, https://www.theguardian.com/books/2016/oct/16/antoine-leiris-you-will-not-have-my-hate-interview-paris-attacks-helene-bataclan

8 A Warehouse of Souls

1. S. Bjelotomic, 'Death of the Balkan route: UNHCR and IOM's strategy in Serbia', 25 January 2017, http://serbianmonitor.com/en/featured/29317/death-of-the-balkan-route-unhcr-and-ioms-strategy-serbia/; 'Enough is enough:deaths on the western Balkans route', 22 March 2017, http://www.irr.org.uk/news/enough-is-enough-deaths-on-the-western-balkans-route/

2. 'Napoleon Bonaparte quotes', http://www.azquotes.com/author/1621-Napoleon_Bonaparte
3. 'Paris attacks: Who was Hasna Ait Boulahcen?', 22 November 2015, http://www.bbc.com/news/world-europe-34877374
4. Muhammad Awzal d. AD 1749, http://www.worldcat.org/identities/lccn-nr97034325/; 'The Berber literary tradition of the Sous – with . . . "The Ocean of Tears" by Muhammad Awzali (d. 1749)', https://www.amazon.com/Berber-Literary-Tradition-Sous-Translation/dp/3896459996
5. 'Islamic State can make fake Syrian passports: US report', 11 December 2015, https://www.reuters.com/article/us-mideast-crisis-usa-passports/islamic-state-can-make-fake-syrian-passports-u-s-report-idUSKBN0TV02820151212
6. 'Macedonia to grant passage only to migrants allowed in EU, says Poposki', 23 November 2015, http://www.mia.mk/en/Inside/RenderSingleNews/328/132908028 (Macedonia to grant passage only to 3 nationalities)
7. 'Abandoned Athens Olympic 2004 venues, 10 years on – in pictures', 13 August 2014, https://www.theguardian.com/sport/gallery/2014/aug/13/abandoned-athens-olympic-2004-venues-10-years-on-in-pictures
8. 'Greece "will not become Lebanon of Europe"', 25 February 2016, https://www.theguardian.com/world/2016/feb/25/greece-wont-be-lebanon-of-europe-yannis-mouzalas-refugees-eu
9. L. Hart, N. Graviano and S. Klink, *Assisted Voluntary Return and Reintegration: At a Glance 2015*, 2015, https://www.iom.int/sites/default/files/our_work/DMM/AVRR/AVRR-at-a-glance-2015.pdf; 'Assisted Voluntary Return and Reintegration 2015 Key Highlights', 2016, https://publications.iom.int/books/assisted-voluntary-return-and-reintegration-2015-key-highlights
10. 'Johannes Pfuhl', https://en.wikipedia.org/wiki/Johannes_Pfuhl; 'Eurytion', http://www.theoi.com/Georgikos/KentaurosEurytion1.html
11. '10 Commission priorities for 2015–19', https://ec.europa.eu/commission/priorities/migration_en

9 The EU–Turkey Deal

1. 'Mass sexual assault in Egypt', https://en.wikipedia.org/wiki/Mass_sexual_assault_in_Egypt
2. 'Investigation committee opens first meeting on Cologne N[ew] Y[ear's] E[ve] assaults', 18 February 2016, http://www.dw.com/en/investigation-committee-opens-first-meetingon-cologne-nye-assaults/a-19055748; 'Cologne attacks: first trial for sexual assault on New Year's Eve begins', 6 May 2016, http://www.bbc.com/news/world-europe-36225177
3. 'Report: Cologne New Year's Eve attacks "could have been prevented"', 17 March 2017, http://www.dw.com/en/report-cologne-new-years-eve-attacks-could-have-been-prevented/a-37979296
4. 'Copper – a driving force behind the automotive industry', http://www.makin-metals.com/about/uses-of-copper-in-cars/
5. 'Aksaray, Fatih', https://en.wikipedia.org/wiki/Aksaray,_Fatih
6. 'Syrian refugee entrepreneurs boost Turkey's economy', 16 May 2016, https://www.ft.com/content/93e3d794-1826-11e6-b197-a4af20d5575e
7. 'DR Congo: 24 killed since election results announced', 21 December 2011, https://www.hrw.org/news/2011/12/21/dr-congo-24-killed-election-results-announced
8. 'Protests in Congo over president's future', 20 January 2015, https://www.theguardian.com/world/2015/jan/20/-sp-deadlyprotests-democratic-republic-congo-drc-president-kabila
9. For a more recent assessment of the situation in DR Congo, see: 'Democratic Republic of Congo in crisis', 9 April 2018, https://www.hrw.org/blog-feed/democratic-republic-congo-crisis

10. 'The organisation of Asylum and migration policies. Factsheet: France', https://www.immi-gration.interieur.gouv.fr/content/download/39552/303018/file/8.FRANCE_Factsheet_Institutional_Chart_October2012.pdf; http://www.asylumineurope.org/reports/country/france/asylumprocedure/general/short-overview-asylum-procedure
11. 'Some Syrians chart pre-approved path to European asylum', https://www.apnews.com/dc5ece27b897426ca92569c4faa55306
12. D. Bilefsky, 'Sweden and Denmark add border checks to stem flow of migrants', 4 January 2016, https://www.nytimes.com/2016/01/05/world/europe/sweden-denmark-border-check-migrants.html
13. M. Dettmer and C. Reiermann, 'Budget battle begins over Germany's new residents', 29 February 2016, http://www.spiegel.de/international/germany/budget-battle-begins-over-refugees-in-germany-a-1079864.html
14. 'Germany spent 20 billion euros on refugees in 2016', 24 May 2016, http://www.dw.com/en/germany-spent-20-billion-euros-on-refugees-in-2016/a-38963299
15. 'Demography, Immigration, Refugees', https://www.iwkoeln.de/themen/demografie/zuwanderung/fluechtlinge.html
16. 'Turkey's PM plays hardball at EU summit', 7 March 2016, https://euobserver.com/migration/132579
17. EU–Turkey Statement, 18 March 2016, http://www.consilium.europa.eu/en/press/press-releases/2016/03/18/eu-turkey-statement/
18. 'EU and Turkey reach refugee deal', 20 March 2016, https://www.politico.eu/article/eu-and-turkey-finalize-refugee-deal/
19. 'EU Minister: Turkey won't take back migrants already on Greek islands', 10 March 2016, http://www.hurriyetdailynews.com/eu-minister-turkey-wont-take-back-migrants-already-on-greek-islands-96265
20. M. Cheresheva, 'Bulgarian, Turkish premiers seek solution on migrants', 26 August 2016, http://www.balkaninsight.com/en/article/bulgaria-s-borissov-meets-turkish-pm-to-seek-partnership-on-migration-08-25-2016
21. 'EU–Turkey deal a historic blow to rights', 18 March 2016: https://www.amnesty.org/en/latest/news/2016/03/eu-turkey-refugee-deal-a-historic-blow-to-rights/
22. 'Erdogan blasts the West's response to Turkey coup, refugee crisis', 8 August 2016, http://www.businessinsider.de/erdogan-blasts-international-response-to-turkey-coup-refugee-crisis-2016-8?r=UK&IR=T
23. 'Saxony-Anhalt state election 2016', https://en.wikipedia.org/wiki/Saxony-Anhalt_state_election,_2016
24. Conversations between Gerald Knaus and the author, August 2018.

10 The Street of Four Winds

1. 'Interview: Pope Francis', 17 May 2016, https://www.la-croix.com/Religion/Pape/interview-Pope-Francis-2016-05-17-1200760633
2. 'On the run from Isis: Jihadists "targeting Paris attacker Salah Abdeslam for chickening out of killings"', 19 November 2015, http://www.independent.co.uk/news/world/europe/paris-attack-eighth-attacker-salah-abdeslam-could-also-be-on-the-run-from-isis-amid-fears-the-group-a6740781.html
3. T. Miles, 'More Europe-bound migrants may be dying in Sahara than at sea: report', 15 July 2016, https://www.reuters.com/article/us-europe-migrants-sahara/more-europe-bound-migrants-may-be-dying-in-sahara-than-at-sea-report-idUSKCN0ZV22C
4. ' "Six thousand migrant arrivals is not an invasion": Renzi', 15 April 2016, https://www.thelocal.it/20160415/nearly-6000-migrants-reach-italy-since-tuesday
5. 'Libya: Humanitarian support to migrants and IDPs', 30 January 2016, https://www.iom.int/sites/default/files/situation_reports/file/IOM-LBY-Situation-Report-Jan-2016.pdf
6. 'Italian PM Renzi says Austrian border plans are shameless', 27 April 2016, https://www.reuters.com/article/us-europe-migrants-brenner-renzi/italian-pm-renzi-says-austrian-

313

border-plans-are-shameless-idUSKCN0XO1OL; I. Oliveira, 'Angela Merkel warns against Brenner pass closure', 5 June 2016, https://www.politico.eu/article/angela-merkel-warns-against-brenner-pass-closure-austria-italy-refugees-migrants-crisis/

7. 'Why is Pope Francis going to Lesbos?', 16 April 2016, http://www.bbc.com/news/world-europe-36053880

8. UNHCR, *Lesvos Island – Greece*, Factsheet, 12 November 2015, http://www.unhcr.org/protection/operations/5645ddbc6/greece-factsheet-lesvos-island.html

9. R. Schoenbauer, 'Volunteers who saved lives on Lesvos nominated for Nobel Peace Prize', 7 October 2016, http://www.unhcr.org/afr/news/latest/2016/10/57f7732d4/volunteers-saved-lives-lesvos-nominated-nobel-peace-prize.html

10. 'Interview: Pope Francis', 17 May 2016, https://www.la-croix.com/Religion/Pape/interview-Pope-Francis-2016-05-17-1200760633

11. *EASO Newsletter*, April 2016, https://www.easo.europa.eu/sites/default/files/newsletters/EASO-Newsletter-April-2016.pdf; 'Greece: Refugees detained in dire conditions amid rush to implement EU–Turkey deal', 7 April 2016, https://www.amnesty.org/en/latest/news/2016/04/greece-refugees-detained-in-dire-conditions-amid-rush-to-implement-eu-turkey-deal/

12. G. Soros, 'Europe: a better plan for refugees', 9 April 2016, http://www.nybooks.com/daily/2016/04/09/europe-how-pay-for-refugees/

13. 'Prayer, food, sex and water parks in Iran's holy city of Mashhad', 7 May 2015, https://www.theguardian.com/world/iran-blog/2015/may/07/prayerfood-sex-and-water-parks-in-irans-holy-city-of-mashhad; https://en.wikipedia.org/wiki/Mashhad

14. Proposal for a regulation of the European Parliament and of the Council establishing criteria and mechanisms for determining the Member State responsible for examining an application for international protection lodged in one of the Member States by a third-country national or a stateless person, 4 May 2016, https://eur-lex.europa.eu/legal-content/EN/TXT/PDF/?uri=CELEX: 52016PC0270(01)&from=EN

15. D. McLaughlin, 'Central European states deride new EU refuges plan', 5 May 2016, https://www.irishtimes.com/news/world/europe/central-european-states-deride-new-eu-refugee-plan-1.2636647

16. 'Remarks by First Vice-President Timmermans and Commissioner Avramopoulos to the European Parliament Plenary Session', europa.eu/rapid/press-release_SPEECH-16-1726_en.pdf

17. 'EU states face charge for rejecting refugees', 3 May 2016, https://www.ft.com/content/346ba28a-10b8-11e6-bb40-c30e3bfcf63b

11 Keep Calm and Think of England

1. 'PM Orban's Brexit stance "bears weight" in the EU', 21 June 2016, http://abouthungary.hu/news-in-brief/pm-orbans-brexit-stance-bears-weight-in-the-eu/

2. 'Orban has already drawn the conclusions of the Brexit decision', 24 June 2016, https://www.napi.hu/magyar_gazdasag/orban_maris_levonta_a_kovetkezteteset_a_brexit_utan. 616695.html

3. M. Pantovic, 'Violence against migrants on rise in Balkans', 1 August 2016, http://www.balkaninsight.com/en/article/msf-increase-of-violence-towards-migrants-on-balkan-route-07-29-2016; Jesuit Refugee Service Europe, *Annual Report 2016*, https://jrseurope.org/Assets/Publications/File/JRS_Europe_annual_report_2016.pdf; Médecins Sans Frontières, *Serbia: Games of Violence – Unaccompanied Children and Young People Repeatedly Abused by EU Member State Border Authorities*, 3 October 2017, http://www.msf.org/sites/msf.org/files/serbia-games-of-violence-3.10.17.pdf

4. N. Thorpe, 'Hungary deploys army to push migrants back to Serbia', 14 July 2016, http://www.bbc.com/news/world-europe-36786438

5. 'Kenya al-Shabab attack: security questions as dead mourned', 4 April 2015, https://www.bbc.com/news/world-africa-32177123

6. 'Radomir Putnik', https://hu.wikipedia.org/wiki/Radomir_Putnik

7. 'The German minority in Hungary, 1938–48': http://www.konfliktuskutato.hu/index. php?option=com_content&view=article&id=358:a-nemet-kisebbseg-magyarorszagon-1938-1948&catid=43:etnikai-konfliktusok&Itemid=214;

8. ICRC 2016 report, *Western Balkans (regional)*, http://www.refworld.org/pdfid/59490da77. pdf

9. 'Erdogan's Turkey', 13 April 2017, http://www.bbc.co.uk/news/resources/idt-sh/Erdogans_ Turkey

12 The Women of Adaševci

1. UN Summit for refugees and migrants 2016, https://refugeesmigrants.un.org/summit

2. Serbia: Factsheet, http://ec.europa.eu/echo/files/aid/countries/factsheets/serbia_en.pdf

3. 'Syrian refugees: a journey through mud, fire and cold', 8 August 2016, https://www.care-international.org.uk/stories/syrian-refugees-journey-through-mud-fire-and-cold

4. G. Baczynska, 'Hungary, Slovakia challenge quotas on asylum-seekers at top EU court', 10 May 2017, https://www.reuters.com/article/us-europe-migrants-slovakia-hungary/hungary-slovakia-challenge-quotas-on-asylum-seekers-at-top-eu-court-idUSKBN186222; 'At Bratislava summit, key question is the future of the EU', 15 September 2016, http://hu.euronews.com/2016/09/15/pozsonyi-eu-csucs-a-fo-kerdes-az-unio-jovoje

5. 'Angela Merkel admits mistakes over asylum seekers after disastrous election', 19 September 2016, https://www.theguardian.com/world/2016/sep/19/angela-merkel-admits-mistakes-asylum-seekers-election

6. 'Orbán and Kaczyński are for counter-cultural revolution in Europe', 9 September 2016, https://visegradpost.com/en/2016/09/09/orban-and-kaczynski-are-for-counter-cultural-revolution-in-europe/

7. E. Zalan, 'EU migrant quota idea is finished, Fico says', 27 September 2016, https://euobserver.com/migration/135245

8. UN Summit for refugees and migrants 2016, http://refugeesmigrants.un.org/summit

9. 'Figures of the week: UN Summit for refugees and migrants calls for international action', 23 September 2016, https://www.brookings.edu/blog/africa-in-focus/2016/09/23/figures-of-the-week-un-summit-for-refugees-and-migrants-calls-for-international-action/

10. Foreign Minister speaks in general debate of UN' 23 September 2016, http://www.kormany.hu/hu/kulgazdasagi-es-kulugyminiszterium/hirek/szijjarto-peter-felszolal-az-ensz-kozgyulesenek-altalanos-vitajan

11. 'Remarks by President Obama at leaders summit on refugees', 20 September 2016, https://obamawhitehouse.archives.gov/the-press-office/2016/09/20/remarks-president-obama-leaders-summit-refugees

12. 'UN summit on refugees fails to deliver real solutions', 20 September 2016, https://www.oxfam.org/en/pressroom/reactions/un-summit-refugees-fails-deliver-real-solutions

13. New York Declaration for Refugees and Migrants, 19 September 2016, http://www.unhcr.org/new-york-declaration-for-refugees-and-migrants.html

14. 'Orban's border blocking policies are comprehensible', 23 September 2016, https://derstandard.at/2000044795966/Bundeskanzler-Kern-Orbans-Politik-der-Grenzsperren-verstaendlich

15. 'Pangloss in Brussels – How (not) to implement the Aegean Agreement', 7 October 2016, https://www.esiweb.org/index.php?lang=en&id=156&document_ID=177

16. Communication from the Commission to the European Parliament, the European Council and the Council, 28 September 2016, https://ec.europa.eu/home-affairs/sites/homeaffairs/files/what-we-do/policies/european-agenda-migration/proposal-implementation-package/docs/20160928/3rd_report_on_the_progress_made_in_the_implementation_of_the_eu-turkey_statement_en.pdf

17. National Election Office statement on 2 October referendum results, http://www.valasztas.hu/dyn/onepsz201610/szavossz/en/eredind_e.html

18. 'It turned out just how much pain the quota referendum caused the government', 3 October2016,http://nol.hu/belfold/kiderult-mennyibe-fajt-a-kvotanepszavazas-1634635; 'The weapon will be powerful enough – Viktor Orban', 2 October 2016, https://www.hirado.hu/2016/10/02/orban-a-fegyver-eleg-eros-lesz-brusszelben-is/

19. Personal communication from source close the government, on Orban's disappointment.

20. E. Zalan, 'Orban spins migrant vote result, as EU celebrates', 3 October 2016, https://euobserver.com/migration/135329

13 A Slow and Painful Europe

1. 'New Year's address by Federal Chancellor Angela Merkel', 31 December 2016, https://www.bundesregierung.de/Content/EN/Pressemitteilungen/BPA/2016/2016-12-31-neujahrsansprache-podcast_en.html

2. 'Körmend priest accepted refugees', 14 December 2016, https://www.magyarkurir.hu/hirek/menekulteket-fogadott-be-kormendi-plebanos

3. 'Bamenda protests: mass arrests in Cameroon', 23 November 2016, www.bbc.com/news/world-africa-38078238

4. Cancer Moonshot webpage, https://www.cancer.gov/research/key-initiatives/moonshot-cancerinitiative

5. '"Shockingly high" losses for Afghan forces over winter', 1 May 2017, https://www.aljazeera.com/news/2017/05/high-losses-afghan-forces-winter-170501041116344.html

6. 'Joint way forward on migration issues between Afghanistan and the EU', 2 October 2016, https://eeas.europa.eu/sites/eeas/files/eu_afghanistan_joint_way_forward_on_migration_issues.pdf

7. 'Deportations from Germany to Afghanistan', 12 September 2017, http://www.dw.com/en/deportations-from-germany-to-afghanistan/g-40465731

8. N. Nielsen, 'EU steps up efforts to repatriate Afghans', 4 October 2016, https://euobserver.com/migration/135349

9. 'Germany restarts Afghan deportations, returns eight rejected asylum seekers', 13 September 2017, https://www.rferl.org/a/germany-afghan-deportations-eight-rejected-asylum-seekers/28733437.html

10. 'Exodus: Our Journey', BBC TWO, three episodes, http://www.bbc.co.uk/programmes/b07ky6ft

11. https://en.wikipedia.org/wiki/Murder_of_Maria_Ladenburger

12. 'Hungary: Key Asylum Figures as of 1 September 2016': https://www.helsinki.hu/wp-content/uploads/HHC-Hungary-asylum-figures-1-September-2016.pdf

13. 'Pope Francis sends a message to Trump', 20 January 2017, https://www.washingtonpost.com/local/2017/live-updates/politics/live-coverage-of-trumps-inauguration/pope-francis-sends-a-message-to-trump/?utm_term=.a4e539161bda

14. 'Migration: Thousands trapped in freezing temperatures in Greece and the Balkans', 9 January 2017, http://www.msf.org/en/article/migration-thousands-trapped-freezing-temperatures-greece-and-balkans

14 Borderlands

1. Asylum statistics in Romania: https://www.asylumineurope.org/reports/country/romania/statistics

2. Emergency Transit Centre, Timişoara: http://www.unhcr.org/ceu/100-enwhat-we-doresettlementetc-timisoara-html.html

3. For video and text reports on their stories, see: https://www.bbc.com/news/world-europe-45340715

4. Asylum requests in Germany, to May 2018, https://www.bmi.bund.de/SharedDocs/pres-semitteilungen/DE/2018/06/asylantraege-mai-2018.pdf?blob=publicationFile&v=5; Asylum quarterly report, 15 June 2018, http://ec.europa.eu/eurostat/statistics-explained/index.php/Asylum_quarterly_report

15 Wish You Were Here

1. http://www.cedarnetwork.org/2017/01/13/difference-demons-adam-b-seligman/
2. BAMF (Federal Office for Migration and Refugees), 'Child benefit and other benefits', http://www.bamf.de/EN/Willkommen/KinderFamilie/Kindergeld/kindergeld-node.html
3. 'Insight: After chemical horror, besieged Syrian suburb defiant', 4 October 2013, https://www.reuters.com/article/us-syria-crisis-zamalka-insight/insight-after-chemical-horror-besieged-syrian-suburb-defiant-idUSBRE9930E420131004
4. 'Expulsion of Germans from Czechoslovakia', https://en.wikipedia.org/wiki/Expulsion_of_Germans_from_Czechoslovakia
5. 'Ansbach suicide bombing-Islamism', http://www.zeit.de/gesellschaft/zeitgeschehen/2016-07/ansbachselbstmordanschlag-islamismus/komplettansicht
6. 'Ansbach attacker: asylum seeker to IS suicide bomber', 25 July 2016: http://www.bbc.com/news/world-europe-36886647
7. 'New refugee homes open on Bruchsal industrial estate',1 September 2015, https://www.ka-news.de/region/bruchsal/asyl-karlsruhe./Auf-Bruchsaler-Fabrikgelaende-Neue-Fluechtlingsheime-eroeffnet;art6011,1720912
8. 'Brigade La Fayette', https://fr.wikipedia.org/wiki/Brigade_La_Fayette; J.-D. Merchet, 'Depuis un an, l'armée française a "éliminé" environ 150 insurgés en Kapissa', 28 January 2015, http://secretdefense.blogs.liberation.fr/2009/10/26/depuis-un-anlarmee-francaise-a-elimine-environ-150-insurges-en-kapissa/
9. 'Captain Teacher, un journaliste en uniforme français pour monter une radio afghane', 1 October 2013, http://www.guerres-influences.com/captain-teacher-journaliste-reserviste-radio-surobi-afghanistan/
10. 'Calais "jungle" cleared of migrants French prefect says', 26 October 2016, http://www.bbc.com/news/world-europe-37773848
11. AIDA, France: country report, http://www.asylumineurope.org/reports/country/france, last updated 28 February 2018.
12. Swiss Refugee Council, 'Short overview of the asylum procedure', http://www.asylumineurope.org/reports/country/switzerland/asylumprocedure/general/short-overview-asylum-procedure
13. 'The 2015 Swiss elections: a landslide win for the right, despite limited changes in vote shares', 24 October 2015, http://blogs.lse.ac.uk/europpblog/2015/10/24/the-2015-swiss-elections-a-landslide-win-for-the-right-despite-limited-changes-in-vote-shares/
14. Swiss Confederation, *Migration Report 2016*, https://www.sem.admin.ch/dam/data/sem/publiservice/berichte/migration/migrationsbericht-2016-e.pdf

Afterword

1. John Berger, *Hold Everything Dear: Dispatches on Survival and Resistance* (Verso, 2007).
2. 'Migration: supporting a robust, realistic and fair EU policy', https://ec.europa.eu/commission/ sites/beta-political/files/budget-may2018-fair-migration-policy_en.pdf
3. 'On the edge of the Sahara, people mourn the decline of people-smuggling', *Economist*, 5 July 2018, https://www.economist.com/middle-east-and-africa/2018/07/05/on-the-edge-of-the-sahara-people-mourn-the-decline-of-people-smuggling
4. 'Turkey–Syria border wall to be completed by spring', 18 December 2017, http:// www.hurriyetdailynews.com/turkey-syria-border-wall-to-be-completed-by-spring-124303

5. 'A warning against mass returns to Syria', Norwegian Refugee Council, 12 March 2018, https:// www.nrc.no/news/2018/march/a-warning-against-mass-returns-to-syria/

6. Ivan Krastev, *After Europe* (University of Pennsylvania Press, 2017).

7. German Federal Elections, final result, https://www.bundeswahlleiter.de/en/bundestag-swahlen/ 2017/ergebnisse/bund-99.html

8. 'Austrian Foreign Minister Kurz: "Europe's values cannot be negotiable"', interview by W. Mayr and M. von Rohr, 1 June 2016, http://www.spiegel.de/international/europe/interview-with-austrian-foreign-minister-sebastian-kurz-a-1094931.html

9. Italian statistics for asylum-seekers, https://www.asylumineurope.org/reports/country/italy/

10. J. Reynolds, 'Italy election: what does the result mean?' 5 March 2018, https://www.bbc.com/news/world-europe-43291390

11. 'Italy government: Guiseppe Conte to head populist coalition', 1 June 2018, https:// www.bbc.com/news/world-europe-44322429

12. 'Stranded migrants: Macron scolds Italy over Aquarius ship', 12 June 2018, https:// www.bbc.com/news/world-europe-44452760; 'Spain foreign minister calls for more EU ambition', 12 June 2018, https://www.ft.com/content/ 3eb1891e-6e83-11e8-92d3-6c13e5c92914

13. Krastev, *After Europe*.

14. 'Germany: Crime rate drops, but fear rises', 7 May 2018, https://www.dw.com/en/germany-crime-rate-drops-but-fear-rises/a-43692277

15. *Laudato Si*, Encyclical Letter of Pope Francis, 18 June 2018, https://www.romereports.com/en/ 2015/06/18/read-full-text-of-the-pope-s-encyclical-laudato-si/

16. Jytte Klausen, *The Islamic Challenge: Politics and Religion in Western Europe* (Oxford University Press, 2005).

SELECT BIBLIOGRAPHY

Berger, John, *Hold Everything Dear: Dispatches on Survival and Resistance* (Verso, 2007).

Betts, Alexander and Paul Collier, *Refuge: Transforming a Broken Refugee System* (Allen Lane, 2017).

Carr, Matthew, *Fortress Europe: Inside the War Against Immigration* (C. Hurst & Co., 2012).

Demetriou, Olga, *Capricious Borders: Minority, Population and Counter-conduct between Greece and Turkey* (Berghahn Books, 2013).

Ignatieff, Michael, *The Ordinary Virtues: Moral Order in a Divided World* (Harvard University Press, 2017).

Kingsley, Patrick, *The New Odyssey: The Story of Europe's Refugee Crisis* (Guardian Books and Faber & Faber, 2016).

Kirby, Emma-Jane, *The Optician of Lampedusa* (Penguin, 2017).

Klausen, Jytte, *The Islamic Challenge: Politics and Religion in Western Europe* (Oxford University Press, 2005).

Krastev, Ivan, *After Europe* (University of Pennsylvania Press, 2017).

Marrus, Michael R., *The Unwanted: European Refugees from the First World War Through the Cold War* (Oxford University Press, 1985).

Miliband, David, *Rescue: Refugees and the Political Crisis of Our Time* (TED Books, Simon & Schuster, 2017).

Popoola, Olumide and Annic Holmes, *Breach* (Peirene Press, 2016).

Ruthven, Malise, *Encounters with Islam: On Religion, Politics and Modernity* (I.B. Tauris, 2012).

Ruthven, Malise, *A Fury for God: The Islamist Attack on America* (Granta Books, 2002).

Shukla, Nikes, *The Good Immigrant* (Unbound, 2016).

Sigona, Nando, Heaven Crawley, Franck Duvell, Katharine Jones, Simon McMahon, *Unravelling Europe's 'Migration Crisis': Journeys over Land and Sea* (Policy Press, 2017).

Trilling, Daniel, *Lights in the Distance: Exile and Refuge at the Borders of Europe* (Picador, 2018).

INDEX

INDEX

INDEX